Caney's
THE LAW OF SURETYSHIP
IN SOUTH AFRICA

PROF FJ VAN ZYL BOOK AWARD

for

Outstanding Performance

in

Law of Contract and Specific Contracts by a Final Year LLB Student

Awarded to

Tamryn Jensen
(91%)

(sponsored by Professor Christo van Loggerenberg)

Caney's
THE LAW OF SURETYSHIP
IN
SOUTH AFRICA

SIXTH EDITION

by

C F FORSYTH

BSc LLB (Natal) LLB PhD (Cantab)
Professor of Public Law and Private International Law,
University of Cambridge
Extraordinary Professor of Law,
University of Stellenbosch,
Fellow of Robinson College
Advocate of the High Court of South Africa
Of the Inner Temple, Barrister

and

J T PRETORIUS

BIuris (Pret) LLB (Natal) LLM (Cape Town) LLM (London) LLD (RAU)
Professor of Law in the Department of Mercantile Law,
University of South Africa
Life Member, Clare Hall, University of Cambridge
Attorney of the High Court of South Africa

First Published 1936
Second Edition 1970
Third Edition 1982
Fourth Edition 1991
Fifth Edition 2002
Second Impression 2006
Third Impression 2007
Fourth Impression 2008
Sixth Edition 2010

© Juta & Co, Ltd
1st floor, Sunclare Building, 21 Dreyer Street, Claremont 7708

This book is copyright under the Berne Convention. In terms of the Copyright Act, No 98 of 1978, no part of this book may be reproduced or transmitted in any form or by any means, electronic or mechanical, including photocopying, recording or by any information storage and retrieval system, without permission in writing from the Publisher.

Although every care is taken to ensure the accuracy of this publication, supplements, updates and replacement material, the authors, editors, publishers and printers do not accept responsibility for any act, omission, loss, damge or the consequences thereof occasioned by a reliance by any person upon the contents hereof.

Set in 10/12 pt Baskerville Classico

ISBN: 978-0 7021 8456 7

Cover design by Drag and Drop

Typesetting by ANdtp Services, Cape Town

Print management by Print Communications

Preface

The courts have been busy since the publication of the last edition of this book in 2002. One significant development is that the Supreme Court of Appeal has at last spoken on the vexed question of whether interruption of prescription against the debtor also interrupted prescription against the surety. In a learned and principled judgment in *Rand Bank v De Jager* 1982 (3) SA 418 (C) Baker J had held that the surety's and the debtor's obligations prescribed separately. But this has now been overruled by the SCA in *Jans v Nedcor Bank Ltd* 2003(6) SA 646 (SCA). It is now clear that these two obligations prescribe together. (See the discussion below at p. 200) This is a question that has been robustly debated in the scholarly literature and in the provincial divisions over many years. It is in the public interest that it has at last been settled. Clarity in the law is no small thing.

However, the SCA's decision nowhere shows where Baker J was in error but instead is based, it seems to us, in part on considerations of practical convenience and in part on a judgment of where the balance should be struck between the interests of the surety and the interests of the creditor. As Scott JA remarked: 'By its very nature a contract of suretyship is burdensome. The surety undertakes responsibility for the fulfilment of another's obligation. No doubt for this reason the law affords protection to a surety in a number of different ways....But a balance must be struck. Sureties do not assume the obligations of others against their wills, but with their free consent. Once having done so they cannot expect to be entitled simply to disabuse their minds of the fortunes of the principal debtor's liability and then require the law to protect them against their ignorance. If prescription in favour of the principal debtor is delayed or interrupted without their knowledge, they generally have themselves to blame...' (in para 30). The balance, it seems to us, has been shifted a little closer towards the creditor by this decision.

Another area where clarity has grown but the balance between creditor and surety may have shifted, or be in the process of shifting, is the following. It has long been a vexed question whether there exists a 'long stop' defence to protect the surety where the creditor seeks to use the suretyship for a purpose never contemplated by the parties. The *exceptio doli generalis*, which was long thought to provide such a defence, was ejected from the law in 1988 (in *Bank of Lisbon and South Africa Ltd v De Ornelas and Another* 1988 (3) SA 580 (A)). The alternative candidates to ground such a defence were either the doctrine of public policy or the principle of good faith which permeates all contracts and, it was said, justifies the courts in developing new and fair rules applicable in situations where there would otherwise be injustice. But it is now clear following *Brisley v Drotsky* 2002(4) SA 1 (SCA) and *Afrox Healthcare Bpk v Strydom* 2002 (6) SA 21 (SCA) that the abstract principle of good faith does not justify the development of fresh rules to secure fairness in the way described. Thus the 'long stop' defence rests on the doctrine of public policy alone. (See the discussion below at p. 210)

The interesting and significant point is that the concept of public policy has itself been in the process of transformation through the influence of constitutional values. As Ngcobo J said in the Constitutional Court in *Barkhuizen v Napier* 2007 (5) SA 323 (CC) '...the proper approach to the constitutional challenges to contractual terms is to determine whether the term challenged is contrary to public policy as evidenced by the constitutional values, in particular, those found in the Bill of Rights. This approach leaves space for the doctrine of *pacta sunt servanda* to operate, but at the same time allows courts to decline to enforce contractual terms that are in conflict with the constitutional values even though the parties may have consented to them.' It is too early to assess in the context of suretyship the impact of this constitutionalisation of the doctrine of public policy but at least it can be said that here is a secure basis for the 'long stop' defence.

That the contract of suretyship is inherently and rightly 'burdensome' is not in doubt. But the question is how burdensome ought it to be. As we have remarked before in most cases the creditor dictates to the surety the terms of the contract and, in the nature of things, those terms will favour the creditor. There should be no easy release of the surety when the debtor has not performed what he has undertaken to do. But in recognition of this disparity of bargaining power the balance between creditor and surety should shift towards the surety rather than away from him or her. Perhaps this is already happening with the constitutionalisation of the doctrine of public policy. If so, it is a welcome development.

We would like particularly to thank Mr Selwyn Cohen of the firm Eversheds who was kind enough to read and comment on an earlier version of this edition. We would also like to thank Ria de Kock and Patty Searle of Juta & Co for their sterling work in editing this edition.

The text reflects the authors' view of the law as at the 1st of January 2010.

Christopher Forsyth
University of Cambridge
March 2010

JT Pretorius
University of South Africa, Pretoria
March 2010

Contents

	Page
Preface	v
Mode of Citation	ix
Table of Cases	xi

PART ONE
THE NATURE OF SURETYSHIP AND THE FORMATION AND OPERATION OF THE CONTRACT

Chapter

I	The Roman Law: Foundations of our Law of Sureties	3
II	Definition and Nature of Suretyship	26
III	The Principal Obligation	38
IV	The Surety	51
V	The Formation of the Contract of Suretyship	61
VI	The Interpretation of the Contract	87
VII	The Obligations of the Surety	101

PART TWO
THE RIGHTS OF THE SURETY

VIII	The Benefit of Excussion	125
IX	The Benefit of Division Amongst Co-Sureties	138
X	The Benefit of Cession of Actions	145
XI	The Surety's Right of Recourse	159
XII	The Right to Contribution by Co-Sureties	171

PART THREE
THE RELEASE OF THE SURETY

XIII	Discharge of the Surety	187

General Index	215

Mode of Citation

B:	W Burge *Commentaries on the Law of Suretyship* (1849)
BMI:	W Buckland *Main Institutions of Roman Law* (1931)
BTB:	W Buckland *Textbook of Roman Law* 3 ed by P Stein (1963)
C:	*Codex* of Justinian
Cens For:	CFS van Leeuwen *Censura Forensis* (1962), translated by SH Barber and WA Macfayden (1896)
D:	*Digesta* of Justinian
De Zulueta:	F de Zulueta *The Institutes of Gaius* (1946) vol II 30l.
Dictata:	DG van der Keessel *Praelectiones Iuris Hoderni ad Hugonis Grotii introductionem ad jurisprudentianum hollandicam* translated into Afrikaans by P van Warmelo and others (1961). Cited as Lee *ad Gr.*
Domat:	Jean Domat *The Civil Law in its Natural Order* translated by W Strahan (1850)
G:	*The Institutes of Gaius*
Gr.	Hugo de Groot *Inleiding tot de Hollandsche Rechtsgeleertheyt* (1767)
Groen:	Simon à Groenewegen van der Made *Tractatus de legibus abrogatis et inusitatis* (1649) translated by B Beinart and ML Hewett
Huber:	U Huber *Heedendaegse Rechtsgeleertheyt* (1768)
Inst:	*The Institutes of Justinian*
Jolowicz:	HF Jolowicz *Historical Introdudion to the Study of Roman Law* 2 ed (1952)
Kaser:	Max Kaser *Das Römische Privatrecht* 2 ed (1975)
Lee:	RW Lee *Elements of Roman Law* 4 ed (1956)
Lee *ad* Gr:	*Commentary on Grotius's Introduction* (1936) by RW Lee
Lee *Intro*:	RW Lee *Introduction to Roman-Dutch Law* 5 ed (1953)
Nov:	*The Novels of Justinian*
P:	RJ Pothier *Traité des obligations,* translated by WD Evans (1806)
Sande:	JA Sande *Commentary on the Cession of Actions,* translated by PC Anders (1906)
Sch:	W Schorer *Annotations of Grotius's Introduction* (1767), translated by AFS Maasdorp (1903)
V:	*Commentarius ad Pandectas* (1698), translated by P Gane as *The Selective Voet* (1955)
VdK:	DG van der Keessel *Select Theses,* translated by CA Lorenz (1855)
Vdl:	J van der Linden *Koopmans Handbook* (1806)
VL:	S van Leeuwen *Het Roomsch Hollandsch Recht* (1664)
Wessels:	Sir JW Wessels *The Law of Contract* 2 ed by AA Roberts (1951)
Zimmermann:	Reinhard Zimmermann *The Law of Obligations* (1990)

Table of Cases

A

Absa Bank Ltd v The Master 1998 (4) SA 15 (N) 170
ABSA Bank Bpk v De Villiers 2001 (1) SA 481 (A) 200, 202
ABSA Bank Ltd t/a Volkskas Bank v Page and Another 2002 (1) SA 617 (SCA) ... 115
ABSA Bank Ltd v Davidson 2000 (1) SA 1117 (A)...................... 206
Absa Bank Ltd v Scharrighuisen [2000] 1 All SA 318 (C).. 163, 165, 166, 168, 169, 170
ABSA Bank v De Villiers 1998 (3) SA 920 (O)........................ 202
ABSA Bpk v De Goede 1997 (4) SA 66(A)........................... 53, 54
ABSA Bpk v Lydenburg Passasiersdienste BK 1995 (3) SA 314 (T) 54
Ackerman v Colonial Government 1869 NLR 155 209
Acutt v Bennett (1906) 27 NLR 716............................ 32, 129, 139
Adams v SA Motor Industry Employers Association 1981 (3) SA 1189 (A).... 163
Administrateur, Natal v Trust Bank van Afrika Bpk 1979 (3) SA 824 (A) 99
Administrator-General, South West Africa v Trust Bank of Africa Ltd 1982 (1) SA 635 (SWA).. 210
Adrianatos v Caradas' Estate and Another 1946 CPD 455................... 77
African Guarantee and Indemnity Co Ltd v Rabinowitz 1934 WLD 151 25
African Guarantee & Indemnity Co Ltd v Thorpe 1933 AD 330.. 39, 147, 148, 152, 153, 159, 204
African Life Property Holdings (Pty) Ltd v Score Food Holdings Ltd 1995 (2) SA 230 (A)... 30, 38, 62, 81
African Lumber Co (Pvt) Ltd v Katz 1978 (4) SA 432 (C) 71, 72
Afrox Healthcare Bpk v Strydom 2002 (6) SA 21 (SCA) 88, 91, 212, 213
Alagerysamy v Kvalsig 1912 NPD 25 .... 116, 117
Albert v Papenfus 1964 (2) SA 713 (E) 39, 41
Alexander NO v Administrator, Transvaal 1974 (2) SA 248 (T) 109
Alfred McAlpine & Son (Pty) Ltd v Transvaal Provincial Administration 1974 (3) SA 506 (A).. 91, 92
American Surety Co of New York v Wrightson (1910) 16 Com Cas 37 at 55, (1910) 103 LT 663.. 181
Amod Moussa v Loterijman & Co (1894) 1 OR 326..................... 126
Anglo African Shipping Co (1936) Ltd v Harris 1977 (2) SA 213 (W)........ 183
Arenson v Bishop 1926 CPD 73, 6 PH A48................. 43, 96, 190, 194
Arnoldi v Klazenga, Albers and Dreyer 1905 TS 533 136
ASA Investments (Pty) Ltd v Smit 1980 (1) SA 897 (C) 171, 176, 178, 179
Asco Carbon Dioxide Ltd v Lahner 2005 (3) SA 213 (N) 71, 130, 133
Astra Furnishers (Pty) Ltd v Arend and Another 1973 (1) SA 446 (C) 114

B

Baillie v Transvaal Assets Ltd 1923 (2) PH A21 (W).................. 157, 195

Bankkorp Ltd v Hendler and Another 1992 (4) SA 375 (W) 114
Bank of Africa v Hampson and Others (1884) 3 HCG 1 . . . . 129, 130
Bank of Africa v Vom Dorp (1909) 26 SC 143. 195
Bank of Lisbon and South Africa Ltd v De Ornelas and Another 1988 (3) SA
    580 (A). 4, 21, 22, 74, 94, 113, 211
Bank of Lisbon and South Africa Ltd v The Master 1987 (1) SA 276 (A). 170
Bank of the Orange Free State v Cloete 1985 (2) SA 859 (EC). 202
Bankorp Ltd v Hendler and Hendler 1992 (4) SA 375 (W) 201
Barclays Mortgage Nominees (Pty) Ltd v Brown 1979 (2) PH A50 (N) 75
Barclays National Bank Ltd and Others v Traub; Barclays National Bank Ltd v
    Kalk 1981 (4) SA 291 (W). 192
Barclays National Bank Ltd v Lockhat 1978 (3) SA 922 (D). 95
Bardays Bank (DCO) v Bolton 1952 (2) PH A65 (C) 74
Bardopoulos and Macrides v Miltiadous 1947 (4) SA 860 (W). 77
Barkhuizen v Napier 2007 (5) SA 323 (CC). 212, 213
Barkhuizen v Napier 2006 (4) SA 1 (SCA) 212
Barlows Tractor Co (Pty) Ltd v Townsend 1996 (2) SA 869 (A). 157, 158
Barnard v Laas 1929 TPD 349 . . . . 116, 117
Barrett NO v Hassim Moti 1925 (1) PH K6 (T). 117
Basil Read (Pty) Ltd v Beta Hotels (Pty) Ltd and Others 2001 (2) SA 760
    (C) 28, 32, 98
Baumann v Thomas 1920 AD 428 . . . . 85, 86, 105
Beaufort West Municipality v Krummeck's Trustees and Others. 43, 96
Beer v Roach 1950 (4) SA 370 (C). 208
Bekker NO v Total South Africa (Pty) Ltd 1990 (3) SA 159 (T) 88
Bell qq Colonial Government v McDonald and Breda (1836) 2 Menz 28. . 157, 208
Benson v SA Mutual Life Assurance Society 1986 (1) SA 776 (A). 107, 108
Bentley Maudesley & Company Ltd v 'Carburol' (Pty) Ltd and Another 1949
    (4) SA 873 (C) 83
Beplat v Dold & Stone (1909) 26 SC 160 95
Bermann en 'n Ander v Administrasie van Suidwes-Afrika 1966 (2) PH A85
    (SWA). 109
Berzack Brothers Ltd v Iesberts and Others 1973 (2) SA 196 (W) . . . 147, 148, 153,
    175, 180
Bester v Cape Finance Corporation 1955 (1) PH A29 (C). 95
Bethlehem v Zietsman 1908 EDC 367. . . . . 127, 135
Bevern v Jacobse (1889) 7 SC 65. 135
Bevray Investments (Edms) Bpk v Boland Bank Bpk en Andere 1993 (3) SA
    597 (A). 42
Birch v Divisional Council of Jansenville (1890) 7 SC 314. . . . . 116, 131
BK Tooling (Edms) Bpk v Scope Precision Engineering (Edms) Bpk 1979 (1)
    SA 391 (A). 109
Blackshire v Stegman, Esselen and Roos 1906 TS 768 95
Blom v Auret (1907) 24 SC 48. 35
Blue Chip Consultants (Pty) Ltd v Shamrock 2002 (3) SA 231 (W) 66
Board of Executors v Ross (1888) 6 SC 48 131

TABLE OF CASES xiii

Board of Executors v Ross (1888) 6 SC 52 129
Board v De Villiers (1840) 2 Menz 55 104
Bock and Others v Duburoro Investments (Pty) Ltd 2004 (2) SA 242 (SCA). . 88, 206
BOE Bank Ltd v Bassage 2006 (5) SA 33 (SCA) 169
Boland Bank v Loeb and Others 1995 (2) SA 142 (C). 106
Boonzaier v Kiley 1981 (2) SA 618 (W) 136
Boshoff v South African Mutual Life Assurance Society 2000 (3) SA 597 (C). . 189
Botha (now Griessel) and Another v Finanscredit (Pty) Ltd 1989 (3) SA 773
    (A) 113, 114, 188, 205, 213, 214
Botha v Nedbank 1981 (4) SA 949 (NC) 79
Bourke v Buxton and De Villiers (1899) 3 SAR 39 100
Bouwer v Lichtenburg Cooperative Society. 100
Bowe v Colmar Garage (Pty) Ltd 1955 (1) PH F34 (W) 133
Boyce NO v Bloem and Others 1960 (3) SA 855 (T). 194
BP Lesotho (Pty) Ltd v Lucy Mabathoana and others (High Court of Lesotho,
    unreported, 15th November 2004). 25
Brandt v Weber (1886) 2 SAR 98. . . . . 41, 126
Brinkman v McGill 1931 AD 303 . . . . 206, 207, 210
Brink v Humphries & Jewell (Pty) Ltd 2005 (2) SA 419 (SCA. 66
Brisley v Drotsky 2002(4) SA 1 (SCA) 88, 91, 212, 213, 214
Brook v Jones 1964 (1) SA 765 (N) 48
Brown & Co v Jacobson 1915 OPD 42 63
Brown, Greisler (Pty) Ltd v Wootton 1937 (1) PH A8 (W) 36, 99
Buerger v Doll 1923 SWA 5 . . . . 150, 153, 176, 180
Bulsara v Jordan & Co Ltd 1996 (1) SA 805 (A). 202, 203
Burton v Barlow Rand Ltd, t/a Barrows Tractor and Machinery Co, Burton v
    Thomas Barlow & Sons (Natal) Ltd 1978 (4) SA 794 (T). 198
Business Buying & Investment Co Ltd v Linaae 1959 (3) SA 93 (T) . . . 57, 58, 148,
    154, 157, 158, 208
Buyskes and Others, Trustees of Du Toit v De Kock and Others (1832) 2 Menz
    12 . . . . 47, 85, 86, 105
Byron v Duke Inc 2002 (5) SA 483 (SCA). 111

C

Cairns (Pty) Ltd v Playdon & Co Ltd 1948 (3) SA 99 (A). 90, 91
Cape Produce Co (PE) (Pty) Ltd v Dal Maso and Another NNO 2001 (2) SA
    182 (W) 188, 190
Capnorizas v Webber Road Mansions (Pty) Ltd and Another 1966 (1) PH A22
    (W). 46
Carrim v Omar [2001] 3 All SA 71 (W). 28, 29, 32, 34, 34
Cassiem v Standard Bank of South Africa Ltd 1930 AD 366. 84
Cazalet v Johnson 1914 TPD 142. . . . . 34, 35
Cecil Nurse (Pty) Ltd v Nkola 2008 (2) SA 441 (SCA). 81
Chase v Cloete (1828) 2 Menz 4. 128
Choonora v Rahim 1960 (2) SA 504(W) 57
Churchwardens of Uitenhage v Meyer and Barnard (1835) 2 Menz 21. 105

Cinema City (Pty) Ltd v Morgenstern Family Estates (Pty) Ltd and Others 1980
(1) SA 796 (A) 89
Cloete v Eksteen (1834) 1 Menz 71 183
Coca-Cola Sabco (SA) (Pty) Ltd v Muller 1999 (4) SA 829 (E) 70
Coetzee v Tiran (1880) Foord 42 135
Cohen v Louis Blumberg (Pty) Ltd 1949 (2) SA 849 (W) 111
Colonial Government v Du Toit and Muller (1855) 2 Searle 225 .... 98, 105
Colonial Government v Edenborough and Another (1886) 4 SC 290 .. 27, 157, 188, 195, 198, 206, 207, 208
Colonial Government v Goch and Chapman (1885) 3 HCG 216............. 105
Colonial Government v Sandenberg, Executors of Matthiesson, and Jan W Klerk
(1834) 2 Menz 18... 105
Colonial Treasurer v Swart 1910 TPD 552.......... 131, 134, 142, 194, 208, 209
Colonial Trust Corporation Ltd of Graaff Reinet v The School Board of Pearston
and Others 1916 CPD 275 .... 107, 108, 109
Coloured Development Corporation Ltd v Sahabodien 1981 (1) SA 868 (C) ... 142
Commercial Bank of Namibia Ltd v Trans Continental Trading (Namibia) and
Others 1992 (2) SA 66 (Nm) 78, 79
Commercial Union Assurance Co Ltd v Hayden [1977] 1 QB 804 (CA) 816,
[1977] All ER 441 .... 181, 182
Commissioner for Customs and Excise v Standard General Insurance
Company Ltd. [1998] 4 All SA 46 (W) 202
Compaan v Dorbyl Structural Engineering (Pty) Ltd t/a Brownbuilt Metal
Sections 1983 (4) SA 107 (T)..................................... 69, 72
Conradie v Rossouw 1919 AD 279.................................... 63
Consolidated Agencies v Agjee 1948 (4) SA 179 (N) 85
Consolidated Textile Mills Ltd v Weiniger 1961 (3) SA 335 (O).............. 120
Copestake and Others v Alexander, In re Fisher (1882) 2 SC 137............ 165
Cope v Atkinson's Motor Garages Ltd 1931 AD 366............. 47, 89, 103, 110
Corrans and Another v Transvaal Government and Coull's Trustee 1909 TS
605 .... 27, 29, 43, 107, 108, 148, 152, 153, 154, 159, 163
Credit Corporation of SA Ltd v Botha 1968 (4) SA 837 (N) 79
Credit Corporation of SA Ltd v Du Preez 1961 (4) SA 515 (T)............... 67
Credit Guarantee Insurance Corporation of South Africa Ltd v Schreiber 1987
(3) SA 523 (W)... 70
Cronin v Meerholz 1920 TPD 403 .... 197, 201
Cullinan v Noordkaaplandse Artappelkernmoerkwekers Koöperasie Bpk 1972
(1) SA 761 (A)... 46, 50
Cullinan v Union Government 1922 CPD 33........................... 105

D

Davids en Andere v ABSA Bank Bpk 2005 (3) SA 361 (C)............... 64, 66
De Beers Mining Board v Olsen (1882) 1 HCG 103 .... 206, 208
De Beer v Bosman (TPD 27 November 1990 (case 1993/90) unreported) .. 55, 172, 173, 179, 181, 182
De Charmoy and St Pol v Dhookoo 1924 NPD 254................... 156, 194

TABLE OF CASES xv

De Kock v Russouw and Van der Poel (1841) 1 Menz 78 135
Delfs v Kuehne & Nagel (Pty) Ltd 1990(1) SA 82 (A) 92
Delmas Milling Co Ltd v Du Plessis 1955 (3) SA 447 (A) 89, 90
D Engineering Co (Pty) Ltd v Morkel and Others (TPD 27 March 1992
    (A813/91); (1992) 3 Commercial Law Digest 228 (T) 114, 213
De Pass v Colonial Government and Others (1886) 4 SC 383. 55
Devenish v Johnstone (1847) 2 Menz 82 164
De Villiers v Conradie and De Vos (1864) 5 Searle 68. . . . . 47, 62
De Villiers v Nefdin Bank, A Division of Nedcor Bank Ltd 1997 (2) SA 76 (E). . 71
Dewar v De Witt & Dickens NO 1948 (4) SA 898 (GW) 107
De Wet Bros v The Master and Another 1934 CPD 427 120
De Wet NO v Jurgens 1970 (3) SA 38 (A) 44
De Wet v Joubert 1931 CPD 123 84
Dickinson v South African General Electric Co (Pty) Ltd 1973 (2) SA 620
    (A) 84, 135
Diners Club SA (Pty) Ltd v Livingstone and Another 1995 (4) SA 493 (W). 65
Diners Club SA (Pty) Ltd v Thorburn 1990(2) SA 870(C). 65
Diners Club South Africa (Pty) Ltd v Durban Engineering (Pty) Ltd 1980 (3)
    SA 53 (A). 34, 112
Dirck's Estate v Gwadiso & Komanis' Estates 1936 EDL 303 . . . . 54, 157
Director of Public Works v Lewis, Blundell and Roberts 1908 ORC 14 . . . 104, 120,
    134
Divine Gates & Co v African Clothing Factory 1930 CPD 238. 198
Donelly v Barclays Bank Ltd 1995 (3) SA 1 (A) 214
Donelly v Barclays National Bank Ltd 1990 (1) SA 375 (W) 114, 214, 213
Dorman v Perring 1922 EDL 137. 35
Douglas v Baynes [1908] AC 477, 1908 TS 1207 92
Dowson & Dobson Industrial Ltd v Van der Werf and Others 1981 (4) SA 417
    (C). 43
Dreyer v Smuts (1828) 1 Menz 308 . . . . 95, 115
Du Plessis v Greef and Walter (1905) 22 SC 580. . . . . 129, 135, 143
Du Plessis v Miller and Carlie 1906 TS 150. 208
Durity Alpha (Pty) Ltd v Vagg 1991 (2) SA 840 (A) 72
Du Toit en 'n Ander v Barclays Nasionale Bank Bpk 1985 (1) SA 563 (A) . . 46, 71
Dwyer v Goldseller 1906 TS 126. . . . . 156, 194
Dyamola v Cohen 1927 (1) PH A20 (E). 116

E

EA Gani (Pty) Ltd v Francis 1984 (1) SA 462 (T) 203
Eager v Clarke and Others (1933) 2 Menz 15 86
Eaton & Louw v Arcade Properties (Pty) Ltd 1961 (4) SA 233 (T). 46
Eaton Robins & Co v Nel (2) (1909) 26 SC 624 . . . . 41, 197
Edgcome v Maunsell 1911 CPD 521 . . . . 34, 35
Eerste Nasionale Bank van Suidelike Afrika Bpk v Noordkaap Lewendehawe
    Kooperasie Bpk 1997 (1) SA 299 (A) 53

Eerste Nasionale Bank van Suidelike Afrika Bpk v Saayman NO 1997(4) SA 302
(A) 51, 63, 211
Eley (formerly Memmel) v Lynn & Main Inc 2008 (2) SA 150 (SCA)........ 203
Ellesmere Brewery Company v Cooper and Others [1896] 1 QB 75...... 181, 182
Ellis v Trust Bank of Africa Ltd 1981 (1) SA 733 (N) 73, 78
Estate Liebenberg v Standard Bank of South Africa Ltd 1927 AD 502.. 137, 163, 208, 209
Estate Silbert & Co v De Jager 1933 CPD 88 .... 84, 85, 163
Estate Smuts v Behrens 1872 NLR 71 209
Estate Steer v Steer 1923 CPD 354............... 134, 154, 158, 175, 173, 177
Estate Tudhope v Sand (1907) 24 SC 614 .... 148, 157
Estate Van der Lith v Conradie & Others (1903) 20 SC 241 .... 40, 188
Ewers v The Resident Magistrate of Oudtshoorn and Another (1880) Foord 32 . 163
Executors Estate Watson v Huneberg & Leathern 1915 NPD 571..... 56, 172, 180
Executors of Hoets v De Vos (1837) 2 Menz 53......................... 208
Executors of Watermeyer v Executor of Watermeyer (1870) 2 Buch 69 ... 158, 193, 208
Ex parte Currie NO 1966 (4) SA 546 (D)............................. 168
Ex parte Goldman and Kalmer NNO 1965 (1) SA 464 (W).................. 69
Ex parte Minister of Justice: in Re Nedbank Ltd v Abstein Distributors (Pty)
Ltd and Others 1995 (3) SA 1 (A) 214

F

Farthing and Another v Pieters & Co 1913 CPD 771.................. 148, 168
Farthing v Pieters and Co 1912 CPD 215.......................... 128, 148
Fauresmith Board of Executors v Blommestein (1887) 4 CLJ 290 95
Faure v Bosman (1864) 5 Searle 9 .... 164, 193, 205
Featherstone v Peel (1909) 26 SC 417 .... 129, 136
Featherstone v Trustees of East London Angling Society and Peel (1906) 16
CTR 112.. 58
Fedbond Nominees (Pty) Ltd v Meier 2008 (1) SA 458 (C) 59
Federated Timbers (Pretoria) (Pty) Ltd v Fourie 1978 (1) SA 292 (T)....... 62, 71
Feldman Ltd v Sulski 1954 (4) SA 665 (W)..................... 86, 98, 105
Ferreira and Others v SAPDC (Trading) Ltd 1983 (1) SA 235 (A) 81, 113
Finansbank Bpk v Klopper 1981 (1) SA 106 (T) 208, 209
Fircone Investments (Pty) Ltd v Bank of Lisbon and South Africa and Another
1982 (3) SA 700 (T)......................... 163, 180, 173, 175, 176, 179
Fircone Investments (Pty) Ltd v Bank of Lisbon and South Africa Ltd and
Another 1981 (3) SA 141 (W) 55, 169, 172
First Consolidated Holdings (Pty) Ltd v Bissett and Others 1978 (4) SA 491 (T). 48
First National Bank of SA Ltd v Lynn NO and Others 1996 (2) SA 339 (A). 48, 111
Firstrand Bank Ltd v Carl Beck (Pty) Ltd and Carl Beck 2009 (3) SA 384 (T). . 193
First Rand Bank of Southern Africa Ltd v Pretorius and Another 2002 (3) SA
489 (C)... 75
Fitzgerald v Argus Printing and Publishing Co Ltd (1907) 3 Buch AC 152 .. 27, 99, 131, 132, 142

TABLE OF CASES xvii

FJ Hawkes & Co Ltd v Nagel, 1957 (3) SA 126 (W).............. 92, 93, 94, 103
FJK Syndicate v Du Preez and Smit 1943 WLD 116............ 28, 83, 136, 155
FJ Mitrie (Pty) Ltd v Madgwick and Another 1979 (1) SA 232 (D) 72, 73
Fluxman v Brittian 1941 AD 273...................................... 115
Form-Scaff (Pty) Ltd v Fischer (D), unreported 21 August 1992 65
Fourlamel (Pty) Ltd v Maddison 1977 (1) SA 333 (A) ... 68, 69, 72, 73, 77, 78, 79
Fourlamel (Pty) Ltd v Penguin Heating and Air Conditioning (Pty) Ltd and
 Others 1975 (4) SA 501 (W) 77
Fraser and Another v Viljoen 2008 (4) 106 (SCA)......................... 75
Freedman and Rossi (Pty) Ltd v Geustyn and Others.................. 190, 191
French v Sterling Finance Corporation (Pty) Ltd 1961 (4) SA 732 (A)........ 195
Friedman v Bond Clothing Manufacturers (Pty) Ltd 1965 (1) SA 673 (T) .. 48, 168,
194, 195, 197
Froman v Robertson 1971 (1) SA 115 (A).............................. 63
Fry and Another v First National Bank of South Africa Ltd 1996 (4) SA 924
 (C).. 206, 207
Fryde v Fryde 1944 CPD 407.................................... 161, 162

G

Gaba v Ordra Trust and Investments (Pty) Ltd and Another 1954 (2) SA 129 (T).....
 129, 136, 143
General Accident Insurance Company SA Ltd v Dancor Holdings (Pty) Ltd and
 Others 1981 (4) SA 968 (A)...................................... 71, 72
George v Fairmead (Pty) Ltd 1958 (2) SA 465 (A) 64
Gerber v Wolson 1955 (1) SA 158 (A)... 27, 54, 131, 139, 142, 146, 147, 150, 151,
152, 167, 171, 174, 180
G & H Montage Gmbh v Irvani [1990] 1 WLR 667 (CA).................. 83
Gie v De Villiers (1835) 1 Menz 63 183
Glenn Brothers v Commercial General Agency Co Ltd 1905 TS 737 . 46, 87, 88, 89,
110
Glolec Bpk v Van Rensburg en 'n Ander 1983 (2) SA 192 (O) 135
Goldschmidt NO v Kinnear (1885) 2 SAR 1 .... 126, 130
Goode, Durrant and Murray Ltd v Hewitt and Cornell NNO 1961 (4) SA 286
 (N) 63
Gould v Ekermans 1929 TPD 96 .... 84, 85, 158, 208, 210
Green v Beveridge (1891) 8 SC 155.................................... 97
Grootchwaing Salt Works Ltd v Van Tonder 1920 AD 492 199
Gurland v Caltex (Africa) Ltd 1965 (2) SA 659 (SR) 57

H

Haffajee v Ramdhani 1947 (1) SA 823 (A) 85, 195, 197, 208
Hanekom v Builders Market Klerksdorp (Pty) Ltd and Others 2007 (3) SA 95
 (SCA)... 52, 62
Harcourt v Eastman NO 1953 (2) SA 424 (N)............................ 52
Hare qq v Croeser (1828) 1 Menz 293.............................. 128, 129
Harman's Estate v Bartholomew 1955 (2) SA 302 (N) 34, 155

xviii   TABLE OF CASES

Hart v Corder 1973 (3) SA 11 (N) 55, 172, 173, 177
Hasson Trading Co v Hopkinson and Hopkinson 1961 R & N 161............ 48
Hastie v Dunstan (1892) 9 SC 449...................................... 197
Hattingh & Co v De Wet (1904) 21 SC 212.............................. 118
Hawkes, FJ, & Co Ltd v Nagel 1957 (3) SA 126 (W) 92, 83, 94, 103
Hazis v Transvaal and Delagoa Bay Investment Co Ltd 1939 AD 372 98
Heathfield v Maqelepo 2004(2) SA 636 (SCA) 33
Hedy (Pty) Ltd v Wellcut Garment Manufacturing Co (Pty) Ltd and Another
    1953 (2) SA 236 (C)... 130, 136
Henwood & Co v Westlake and Coles (1887) 5 SC 341 .... 55, 167
H Maisels & Co (Pty) Ltd v Zirzow 1971 (3) SA 523 (SWA).............. 131
Hodgetts Timbers (East London) (Pty) Ltd v HBC Properties (Pty) Ltd and
    Another 1972 (4) SA 208 (E)....................................... 80
Hoyer v Martin and Others 1968 (2) PH A53 (D) 177
Hubbart v Rogers 1915 WLD 39 .... 34, 35, 131
Humphreys v Bredell 1913 TPD 86 136
Huneberg and Others v Watson's Estate 1916 AD 116................ 56, 58, 173
Hurley v Marais (1882) 2 SC 155........................ 116, 117, 125, 127
Hutchinson v Hylton Holdings and Another 1993 (2) SA 405 (T). 27, 33, 35, 42, 89,
                                                                              98

                                        I

Ideal Finance Corporation v Coetzer 1969 (4) SA 43 (O) 57, 131, 142
Ideal Finance Corporation v Coetzer 1970 (3) SA 1 (A) 131, 142, 188
Imperial Cold Storage and Supply Company Ltd v Julius Weil and Co 1912 AD
    747 .... 32, 35, 38
Incorporated General Insurances Ltd v Saayman en Andere 1982 (1) SA 739
    (T).. 164
Indac Electronics (Pty) Ltd v Volkskas Bank Ltd 1992 (1) 8A 783 (A)......... 99
Industrial Development Corporation of SA Ltd v See Bee Holdings (Pty) Ltd
    and Others 1978 (4) SA 136 (C) 80, 143, 156, 171
Industrial Development Corporation of SA (Pty) Ltd v Silver 2003 (1) SA 365
    (SCA)... 70, 72, 73
Inglis v Durban Navigation Collieries Ltd (1908) 29 NLR 436........... 27, 104
In re Brink, ex parte Porter, Hodgson & Co (1865) 1 Roscoe 305............ 120
In re Deneys (1846) 3 Menz 309 .... 57, 120
In re Sydserff (1866) 5 Searle 193 120
In re Trollip (1895) 12 SC 243..................................... 69
Intercontinental Exports (Pty) Ltd v Fowles 1999 (2) SA 1045 (A)   44, 74, 75, 76, 77
Inter Industria Bpk v Nedbank Bpk en 'n Ander 1989 (3) SA 33 (NC) 164, 198,
                                                                         199, 204
Inter-Union Finance Ltd v Dunsterville 1956 (4) SA 280 (D) 48
Inter-Union Finance, Ltd v Franskraalstrand (Edms) Bpk and Others 1965 (4) SA
    180 (W) 47
Inventive Labour Structuring (Pty) Ltd v Corfe 2006 (3) SA 107 (SCA) . 74, 75, 76
Irwin v Davies 1937 CPD 442 .... 154, 157, 195, 206, 207, 210

TABLE OF CASES xix

Iscor Pension Fund v Marine and Trade Insurance Co Ltd 1961 (1) SA 178 (T) 31, 36
Israelsohn v Newman & Sons Ltd 1949 (4) SA 300 (C) 84, 156

J

Jans v Nedcor Bank Ltd 2003 (6) SA 646 (SCA) 202, 203
Jayber (Pty) Ltd v Miller and Others 1981 (2) SA 403 (N) 96
Jeeva Mahomed v Mahomed Valli 1922 TPD 124 .... 127, 132
Jenkins & Co v TN Price (1903) 24 NLR 112 .... 112, 205
J McNeil v Insolvent Estate of R Robertson (1882) 3 NLR 190 48
Johannesburg Coal Agency v Hyman 1915 WLD 98 197
Johannesburg Town Council v Union Assurance Society Ltd 1928 AD 294 .. 106, 110, 208, 210
Jonnes v Anglo-African Shipping Co (1936) Ltd 1972 (2) SA 827 (A) ... 88, 89, 90
Joosab v Tayob 1910 TS 486 196
Jordan & Co Ltd v Hamant Bulsara 1992 (4) SA 457 (E) 202, 203
Joubert v Vermooten 1912 TPD 537 .... 116, 117
JPS Nominees (Pty) Ltd v Kruger 1976 (1) SA 89 (W) 71
JR & M Moffett (Pty) Ltd v Kolbe Eiendoms Beleggings (Edms) Bpk and Another 1974 (2) SA 426 (O) 131, 142, 198, 199
J & T Anderson v Patrick & Plowright (1904) 25 NLR 75 ..... 105, 131, 135, 142
Jungers v List 1978 (1) SA 1200 (SWA) 34
Jurgens and Others v Volkskas Bank Ltd 1993 (1) SA 214 (A) 61, 78, 79
Just Names Properties 11 CC and Another v Fourie and Others 2008 (1) 343 (SCA) 75

K

Kalil v Standard Bank of South Africa Ltd 1967 (4) SA 550 (A).. 55, 112, 119, 120, 121
Kaplan v ER Syfret & Co 1914 CPD 1104 .... 102, 131, 142
Karstein v Moribe and Others 1982 (2) SA 282 (T) 46
Keens Group Co (Pty) Ltd v Lötter 1989 (1) SA 585 (C) 63, 64
Kennedy NO v Haarhoff (1884) 2 HCG 215 105
Kessoopersadh en 'n Ander v Essop en 'n Ander 1970 (1) SA 265 (A) 49
Khan v Naidoo 1989 (3) SA 724 (N) 64
Kilroe-Daley v Barclays National Bank Ltd 1984 (4) SA 609 (A) 131, 143, 202
Kistan and Others v Komarasamy 1940 NPD 56 55
Klopper v Van Straaten (1894) 11 SC 94 .... 55, 116, 117, 127, 134, 135, 138, 143
Knightsbridge Investments (Pvt) Ltd v Gurland 1964 (4) SA 273 (SR) 42
Kotze v Meyer (1830) 1 Menz 466 .... 154, 157
Kowarsky & Co v Sable 1923 WLD 156 85
Kroon v Enschede and Others 1909 TS 374 ...... 55, 145, 148, 159, 172, 175, 177

L

Lalia v Bodasirg 1955 (1) PH F49 (D) 197
Lange Accessories (Pvt) Ltd v Fisher and Another 1974 (1) SA 61 (R) 130

Langeberg Koöperasie Bpk v Inverdoorn Farming and Trading Company Ltd
  1965 (2) SA 597 (A).   27
Langeveld v Union Finance Holdings (Pty) Ltd 2007 (4) SA 572 (W)   66
Langston Clothing (Properties) CC v Danco Clothing (Pty) Ltd 1998 (4) SA 885
  (A) 106, 112
Larkins and Green v Bok NO (1886) 2 SAR 108. . . . .   206, 210
Lategan and Another NNO v Boyes and Another 1980 (4) SA 191 (T). . .   63, 69, 71,
  206
Lazarus v Gorfinkel 1988 (4) SA 123 (C). 75, 77
Leathern v Henwood & Co (1887) 8 NLR 29 . . . .   107, 108, 109, 166
Lee en 'n Ander v Maraisdrif (Edms) Bpk 1976 (2) SA 536 (A).   45
Leipsig v Bankorp Ltd 1994 (2) SA 128 (A)   200
Lever v Buhrmann 1925 TPD 254 . . . .   36, 55, 86, 172, 173, 174, 176
Levitan NO v Petrol Conservation (Pty) Ltd and Another 1962 (3) SA 233 (W) .   68
Levi v Almog 1990 (1) SA 541 (W). 72, 85, 163, 167
Lewin & Adamstein v Burger (1908) 18 CTR 160. . . . .   67, 204
Lewis & Friedland Ltd v Tinn Bros & Lawrie 1931 (2) PH A95 (T).   110
Leyland Finance Co Ltd v Van Rensburg 1970 (4) SA 145 (T)   112
Leyland South Africa (Pty) Ltd v Booysen and Clark Motors (Pty) Ltd 1984 (3)
  SA 480 (W)   136
Liebenberg NO v MGK Bedryfsmaatskappy (Pty) Ltd 2003 (2) SA 224 (SCA). .   53
Linden Duplex (Pty) Ltd v Harrowsmith 1978 (1) SA 371 (W). .   188, 190, 191, 193
Lindley v Ward 1911 CPD 21. . . . .   104, 129, 154, 208
Linford v Heynes Mathew Limited 1915 CPD 531 . . . .   87, 90
Lion Mill Manufacturing Co (Pty) Ltd and Another v New York Shipping Co
  (Pty) Ltd 1974 (4) SA 984 (T).   83
Lippert & Co v Van Rensburg (1877) 7 Buch 42   154
Lipschitz NO v UDC Bank Ltd 1979 (1) SA 789 (A) 39, 41
Liquidator of the Owl Syndicate v Bright (1909) 26 SC 12. . . . .   129, 139
Liquidators, FH Clarke & Co Ltd v Nesbitt 1906 TS 726   189
List v Jungers 1979 (3) SA 106 (A) 29, 32, 88, 89, 98
Litecor Voltex (Natal) (Pty) Ltd v Jason 1988 (2) SA 78 (D).   75
London and South Africa Bank v Behrens 1869 NLR 189   208
Louw v WP (Kooperatief) Bpk 1998 (2) SA 418 (A).   202
LTA Construction Bpk v Administrateur, Transvaal 1992 (1) SA 473 (A). .   111, 116

M

Maasdorp v Graaff-Reinet Board of Executors (1909) 3 Buch AC 482. . .   24, 57, 84,
  131, 135, 142
Maasdorp v Morkel's Executor (1828) 1 Menz 293.   128
Machanick v Simon 1920 CPD 333   63
Mackenzie v Basckin 1925 CPD 257. . . . .   154, 163
Madnitsky v Kantor 1952 (3) SA 491 (W).   136
Mahadi v De Kock and Hyde (1883) 1 HCG 344   24
Maharaj v Barclays National Bank Ltd 1976 (1) SA 418(A).   77
Mahomed v Lockhat Brothers & Co Ltd 1944 AD 230 . . . .   57, 134

TABLE OF CASES xxi

Makda v Kalsheker 1954 (4) SA 185 (SR)............................ 129
Malcolm v Cooper and Others 1974 (4) SA 52 (C) 39
Malmesbury Board of Executors and Trust Co v Duckitt and Bam 1924 CPD 101 . 27
Managers of Oudtshoorn Public School v White (1893) 10 SC 203 46
MAN Truck & Bus (SA) (Pty) Ltd v Singh and Another (2) 1976 (4) SA 266
  (N) 102
Manufacturers Development Co (Pty) Ltd v Repcar Holdings (Pty) Ltd and
  Others 1975 (2) SA 779 (W) 80, 143, 156, 171
Mapenduka v Ashington 1919 AD 343................................. 86
Marshall's Industrials Ltd v Khan and Another 1959 (4) SA 684 (D) 52
Mason & Co v Booth & Co (1903) 20 SC 645........................... 127
Maxwell Furnishers v Hume 1971 (3) SA 636 (T)....................... 69
McDonald v Bell 3 Moo PCC 315 157
McLean v McLean's Trustee 1923 AD 141 120
Meer v General Industrial Credit Corporation (Pty) Ltd 1947 (4) SA 330 (C)   56, 83,
                          131, 142, 147, 148, 150, 155, 156, 172, 200, 204
Metequity Ltd NO and Another v Heel 1997 (3) SA 432 (W)............ 41, 203
Meyer v Coetzee (1892) 4 SAR 252................................. 100, 129
Meyer v Coetzee 1893 OR 25..................................... 116, 208
Meyer v Low (1832) 2 Menz 8...................................... 157, 158
Meyer v Merchants' Trust Ltd 1942 AD 244 74
Mignoel Properties (Pty) Ltd v Kneebone 49
Miller's Trust Foreshore Properties (Pty) Ltd v Kasimov 1960 (4) SA 953 (C) . 154
Miller v Muller 1965 (4) SA 458 (C) 41, 198, 208
Miller v Trust Bank of South Africa 1965 (2) SA 447 (T) 157
Millman and Another NNO v Masterbond Participation Bond Trust Managers
  (Pty) Ltd (under curatorship) and Others 1997 (1) SA 113 (C)....... 4, 13, 168
Millman NO and Stein NO v Kamfer 1993 (1) SA 305 (C)............. 191, 192
Millman v Masterbond Participation Trust 1997 (1) SA 113 (C)........... 56, 57
Milne NO v Cook and Others 1956 (3) SA 317 (D).................... 47, 105
Minister of Community Development v SA Mutual Fire and General Insurance
  Co Ltd 1978 (1) SA 1020 (W)......................... 206, 207, 210
Minister van Landbou-Tegniese Dienste v Scholtz 1971 (3) SA 188 (A) 91
Mitchell Cotts & Co v Commissioner of Railways 1905 TS 349............. 148
Mmabatho Food Corporation (Pty) Ltd v Fourie en Andere 1985 (1) SA 318 (T). 46
Moodliar v Moodley 1958 (1) PH F44 (N)............................. 40
Moosa v Mahomed 1939 TPD 271........... 55, 63, 84, 127, 154, 156, 172, 177
Moosa v Schindler Lifts (SA) Ltd 1955 (2) PH A56 (A).................... 85
Moraitis v De Canha and Another 1984 (1) SA 420 (W).................. 136
Moreriane v Trans-Oranje Finansierings- en Ontwikkelingskorporasie, Bpk
  1965 (1) SA 767 (T).. 95, 196
Morgan and Another v Brittan Boustred Ltd 1992 (2) SA 775 (A) 81, 112, 113
Moss & Page Trading Co (Pty) Ltd v Spancraft Furniture Manufacturers &
  Shopfitters (Pty) Ltd & others 1972 (1) SA 211 (D) 48
Moti & Co v Cassim's Trustee 1924 AD 720 ... 31, 82, 83, 132, 135, 136, 143, 159,
                                                168, 188, 194, 195

Mouton v Mynwerkersunie 1977 (1) SA 119 (A). 28, 32, 98, 131, 142
Muller and Others v Botswana Development Corporation Ltd [2002] 3 All SA
    663 (SCA) 131, 142, 199
Murray and Burrill v Buck and Buck 1870 NLR 155 27
Musgrove & Watson (Rhod) (Pvt) Ltd v Rotta 1978 (2) SA 918 (R). 63, 64
Musgrove & Watson (Rhodesia) Ltd v Rotta 1978 (4) SA 656 (RA). 67
Mutual and Federal Insurance Co Ltd v Oudtshoorn Municipality 1985 (1) SA
    419 (A). 31
Mutual Construction Co v Victor [2002] 3 All SA 807 (W). 61, 74

N

Natal Bank v Banfield & Co (1885) 6 NLR 178 195
Nathanson and Another v Dennill 1904 TH 289. . . . . 157, 206
National Acceptance Co (Pty) Ltd v Robertson and Another 1938 CPD 175 83
National Bank of ORC v Salkinder 1907 OR 69 158
National Bank of South Africa Ltd v Seligson 1921 WLD 108. 83
National Board (Pretoria) (Pty) Ltd and Another v Estate Swanepoel 1975 (3)
    SA 16 (A). 73
National Industrial Credit Corporation Ltd v Zachareas 1949 (4) SA 790 (W). . . 25
National Industrial Credit Corporation (Rhod) Ltd v Gumede and Another (2)
    1964 (4) SA 258 (SR). 57
NBS Boland Bank Ltd v One Berg River Drive CC 1999 (4) SA 928 (A) 212
Neale v Edenvale Plastic Products (Pty) Ltd 1971 (3) SA 860 (T) 62
Nedbank Ltd v Abstein Distributors (Pty) Ltd and Others 1989 (3) SA 750
    (T). 114, 214
Nedbank Ltd v Van der Berg and Another 1987 (3) SA 449 (W). 114, 214
Nedbank Ltd v Van Zyl 1990 (2) SA 469 (A). 28, 40, 44, 45, 46, 56, 62, 76
Nedcor Bank Ltd v Sutherland 1998 (4) SA 32 (N). 202
Nedfin Bank Ltd v Muller and Others 1981 (4) SA 229 (N) 81
Neethling qq v Minnaar (1830) 1 Menz 535 149
Neethling v Hamman (1834) 1 Menz 71 183
Nelson v Hodgetts Timbers (East London) (Pty) Ltd 1973 (3) SA 37 (A). . . 80, 156,
    172
Neon and Cold Cathode Illuminations (Pty) Ltd v Ephron 1978 (1) SA 463 (A) . 57,
    131, 134, 142
Neugarten and Others v Standard Bank of SA Ltd 1989 (3) SA 797(A) 42
Neuhoff v York Timbers Ltd 1981 (4) SA 666 (T). 74, 112, 113, 210
Niel & Co v Quin & O'Hea 1903 TH 458 63
Nisbet and Dickson v Thwaites (1829) 1 Menz 427. 158
Noakes v Whiteing 1968 (1) SA 302 (R) 177
Norex Industrial Properties (Pty) Ltd v Monarch South Africa Insurance Co Ltd
    1987 (1) SA 827 (A). 96, 189
Northern Assurance Co Ltd v Delbrook-Jones and Another 1966 (3) SA 176
    (T). 24, 35
Northern Cape Co-operative Livestock Agency Ltd v John Roderick & Co Ltd
    1965 (2) SA 64 (O). 69, 74, 75, 114, 115, 194

TABLE OF CASES

Norton v Statchwell (1840) 1 Menz 77. 135
Nosworthy and Another v Yorke 1921 OPD 404 .... 172, 177
Nuform Formwork & Scaffolding (Pty) Ltd v Natscaff CC and Others 2003 (2)
    SA 56 (D). 76

O

Oak v Lumsden (1884) 3 SC 144. .... 24, 85
Oceanair (Natal) (Pty) Ltd v Sher 1980 (1) SA 317 (D). 81, 112, 210
Odendaal v Van Oudtshoorn 1968 (3) SA 433 (T) 160
Oranjerivier Wynkelders (Koöp) Bpk v Von Wieligh [2002] 1 All SA 449 (C)... 71
Orkin Lingerie Co (Pty) Ltd v Melamed & Hurwitz 1963 (1) SA 324 (W) 28, 38, 68
Orlando Hosking v Standard Bank of SA Ltd (1892) 13 NLR 174 .... 31, 67
Orphan Chamber v Cloete (1833) 3 Menz 157. 105
Oslo Land Co Ltd v Temple Nourse 1930 TPD 35. 127
Ottosdal Ontwikkelingsmaatskappy (Edms) Bpk v KNT Bouers (Edms) Bpk 1974 (1)
    SA 712 (T). 89
Overbeek v Cloete (1831) 1 Menz 523. 209

P

Paddock Motors (Pty) Ltd v Igesund 1976 (3) SA 16 (A) 211
Page v ABSA Bank Ltd t/a Volkskas Bank and Another 2000 (2) SA 658 (EC) . 194
Papageorgiou v Kondakis & others 1968 (1) SA 85 (O) 25
Parijs Municipality v AS le Roux and EH le Roux 1916 EDL 215 95
Parker Wood & Company Ltd v Richards and Another 1925 NLR 277.... 104, 134
Patel v Patel and Another 1968 (4) SA 51 (D) 87, 88, 91, 93, 94
Pearce and Another v De Jager 1924 CPD 455 .... 147, 148, 153, 173
Peimer v Finbro Furnishers (Pty) Ltd 1936 AD 177. .... 57, 83, 84, 136, 155
Pendlebury v Walker (1841) 4 Y & C Ex 424 181
Peri-Urban Areas Health Board v The South British Insurance Co Ltd 1966 (2)
    PH A66 (T). 42, 206, 209
Pfeiffer v First National Bank of SA Ltd 1998 (3) SA 1018 (SCA). 115, 116
Pheasant v Warne 1922 AD 481 51
Pizani and Another v First Consolidated Holdings (Pty) Ltd 1979 (1) SA 69 (A). 48,
    71, 79, 96
Plascon-Evans Paints (Transvaal) Ltd v Virginia Glass Works (Pty) Ltd and
    Others 1983 (1) SA 465 (O). 70, 81, 113
Postmaster General v Taute 1905 TS 582. 198
Potgieter en 'n Ander NNO v Shell Suid-Afrika (Edms) Bpk 2003 (1) SA 155
    (SCA). 53, 89
Prins v ABSA Bank Ltd 1998 (3) SA 904 (C) 64
Pritchard Properties (Pty) Ltd v Koulis 1986 (2) SA 1 (A) 89
Progress Knitting and Textiles Ltd v Nefic Investments (Pty) Ltd and Others
    1992 (4) SA 105 (N). 78
Proksch v Die Meester en Andere 1969 (4) SA 567 (A). 163, 168, 169, 170
Putter v Provincial Insurance Co Ltd and Another 1963 (3) SA 145 (W) 69

R

Rand Bank Ltd v De Jager 1982 (3) SA 418 (C) 4, 196, 201, 202, 203
Rand Bank Ltd v Rubenstein 1981 (2) SA 207 (W). 113, 210
Reichmans (Pty) Ltd v Ramdass 1985 (2) SA 111 (D).   44
Renou v Walcott (1909) 10 HCG 246. . . . .   35, 100
Republican Press (Pty) Ltd v Martin Murray Associates CC and Others 1996 (2) SA 246 (N). 76, 77
Rich and Others v Lagerwey 1974 (4) SA 748 (A)   136
Richter v Bloemfontein Town Council 1922 AD 57.   89
Ridley v Anderson 1911 EDL 13 . . . .   127, 135, 208
Robb NO v Standard Bank Ltd and Another 1979 (2) SA 420 (R)   94
Robertson v Onkruyt (1842) 2 Menz 59.   157
Robinson v Hay 1930 (1) PH E3 (N)   52
Rogerson NO v Meyer and Berning (1837) 2 Menz 38 .   59, 120, 127, 128, 129, 131, 134, 208
Roodt v Botha (1905) 22 SC 189 . . . .   98, 105
Roomer v Wedge Steel (Pty) Ltd 1998 (1) SA 538 (N)   65
Roos v Coetzee (1846) 2 Menz 74 . . . .   57, 144
Ross & Co v Smith (1905) 22 SC 535   116
Rosseau v Bierman (1828) 1 Menz 338   157
Rossi (Pty) Ltd v Geustyn and Others 1986 (4) SA 762 (W).   190
Rossouw and Rossouw v Hodgson & Others 1925 AD 97. . .   31, 159, 163, 166, 168, 170
Royal Bank of Scotland plc v Etridge (No. 2) [2001] 4 All E.R. 449   65
Rudd, Milton & Co v Dolley & Co (1884) 3 EDC 351 . . . .   114, 210
Rutowitz's Flour Mills v The Master and Others 1934 TPD 163. . . . .   163, 165
Ryan Nigel Corporation (Cape) (Pty) Ltd v Peires and Another 1976 (3) SA 660 (C)   80

S

Saambou-Nasionale Bouvereniging v Friedman 1979 (3) SA 978 (A)   63
SA Breweries Ltd v Van Zyl 2006 (1) SA 197 (SCA) 48, 111
SA General Electric Co (Pty) Ltd v Sharfman and Others NNO 1981 (1) SA 592 (W). 110, 112, 119
Sampson v Union and Rhodesia Wholesale Ltd (in liquidation) 1929 AD 468. .   149
SAPDC (Trading) Ltd v Ferreira and Others 1980 (3) SA 507 (T)   210
Sapirstein and Others v Anglo African Shipping Co (SA) Ltd 1978 (4) SA 1 (A) 28, 69, 71, 72
SA Produce, Wine and Brandy Co v Mihnert (1908) 18 CTR 700.   114
Sasfin Bank Ltd v Soho Unit 14 CC.   50
Sasfin (Pty) Ltd v Beukes 1989 (1) SA 1 (A). 114, 213, 214
Sassoon Confirming and Acceptance Co (Pty) Ltd v Barclays National Bank Ltd 1974 (1) SA 641 (A). 32, 34, 88
Schoeman v Moller 1949 (3) SA 949 (O).   195
Schoeman v Moller 1951 (1) SA 456 (O). 34, 35, 131, 206, 207, 208, 209
Schoenfeldt v Myer and Co 1928 TPD 468   110

Schonfrucht v King 1934 (2) PH A35 (W)	195, 209
Scottish Union & National Insurance Co Ltd v Native Recruiting Corporation Ltd 1934 AD 458	88
Segell v Kerdia Investments (Pty) Ltd 1953 (1) SA 20 (W)	43, 90, 96, 103, 110, 116
Senekal v Trust Bank of Africa Ltd 1978 (3) SA 375 (A)	114
Serrurier v Langeveld (1828) 1 Menz 316	128, 134
Shaw v Kirby 1924 GWL 33	34
Shell SA (Pty) Ltd v Guarantee Exchange International 1986 (4) SA 7 (C)	129
Shuter v Ridgway 1926 NPD 149	58, 84
Silver Garbus & Co (Pty) Ltd v Teichert 1954 (2) SA 98 (N)	67
Simon v Sacks and Another 1927 WLD 162	136
Snaid v Volkskas Bank Ltd 1997 (1) SA 239 (W)	111, 115
Sneech v Hill Kaplan Scott and Partners 1981(3) SA 332(A)	72
Société Commerciale de Moteurs v Ackermann 1981 (3) SA 422 (A)	80, 98
Somchem (Pty) Ltd v Federated Insurance Co Ltd and Another 1983 (4) SA 609 (C)	96
Sonfred (Pty) Ltd v Papert 1962 (2) SA 140 (W)	82
Soomar v Jeewa and Others 1958 (4) SA 24 (N)	143
South African Bank v Forde (1886) 4 SC 287	105
South African Forestry Co Ltd v York Timbers Ltd 2005 (3) SA 323 (SCA)	91
South African Independent United Order of Mechanics and Fidelity Benefit Lodge v General Accident Fire and Life Assurance Corporation Ltd 1916 CPD 457	105, 116
South African Scottish Finance Corporation Ltd v Wassenaar 1966 (2) SA 723 (A)	47
Speech v Hill Kaplan Scott and Partners 1981 (3) SA 332 (A)	70
Spindrifter (Pty) Ltd v Lester Donovan (Pty) Ltd 1986 (1) SA 893 (A)	64
Spur Steak Ranch Ltd v Mentz 2000 (3) SA 755 (C)	206
Stainbank v National Bank of South Africa Ltd (1906) 27 NLR 465	24
Standard Bank of SA Ltd v Cohen (1) 1993 (3) SA 846 (SE)	73
Standard Bank of SA Ltd v Cohen (2) 1993 (3) SA 854 (SE)	75, 210
Standard Bank of SA Ltd v Durban Security Glazing (Pty) Ltd 2000 (1) SA 146 (D)	92, 93
Standard Bank of SA Ltd v Jaap de Villiers Beleggings (Edms) Bpk 1978 (3) SA 955 (W)	78, 79
Standard Bank of SA Ltd v Lewis 1922 TPD 285	97, 195
Standard Bank of SA Ltd v Lombard and Another 1977 (2) SA 808 (W)	45
Standard Bank of SA Ltd v Neugarten and Others 1987 (3) SA 695 (W)	42, 114, 214
Standard Bank of SA Ltd v SA Fire Equipment (Pty) Ltd and Another 1984 (2) SA 693 (C)	131, 142, 188, 189, 198, 199
Standard Bank of SA Ltd v Wilkinson 1993 (3) SA 822 (C)	213
Standard Bank of South Africa Ltd v Bhamjee and Another 1978 (4) SA 39 (W)	69
Standard Bank of South Africa Ltd v Oneanate Investments (Pty) Ltd (in Liquidation) 1998 (1) SA 811 (SCA)	115

Standard Bank v Du Plooy and Another; Standard Bank v Coetzee and
  Another (1899) 16 SC 161 67
Standard Bank v Lowry and Another 1926 CPD 338 195
Standard Building Society v Kellerman 1930 TPD 796 24
Standard Credit Corporation Ltd v Laycock 1988 (4) SA 679 (N) 195
Steenkamp v Webster 1955 (1) SA 524 (A) 69
Stephan Brothers v Engelbrecht (1894) 11 SC 248 135
Stewart & Lloyds of SA Ltd v Croydon Engineering Mining Supplies (Pty) Ltd
  and Others 1981 (1) SA 305 (W) 78
Steyn NO v Borckenhagen and Venter (1897) 14 CLJ 202 95
Steytler v Saunders (1883) 2 Menz 15 95
St Patricks Mansions (Pty) Ltd v Grange Restaurant (Pty) Ltd and Another
  1949 (4) SA 57 (W) 88, 92, 96, 103, 112, 116, 117, 190, 194
Strachan v Fawcett 1933 NPD 639 .... 153, 172, 177, 180
Stratton v Cleanwell Dry Cleaners (Pvt) Ltd and Another 1960 (1) SA 355
  (R) 47
Stride v Wepener 1903 TH 383 .... 24, 67
Strydom v Goldblatt 1976 (2) SA 852 (W) 96
Strydom v Protea Eiendomsagente 1979 (2) SA 206 (T) 45
Sulski v Feldman Ltd 1956 (1) SA 759 (A) 60, 86, 98, 105
Swadif (Pty) Ltd v Dyke NO 1978 (1) SA 928 (A) 196
Swart en 'n Ander v Cape Fabrix (Pty) Ltd 1979 (1) SA 195 (A) 88, 89, 90
Sweets from Heaven (Pty) Ltd and Another v Ster Kinekoor Films (Pty) Ltd
  and Another 1999 (1) SA 796 (W) 93
Swiftair Freight CC v Singh 1993 (1) SA 454 (D) 70
Sydney Road Holdings (Pty) Ltd v Simon 1981 (3) SA 104 (D) 96

T

Taylor and Thorne NNO and Others v The Master 1965 (1) SA 658 (N) ... 58, 131,
  142, 160, 163, 165, 168
Techni-Pak Sales (Pty) Ltd v Hall 1968 (3) SA 231 (W) 92
Television & Electrical Distributors (Pty) Ltd v Coetzer en Andere 1962 (1) SA
  747 (T) 39
Tesoriero v Bhyjo Investments Share Block (Pty) Ltd 2000 (1) SA 167 (W) . 53, 64,
  65
Tesven CC and Another v South African Bank of Athens 2000 (1) SA 268 (A) . 74, 77
Texas Co (SA) Ltd v Webb and Tomlinson 1927 NPD 24 .... 86, 114, 210
The Divisional Council of Middelburg v Close (1885) 3 SC 411 95
The Master v General Accident, Fire and Life Assurance Corporation 1935 CPD
  389 210
The Master v Ocean Accident and Guarantee Corporation Limited 1937 CPD
  302 97
The Master v Western Australian Assurance Co Ltd 1925 CPD 314 102
The National Bank of South Africa v Graaf and Others (1904) 21 SC 457 . 111, 115
Theodore v Deaconos 1958 (3) SA 807 (SR) 208, 209

TABLE OF CASES xxvii

Theunissen en Andere v Transvaalse Lewendehawe Koöp Bpk 1988 (2) SA 493
 (A) 69, 72
Townsend v Barlows Tractor Co (Pty) Ltd and Another 1995 (1) SA 159 (W) . . 158
Trans-Africa Credit and Savings Bank Ltd v Union Guarantee and Insurance
 Co Ltd 1963 (2) SA 92 (C). 36
Trans-Drakensberg Bank Ltd v Guy 1964 (1) SA 790 (D). 31, 38, 67, 95, 101
Trans-Drakensberg Bank Ltd v The Master and Others 1962 (4) SA 417 (N). . 57, 104,
 120, 190
Traub v Barclays National Bank Ltd; Kalk v Barclays National Bank 1983 (3)
 SA 619 (A) 192, 204
Trust Bank of Africa Ltd v Cotton 1976 (4) SA 325 (N) 72, 73
Trust Bank of Africa Ltd v Frysch 1976 (2) SA 337 (C) 74
Trust Bank of Africa Ltd v Frysch 1977 (3) SA 562 (A) 28, 39
Trust Bank van Afrika Bpk v Eksteen 1964 (3) SA 402 (A) 42, 79
Trust Bank van Afrika Bpk v Sullivan 1979 (2) SA 765 (T) 73
Trustees of Du Toit v Executors of Smuts and De Kock (1835) 2 Menz 24 . 57, 115,
 144
Trustees of Port Elizabeth Bank v Ogilvie (1866) 1 Roscoe 339 208
Tsaperas and Others v Boland Bank Ltd 1996 (1) SA 719 (A). 81, 91, 113, 188
Tucker and Another v Carruthers 1941 AD 251 55
Turkstra v Massyn 1959 (1) SA 40 (T) 31, 62, 148, 159, 160
TV and Radio Guarantee Co (Pty) Ltd v Du Preez 1986 (3) SA 866 (W) . . 130, 135,
 137

U

Ullman Bros and Davidson v Railton 1903 TS 596 . . . . 127, 135
Union Government v Pearl Assurance Co Ltd 1933 (1) PH A12 (T) 188
Union Government v Van der Merwe 1921 TPD 318 . . . . 27, 38, 57, 131, 134,
 136, 142, 188, 201
Union Share Agency & Investment Ltd v Spain 1928 AD 74 136
Union Trust Maatskappy (Edms) Bpk v Thirion 1965 (3) SA 648 (GW). . . . 55, 155
United Dominions Corporation (SA) Ltd v Rokebrand 1963 (4) SA 411 (T) . 39, 41,
 47

V

Vaid v Ameen 1962 (2) PH A33 (N) 195, 206, 208, 209
Van Aswegen v Van Eetveld and Du Plessis 1925 (2) PH A37 (C) . . . 195, 206, 207
Van den Berg v Malherbe (1829) 1 Menz 429 . . . . 98, 105
Van der Byl v Munnik (1845) 2 Menz 73 . . . . 57, 208
Van der Riet v Pieters 1879 OFS 1 95
Van der Spuy v Levy 1921 TPD 581 84
Van der Vyver v De Wayer and Others (1861) 4 Searle 27 . . 55, 58, 131, 136, 138, 142
Van der Walt's Trustees v Van Coller 1911 TPD 1173 . . . . 163, 165
Van Eeden v Sasol Pensioenfonds 1975 (2) SA 167 (O) 39, 42
Van Niekerk v Smit and Others 1952 (3) SA 17 (T) 69
Van Oosterzee v McRaie qq Carfrae & Co (1828) 1 Menz 305 157

Van Rensburg v City Credit (Natal) (Pty) Ltd 1980 (4) SA 500 (N) 89
Van Wyk v Rottcher's Saw Mills (Pty) Ltd 1948 (1) SA 983 (A) 75
Vermaak v Cloete (1836) 2 Menz 35 . . . . 156, 208
Versfeld & Co v Southern Timber (Pty) Ltd 1935 (2) PH A38 (C) 34, 38
Verster, Van Wijk & Company v Pienaar (1904) 21 SC 386 . . . . 126, 135, 136
Versveld & Co v Southern Timber (Pty) Ltd 1935 (2) PH A38 . . . . 35, 100
Villiers v Villiers (1843) 2 Menz 7 60
Visser v Theodore Sassen & Son (Pty) Ltd 1982 (2) SA 320 (C). 81, 172
Vitamax (Pty) Ltd v Executive Catering Equipment CC and Others 1993 (2)
  SA 556 (W) 70, 89
Volkskas Beperk v Mohamed 1955 (1) SA 453 (T) 129, 130, 136
Volkskas Bpk v Meyer 1966 (2) SA 379 (T) 111, 114, 115
Volkskas Bpk v The Master 1975 (1) SA 69 (T). 201
Volkskas Spaarbank Bpk v Van Aswegen 1990 (3) SA 978 (A). 63, 201

W

Walker's Fruit Farms Ltd v Sumner 1930 TPD 394 98
Walker v Syfret NO 1911 AD 141 149
Wallace v 1662 G & D Property Investments CC 2008 (1) SA 300 (W) 70
Watermeyer qq v Theron and Meyring (1832) 2 Menz 14 157
Webb v Shell Zimbabwe (Pvt) Ltd 1982 (2) SA 763 (Z) 94
Weinerlein v Goch Buildings Ltd 1925 AD 282 211
Wessels v The Master of the High Court (1891) 9 SC 18. . . . . 102, 105
Western Bank Ltd v Pretorius 1976 (2) SA 481 (T) 136
Western Bank Ltd v Wood 1969 (4) SA 131 (D) 104
Whitaker, Paterson & Brooks Ltd v Slater (1905) 19 EDC 103. 134
Whitnall v Goldschmidt (1884) 3 SC 314 24
Wides v Butcher and Sons (1905) 26 NLR 578 . . . . 194, 195
Wiehahn NO v Wouda 1957 (4) SA 724 (W). 38, 57, 136, 188
Wilkins NO v Voges 1994 (3) SA 130 (A) 92
Willems v Widow Schendeler (1835) 2 Menz 20 . . . . 57, 104
Wolfson v Crowe 1904 TS 682. . . . . 125, 126, 129
Wollach v Barclays National Bank Ltd 1983 (2) SA 543 (A) 110, 114
Woolfsons Credit (Pty) Ltd v Holdt 1977 (3) SA 720 (N) 136
Worthington v Wilson 1918 TPD 104. . . . . 125, 126, 127, 129, 132, 188, 189

Y

Yorkshire Insurance Co Ltd v Barclays Bank (DC&O) Ltd 1928 WLD 199. . . . 148
Yorkshire Insurance Co Ltd v Dippenaar and Others 1963 (3) SA 414 (W) 37

Z

Zietsman v Allied Building Society 1989 (3) SA 166 (O) 89, 91, 115, 194
Zimbabwe Football Association v Mafurusa 1985 (3) SA 1050 (2). 196
Zuurbekom Ltd v Union Corporation Ltd 1947 (1) SA 514 (A) 211

PART ONE

The Nature of Suretyship and the Foundation and Operation of the Contract

CHAPTER I

The Roman Law: Foundations of our Law of Sureties

	Page
1. Introduction.	3
2. Early Roman forms of suretyship: born out of the procedure for enforcing claims	4
3. The first stipulatory suretyships: *sponsio* and *fidepromissio*	7
4. Stipulatory suretyship: *fideiussio*.	10
5. Justinian's legislation.	16
6. Other *Roman* forms of suretyship: mandate and *constitutum*	17
7. From Roman to Roman-Dutch law.	21
8. The rise and fall of the women's suretyship benefits.	23

1. Introduction

If this book were botanical and suretyship a tree, this chapter could be said to describe rather more that just the roots of suretyship: the trunk at least is also included. For while the roots of the modern South African law of sureties lie deep in Roman law, something more than the roots are to be found in there. By the time Justinian had left it, Roman law had developed a law of sureties whose principles are substantially those of our modern law.

Although in the early days after the fall of the Western Roman Empire, Germanic law returned to a more primitive concept of suretyship in which the tendency was to make the surety directly responsible to the creditor and the debtor to the surety,[1] the revival of Roman law brought with it a return to the Roman law, in particular the Roman law of *fideiussio*.[2] The primary Roman-Dutch writers all draw their expositions of the law of suretyship directly from the *Corpus Iuris*,[3] and though the commentators and Roman-Dutch writers were undoubtedly responsible themselves for important developments, they handed on a law of suretyship whose principles were profoundly Roman. Those principles still provide the firm foundations for this branch of our modern law. A glance at the judgments of the leading South African

---

[1] Wessels para 3776. See also Willis D Morgan 'The History and Economics of Suretyship' (1927) 12 *Cornell LQ* 153 and Donald E Phillipson 'Development of the Roman Law of Debt Security' (1968) 20 *Stanford LR* 1230.
[2] Wessels para 3777.
[3] See, especially, Grotius *Introduction to Dutch Jurisprudence* bk 3, ch 3 (Gr) (and see Groenewegen's references and Schorer's and Van der Keessel's Notes thereto), Van Leeuwen's *Commentaries of Roman Dutch Law* bk IV, ch IV (VL) (and see Decker's Notes thereto); Voet *Commentary on the Pandects* 46.1 (V); and Van der Linden's *Institutes of Holland* 1.14.10 (VdL).

cases will quickly convince the sceptical;[4] hence the importance of this chapter for the reader seeking a full understanding of the modern law.

However, the Roman roots of the modern law are gnarled and complex, so it may be helpful if, before turning to a full exposition of the Roman law, the basic structure of the history is set out here. First, the concept of one person being responsible for the obligation of another is born in the technicalities of the *legis actio* procedure with the development of the three ancient forms of suretyship: the *vindex, vades,* and *praedes.* Secondly, here too was born *stipulatio* and the first two forms of stipulatory suretyship: *sponsio* and *fidepromissio.* Great strides were made with these forms—concerning chiefly the redress the surety who had paid the creditor had against the principal debtor. However, legislation during the Republic designed to regulate the position of sureties *inter se* overshot its mark and cast too great a burden upon the surety. Hence, thirdly, there developed *fideiussio,* the final form of stipulatory suretyship, which was free of these burdens. There were other forms of suretyship but these were assimilated to *fideiussio,* and *fideiussio* freed of formality and overlaid with legislation by Hadrian and Justinian forms the basis of the modern Roman-Dutch law as well as other civilian systems of law of suretyship. Let us now turn to the detail of this tale.

2. Early Roman forms of suretyship: born out of the procedure for enforcing claims

We know little of suretyship prior to the Twelve Tables. Indeed, we know little of law at that time.[5] Still, we do know that some forms of primitive suretyship were known in Roman law as early as the Twelve Tables and were enmeshed in the technicalities of litigation. Thus we know of a *vindex*[6] who could release a defendant from his obligation to attend his opponent when summoned before the praetor by standing in for the defendant and later merely by standing guarantor for the defendant's appearance.[7] We also know of the *vades* who 'went bail' for the

---

[4] *Rand Bank Ltd v De Jager* 1982 (3) SA 418 (C) provides a good example of a modern suretyship case turning on the interpretation of Roman Law. It is discussed below in Chapter XIII. See also *Bank of Lisbon and South Africa Ltd v De Ornelas and Another* 1988 (3) SA 580 (A) for a more modern suretyship case turning on ancient Roman principles. There is an interesting historical discussion of the law of suretyship in *Millman and Another NNO v Masterbond Participation Bond Trust* 1997 (1) SA 113 (W) at 116-118.

[5] Attempts to reconstruct the Twelve Tables have been made, but they are gleaned from passages in much later writings as well as scattered references in the Digest. For a discussion of modern research into the Twelve Tables generally, see HF Jolowicz *Historical Introduction to the Study of Roman Law* 2 ed (1952) (hereinafter Jolowicz) ch VII.

[6] Twelve Tables 1-4; see generally Jolowicz 179-80; and F de Zulueta *The Institutes of Gaius* (1946) vol II 301.

[7] As Jolowicz 180 note 1 observes, scholars are at variance on the question whether the *vindex* became a substitute for the defendant or was at all times merely a guarantor for his appearance. The Twelve Tables apparently provided that if the defendant was of the wealthier (tribute-paying) class only a man of similar class could be his *vindex*, which perhaps suggests that at least in the earliest period the *vindex* became a mere 'surety' for the defendant's appearance.

Also a *vindex* could come forward and release the defendant not only at the stage at which he was initially summoned to the praetor, but it seems also at a later stage, when a defendant was finally summoned before the praetor under the *manus iniectio* procedure to fulfil the judgment debt or face condemnation to captivity in the creditor's private prison. G 4.21; see De Zulueta 242 ff.

THE ROMAN LAW: FOUNDATIONS OF OUR LAW OF SURETIES 5

reappearance of the defendant when there was an adjournment of proceedings after *litis contestatio*.[8]

We also know of other sureties of ancient date[9]—the *praedes*. Gaius[10] tells us of two kinds: the *praedes sacramenti causa* and the *praedes litis et vindiciarum*. When a thing was claimed by way of the *legis actio sacramenti in rem* procedure the thing in dispute or a symbol of it[11] would be brought before the praetor and both parties would lay claim to it. The praetor then instructed both parties to release the thing and each party then made a *sacramentum*, originally probably a religious oath,[12] that the thing was his. The oath was fortified by an undertaking to pay a fixed sum of money to the public treasurer[13] in the event of adverse judgment. The matter was then sent to the *iudex* to determine which of the oaths was justified[14] and interim possession was granted by the praetor pending the decision of the case. The *praedes sacramenti causa* were taken by the praetor to ensure the payment of the *summa sacramenti* to the treasury,[15] and the *praedes litis et vindiciarum* were given by the interim possessor to his opponent for the delivery of the thing in the event of judgment finally going against the interim possessor.[16]

Where the claim was not to a thing, but *in personam*, the appropriate *legis actio* was originally the *legis actio per sacramentum in personam*,[17] which was sent to trial on a similar procedure except that there was, of course, no dispute over title

---

[8] Twelve Tables 1.10; see generally Jolowicz 187; and De Zulueta 302. The giving of *vades* was necessary only where there was an adjournment during the *in iure* proceedings. Once the *iudex* had been appointed, he could give judgment by default against a defendant who failed to appear on the appointed day, so that no security for his appearance at that stage was necessary. The object of taking *vades* was thus merely to save the necessity for a new *in ius vocatio*. Since the indications in old fragments and in comparative studies are that the praetor would originally have been expected to dispose of the *in iure* proceedings on the day of summons, we can expect the *vades* to have been a later development than the *vindices*.

The manner in which the *vades* engaged themselves is not really known (see DeZulueta 303). R Sohm *The Institutes of Roman Law* 3 ed translated by JC Ledlie (1907) at 384 note 3 has suggested that it was by a 'solemn promise' to pay a specified penalty in the event of the defendant failing to reappear. This was not really suretyship in the modern sense, since the obligation of the *vas* was to pay the specified penalty if the principal failed to do what he was obliged to do.: It was not an undertaking to fulfil the same or part of the same obligation as that imposed upon the principal (Sohm *loc cit*). But it was a step towards the birth of true suretyship, for the *vades* were never merely 'substitutes' for the principal debtor.

[9] We are not specifically told by Gaius that the *praedes* date back as far as the Twelve Tables, but the language of his texts gives no hint that they were a later innovation in the *legis actio* procedure. There is, therefore, no reason to doubt they were at least as old as the Twelve Tables.

[10] G 4.13 and 16.
[11] G 4.17.
[12] DeZulueta 235, where reference is made to ancient and modern authorities.
[13] The reason why payment was made to the public treasury is a matter of much scholarly conjecture (see DeZulueta 235-6). It is clear that the *sacramentum* was in some way an important factor in involving the State, originally through the King, in the dispute between the parties. The sacramental procedure survived into the classical period when the action was brought before the *centumviri* (G 4.95), but the sum involved was settled at 125 *sesterces*, by then a nominal sum. Under the formulary procedure an analogous procedure under which the parties solemnly promised to pay each other a given sum if the property in dispute was not theirs, was evolved, but by Gaius's time payment of the sum (a nominal 25 *sesterces*) was not exacted (G 4.94).
[14] Cicero *pro Caec* 33.97.
[15] G 4.16.
[16] G 4.16.
[17] G 4.13.

to a thing and hence *praedes sacramenti causa* were given but not *praedes litis et vindiciarum*.[18]

The scant knowledge we have of the *vindices* and the *vades*,[19] and the evidence available in regard to the history of *praedes*[20] is consistent with what we surmise about dispute resolution in the earliest times. Self-help was the starting point. The person who had suffered a wrong went personally to the wrongdoer; and, supported by other members of his *gens* would capture him. In the earliest times, no doubt, the aggrieved would not release the wrongdoer until the latter redressed the wrong. But even then pecuniary composition was often accepted as a proper method of giving redress [in many cases].[21] But what if the wrongdoer could not provide immediate composition? At an early date it would appear that the provision of a 'hostage' from his own family or *gens* became an accepted method of obtaining release for the wrongdoer while ensuring that he would come back to fulfil his undertaken composition. What was common in the practice of inter-tribal warfare and tribal peace treaties was no doubt equally true of the earliest litigation.[22]

The surety was thus born as a hostage and perhaps *stipulatio* itself was born of the composition agreement. Certainly the earliest form of *stipulatio* was '*sponsio*' (the stipulator asked the promissor 'Do you undertake ...?' *spondes*? and the promissor replied 'I do undertake ...' *spondeo*).[23] And the term 'sponsor' from the earliest times down even to the latter days of Roman law meant 'surety'.[24] There are therefore many who see the birth of *stipulatio* linked with early suretyship,[25] but the exact history is obscure and no suggested conclusions have won universal acceptance among scholars.

At all events, by the time of the Twelve Tables, some forms of contractual obligation could be undertaken by *stipulatio* and some forms of suretyship were known. But whatever the position then, Roman law soon took the further step

---

[18] We do not really know a great deal about the *praedes*, but they do seem to fit in with the pattern seen in the *vindices* and *vades* in this respect, that originally they do seem to have engaged themselves in place of the principal debtor rather than merely as accessory to them. At least, execution would normally proceed against *them*, for it was to that end that they were introduced. Later, under the formulary procedure, their role in litigation was taken over by ordinary stipulatory sureties; see G 4.88-95, De Zulueta 276.

[19] See notes 7 & 8 above.

[20] See Jolowicz 294 and 413; see also Buckland in BTB 407, and BMI 236; and cf note 18 above.

[21] In general the Twelve Tables prescribed a given sum as pecuniary composition: but at least in the cases of *membrum ruptum* and manifest theft the complainant was allowed to exercise more direct forms of physical vengeance unless he chose to accept a composition—see D 2.14.7.14 end 176.

[22] Indeed there is evidence in the case of *sponsio* of a close association between the formal undertaking of treaty obligations and the related institution of the civil law—cf G 3.94 and cf Mommsen *Staatsrecht* I, 249. Cf also Festus's derivation of the word *spondere*—Bruns *Fontes* II.40.

[23] G 3.92 and 93, I 3.15.1.

[24] D Daube '*Sponsor* and the History of Contract' (1946) 62 *LQR* 266-72 doubts whether much weight can be attached to the fact that the word *sponsor* always bore the meaning 'surety'. The argument is that the meaning of a verbal noun is not necessarily a safe guide to the meaning of the verb—to borrow a phrase, not everyone who undertakes is an undertaker. *Sed quaere*. See, by contrast, Jolowicz 295.

[25] This view was originally propounded by Mitteis. Generally see Jolowicz 294 ff, and also at 563-4. Cf also. R Sohm *The Institutes of Roman Law* 3 ed translated by JC Ledlie (1907) s 12, 64 note 16. See also generally Max Kaser *Das Römische Privatrecht* 2 ed (1975) s 57.3.1.

of acknowledging that a 'surety' could do something quite different from merely stepping into a defendant's shoes when the latter was sued. It came to acknowledge that a 'surety' could by *stipulatio* support a debtor's obligation to pay his creditor. This was the birth of the idea of suretyship as accessory to the principal obligation.

In due course the older forms of suretyship disappeared into the pages of the antiquarians. The *vades* were finally abolished by the *lex aebutia*.[26] The others would, in any event, have disappeared when the *legis actio* procedure was replaced with the formulary procedure.[27]

3. The first stipulatory suretyships: *sponsio* and *fidepromissio*

The ancient forms of suretyship had, however, paved the way for the development of the more general stipulatory forms and by the end of the Republican period, the securing of debts by stipulatory suretyship had become a legal and social institution of major importance.[28]

There were three kinds of stipulatory suretyship; the two oldest will be discussed now and the third in the next section. The oldest was *sponsio*—that is, the surety undertook his obligation by entering into a *stipulatio* with the creditor, the question and answer being framed in the formal terms of the Quirital law: *idem dari spondes? idem dari spondeo*.[29] This was a form of suretyship which could be

---

[26] A *lex* of uncertain date but probably passed in the second century BC. See Gellius *Noctes Atticae* XVI, 10.8. See also Jolowicz *loc cit* where the modern authorities are canvassed.

[27] G 4.30, and generally see Jolowicz 226 ff. The abolition of the *legis actio* was achieved partly by the *lex aebutia* and finally by legislation passed under Augustus shortly before the end of the first century BC.

[28] Indeed personal security was preferred by the Romans to real security—see Kaser s 31.1.1 and ss 57.2.1; Buckland & McNair *Roman Law and Common Law* (2 ed) 324; and BMI 320 (s 116). As the passage referred to in Horace's *Satires* (Sat II.VI.1.23) hints, it was a social obligation to go surety for a friend—a vestige, no doubt, of the ancient history of suretyship, for it was born of the solidarity of the *gens*. Moreover, the ferocity of the *manus iniectio* procedure for the enforcement of personal obligations meant creditors would generally be content when a person of substance stood surety (see Reinhard Zimmermann *The Law of Obligations* (1990) (hereinafter Zimmermann) 115-17) for the surety would be unlikely to default.

Real security, on the other hand, presented many problems. In its earliest recognized form, *fiducia cum creditore*, ownership was passed to the creditor subject to an obligation in good faith (*fiducia*) to hold the thing and restore it to the debtor on payment. However, since ownership had passed, the debtor's position was a precarious one, and in any event, if he did not repay the debt, he lost the thing altogether, whatever its value in comparison to the debt. *Pignus*, or pledge, was more fair to the debtor, but the ordinary pledging of movables by delivery of possession of them to the creditor would not, in the nature of things, afford a universal or flexible method of obtaining security for debts. The development of pledge without transfer of possession (called *hypotheca*) was a great advance in the law relating to securities, but *hypotheca* became so bedeviled with the growth of tacit hypothecs, which were given priority, that it became a distinctly precarious form of security for the creditor (generally see BMI *loc cit,* and Kaser' s 31.1.1 and Zimmermann *loc cit*). Thus personal security remained the primary form of security throughout the long history of Roman law. Cf Horace *Sat* II.VI.1.23 (*Romae sponsorem me rapis*).

[29] G. 3.116.

concluded only between Roman citizens.[30] Moreover, the principal obligation must also have been contracted between Roman citizens.[31]

The second kind of stipulatory suretyship was *fidepromissio*. This was undertaken by a *stipulatio* between the surety and the creditor, the question and corresponding answer, however, being framed in the less formal terms: *idem fidepromittis*? (Do you promise the same thing on your honour?) *fidepromitto* (I do promise).[32] This form of suretyship was not restricted to Roman citizens,[33] but like *sponsio* it could be undertaken only to secure performance of an obligation itself embodied in some form of *stipulatio*.[34]

Both these forms of suretyship are of ancient date. Their antiquity is evidenced[35] by the fact that neither the *sponsor's* nor the *fidepromissor's* liability descended to his heir.[36]

The first question which arises in regard to these forms of suretyship is the nature of the redress which the surety had against the principal debtor. Gaius[37] tells us that the *sponsor* who was compelled to pay the creditor was given redress against the principal debtor under a certain *lex publilia* by an action called the *actio depensi*.[38] If the principal debtor denied liability but was in due course condemned

---

[30] G. 3.93.

[31] In the very earliest times, in Mitteis's view, the *sponsor* would have contracted the principal and not an accessory obligation (see note 27 above). Whatever the original position, however, the law (at a still very early date) reached the point where the *sponsor* would be liable alongside the debtor (whose obligation emerged only gradually as the principal obligation). Probably the *sponsio* of the surety had therefore, in early times, to be undertaken during the same formal 'ceremony' when the debtor undertook his stipulation (cf Jolowicz 314 note 6 and R Sohm *The Institutes of Roman Law* 3 ed translated by JC Ledlie (1907) 384-5 note 3). It would therefore be inappropriate to enter a *sponsio* where the 'principal debtor' was not also a *civis*.

The classical texts, however, go no further; they simply tell us that the *sponsor* could be a surety for only a verbal (stipulatory) obligation—cf G 3.119.

As regards the requirement that the *sponsio* be undertaken contemporaneously with the principal obligation, this must have disappeared at least by the later years of the Republic, for otherwise the *lex cicereia* would scarcely have been necessary.

[32] G 3.116.

[33] G 3.93.

[34] G 3.119.

[35] BTB 445 and BMI 238.

[36] G 3.120.

[37] G 3.127.

[38] BTB 446; cf Kaser s 57.2.4a. The name of the action indicates that it derives from very early times, for the name implied a 'weighing out', and perhaps refers to the payment *per aes et libram* by the surety to the creditor when the latter had under the old procedure obtained a judgment against the surety. Presumably this judgment then entitled the surety to proceed against the principal debtor, for it is clear from G 4.22 that a surety could proceed by way of *manus iniectio* against the principal debtor. Whether this whole procedure derived from the *lex publilia* is uncertain (see 201 note 6 and the authorities there referred to and also Kaser *loc cit*). But it was subsequent to the Twelve Tables and earlier than the beginning of the second century BC (Jolowicz *loc cit*). PF Girard *Manual Elementaire de Droit Romain* 8 ed by F Senn (1929) at 808 and Jolowicz 201 note 6 regard the *lex publilia* as one of the series of *leges* in connection with suretyship passed about the end of the third or beginning of the second century BC, but the terms of Gaius's text suggest that it was the earliest of the statutes after the Twelve Tables to provide for automatic execution by way of *manus*

under the *actio depensi*, he had to pay *in duplum*,[39] a feature deriving from the association of this action with the *manus iniectio* procedure.[40]

The redress afforded to *the fidepromissor* who was compelled to pay the creditor is less certain. It seems clear that by the end of the Republican period, he was afforded redress by an *actio mandati* against the principal debtor.[41] *Fidepromissio* however, is older than the *actio mandati*, and it seems difficult to believe that before the emergence of the *actio mandati*, the surety would have had no redress against the principal debtor. Lenel found a hint in Digest 17.1.10.11 and related texts of an earlier praetorian *actio infactum* based, he said, on the idea of *pecuniam abesse*. But here we are on uncertain ground.[42]

The second central question which arises relates to the position of sureties *inter se*. Once suretyship had emerged from the primitive form in which the surety or hostage took the liability of the principal on himself, and became, instead, liable under an obligation accessory to the obligation of the principal debtor, there was no reason why there should not be a multiplicity of sureties. If so, however, what were their relations *inter se*?

At first, the creditor could proceed against the surety of his choice for the full amount. Later, it seems, it was thought to be unfair to allow him to do so and a series of three *leges* were passed in the period between 240 and 170 BC regulating the position. The three *leges* in point (in chronological order) were the *lex apuleia*, the *lex furia de sponsu*, and the *lex cicereia*.[43] All three applied both to *sponsio* and *fidepromissio*, but did not refer[44] to the third form of stipulatory suretyship, *fideiussio* (discussed below).

The *lex apuleia* enacted that where there were several *sponsors* or *fidepromissors*, any one of them who had paid more than a proportionate share of the debt might

---

iniectio and the terms of G 4.9 and G 4.171 (where the action under the *lex publilia* is referred to alongside the *actio legis Aquiliae*) may be taken to suggest that the *lex publilia* was older than the *lex Aquilia*. It should also be remembered that Chapter II of the *lex Aquilia* provided a special remedy where an *'adstipulator'* released the debtor in fraud of the principal (see GH 3.215), and therefore it need not surprise us if the law had already provided a special remedy where the *sponsor* had paid off the debt owed by the principal, which, after all, would be a more usual case than that dealt with in Chapter II of the *lex Aquilia*. If some remedy existed prior to the *lex publilia*, this argument would of course be somewhat less cogent.

[39] G3.127 read alone might suggest that the *actio depensi* would involve judgment *in duplum* even if liability were not denied; but G 4.171 indicates quite clearly that this was not so—see DeZulueta 230 note 4.

[40] G 3.127; 4.9; 4.171; DeZulueta 190-1, 230 and 246.

[41] The existence of redress by way of *actio mandati* in the classical law is perfectly clear—see G 3.127 and the numerous texts referring to it in D 17.1. The only question is whether the *actio mandati* was available to the surety by the end of the Republican period. That mandate had emerged as an accepted legal institution before the end of the Republican period is clear (though the exact period of its emergence is much debated—generally see A Watson *Mandate in Roman Law* (1961) 16-23). On principle, therefore, one would have expected the *actio mandati* to be available to the surety by the end of the Republic period and certain texts in the Digest indeed seem to imply that such a remedy was known when Quintus Mucius Scaevola was writing (the beginning of the first century BC—see Jolowicz 90)—see D 17.48 and D 17.62.

[42] *Edictum Perpetuum* (3 ed) pp 296-7.

[43] Generally see A Watson *Mandate in Roman Law* (1961) 84-5 (who supports Lenel, but indicates that the weight of scholarly opinion still tends to be against him).

[44] G 3.121-3.

recover the excess from his co-sureties.[45] This *lex* applied to the provinces as well as to Italy.[46] The *lex furia de sponsu* provided that the debt should be divided by the number of *sponsors* or *fidepromissors* living at the time the debt fell due[47] and gave any surety who had paid more than his share an action against the creditor for recovery of the excess.[48] Under the *lex furia,* the surety could proceed against the creditor immediately by *manus iniectio*[49] so that, if the action was defended unsuccessfully, judgment would be *in duplum.* The *lex furia* applied only in Italy,[50] where its practical effect was to displace the remedies provided by the *lex apuleia.*[51] The *lex apuleia* remained of importance in the provinces.[52]

The *lex cicereia* completed the system by requiring the creditor to state openly the amount of the debt and the number of sureties.[53] If he did not, the surety could secure his release.[54]

4. Stipulatory suretyship: *fideiussio*

This restrictive legislation, designed to lighten the burden cast upon sureties, overshot its mark by reducing too greatly the value of the surety to the creditor.[55] He could only proceed against each surety for his proportionate share, even though the value of other sureties might prove illusory. Consequently a new form of stipulatory suretyship emerged—the so-called *fideiussio* (the surety was asked: '*id(em)*[56] *fide tua esse iubes?*'[57]).

---

[45] G 3.121-3.

[46] G 3.122. We accordingly know that this *lex* must have been passed later than 227 BC, the date of the first Roman province, Sicily, shortly thereafter followed by Sardinia and Corsica—see Cary *A History of Rome* (2 ed) 153.

[47] G 3.121.

[48] G 3.121.

[49] There is some debate whether the action under the *lex furia* was available only where the surety had been forced to pay by a judgment secured in an action against him. If not, the *manus iniecto* procedure would appear to be inappropriate, but the dominant view is that *any* payment in excess of the proper share could be so recovered.

[50] G 4.22.

[51] When it is said that the *lex furia* applied only in Italy, this must be understood to mean that it applied to any surety given in Italy, even if the principal obligation was contracted elsewhere—see BTB 447.

[52] G 3.122. The *lex furia* provided also that the liability of *sponsores* and *fidepromissores* should be discharged after two years—see G 3.121. Buckland (BTB 447) takes this to mean two years from the due date. See also G 3.122.

[53] G 3.123.

[54] G 3.122.

[55] Jolowicz 316; Zimmermann 121. Zimmermann's reference to 'legislation designed to achieve better protection of the *debtor*' must be a slip of the pen for 'surety'.

[56] There is doubt whether the right word is *id* or *idem*—cf D 45.1.75.6 and see De Zulueta's textual note to G 3.116. See also Jolowicz 316. If *id* is indeed to be preferred the significance of this difference between *fideiussio* and the two older forms of suretyship is debated—see Jolowicz *loc cit,* and the authorities there cited.

[57] G 3.116.

Fideiussio appears to have been born in the later years of the Republic.[58] With the advent of *fideiussio,* the Roman law of sureties began to attain maturity for, unlike *sponsio* and *fidepromissio* which as noted above could be used only to secure stipulatory obligations, this was a form of suretyship which was available to secure any recognized form of obligation.[59] Indeed, the principal obligation need not be a civil obligation. By *fideiussio,* even a natural obligation[60] could validly be secured[61] unless the enforceability of the undertaking would offend against the policy of the law or rule which made the principal obligation unenforceable.[62]

As might be expected, *fideiussio,* in practice, had overtaken *sponsio* and *fidepromissio* by the end of the classical period.[63] By Justinian's day the two older forms had become entirely obsolete and are omitted from the *Corpus Iuris.*[64]

The new form of suretyship was a great advance, but there were many latent problems in the relationship between the obligation of the surety and the obligation of the principal debtor which had still to be tackled, for the notion of an 'accessory obligation' was laden with many difficulties. Moreover, the new form of suretyship having been designed to circumvent the restrictions introduced by

---

[58] Gaius (G 3.124.) tells us that the *lex cornelia* applied to this form of suretyship as well as to *sponsio* and *fidepromissio.* The *lex cornelia* appears to be the last of the series of Republican *leges* which were intended to alleviate the position of surety (G 3.124; BTB 447; Jolowicz 315 note 3; Kaser s 57.2.3b.). It restricted the amount in which any one man could go surety for any one other in the same year to 20 000 *sesterces,* subject to certain exceptions. The *lex cornelia* disappeared under Justinian (see Kaser s 57.2.3b; BTB 448). The passage in Gaius appears to imply that *fideiussio* was already known at the date of this *lex,* and it has been conjectured by Jolowicz *(loc cit;* BTB *loc cit.)* that the *lex* may be due to Sulla and would accordingly be dated about 81 BC. On the other hand, Jolowicz indicates that Cicero gives us no hint of the existence of *fideiussio* in his time and Jolowicz accordingly follows Levy *(Sponsio, fidepromissio, fideiussio* at 118-23) in his conjecture that *fideiussio* was invented by Labeo (a jurist in the Augustan period). See Jolowicz 391. Kaser s 57.2.2c accepts a date 'during the last century BC'. It seems most likely that it emerged early in that century, though it was probably not until considerably later that it replaced *sponsio* as the standard form of security for Roman citizens (cf the reference to Horace *Sat* II. VI.1.23 above).

[59] G 3.119 says that *the fideiussor* can become surety for any kind of obligation, but adds, 'that is whether it arises from real, verbal, literal or consensual contract' *(id est sive re sive verbis sive litteris sive consensu contractae fuerint obligationes).*

D46.1.8, especially 5 and 6; D 46.1.70.5; D 46.1.56.3 make it clear, however, that this form of suretyship was available even where the principal obligation was not contractual. The terms of the texts, however, suggest that there was a development here and perhaps it was not until classical times that the jurists accepted the extension of this form of suretyship to non-contractual obligations. For fuller discussion see De Visscher in *Etudes* 279.

[60] And, *a fortiori,* a praetorian liability, cf D 46.1.8.2.

[61] Of course there can be no valid suretyship where there is no principal obligation at all—ie where the principal debtor is not even placed under a natural obligation—cf D 46.1.25 (where the principal debtor is insane); D 46.1.29 (principal obligation subject to impossible condition); D 46.1.47 pr (principal debtor deported before surety taken). The rule appears to be different, however, where the surety is taken and the principal debtor subsequently becomes insane, or is deported, or the condition becomes impossible—see D 16.3.1.14 *ad fin* and generally see BTB 446 note 1; BMI 320 (s 115 *ad fin*).

It should be noted that it would appear from G 3.119 that *sponsores* and *fidepromissores* might be bound in certain cases even where the principal 'debt' did not create a natural obligation—see BTB 445, where it is suggested that this may be traceable to the very early history of suretyship when the undertaking by the surety was in fact the principal obligation.

See also G 3.119; D 46.1.6.2; D 46.1.16.3 and 4.

[62] D 46.1.46 and generally see Voet's analysis of the Roman texts—V 46.1.9.

[63] Kaser s 57.2.5.

[64] Kaser *loc cit;* Lee 366.

the *lex apuleia* and *lex furia,* the position of sureties *inter se* had to be worked out anew. The classical jurists tackled the problems, but the development of the law was not completed until Justinian's day.

The classical jurists accepted that *fideiussio* could be undertaken to secure all kinds of principal obligations, civil or natural. They concluded that it could validly be undertaken after[65] and even before[66] the principal obligation was undertaken. It had, however, to be undertaken to the same creditor, and had to relate to the very obligation undertaken by the principal debtor.[67]

Because the obligation of the surety was accessory, it could not embrace more than the principal obligation, though it could embrace less.[68] By the same token, the surety's obligation could be conditional or *ex die* while the principal obligation was *pura* but not vice versa.[69] In this matter, theory appears to have been strictly applied by the classical jurists. If the obligation of the surety purported to be for more than the principal obligation it could not be accessory to the latter. Since it was intended to be only accessory and not principal, it must therefore be wholly invalid. This, at least, was Ulpian's conclusion,[70] though there are texts (not relating *to fideiussio* but to *constitutum*)[71] which show a tendency to sustain the obligation for the lesser amount.[72] There is nothing, however, to suggest that the rigour of the rule was ever qualified in relation to *fideiussio* by the classical or post-classical law. In his Institutes, Justinian simply restates the classical rule.[73]

The greatest problem arising out of the accessory nature of the surety's obligation, however, related to the situation where the principal obligation was

---

[65] D 46.1.6 pr.
[66] D 46.1.6.2.
[67] Cf D 46.1.8.8 *in med.*
[68] G 3.126; D 46.1.8.7.
[69] Generally the surety would be bound if the terms of his undertaking were in some way less onerous than those of the principal debt (D 46.1.8.11) but not vice versa (cf D 46.1.8.8). The relevant term should in any event not be such as would render the surety's obligation a 'different' one from that of the principal (cf D 46.1.8.8 *in med*)—it must still be capable of being treated as 'accessory' to the principal debt, but this particular question was sometimes a matter of no small subtlety—cf D 46.1.116.5.
[70] D 46.1.8.7 following Julian—D 46.1.8.8 and D 46.1.16.1 and 2.
[71] D 13.5.11.1 and D 13.5.12.
[72] The relevant texts relating to *constitutum* do not actually refer to the situation where a surety was taken. They refer to a case where the *constituens* himself undertook to pay what he owed under other transactions, but in so doing undertook to pay more than he actually owed or to pay on more onerous terms and conditions. The texts hold him liable for the amount actually owed or on the same terms and conditions as the original debt was owed. There is no reason, however, to believe that the principal would not equally apply where a surety was taken by way of *constitutum*.

That, however, does not imply that the same development should have been expected in the case of *fideiussio,* for it had a different legal background, as appears later in this chapter.

It is interesting, however, that something of a compromise solution does appear to have been supported by Julian (if the text of D 46.1.16.5 is reliable). In that text Julian considers the case where the principal debtor is liable *ex die* and the surety purports to bind himself not *ex die* but *sub conditione.* He concludes that if the condition does not mature before the given date, the surety will be liable, but not vice versa.
[73] I 3.20.5.

extinguished. In that event the accessory obligation must also be extinguished.[74] This rule did not apply, of course, where the principal obligation was not actually extinguished, but the principal debtor merely afforded some personal defence.[75] The more modern difficulties which arise in connection with the prescription of the principal obligation do not appear to have concerned the classical jurists much,[76] for in their time contractual obligations including *fideiussio*[77] were perpetual obligations, for they gave rise to civil actions.[78]

A more acute aspect of the problem arose when the creditor had to decide whether to bring action first against the principal debtor or against one of the sureties. At this stage of the law's development the surety and the principal debtor 'were liable on an equal footing and not the one only if satisfaction could not be obtained from the other'.[79] A text[80] attributed to Gaius's Commentary on the Provincial Edict, however, suggests that the creditor would normally be obliged to proceed first against the principal debtor, for it might constitute an actionable *iniuria* to proceed against the sureties if the principal debtor was *paratus solvere*.[81]

Litis contestatio, however, would extinguish the principal obligation, replacing it with the new obligation embodied in the formulated cause of action.[82] It followed that action against the principal debtor would release the sureties.[83] Two methods of circumventing this most inconvenient result were found. Celsus,[84] writing in the early classical period,[85] made reference to a stipulation in terms of which a creditor stipulated for the amount of a debt which he might fail to collect from the principal debtor. Such a stipulation would oblige the promissor to pay just what the principal debtor failed to pay. It is probable, however, that this was originally

---

[74] Observe however, as indicated above, that the mere disappearance of the debtor, eg by death without heirs or by deportation, did not render ineffective a contract of suretyship which had already been concluded. Many, however, argue that in classical law it did do so. Generally see BMI 320, and Buckland & McNair *Roman Law and Common Law* (2 ed) 236 who reject their argument.

[75] D 2.14.22 and D 2.14.32. Cf also 4.4.13 pr. But the tests are subtle. See, by comparison, D 2.14.21.5, and generally see BTB 446.

[76] There were special cases where the problem of time-barring did arise. D 46.3.38.4. BTB 446 note 6, simply concludes that in principle the surety would be released if action against the principal was time-barred absolutely.

[77] The two-year limitation period provided for by the lex *furia* (see note 63 above) did not apply to *fideiussio* (nor, for that matter, to *mandate* or *constitutum*). See G 3.121.

[78] G 4.110 and DeZulueta 278.

[79] Zimmermann, 130 approved in *Millman and another NNO v Masterbond Participation Bond Trust* 1997 (1) SA 113 (W) at 116B. Although it would be usual to proceed against the debtor first it was thus only with the development of the benefit of excussion that the surety's obligation became subsidiary to that of the principal debtor.

[80] D 47.10.19.

[81] Imperial legislation shortly after the end of the classical period (the Constitution is attributed to Diocletian and Maximian) appears to have given the creditor an 'election' to proceed against the sureties or the principal debtor (C 8.40(41).19). Earlier legislation attributed to Antoninus Pius towards the end of the classical period, however, appears to have been designed to make the principal debtor a party if the sureties were sued, unless the contrary had been agreed (C 8.40(41).5). Since Justinian did set out to reform this branch of the law, it is at least possible that he doctored these constitutions when they were incorporated in the Code.

[82] G 3.180 and generally see De Zulueta 195 and Zimmermann 125-6.

[83] BTB 450 *ad fin* and note 10 where the Roman authorities are cited.

[84] D 12.1.42 pr.

[85] See Jolowicz 394.

regarded as a special form of conditional stipulation[86] and it was, perhaps, only somewhat later that it became assimilated *with fideiussio* to give birth to what the commentators described *as fideiussio indemnitatis*.[87]

The second method, which apparently became usual in later law,[88] was for sureties to agree not to avail themselves of the extinction of their accessory obligations by *litis contestatio* in a suit against the principal debtor. If this were done, then a plea of *res judicata* in a suit against the sureties would be defeated by the praetorian *replicatio pacti conventi*.[89]

Justinian in due course legislated to ensure that *litis contestatio* in an action against one co-debtor did not release the others until the creditor had been paid in full.[90]

But what of the converse situation: would action against a surety release the principal debtor and the other sureties? Here, there is dissention among the writers. On the one hand, Levy[91] contends that the surety and the debtor's obligation were *eadem res* and thus an action against the surety released the debtor. Buckland,[92] however, argues that *litis contestatio* supplanted only the particular surety's accessory obligation and the same logic does not necessarily apply in the case where the principal was sued. Accordingly he argues that in classical law the action against the surety would not release the principal debtor and the other sureties.[93]

The *fideiussor* inherited from the *fidepromissor* recourse against the principal debtor by way of the *actio mandati*.[94] Moreover, the classical tests indicate that even where the surety received no mandate from the principal debtor he could proceed against the principal debtor to the extent to which the latter was benefited, by an action based on *negotiorum gestio*.[95] Thus the surety was without recourse against the principal debtor only if he had actually stood surety against the wishes of the principal debtor.[96] In the special case where he stood surety in an

---

[86] See D 45.1.116 and D 46.2.6 pr.

[87] The terms of D 45.1.116 suggest that this development was post-classical, for in that text (interpolated though it appears to be) we are told that Paul treated this arrangement as consisting theoretically of two independent *stipulationes* linked by the special terms of the condition to which the latter was subject. He did not, therefore, treat them strictly as principal and accessory obligations. The probable interpolation of the term *fideiussio* in D 46.2.6 pr is also in accord with this view. See also BTB 451 note 8.

[88] See Code 8.40(41).28.

[89] BTB 451.

[90] Section 5 of this Chapter below.

[91] E Levy 'Principal and Surety in Classical Roman Law, (1951) 14–15 *Bulletino dell'Institutio di diritto romano* 206 pointing out that in his remedial legislation shortly to be discussed (c 8.40 (41) 28) Justinian provided that 'the barring effect of *litis contestatio* [was] abolished between *reus* [principal debtor] and *fideiussor* as well as between several *fideiussores* regardless of who was sued first'. See also Zimmermann 126 who apparently favours Levy's view.

[92] BTB 451 and Buckland 'Principal and Fideiussor. Consumptio litis' (1941) 53 *Juridical Review* 281. Schultz *Classical Roman Law* (1951) (at 497) agrees but goes further holding that even an action against the debtor did not release the surety.

[93] Earlier (BMI 317 (s 115)) Buckland seems to have accepted that other sureties would in classical law have been released by *litis contestatio* in an action against any one surety.

[94] G 3.127 D 17.1.6.2.

[95] D 17.1.20.1.

[96] D 17.1.40; D 17.1.6.2.

amount in excess of his mandate, he was given an action only up to the amount authorized under the mandate.[97]

That was the position in law; but in fact recourse against the principal debtor would often be illusory if Gaius's text to which reference was made above[98] may legitimately be interpreted (as it is by Buckland)[99] as meaning that the creditor was normally obliged to proceed against the principal debtor unless he was absent or his credit in doubt. In this case the recourse that the surety had against the debtor would usually be without value. Moreover, since the *lex apuleia* and the *lex furia* were inapplicable to *fideiussores*,[100] the creditor could proceed against any surety of his choice for the full amount of the debt, and the latter would be left without recourse against other sureties. This inconvenient result was averted, however, initially by the ingenuity of the jurists, and later by imperial legislation.

From an early date, practice introduced the so-called *beneficium cedendarum actionum*.[101] This was originally designed to give the surety the benefit of other securities held by the creditor, but in due course provided the means by which a surety was enabled to obtain recourse against other sureties.[102]

This benefit consisted of the cession to the surety who was sued of all the creditor's rights and securities against the debtor or other surety.[103] The doctrinal problem that this presented, however, lay again in the fact that *litis contestatio* (or if not *litis contestatio* then certainly payment) extinguished the principal obligation and the other accessory obligations. The actions, therefore, may have been properly ceded, but in theory the whole cause of action was extinguished. This conclusion was evaded by the fiction of treating payment by the surety as a purchase of these rights of action, rather than as a performance of the principal obligation.[104] Buckland,[105] however, points out that this solution would not resolve all the problems, for it is somewhat difficult to see how it could be applied in the case where a surety contested liability but judgment went against him. The texts do not provide a resolution of this difficulty but it disappeared in Justinian's law.

---

[97] The view finally adopted derived from Proculus. Sabinus, however, held a stricter view and would have given the surety no *actio mandati* presumably because he had acted in breach of his mandate. See 13.26.8; *G* 3.161; and cf D 17.1.3.2 and D 17.1.4. See also D 17.1.33. But cf D 17.1.45.6 for a minor qualification of this rule.

[98] D 47.19.19.

[99] BTB 446, 451.

[100] G 3.121-2.

[101] BTB 449. But see K Lipstein, *Critical Studies upon the beneficium cedendarum actionum and venditio nominis* (unpublished PhD thesis, Cambridge, 1936) for the argument that the *beneficium* was not classical. And at any rate in the early years its purpose was simply to transfer to the surety (who had paid the creditor) any other securities (e.g. pledges) held by the creditor. Lipstein's work on the *beneficium* is discussed by Forsyth in the account of Lipstein's scholarly work in *Jurists Uprooted—German-speaking Émigré Lawyers in Twentieth Century Britain* (2004, OUP eds. Beatson and Zimmermann) at 465-467.

[102] BTB 450

[103] D 46.1.17.

[104] D 46.1.17, D 46.1.36 and D 46.3.76.

[105] BTB 449-50. Note, however, that Zimmermann at 135 remarks that 'it was not entirely fair' to object to the unrealistic nature of this fictious sale for it was in the nature of fictions not to deal with facts as they really were. Moreover, Paul in D 46.1.36 by the use of the ablative absolute accepts that *solutio* might precede cession.

The position of sureties was further alleviated by a rescript of Hadrian[106] which may have confirmed or reinforced a praetorian development.[107] This rescript was reminiscent of the *lex furia*, for it provided that the surety might not be sued for more than the debt divided by the number of sureties who were solvent when the action was brought.[108] Hadrian's rescript still forms the basis of the benefit of division.

The procedure, like that of the *lex furia*, was reinforced in practice by the application of the principles of the *lex cicereia*.[109] It differed, however, in certain important respects from the provisions of the *lex furia*, first because the principal debt was to be divided only between the solvent sureties (so they bore the risk of each others' insolvency),[110] and secondly because this was a benefit that had to be pleaded by way of an *exceptio* to the creditor's claim.[111] If it was not pleaded, the rescript would not allow the recovery of any excess paid by the surety to the creditor beyond his proportionate share;[112] nor did the rescript follow the *lex apuleia* in affording the surety a special remedy to recover from co-sureties any excess which he had paid.[113]

Though the benefit of Hadrian's rescript would operate only if pleaded, the texts do not indicate whether it could actually be renounced in the contract of suretyship itself.[114] It is obvious, however, that there might be cases where a creditor would wish to avoid the inconvenience of having to sue all the co-sureties individually for their proportionate share, yet might, at the same time, wish to have the additional security afforded by a plurality of sureties. Here, too, the ingenuity of the jurists found a solution. They invented the so-called *fideiussor fideiussoris*.[115] Instead of taking several co-sureties, one surety might be taken, and another surety called upon to secure the obligation of the first surety. To this situation the rescript of Hadrian did not apply.[116]

5. Justinian's legislation

The classical jurists, therefore, fashioned *fideiussio* to a fairly comprehensive and workable form of personal security, but the difficulties engendered by the accessory nature of *fideiussio* were not all satisfactorily resolved. Where doctrine had wavered, however, Justinian employed the all-powerful wand of legislation. First,

---

[106] G 3.121. See further Zimmermann 131-2.
[107] It may be observed that the rescript was actually issued about the period when the praetor's edict was revised by Julian on Hadrian's direction—see Jolowicz 366-7. Cf Paul's *Sententiae* 1.20.1.
[108] A creditor who brought action against one surety for his share only would not, of course, be barred thereby from proceeding against other sureties for their shares—see BTB 451.
[109] G 3.123 *ad fin*.
[110] G 3.121, I 3.20.4.
[111] D 46.1.28; see BTB 450.
[112] I 3.20.4.
[113] I 3.20.4; C 8.40(41).101; D 46.1.39.
[114] In practice, of course, sureties might well forgo the benefit of division and simply call for a cession of actions. This approach would have the advantage of enabling the surety to obtain cession of any pledges given to the creditor. See Sandars's commentary to I 3.20.4 (TC Sandars *The Institutes of Justinian* 7 ed (1941) at 357). The point is discussed later in this chapter.
[115] D 46.1.8; see BTB 450.
[116] BTB 450.

in his Code he provided that in all cases where several debtors were liable for the same debt, an action against one should not *ipso facto* release the others.[117] Henceforth, therefore, no doctrinal difficulties stood in the way of procuring cession of actions.

Later, in the Novels,[118] he went further and created what the commentators came to call the *beneficium ordinis vel excussionis,* by providing that the principal debtor should in each case be sued first, unless he was absent, in which event the sureties were to be given time to produce him. Only if they did not, could they be sued. Of course, they still had a right to cession of actions against him.

Thus, in Justinian's law we find *in fideiussio* a fully developed law of suretyship. Suretyship has emerged as a method of securing all kinds of obligation and the surety for his part is afforded recourse against the principal debtor by an *actio mandati* or an action based on *negotiorum gestio*. In addition, he is afforded the three central privileges of cession of actions, division and excussion.

6. Other *Roman* forms of suretyship: mandate and *constitutum*[119]

There are, however, two other forms of suretyship which took their place in classical Roman law alongside *fideiussio* and survived to secure a place in the *Corpus Iuris*. The first of these was suretyship undertaken by way of mandate, and the other suretyship undertaken under the so-called *pactum de constituto*.

Mandate dates back to the second century BC[120] and grew out of friendly services undertaken by one person at another's behest.[121] The action was developed on the one hand to enable the mandator to obtain damages if the mandatory failed properly to carry out the request and, on the other hand, to enable the latter to secure reimbursement from the mandator for expenses incurred in carrying out the request.[122] Thus, as we have seen, one who went surety for a principal debtor at the latter's request could utilize an *actio mandati* to recover from the latter whatever he was compelled to pay to the creditor.

But the procedure could be reversed. A (as mandator/surety) could instruct B (mandatory/creditor) to conclude a certain transaction with C (the debtor), for whose debt A intended to stand surety. The effect would be that two independent obligations would be created, that between B (the creditor) and C (the

---

[117] C 8.40(41).28. However, he left several leading texts in the Digest (D 11.1.8 (Paul)) which held that *litis contestatio* against one debtor would in particular circumstances release the other debtors or sureties unchanged. This led the Commentators to draw distinctions between correal obligations—where there was one obligation although several debtors (and where *litis contestatio* effects release)—and solidary obligations where there were several obligations (so *litis contestatio* in proceedings against one did not release the others). This artificial reasoning continues, alas, to find an echo in the modern law. See Chapter XIII, section 2 (k).

[118] Nov 4.1.

[119] See Zimmermann at 138-9 on the use of *emptio venditio* as a form of suretyship. Here a creditor asked the debtor to mandate a third party to buy the creditor's claim (usually at lower price than the amount of the principal debt). If the third party agreed an unsatisfied creditor could sue the third party/surety.

[120] See Jolowicz 311-2, A Watson *Mandate in Roman Law* (1961) 22-3, De Zulueta 181.

[121] D 17.1.1.4; generally see Jolowicz loc cit; A Watson *Mandate in Roman Law* (1961) ch 1; Kaser s 44.1.1; BTB 514.

[122] Jolowicz 311.

debtor) under the relevant transaction, and that between A (the surety) and B (the creditor). A would then be liable to reimburse B for any losses he suffered in consequence of concluding the transaction with C. In this manner a form of suretyship could be effected which avoided the accessory nature of the surety's obligation under *fideiussio,* and in classical times was much used.[123] It was known as *mandatum credendae pecuniae* or, as the commentators called it, *mandatum qualificatum.*[124] It soon became a standard method of suretyship, and was treated alongside *fideiussio* in Hadrian's receipt.[125] The mandator thus had the benefit of division, and it is also clear that from classical times he also had the benefit of cession of actions.[126]

But mandator/surety also had certain special advantages over the *fideiussor,* for the creditor was under a fiduciary obligation to him to preserve any securities he had, and the mandator would be released from any obligation to reimburse the creditor if the latter failed to do so.[127] The *fideiussor,* by contrast, was entitled only to cession of such securities as still existed.[128] On the other hand, the mandator might be liable in cases where the *fideiussor* would not, for the mandator was treated as the originator of the transaction. Thus, for example, where there was a mandate for a loan to a minor who got *restitutio in integrum,* a *fideiussor* would not be liable if he did not know the debtor was a minor, but the mandator would in any event be liable.[129]

From a practical point of view, mandate also had one important advantage over *fideiussio.* It was a consensual contract and therefore did not need to be concluded by *stipulatio.* Although the formalities attaching to *stipulatio* were, during the course of the classical period and later empire, much reduced,[130] the requirement of *unitas actus* survived.[131] Both parties had thus to be present in the same place. By mandate, however, an absent party could undertake suretyship.[132]

---

[123] Jolowicz 316; A Watson *Mandate in Roman Law* (1961) 84. This appears from the many references to it in the Digest, especially D 17.1 (Title on Mandate). Its development in Republican times, indeed, was barred because the mandator appeared to have no interest in the conclusion of the transaction between the creditor and the principal debtor. Servius Sulpicius thus treated this kind of mandate as a mandate *'tua gratia'* and declared it void (G 3.156.). In the early days of the Principate, however, Sabinus upheld the validity of this kind of mandate (C 3.156; I 3.26.6.).
See generally, Zimmermann 139-41.

[124] Lee 334 s 515, and from 367-74.

[125] C 4.18.3; Lee 369 s 579.

[126] The creditor had the additional advantage, of course, that action against the principal debtor did not release the mandator, even in classical law (see D 17.1.27.5), for the mandator's obligation was not accessory to that of the 'principal debtor'.
The mandator in turn had the corresponding advantage that action against him, and even payment by him, did not release the debtor, so that cession of actions could be claimed even if the creditor had sued him (the mandator)—see D 46.3.95.10. See also D 11.1.27.5; and generally see BTB 250.

[127] D 46.3.95.11

[128] See BTB 449 arg C 8.40(41).17.

[129] BTB 520.

[130] The fullest treatment of this very controversial topic is to be found in Riccobono's *Corso di diritto romano: Stipulationes, contractus, pacta* with the material on stipulation conveniently translated into English by Kerr-Wylie, and edited by Beinart *sub nom Stipulation and the Theory of Contract.*

[131] Though even this was severely qualified by Justinian—see I 3.19.12.

[132] D 17.1.1.1 and cf D 17.1.27 pr.

THE ROMAN LAW: FOUNDATIONS OF OUR LAW OF SURETIES 19

On the other hand, there were also serious practical disadvantages: mandate had to be undertaken *before*[133] the principal transaction and even then the mandator was left free to withdraw at any time before the principal contract was undertaken.[134]

Mandate was thus a useful device in many cases for circumventing some of the difficulties inherent in the classical law of *fideiussio*: it could never, however, be a substitute for the latter.

Justinian's legislation had the effect of drawing *mandatum credendae pecuniae* and *fideiussio* closer together.[135] As we have seen, the benefits of cession of actions and of division were already applied to *mandatum credendae pecuniae* in classical times. Justinian also applied the benefit of excussion to it.[136] Moreover, insofar as Justinian's legislation solved the problems created by the accessory nature of *fideiussio,* it correspondingly diminished the special advantages which mandate had over it.

The last form of suretyship, *constitutum,* was a praetorian development. As early as the Twelve Tables, certain informal agreements called *pacta* were recognized as constituting a valid defence to an action,[137] though they did not create an actionable obligation. The praetors soon generalized this rule, so that a pact not to sue was a praetorian defence in any action.[138] Later the praetor went somewhat further and allowed pacts made at the same time as a contract to vary the obligations created under such contract.[139] These were the so-called *pacta adiecta*. Eventually, the praetor went further still and granted certain special actions on particular pacts which were not undertaken as ancillary terms to a principal contract.[140] One of these special actions was the so-called *actio de pecunia constituta*[141] (in one text it is also called the *actio constitutoria,*[142] and in Justinian's Code it is also referred to as the *actio pecuniae constitutae*).[143] This was an action granted upon an informal agreement to pay a sum of money which was owing (the *pactum de constituto*).[144] Originally it was an agreement undertaken by the debtor himself[145] with the credi-

---

[133] There are texts which indicate that ratification of a contract by a principal *after* it has been concluded by the mandatory may suffice to give the parties reciprocal actions under mandate[—cf D 50.17.60]. Why then should the would-be surety not merely purport to 'ratify' the contract of the creditor with the principal debtor? If that could be done, suretyship by way of mandate could be effected *after* the principal obligation had been contracted. That, however, would be possible only if the creditor had purported to lend the money on the mandator's behalf: it could not apply where he had already lent it in his own name—for then the purported mandate would consist merely in an undertaking by the 'mandator' to bear the loss, if any and that in turn would be a clear case of an arrangement '*tua gratia*' and would fail to create any valid mandate. See too D 17.1.12.14.
[134] BTB 520; C 3.159; I 3.26.9; but subject to certain qualifications dictated by equity—see D 17.1.27.2.
[135] Kaser s 57.3.
[136] Nov 4.1.
[137] See DeZulueta 191 note 5, referring to Twelve Tables 8,2; 8,16; 1,7; and 3,5.
[138] DeZulueta 191-2; BTB 527; D 2.14.7.4.
[139] BTB 528.
[140] BTB 529.
[141] I 4.6.8; D 13.5 (Title).
[142] D 13.5.20.
[143] C 4.18.2.
[144] D 13.5.1.1; I 4.6.9.
[145] Cicero *Pro Quinct*, V, 18.

tor with the object of securing a suspension of the principal action.[146] It was also originally available to cover only money debts[147] and it appears to have proved a convenient innovation; its scope was steadily widened. Thus, in the course of its development, it became possible for a third party to promise what was due by the original debtor (without thereby releasing the original debtor)[148] and a form of praetorian suretyship was thus created. The date at which this development occurred is uncertain. Ulpian[149] tells us that Labeo gave the opinion that if a third party undertook a promise to pay on account of someone else he would not be liable if the principal notified him not to pay. The exact situation envisaged by Labeo is not entirely clear, but the text suggests that when he was writing (in the early years of the Principate)[150] the use of *constitutum* by a third party to afford suretyship to a principal debtor had not yet been approved.[151] The earliest writer recorded as approving an action by the creditor against the third party on such a pact is Julian,[152] who wrote in Hadrian's day.[153] Moreover, it seems clear that this was not a standard method of taking sureties at that time, for Hadrian's rescript (introducing the benefit of division), whilst it applied to *fideiussors* and to mandators, did not apply to *constituentes*.[154] Moreover, in the text referred to above,[155] Ulpian refers to Pomponius as the jurist who dissented from Labeo's view. He too was writing about the same period as Julian.[156]

In the later years of the classical period, however, *constitutum* appears to have become quite a common method of taking sureties, for it had certain advantages over *fideiussio*. It was based on an informal agreement and thus could be effected without difficulty by an absent surety.[157] Unlike mandate, moreover, it could, by its very nature, be undertaken after the principal debt. Thus, where it was sought to make an absent party a surety after contracting the principal debt, it was a very useful device.

Moreover, partly because it was praetorian and essentially equitable in nature,[158] and partly because it was never regarded as being strictly a purely accessory obligation, it had two further advantages over *fideiussio* in later classical times: first, after some dispute, it was decided that the action on the pact did not extinguish

---

[146] See Jolowicz 317 note 1.
[147] D 13.5.3.1, BTB 529.
[148] *Constitutum* might also be made to operate as a praetorian novation of the original debt, if that was the intention of the parties—see BTB 530; and cf D 13.5.24. D 13.5.28.
[149] D 13.5.27.
[150] See Jolowicz 391.
[151] A text attributed to Scaevola (writing in the Republican period at the beginning of the first century BC—see 90), namely D 13.5.26, does give an example of a person being liable under the *actio de pecunia constituta*—but the context is a special one, because the *constituens*, we are told by the text, acknowledges that the loan has been made over to him. The text therefore actually favours the view that in Scaevola's day there was no general rule that a third party would, by promising to the creditor what was owed by the debtor, make himself liable to an *actio de pecunia constituta*.
[152] D 13.5.5.3.
[153] See Jolowicz 394-S.
[154] C 4 18 3; Lee 369 s 579.
[155] D 13.s.27.
[156] See Jolowicz 395.
[157] D 13.5.14.3; and cf also D 13.5.26.
[158] D 13.5.1 pr.

the principal obligation;[159] and secondly there are texts which suggest that a pact to pay more than the original obligation, or simply to pay the amount of the debt when the original obligation was conditional, would be valid for the lesser amount[160] or subject to the condition.[161] In this regard, therefore, it was more flexible than *fideiussio*.

Though initially it was applicable only to money debts, it was later made applicable to any obligation to deliver fungibles,[162] but clearly in classical times it was never as comprehensive as *fideiussio*. Moreover, in many cases the action was apparently '*annua*' and prescribed after a year.[163]

In the Code[164] Justinian made *constitutum* applicable to any obligation and made the action based upon it *perpetua*. He also extended to it the benefit of division.[165] In his Novels,[166] moreover, Justinian assimilated *constitutum* to *fideiussio* and mandate in so far as the benefits of excussion, division and cession were concerned.[167]

7. From Roman to Roman-Dutch law[168]

The *Corpus Iuris Justinianus* therefore presents us with a developed though not entirely coherent law of sureties. In its transmission into Western European law and thus into Roman-Dutch law, it underwent certain important changes, but for the most part Roman-Dutch law adhered to the Roman law.[169]

The first important development was that the commentators accepted that an informal agreement could create a binding obligation.[170] The distinction between pacts and formal contracts thus disappeared, and with the disappearance of this distinction, the distinction between *fideiussio* and *constitutum* likewise disappeared.[171] It is accordingly primarily from the Roman texts on *fideiussio* that

---

[159] D 13.5.18.3

[160] It would seem that in one special case there could be an exception to this. If a son was liable in an action *de peculio* and his *paterfamilias* purported to secure his debt in a given sum by *constitutum*, the father was liable only to the same extent as the son would have been liable in the *actio de peculio* (D 13.5.1.8) unless the father undertook the *constitutum* in the name of his son for the full amount of the 'debt'. In that case he would be liable for the full debt (D 13.5.2), presumably because in effect he was treated as ratifying the son's original contract. See also D 13.5.11.1; D 13.5.1.8.

[161] D 13.5.19 pr.

[162] C 4.18.2.

[163] C 4.18.2. (We do not know in exactly what cases it was '*annua*'—see BTB 530.)

[164] C 4.18.2.

[165] C 4 18.3.

[166] Nov 4.1.

[167] In the classical period there was another pact which in many ways was akin to *constitutum*. This was the so-called *receptum argentarii*. It was a special transaction in terms of which a banker undertook a suretyship and in certain respects it was more favourable to the creditor than *constitutum*—generally see BTB 531; TC Sandars *The Institutes of Justinian* 7 ed (1941) 438.

[168] Historical developments since the Roman-Dutch Law came to South Africa will be dealt with in detail in the chapters that follow. See also C F Forsyth, 'Suretyship' in *Southern Cross: Civil Law and Common Law in South Africa* (1996) eds Zimmermann and Visser outlining the historical developments since 1806.

[169] See Zimmermann 142-5; Jones 'Roman Law Bases of Suretyship in Some Modern Civil Codes' (1977) 52 *Tulane Law Review* 129; Slovenko 'Suretyship' (1965) 39 *Tulane Law Review* 427.

[170] See Gr 3.1.52; VL 4.3.1; V 2.14.9; Huber 3.21.2.

[171] V 46.1.1. These developments whereby all contracts became bona fide played a vital part in *Bank of Lisbon and South Africa Ltd v De Ornelas and Another* 1988 (3) SA 580 (A) discussed in detail in Chapter XIII.

the Roman-Dutch writers draw in their construction of the Roman-Dutch law of sureties. Their treatment of the law, however, is infused with the equitable spirit which lay behind *constitutum*. Thus, for example, Voet[172] relies on texts relating to *constitutum* in holding that where a surety undertakes an obligation in excess of the principal obligation, he is bound up to the amount of the principal obligation. Van Leeuwen[173] and Van der Keessel[174] go even further and hold that the creditor would be entitled to advance further sums to the principal debtor up to the full extent of the security which he undertook. Doubtless one would have to interpret the true intention of the parties, for this is an equitable development. Similar equitable considerations were applied where the principal obligation was conditional, and the contract of suretyship unconditional.[175] Likewise the commentators relied on a text relating to mandate in order to develop the equitable doctrine that the creditor was under some obligation to preserve his other securities, and Voet[176] tells us that a creditor who has freed other securities will have his claim against remaining securities proportionately diminished. Again Voet[177] tells us of an equitable development by which sureties could proceed against other co-sureties even though they had failed to take cession of actions before payment, a development which is again in line with the texts on mandate.

Roman-Dutch law, therefore, gradually effected the fusion of the equitable principles underlying mandate and *constitutum* with the *stricti iuris* principles embodied in the Roman law of *fideiussio*.[178] It followed, of course, that *constitutum* and mandate disappeared. Indeed Voet did still refer briefly to mandate,[179] but it does not appear to have been an institution of any importance in relation to suretyship in his day. Moreover, once the law developed a more mature law of agency so that obligations were created directly between the two principals, mandate could hardly function as a method of taking sureties.

There was, however, one other important development in the law of sureties in the course of the transmission of Roman law from the dead letter of the *Corpus Iuris* to the living body of Western European law. Whilst it is clear that in Roman law the surety had to plead the *beneficia* by way of *exceptio*,[180] it is not clear to what degree an agreement not to plead such exception would be valid. We do have a text ascribed to Ulpian[181] in which he purports to decide, contrary to a previous opinion, that there can be a valid agreement that no exception shall be pleaded, but that text does not deal with a benefit specifically created by legislation. Moreover, as late as Justinian's day, it was necessary for the Emperor to decree in a constitution which we find in the Code[182] that if a person purports in

---

[172] V 46.1.4; so too VL 4.4.4.
[173] *Loc cit.*
[174] VdK 499.
[175] V 46.1.4 *ad fin.*
[176] V 46.1.29 (referring to D 46.3.95.11, a text dealing with *mandatum qualificatum*).
[177] V 46.1.30.
[178] So much so that the *exceptio doli generalis* became redundant and did not form part of Roman-Dutch law: *Bank of Lisbon and South Africa Ltd v De Ornelas and Another* 1988 (3) SA 580 (A).
[179] V 46.1.40.
[180] See BTB 450.
[181] D 2.11.4.4; and cf C 8.35(36).6.
[182] C 2.3.29.

THE ROMAN LAW: FOUNDATIONS OF OUR LAW OF SURETIES 23

an agreement to renounce any exception to which he is entitled on account of his rank or prerogative of office, the renunciation will be binding upon him. This is said to be in accordance with the praetor's edict which gave cognizance to pacts 'not contrary to law'. If the text is sound, however, the Code goes on to explain that all this is consistent with a well-established rule that a person may renounce anything that has been provided for his benefit. More specifically as regards the benefit of excussion, the position may be inferred from one of Justinian's Novels[183] which allowed bankers to evade the order of excussion prescribed by Novel 4.1 by taking a renunciation of the benefit of excussion from sureties offered to them by their debtors. The Novel goes on to give two apparently contradictory reasons for this ruling. The first is that the allowance is being granted as a special favour to bankers while the second is that as a matter of general principle every person has a right to renounce any privileges afforded to him by the law. Both Code 2.3.29 and Novel 9.19.1 therefore imply that it was doubted whether legislative provisions creating privileges for persons in a given situation could be avoided by renunciation, but decide that, in certain cases, those benefits may validly be renounced. They include phrases, however, which if they are not subsequent glosses which have found their way into the text, suggest that as a general principle special privileges could be renounced by those for whose benefit they were created. It is, however, doubtful whether so general a rule was fully accepted even in Justinian's day.[184] However, whatever the final position was in Roman law, the commentators regarded Ulpian's text and the above-mentioned Code and Novel as examples of a general principle that persons of full legal capacity could renounce any special privileges which were introduced for their benefit. It followed that sureties could renounce the benefits of cession of actions, division, and excussion. What constituted a sufficient renunciation, however, remained a debated point.[185]

The Roman-Dutch law of sureties, therefore, derives directly from Roman law, but it undoubtedly represents a not inconsiderable advance over the Roman law, for it took three strands and wove them into one. The advance which it made might perhaps be characterized in a phrase by saying that Roman-Dutch law gathered the various Roman forms by suretyship under the rubric of a single consensual contract.

8. The rise and fall of the women's suretyship benefits

From the days of the Roman Empire until 1971 women enjoyed a remarkable degree of protection from the normal consequences of undertaking the obligations

---

[183] Nov 9.19.1.

[184] The only real reason for doubt is, of course, that neither Code 2.3.29 nor Nov 9.19.1 would appear to have been necessary if that principle were generally accepted. As regards C 2.3.29, the explanation may be that it was doubted whether special *privilegia* attaching to certain positions could be renounced: it would be understandable that that should be doubted, for it could be regarded as a special case. That constitution therefore does not necessarily present a real difficulty. But it remains difficult to explain the need for Nov 9.19.1 unless there were a general doubt about the effectiveness of a contractual renunciation of a statutory privilege.

[185] See V 46.1.16: and VL 4.4.12. on the one hand and *contra* VdK 502.

of a surety. In terms of the *propter sexus imbecilitatem*[186] women were prohibited from interceding in respect of a debt of another person by the *Senatusconsultum Velleianum* of about AD 46 and Justinian in AD 556 enacted the *Authentica si qua mulier* which prohibited women from standing surety for their husbands.

Both these enactments were received into the Roman-Dutch law[187] and subsequently formed part of the South African law.[188] Thus, although patently contrary to the tenor of the modern age where sexual equality is, or ought to be, taken for granted, they form a significant part of the history of our law of suretyship. Some account, albeit brief, should be given of them.

The wording of the *Senatusconsultum* is far from clear. It plainly applied to all women, whether married or not, and it applied not only to suretyship but to all forms of intercession. Thus loans to women for the benefit or in the interests of others and other forms of intercession were also hit by the *Senatusconsultum*.[189] But if the precise meaning of the *Senatusconsultum* is diffuse, it clearly had a wide rather than a narrow scope. It did not, however, aid a woman who had made an outright gift to another, nor when she indemnified another for the consequences of his conduct.[190] The *Authentica* is of far more limited scope for it applied only to married women standing surety for their husbands.[191]

A question which has been much disputed is the purpose of the *Authentica*.[192] Since the *Senatusconsultum* of wide scope already existed, why did Justinian find it necessary to enact the more limited *Authentica*? It has been suggested that it was to ensure that the obligations of women who stood surety for their husbands were void rather than voidable;[193] alternatively, the reason may be that the *Authentica*

---

[186] The precise policy behind the *senatusconsultum* has been a matter of some debate. See, for instance, Zimmermann at 146-8 where he rejects the assertion that the *senatusconsultum* was directed against women in an attempt to put them back in their proper place, the home (see H Voigt *Studien zum Senatus Consultum Velleianum* (1952) 6 ff). He also rejects the proposition that the purpose of the *Senatusconsultum* was cognate to the Augustan legislation preventing the husband from selling, without the wife's consent, dotal land in Italy, viz, to protect the wife's fortune from being wasted by a profligate husband (Suzanne Dixon 'Infirmitas Sextus' (1984) 52 *Tijdschrift voor Rechtsgeschiedenis* 356 at 363). Zimmermann settles for the purpose being to protect women from themselves the view being that in the conditions of the time women assumed too easily that they would not be called upon to make good their suretyship undertaking. Thus they could be easily preyed upon by the unscrupulous and those over-optimistic about their financial affairs.

[187] V 16.1.3, 12; Huber 3.27.5.

[188] *Oak v Lumsden* (1884) 3 SC 144; *Whitnall v Goldschmidt* (1884) 3 SC 314; *Mahadi v De Kock and Hyde* (1883) 1 HCG 344; *Maasdorp v Graaff-Reinet Board of Executors* (1909) 3 Buch AC 482; *Standard Building Society v Kellerman* 1930 TPD 796, *inter alia*. Fuller accounts of the womens' suretyship benefits will be found in the third edition of this book at 177- 81 or the second edition at 163-96.

[189] Further examples of intercessions which would be contrary to the *Senatusconsultum* are the following: The woman, not being a debtor, allowing herself to be substituted as such (eg by delegation); or promising jointly (as co-principal debtor); or pledging her credit; or pledging her *res* for the debt of another; or giving a mandate to a person to intercede on behalf of another. See, D 16.1.2 pr., V 16.1.8; Huber 3.27.5, 6, 7, 8.

[190] V 16.1.11; Huber 3.27.14; V 16.1.8; Huber 3.27.15; *Northern Assurance Co Ltd v Delbrook-Jones and Another* 1966 (3) SA 176 (T).

[191] C 4.29.22; Nov 134.8. The suggestion in *Stride v Wepener* 1903 TH 383 that the *Authentica* covers other forms of intercession is plainly wrong.

[192] Zimmermann is, uncharacteristically, unhelpful here. He says simply that the *authentica* 'effectively re-enforced' the policy of the *senatusconsultum* (at 151).

[193] *Oak v Lumsden* (1884) 3 SC 144, *Stainbank v National Bank of South Africa Ltd* (1906) 27 NLR 465 at 476.

was Justinian's attempt to reduce the number of exceptions which were being developed to the *Senatusconsultum*.[194]

Women did not, however, enjoy the protection of the benefits in all circumstances that fell within the terms of the statutes. The benefits could be and frequently were renounced by women when acting as sureties. Controversy raged for centuries, however, over the formalities to be observed in renouncing the benefits[195] but this need not detain us. Where the intercession was to the advantage of the women (for example, where she receives a reward from the transaction) the benefit could not be claimed,[196] and she could not benefit where she was or had been fraudulent in regard to the transaction.[197]

The women's suretyship benefits were abolished in France as early as 1606, the BGB abolished the benefits in 1901 in those parts of Germany which had not already done so, a similar fate befell them in Ceylon in 1924 and in Zimbabwe in 1959, yet only in 1971 was the Suretyship Amendment Act 57 of 1971, which abolished the benefits in South Africa and Namibia, enacted.[198] Thus did the long history of the *Senatusconsultum Velleianum* and the *Authentica si qua mulier* in Roman and Roman-Dutch law come to an end.[199]

---

[194] *Papageorgiou v Kondakis & others* 1968 (1) SA 85 (O) at 87.
[195] And in Natal there was special legislation to govern the formalities of renunciation.
[196] D 16.1.16 pr; D 16.1.21; Gr 3.3.16; *African Guarantee and Indemnity Co Ltd v Rabinowitz* 1934 WLD 151 at 156, 157; *National Industrial Credit Corporation Ltd v Zachareas* 1949 (4) SA 790 (W). The *authentica* contained a specific provision denying the benefit in such circumstances but the similar restriction was only implicit in the *senatusconsultum*.
[197] V 16.1.3, 11; Gr 3.3.15; Huber 3.27.16.
[198] See Ellison Kahn 'Farewell *Senatusconsultum Velleianum* and *Authentica si qua mulier*' (1971) 88 *SALJ* 364 at 364-5.
[199] But it seems that the benefits may yet survive in Lesotho: *BP Lesotho (Pty) Ltd v Lucy Mabathoana and others* (High Court of Lesotho, unreported, 15th November 2004).

CHAPTER II

Definition and Nature of Suretyship

	Page
1. Introduction.	26
2. Definition of the contract of suretyship	28
(a) The accessory nature of the surety's obligation.	29
(b) The parties involved in a suretyship contract and their obligations	30
(c) The right of recourse against the principal debtor by the surety	31
3. Suretyship and the contract of guarantee.	32
4. Other forms of indemnity and intercession and their relationship to suretyship	34
(a) Undertaking liability as principal debtor.	35
(b) Undertaking to indemnify a creditor	35
(c) Suretyship and insurance compared.	36

1. Introduction

Suretyship is only one form of intercession, ie a transaction in which one person undertakes liability for another's debt. Uncertainty can easily arise over whether a particular transaction is in fact suretyship or not.[1] Yet it is often vital to know whether a contract is suretyship. A suretyship will need to comply with the formalities specifically required by the law for contracts of suretyship,[2] but other forms of intercession will not. Also, if a contract is one of suretyship, the surety will be entitled to the suretyship benefits discussed in Part Two, but otherwise not.

---

[1] We will distinguish below between suretyship and the contract of insurance, and between suretyship and the contract of guarantee as well as other undertakings to indemnify another on the happening of a certain event.

[2] Section 6 of the General Law Amendment Act 50 of 1956 laid down that the terms of a 'contract of suretyship' had to be 'embodied in a written [sic] document' for the contract to be valid but did not find it necessary to say what a contract of suretyship was. Section 6 is discussed in detail in Chapter V. See also Susan Scott and Eric Dirix, (2004) 15 *Stell LR* 333 arguing at 343 that section 6 should apply to all forms of personal security. The authors urge legislation if the courts cannot be persuaded to apply section 6 to all forms of personal security. It is true, of course, that the policy considerations that require a contract of suretyship to be in writing apply equally to many other forms of personal security. But this is not yet the law.

DEFINITION AND NATURE OF SURETYSHIP 27

The old authorities did not distinguish themselves in defining the contract of suretyship.[3] However, they do make perfectly clear the crucial point that suretyship is an accessory obligation, ie that a valid principal obligation is essential for suretyship; the suretyship has no independent existence. The judges in the early cases did not always take this much further[4] but in *Corrans and Another v Transvaal Government and Coull's Trustee*[5] Innes CJ said that the definitions of the old authorities came to this, namely, 'that the undertaking of the surety is accessory to the main contract, the liability under which he does not disturb, but it is an undertaking that the obligation of the principal debtor will be dis-

---

[3] Voet (V 46.1.1.) says 'a surety is one who by a stipulation takes upon himself the obligation of another, whilst the latter, the principal debtor, remains bound'. Van der Linden (VdL 1.14.10.) defines suretyship as 'a contract by which a person binds himself on behalf of a debtor, for the benefit of the creditor, to pay him the whole or part of what the debtor owes him, thus joining in the obligation'. Grotius (Gr 33.12.) has it: 'A surety is a person who, for the greater security of debt, binds himself by a promise for a principal debtor.' Van Leeuwen in his *Roman-Dutch Law* (VL 4.4.2.) says 'to bind oneself for another, in other words to become surety, is the binding of oneself by promise for another debtor, in better security (of the debt)'. In *Censura Forensis* 1.4.17.3. he says 'suretyship is an accessory obligation, by which a person, by means of a stipulation, pledges his credit on another's obligation, the principal debtor still remaining bound.' Pothier (P 365) gives the following definition: 'The engagement of a surety is a contract by which a person obliges himself on behalf of a debtor to a creditor for the payment of the whole or part of what is due from such debtor, and by way of accession to his obligation.' While these various remarks do establish clearly that suretyship is an obligation accessory to the obligation of the principal debtor, they do not, with respect, amount to a complete definition of the concept. Further references to the views of the old authorities will be found in Wessels paras 3876-93.

On a number of occasions the courts have approved one or other of the definitions of the old authorities. Voet's definition was approved in *Malmesbury Board of Executors and Trust Co v Duckitt and Bam* 1924 CPD 101 at 108, and the view of Pothier, cited above, was adopted in *Inglis v Durban Navigation Collieries Ltd* (1908) 29 NLR 436 at 447 by the Natal Court, and by the Appellate Division in *Langeberg Koöperasie Bpk v Inverdoorn Farming and Trading Company Ltd* 1965 (2) SA 597 (A) at 60. (See also *Colonial Government v Edenborough and Another* (1886) 4 SC 290 at 296.)

[4] The earliest judicial pronouncement appears to be that of Connor J in *Murray and Burrill v Buck and Buck* 1870 NLR 155 at 156, namely, 'any person is, I apprehend, a surety within the meaning of the term in law, who engages his own liability in respect of another's debt'. This is plainly far too wide. In another early case, *Fitzgerald v Argus Printing and Publishing Co Ltd* (1907) 3 Buch AC 152 at 159, De Villiers CJ said 'the essential requisites of the contract of suretyship are that the surety should incur only an accessory obligation whilst the principal obligation of the debtor remains in full force ...'. These dicta do not take the matter much further than the old authorities had gone.

[5] 1909 TS 605 at 612. This definition was approved in *Hutchinson v Hylton Holdings and Another* 1993 (2) SA 405 (T) at 410H (Van Dijkhorst J). And in *Union Government v Van der Merwe* 1921 TPD 318 at 321 Wessels JP stressed essentially similar points when he said: 'The legal scope of the surety's contract is identical with that of the principal debtor—*accessorium sui principalis naturam sequitur*. The surety undertakes the same obligation as the debtor, and undertakes to perform this same obligation as soon as the debtor, when called upon, fails to perform it. Troplong, *Caut:* 46. It is true there are two contracts, the one between the creditor and the debtor and the other between the creditor and the surety. But the contract between the creditor and the surety is not an independent contract with an obligation of its own but an accessory contract with the very same obligation that exists between the principal debtor and the creditor. It may be observed at this point, in passing, that the obligation of the debtor to the creditor is not necessarily contractual, but may arise out of delict. Moreover, although the obligation of the surety does relate to that of the debtor, it is not necessarily 'the very same obligation', for that of the debtor may be to do something, while that of the surety in that relation may be simply to pay money in indemnification of the creditor for the debtor's not having done it. As Van den Heever JA said in *Gerber v Wolson* 1955 (1) SA 158 (A) at 166, 'the obligation of a surety and that of a principal debtor frequently have the same economic content ... but they are different obligations ...'. See also Huber 3.26.29; Sande 7.5.11. Although the definition of suretyship has on occasion been mentioned in other decided cases nothing of value

charged, and, if not, that the creditor will be indemnified.' Here are contained all the essentials: the contractual nature of suretyship, a principal obligation to which the suretyship is accessory and the undertaking by the surety that the principal obligation will be discharged, upon failure of which the creditor will be indemnified.

Based on this and similar dicta earlier editions of this book have put forward a definition of suretyship. In recent decades that definition has been gathering support and it has now been referred to with apparent approval by the Appellate Division on three occasions;[6] and although it would be wrong to suggest that it is incapable of improvement it should be accepted as a starting point for discussion.

2. Definition of the contract of suretyship

Suretyship[7] is an accessory contract by which a person (the surety) undertakes to the creditor of another (the principal debtor),[8] that the principal debtor, who remains bound, will perform his obligation to the creditor and [9] that if and so

---

seems to have been added to the views already cited. For example, in *Orkin Lingerie Co (Pty) Ltd v Melamed & Hurwitz* 1963 (1) SA 324 (W) at 326 Trollip J said 'a contract of suretyship in relation to a money debt can be said to be one whereby a person (the surety) agrees with the creditor that, as accessory to the debtor's primary liability, he too will be liable for the debt'. This definition is rather too wide and has been criticized. (See 1963 *Annual Survey* 200). And in *FJK Syndicate v Du Preez and Smit* 1943 WLD 116 at 120, Ramsbottom J said 'the plaintiff would have to prove that ... the second defendant agreed [with him] to stand surety for the due fulfilment by the first defendant of the obligation actually undertaken by the latter'.

[6] The citations are: (1) by Corbett JA (Jansen JA concurring) in *Trust Bank of Africa Ltd v Frysch* 1977 (3) SA 562 (A) at 584F; and (2) by Trengove AJA (Wessels ACJ, Jansen, Muller and Joubert JJA concurring) in *Sapirstein and Others v Anglo African Shipping Co (SA) Ltd* 1978 (4) SA 1 (A) at 11H and (3) by Corbett CJ (Hefer, Nestadt, Grosskopf JJA and Nicholas AJA concurring) in *Nedbank Ltd v Van Zyl* 1990 (2) SA 469 (A) at 473I. This definition has been referred to with approval in several cases since—for instance, *Basil Read (Pty) Ltd v Beta Hotels (Pty) Ltd and Others* 2001(2) SA 760 (C) at 766F—but without distinguishing between the Caney definition and other definitions (particularly that in LAWSA Vol 26, para 190 discussed below in the next but one note) which are slightly different. The Caney definition is criticised in the minority judgment of Stegmann J in *Carrim v Omar* [2001] 3 All SA 71 (W) at 81ff; 2001 (4) SA 691 (W). This is discussed more fully below.

[7] In the first and second editions of this work 'suretyship or guarantee' has been referred to at this point, implying that these concepts are interchangeable. Many of the decided cases also use the two words synonymously (see, for example, *Mouton v Mynwerkersunie* 1977 (1) SA 119 (A), where Wessels JA said that 'guarantee' most commonly meant to bind oneself as surety), but this usage has been subjected to growing and justified criticism. Guarantee is a distinct although difficult concept and its precise definition and relationship with suretyship is explored below.

The usage of variants of the word 'guarantee' where suretyship is meant is ingrained in the law reports and the written contracts themselves and very difficult to eradicate. The fact is that sometimes 'guarantee' particularly when used as a verb or a participle is more straightforward and clear, particularly in subordinate clauses, than any obvious alternative. 'The debt which was guaranteed' is much less awkward than 'the debt in respect of which a suretyship has been undertaken'. 'The debt which was secured' is often helpful but leaves uncertain whether real or personal security is intended. It is hoped that in this book the context will always reveal which meaning of 'guarantee' is intended.

[8] In the version of the definition approved by the Appellate Division the word 'primarily' appeared at this point.

[9] In the version of the definition approved by the Appellate Division the word 'secondarily' appeared at this point.

far as the principal debtor fails to do so, the surety will perform it or, failing that, indemnify the creditor.[10]

(a) The accessory nature of the surety's obligation

The fact that the surety's obligation is an accessory obligation is often invested with an air of mystery that apparently justifies without further explanation many aspects of suretyship. In fact the concept is relatively straightforward. It means simply that for there to be a valid suretyship there has to be a valid principal

---

[10] Prior to this edition the definition was in this form: 'Suretyship is an accessory contract by which a person (the surety) undertakes to the creditor of another (the principal debtor), *primarily* that the principal debtor, who remains bound, will perform his obligation to the creditor and, *secondarily*, that if and so far as the principal debtor fails to do so, the surety will perform it or, failing that, indemnify the creditor' (emphasis added). And in that form it was criticised by JG Lotz (revised by JJ Henning) 'Suretyship' in WA Joubert (ed) *The Law of South Africa* vol 26 (first reissue, 1997) para 191 (hereinafter LAWSA). The learned author remarks that it is 'somewhat pointless to say that the surety's primary undertaking is that the principal debtor will perform as that ... does not create a primary (or any) obligation between the creditor and the surety'. There is some force in this criticism. Moreover, the definition has sometimes led to misunderstanding and confusion. See Stegmann J in his dissenting minority judgment in *Carrim v Omar* [2001] 3 All SA 71 (W); 2001 (4) SA 691 (W) supposing that the definition implies that the surety had two obligations—a primary obligation that the debtor would perform and a secondary obligation that the surety would otherwise perform.

It is hoped that the excision of the words 'primarily' and 'secondarily' from the definition will make it plain that the surety has but one obligation (to perform or pay in the debtor's place should the debtor fail to perform).

Although it is tempting to silence the critics by taking the further step of excising any mention of the surety undertaking that the debtor will perform from the definition we resist that temptation for three reasons. First, the formulation in the text is consistent with the best of the judicial definitions (particularly that of Innes CJ in *Corrans and Another v Transvaal Government and Coull's Trustee* 1909 TS 605); see also the judgments of Mason J (the surety 'has promised to secure [the execution of the contract]' (at 627)) and Wessels J in that case. Indeed, the formulation in the text is consistent with all the judicial definitions (for another good example see *List v Jungers* 1979 (3) SA 106 (A) (contract not suretyship because 'no undertaking that principal debtor... will perform his obligations' (at 119G)) except that of Stegmann J in *Carrim v Omar* (who points out that the dicta from *Corrans* cited above are not part of the *ratio*).

Secondly, this approach is not inconsistent with the old authorities discussed above and is consistent with most academic writing: *De Wet en Van Wyk Die Suid-Afrikaanse Kontraktereg en Handelsreg* 5 ed (1992) Vol I by JC de Wet and GF Lubbe (ed) (the surety accepts responsibility 'vir die behoorlike uitvoering van sy verpligtings *deur* die skuldenaar' italics added); GF Lubbe 'Die Onderskeid tussen Borgtog en Ander Vorme van Persoonlike Sekerheidstellings' (1984) 47 *THRHR* 383 (the surety undertakes that 'die hoofskuldenaar sy verpligting teenoor die skuldeiser sal nakom' (at 385)); and NJ Grové *Die Formaliteitsvereiste by Borgstelling* (unpublished LLM dissertation, University of Pretoria (1984)) (the surety undertakes to the creditor that the 'skuldenaar sal presteer in terme van 'n reeds bestaande verbintenis ...' (at 73; *contra, autem* at 77).

And, thirdly, the Caney definition captures a nuance at the heart of suretyship (certainly a suretyship that is gratuitously undertaken) viz, that the surety expects (and thus is willing to accept responsibility there for on pain of having to pay himself) that the debtor will perform. If the surety shared the creditor's scepticism about the debtor's ability to perform few indeed would be the contracts of suretyship gratuitously entered into.

Further discussion of the definition of suretyship will be found in: Forsyth and Du Plessis, 'Suretyship, guarantee and Islamic banking' (2002) 119 *SALJ* 671 and Susan Scott and Eric Dirix, 'To have your cake and eat it' (2004) 15 *Stell LR* 333.

obligation, between the debtor and the creditor.[11] The suretyship is said to be accessory to the transaction which creates the obligation of the principal debtor.[12] Put another way, every suretyship is conditional upon the existence of a principal obligation.

From this flows the fundamental but obvious proposition that in the absence of a valid principal obligation the surety is not bound, so exceptional cases aside,[13] the surety can raise any defence which the principal debtor can raise. More subtly, this means (as Lubbe has pointed out) that in the typical case[14] the surety only takes upon himself the risk of a breach of contract by the principal debtor for the surety is not liable for any non-performance based upon the invalidity or extinction of the obligation in question.[15] This marries well with the idea of a surety as one who promises that the principal debtor will perform, not simply one who will indemnify the creditor for losses caused by non-performance.

By similar reasoning, it follows that a surety is not bound to a person to whom the principal debtor is not liable,[16] even if the surety has made his promise to that person, for there is no principal obligation between principal debtor and creditor to which the suretyship can accede. Nor is a promise to a debtor to pay his debt for him suretyship.[17]

(b) The parties involved in a suretyship contract and their obligations

From the above it is clear that there are three parties involved—the creditor, the principal debtor and the surety; and there are four obligations. The first two are those of the principal debtor to the creditor and, accessory to that, the obligation of the surety to the creditor. The third obligation (of which more in a moment) is that of the principal debtor to reimburse the surety what he pays the creditor. The

---

[11] Or as LAWSA vol 26 para 192 puts it: the causa for a contract of suretyship 'is provided by a valid principal obligation ... if a contract of suretyship is not grafted upon such a principal obligation it is void.' The absence of a principal obligation means that the contract is not suretyship, but it may be some other contract of indemnity. See also *African Life Property Holdings v Score Food Holdings* 1995 (2) SA 230 (A) at 238F quoted in Chapter 111, section 1. See the further discussion of the occasions on which the surety is released through the extinction of the principal obligation in Chapter XIII, section 2.

[12] V 46.1.16.3; Sande 7.11; P 366; B 3. The principal debtor is not, of course, released by the surety's intervention: V 46.1.1; *Cens For* 1.3.17.3; P 367. See also R Korthals Altes *Borgtocht naar Hedendaagsch Nederlandsch Recht* thesis submitted for the degree Doctor in de Rechtsgeleerdheid University of Amsterdam (1933) 20 ff; Wolfgang Mincke *Die Akzessorietät des Pfandsrechts* Habilitationsschrift auf Empfehlung der Juristischen Fakultät Munster gedruckt (1987) 39 ff; Earl C Arnold 'Primary and Secondary Obligations' (1925) 74 *University of Pennsylvania LR* 36 and Léon D Hubert 'The Nature and Essentials of Conventional Suretyship' (1939) 13 *Tulane LR* 519.

[13] See the discussion on the release of the surety in Chapter XIII and in many other parts of this book. An example of a defence which the principal debtor but not the surety could raise would be a defence based upon minority: see Chapter III.

[14] Limiting oneself, for the sake of simplicity, to cases where the principal obligation is based upon contract.

[15] This is clearly set out by GF Lubbe 'Die Onderskeid tussen Borgtog en Ander Vorme van Persoonlike Sekerheidstellings' (1984) 47 *THRHR* 383 at 385-6.

[16] D 46.1.16; V 46.1.3; *Cens For* 1.4.17.5; P 393, 394.

[17] V 46.1.3. The promissor cannot be sued by the creditor, for there is no *nexus* between them, but the debtor may have a cause of action against the promissor to compel payment or for damages.

DEFINITION AND NATURE OF SURETYSHIP 31

fourth obligation falls upon the creditor, namely, to do nothing in his dealings with the principal debtor and with other sureties to the prejudice of the surety.[18]

(c) The right of recourse against the principal debtor by the surety

Although there are three parties involved, there is not necessarily a tripartite agreement or contract; indeed, in practice there seldom is. There is the transaction, as a result of which the principal debtor is bound to the creditor, and there is a contract between creditor and surety by which each is bound to the other.

Thus the principal debtor is not necessarily a party to the contract between the surety and the creditor,[19] but nonetheless, there comes into existence the obligation of the principal debtor to reimburse the surety what he pays the creditor. When the surety intervenes with the consent or knowledge of the principal debtor, the contract of mandate (*mandatum*) comes into existence, either expressly or tacitly;[20] and if he does so without the knowledge of the debtor, the quasi-contract *negotiorum gestorum* regulates their relationship.[21] With the former, *mandatum*, the principal debtor is taken to authorise the surety to perform his obligation on his behalf, with the consequence that the surety has the *actio mandati* for reimbursement of what he pays; with the latter, the surety is taken to act in the interests of the debtor, as *negotiorum gestor*, and entitled consequently to reimbursement from the debtor.

The surety's obligation arises from the making of the contract of suretyship; from then he becomes bound to the creditor and from then he becomes a conditional creditor of the principal debtor in relation to his right of recourse against the latter.[22]

---

[18] Although it has sometimes been suggested (*Iscor Pension Fund v Marine and Trade Insurance Co Ltd* 1961 (1) SA 178 (T)) that suretyship is a contract *uberrimae fidei*, the clear implication in the judgment in *Orlando Hosking v Standard Bank of SA Ltd* (1892) 13 NLR 174 is that suretyship is not such a contract. This conclusion has been fortified by *Mutual and Federal Insurance Co Ltd v Oudtshoorn Municipality* 1985 (1) SA 419 (A) where Joubert JA remarked that *uberrima fides* is an alien, vague, useless expression without any particular meaning in law ... our law of insurance has no need for *uberrima fides* and the time has come to jettison it' (at 433).

Non-disclosure of material information may, nevertheless, on general principles amount to fraudulent concealment justifying rescission. See further Wessels paras 4275-81, and cf *Trans-Drakensberg Bank Ltd v Guy* 1964 (1) SA 790 (D) at 797, 798. See also JE Scholtens 'Suretyship or Insurance: Duty to Disclose Material Facts' (1961) 78 *SALJ* 137 and the 1961 *Annual Survey* 171 and 296. See also 1963 *Annual Survey* 384.

[19] *Turkstra v Massyn* 1959 (1) SA 40 (T).

[20] *Rossouw and Rossouw v Hodgson & Others* 1925 AD 97 at 102. This reference to *mandatum* has no relation to *mandatum credendae pecuniae*, mentioned in the previous chapter as a form of suretyship, in that the surety was the *mandator* and the creditor the *mandatarius*, whilst in the present relation these positions are taken to be occupied by the debtor and the surety respectively: Chapter I. See furtherJE Scholtens 'Rights of Recourse of Sureties and Third Persons Who Paid Another's Debt' (1959) 76 *SALJ* 266 at 268, 269; DH van Zyl *Die Saakwaarnemingsaksie as Verrykingsaksie in die Suid-Afrikaanse Reg* thesis submitted for the degree Doctor in de Rechtsgeleerdheid, University of Leiden (1970) 150-2; JG Lotz 'Suretyship' in WA Joubert (ed) *The Law of South Africa* vol 26 (1986) para 168; DP Visser *Die Rol van Dwaling by die Condictio Indebiti*, thesis submitted for the degree Doctor in de Rechtsgeleerdheid, University of Leiden (1985) 228 ff; Wouter de Vos *Verrykingsaanspreeklikheid in die Suid-Afrikaanse Reg* 3 ed (1987) 214-5.

[21] *Rossouw and Rossouw v Hodgson & Others* 1925 AD 97 at 102.

[22] *Moti & Co v Cassim's Trustee* 1924 AD 720 at 738; *Rossouw and Rossouw v Hodgson and Others* 1925 AD 97. See Chapter XI.

Notwithstanding that a surety binds himself for the debt of another, suretyship is not a contract for the benefit of a third party (a *stipulatio alteri*).[23]

3. Suretyship and the contract of guarantee

In considering the relationship between suretyship and the contract of guarantee it is easiest to say first what is not meant by the word 'guarantee' in this context. It is clear that the word 'guarantee' in common parlance and in many contractual contexts means (and is intended by the parties to mean) simply to undertake the obligations of a surety.[24] This is not what is meant by guarantee in this context, for the contract of guarantee is distinct from suretyship.

On the other hand, a contracting party, typically a vendor, may be said to 'guarantee' some quality in the thing sold, for instance, that a motor vehicle is roadworthy. Here the use of the word simply introduces a term of the contract to that effect. We are not concerned with this use of the word 'guarantee' or with the consequences of a breach of that term.

With a contract of guarantee, on the other hand, the guarantor undertakes a principal obligation to indemnify the promisee on the happening of certain events. The well-worn example is a guarantee that 'the price of cement will not rise this year'. Here the guarantor undertakes a principal obligation to indemnify should the price rise. As a further example, consider *Acutt v Bennett*,[25] where payment of a dividend of 9% by a certain company was guaranteed. This was plainly the undertaking of a principal obligation and not suretyship. In neither of these cases was there a second contract to which the guarantee could be accessory.

Difficulties begin to arise, however, when the event on which the guarantor becomes bound to indemnify the promisee is in fact the performance by a third party of some obligation which that third party owes to the promisee. For instance, in *Sassoon Confirming and Acceptance Co (Pty) Ltd v Barclays National Bank Ltd*[26] the contract involved was a bank 'guarantee' that the bank would pay the appellant a certain sum if final judgment granted in its favour against one Kleiner was not satisfied within seven days. Was this a principal obligation to indemnify the appellants conditional upon non-payment by Kleiner, or had the bank in fact stood surety for Kleiner?

---

[23] Wessels shows this in paras 1743-5; see also *Imperial Cold Storage and Supply Company Ltd v Julius Weil and Co* 1912 AD 747 at 750.

[24] In *Mouton v Mynwerkersunie* 1977 (1) SA 119 (A), for instance, Wessels JA said that 'guarantee' most commonly meant to bind oneself as surety. And in *Basil Read (Pty) Ltd v Beta Hotels (Pty) Ltd and Others* 2001 (2) SA 760 (C) the 'contract guarantee' required by the 'Joint Bulding Contracts Committee' for its standard form building contract was held to be 'in the nature of suretyhsip' (at 766D). However, this is not the inevitable consequence of the use of the word; which must be viewed in its context. Thus in *List v Jungers* 1979 (3) SA 106 (A) it did not mean that a suretyship had been undertaken. See also JT Pretorius 'Borgkontrak of Vrywaringskontrak?' (1982) 45 *THRHR* 73 and the minority judgment of Stegmann J in *Carrim v Omar* [2001] 3 All SA 71 (W) at 81ff; 2001 (4) SA 691 (W).

[25] (1906) 27 NL.R 716.

[26] 1974 (1) SA 641 (A).

One way of answering this question is to assert (as do *De Wet en Van Wyk*[27] that with guarantee 'iemand iets anders as die betaling van 'n skuld deur 'n ander persoon waarborg'. Thus the contract in *Sassoon Confirming* was suretyship not guarantee since the bank had undertaken to indemnify if another person's *debt* was not paid. This resolution of the problem, however, has the smack of dogmatism about it. Contracts of guarantee exist in contexts far removed from securing the payment of debts; why should the existence or otherwise of a debt as the event in respect of which the guarantee is given define the contract? Lubbe and others have rightly been critical of it, pointing out that it is arbitrary to limit the contract of guarantee in this way.[28]

What then is the difference between a guarantee that a debtor will perform and suretyship? Lubbe makes one point of distinction clear: the guarantor's obligation, as an obligation independent of that of the debtor, is to indemnify the creditor in respect of losses suffered through the debtor's non-performance, whereas the surety, as we have seen, is only liable for losses resulting from the debtor's breach of contract. Thus if the creditor suffers grave losses when it turns out that debtor's contract is invalid, the guarantor's obligation remains in force and he will have to pay those losses but the surety's obligation falls away and he will not have to pay a penny.[29] Indeed, even if the debtor's contract is perfectly valid and not breached in any way, the guarantor against loss is bound to make good any losses to the creditor that many none the less result. But a surety will only be bound if the debtor breaches his contract in some way.[30] A second point

---

[27] *De Wet en Van Wyk Die Suid-Afrikaanse Kontraktereg en Handelsreg* 5 ed (1992) Vol I by JC de Wet and GF Lubbe (ed), 391. See also, Cilliers 'Waarborg en Garansie in die Suid-Afrikaanse Kontraktereg' (1962) 25 *THRHR* 244 at 259; Ralph Slovenko 'Suretyship' (1965) 39 *Tulane LR* 427 at 428 ff; Max Radin 'Guarantee and Suretyship' (1929) 17 *California LR* 605, (1929) 20 *California LR* 21.

[28] GF Lubbe 'Die Onderskeid tussen Borgtog en Ander Vorme van Persoonlike Sekerheidstellings' (1984) 47 *THRHR* 383, 391-2. It would be interesting to see how De Wet en Van Wyk would treat the case discussed in the following note. It is clearly not sureyship, yet what was 'guaranteed' was the performance by a third party (*in casu* a non-existent person) of their obligations.

[29] *Hutchinson v Hylton Holdings and Another* 1993 (2) SA 405 (T) well illustrates this. The defendant had signed a document in which he 'guarantee[d] specific performance of this contract [for the sale of land] in my personal capacity' (at 409D). The purchaser of the land was non-existent so there was no principal obligation and no suretyship. The court held that the clause amounted to 'an independent undertaking ... [The defendant] contracts as co-principal debtor and not surety. His undertaking is not dependent upon the non-performance of [the purchaser]...The clause is a form of indemnity. It is not affected by the invalidity of the main contract.' There was no discussion of whether this was guarantee or some other form of indemnity. Similarly, in *Heathfield v Maqelepo* 2004(2) SA 636 (SCA) the defendant has undertaken liability as 'surety and co-principal debtor' for the non-existent purchaser of land but had also undertaken 'irrevocably' to take transfer in his own name. The defendant was held to be a purchaser not a surety. No reference was made to *Hutchinson v Hylton Holdings and Another*.

[30] Thus in *Carrim v Omar* [2001] 3 All SA 71; 2001 (4) SA 691 (W) the creditor (Omar) had invested money with the Islamic Bank which she had lost when the bank failed. As a devout Muslim wishing to avoid being paid interest Mrs Omar had invested the funds pursuant to a *mudhaarabah* contract which was a form of partnership in which the creditor and debtor shared profits and losses. If the joint investments with the bank did badly Mrs Omar could thus lose every penny without there being any breach of contract by the bank. A director of the bank (Carrim) had promised orally to repay the investment to her if the bank failed to repay. In these circumstances the majority of the court (Willis J and Shakenovsky AJ) concluded that Carrim had guaranteed Mrs Omar against loss. He had not stood surety for the bank (which would have required writing (see Chapter V) and would not protect her if the moneys were lost without breach of contract by the bank). Carrim's

of distinction is this: as we have seen, a surety undertakes that the debtor himself will perform, and only that if he fails to perform that the surety will do so. With guarantee, on the other hand, the guarantor undertakes to pay on the happening of a certain event but does not promise that that event will not happen.[31]

However, if the theoretical difference between suretyship and guarantee is now clear, it remains difficult to tell them apart particularly where the event guaranteed is the performance of a contractual obligation. As Hahlo and Kahn remark 'the distinction often turns on a knife edge'.[32]

4. Other forms of indemnity and intercession and their relationship to suretyship

There are several ways other than by entering into a contract of suretyship or guarantee in which one person may undertake responsibility for another's debt or to indemnify another for some harm which may be suffered. Some of these may be discussed briefly here.

(a) Undertaking liability as principal debtor

A person who undertakes to pay another's debt may intend to take upon himself the obligation of a debtor to the creditor, as a principal, either alone (ie replacing the existing debtor) or as co-principal debtor with an existing debtor. If he assumes liability for the debt of another as a co-principal debtor or if he does so in place of the other by a process of novation, his undertaking is an *intercessio*,

---

obligation was a principal not an accessory obligation.

[31] In *Sassoon Confirming and Acceptance Co (Pty) Ltd v Barclays National Bank Ltd* 1974 (1) SA 641 (A) the bank 'guarantee' appears to be just that: an undertaking to pay if Kleiner failed to pay, not an undertaking that Kleiner would pay. One wonders why the Appellate Division thought that this was not 'a guarantee (in its ordinary sense)' (at 646D). As adumbrated, however, *De Wet en Van Wyk,* because of their restricted concept of guarantee, consider that this was 'amper 'n klassieke voorbeeld van borgtog' (at 392).

[32] HR Hahlo and Ellison Kahn *The Union of South Africa: the Development of Its Laws and Constitution* (1960) 705-6. In the following cases it was held that the contract concerned amounted to an original or primary obligation to pay, and not the accessory obligation of suretyship: *Edgcome v Maunsell* 1911 CPD 521; *Hubbart v Rogers* 1915 WLD 39; *Cazalet v Johnson* 1914 TPD 142; *Shaw v Kirby* 1924 GWL 33; *Versfeld & Co v Southern Timber (Pty) Ltd* 1935 (2) PH A38 (C); *Schoeman v Moller* 1951 (1) SA 456 (O) at 472; *Harman's Estate v Bartholomew* 1955 (2) SA 302 (N) at 303, 309; *Jungers v List* 1978 (1) SA 1200 (SWA). *Diners Club South Africa (Pty) Ltd v Durban Engineering (Pty) Ltd* 1980 (3) SA 53 (A) deserves special mention here. The court was concerned with the termination of the legal relationship between the issuer of a credit card and a company which had undertaken joint and several liability for the debts to the issuer incurred by a sometime employee of the company. A majority of the court held that, whatever the nature of the relationship, it had been terminated. A difference of opinion, however, manifested itself in regard to the nature of the relationship. Rabie JA (with Joubert JA) felt that the court was concerned with liability as surety and co-principal debtor under a continuous suretyship. Viljoen AJA, on the other hand, found that the company had undertaken a principal obligation to the card issuer. Neither Kotzé JA nor Botha AJA found it necessary to decide on the nature of the relationship.

It is submitted that the writer in 1980 *Annual Survey* 157 is correct to prefer the view of Viljoen AJA. After all, in the extensive analysis of the evidence there is no indication that the company had undertaken that the employee would pay his debts to the issuer, ie had undertaken liability as a surety. See also JT Pretorius 'Borgkontrak of Vrywaringskontrak?' (1982) 45 *THRHR* 73 and the minority judgment of Stegmann J in *Carrim v Omar* [2001] 3 All SA 71 (W) at 81ff; 2001 (4) SA 691 (W).

because he takes upon himself the obligation to meet a debt originally payable not by him but by another.[33] He is liable whenever and howsoever the debtor whose place he takes would be liable.

(b) Undertaking to indemnify a creditor

A person may undertake a principal obligation to indemnify another should that other suffer loss as a result of undertaking a particular activity, for example, the undertaking may be against loss to be incurred in the doing of business with a third person or in giving a third person credit. This is plainly not a suretyship in the absence of an accessory undertaking that the third person will perform his obligation.[34] Plainly it is not novation; the indemnifier's liability is in addition to that of the original debtor not instead of it.[35] Such undertakings have often been recognized and enforced by the courts (although not always by the name of indemnity),[36] and they can, but do not necessarily, amount to *intercessio*.

The difficulty here is deciding whether there is any significant difference between a guarantee and such a contract of indemnity. Lubbe apparently equates guarantee with a 'contract of indemnity'[37] while Grové sees indemnity simply as a form of guarantee.[38] It is submitted that such differences as exist are only of nuance and degree. There is no difference in principle between indemnity and guarantee. In essence both indemnity and guarantee are contracts in which the promissor undertakes a principal obligation to compensate another for the losses sustained by that other on the occurrence of a particular event, whatever the nature of that event.

---

[33] *Schoeman v Moller* 1951 (1) SA 456 (O) at 467. Wessels deals with the various forms of intercession in paras 3778-83. See also 1966 *Annual Survey* 136. The example of suretyship stated at the outset of the article is, however, not accurate; a surety undertakes that the debtor will perform his obligations and that, if he does not, the surety will do so or will indemnify the creditor. An important point of distinction is that the liability of one who has interceded as a co-principal debtor is not dependent on failure to pay on the part of the original debtor: *Schoeman v Moller* 1951 (1) SA 456 (O) at 467. See also JSA Fourie 'Die Aanspreeklikheid van die Borg en die Hoofskuldenaar' (1978) 41 *THRHR* 307. See *Hutchinson v Hylton Holdings and Another* 1993 (2) SA 405 (T), discussed in section 3, for an example of a party taking upon himself the liability of a debtor.

[34] Cf *Imperial Cold Storage and Supply Company Ltd v Julius Weil and Co* 1912 AD 747 at 750, 754: 'A contract to indemnify a person against the consequences of his own act or omission is not suretyship. If that person be regarded as a creditor, there is no principal debtor, other than the indemnifier'—per Snyman J in *Northern Assurance Co Ltd v Delbrook-Jones and Another* 1966 (3) SA 176 (T) at 180, quoting from the first edition of this book. At 181 he said 'indemnity is a form of suretyship'; this is obviously a 'slip of the pen', for the proposition is inverted: he no doubt intended to say 'suretyship is a form of indemnity'.

[35] See GF Lubbe 'Die Onderskeid Tussen Borgtog en Ander Vorme van Persoonlike Sekerheidstelling' |(1984) 47 *THRHR* 383 388-9.

[36] See JT Pretorius 'Die Formaliteitsvereiste by Borgstelling' (1988) 10 *MB* 122 at 127, pointing to cases such as *Hubbart v Rogers* 1915 WLD 39; *Versfeld & Co v Southern Timber (Pty) Ltd* 1935 (2) PH A38 (C); *Edgcome v Maunsell* 1911 CPD 521; *Renou v Walcott* (1909) 10 HCG 246; *Blom v Auret* (1907) 24 SC 48; *Schoeman v Moller* 1951 (1) SA 456 (O); *Cazalet v Johnson* 1914 TPD 142; *Dorman v Perring* 1922 EDL 137.

[37] GF Lubbe 'Die Onderskeid tussen Borgtog en Ander Vorme van Persoonlike Sekerheidstellings' (1984) 47 *THRHR* 383, 391.

[38] NJ Grové *Die Formaliteitsvereiste by Borgstelling* (unpublished LLM dissertation, University of Pretoria (1984)) at 78-9. The author restricts indemnity to the case where the indemnifier promises that a third party will not exercise his rights against the person indemnified.

(c) Suretyship and insurance compared

It has been said that suretyship and insurance 'have very much in common, so that it is often difficult to determine into which class a particular contract falls'.[39] The apparent similarity seems to stem from the fact that each involves an element of indemnity. Troplong[40] states the differences to be threefold:

(a) in suretyship the obligation is unilateral, on the part of the surety alone, whilst in insurance there are bilateral obligations in that the insurer's obligation is reciprocal to that of the proposer of the insurance who is obliged to pay a premium (we interpolate here that the creditor, as the consequence of the suretyship and in consideration of it, agrees to give or do something to or for the principal debtor, that is to say, to give him credit or to extend an existing credit);

(b) suretyship is an accessory contract whilst insurance is a principal contract; and

(c) suretyship is a contract of 'benevolence', in the sense, apparently, that no consideration passes from the creditor to the surety,[41] whilst insurance is a matter of business negotiation between insured and insurer.

In this relation, an insurer is hardly in a position to know the risks attached to the venture, whilst a surety may be expected to protect himself by inquiry and, indeed, is in all likelihood in some way associated with the principal debtor before he takes the suretyship upon himself. In commercial affairs it is not unknown for a creditor to pay a fee to a surety (or more commonly a guarantor) for providing his undertaking.[42]

A further point of distinction is that while the surety's right of recourse against the debtor exists irrespective of whether cession of the creditor's actions against the debtor is taken,[43] an insurer in seeking to recover from the third party what he has paid is subrogated to the remedies of the insured.[44]

---

[39] *Trans-Africa Credit and Savings Bank Ltd v Union Guarantee and Insurance Co Ltd* 1963 (2) SA 92 (C) at 98.

[40] *Caut* 35 and 36. The paragraphs from Troplong mentioned above are to be found translated in *Iscor Pension Fund v Marine and Trade Insurance Co Ltd* 1961 (1) SA 178 (T) at 183. See also the discussion on the two paragraphs in *Trans-Africa Credit and Savings Bank Ltd v Union Guarantee and Insurance Co Ltd* 1963 (2) SA 92 (C) at 98, 99.

[41] Though the principal debtor may reward the surety for providing his undertaking (*Lever v Buhrmann* 1925 TPD 254 at 263).

[42] V 46.1.32. See, for instance, *Brown, Greisler (Pty) Ltd v Wootton* 1937 (1) PH A8 (W).

[43] See above Chapter II or Chapter XI.

[44] JP van Niekerk *Subrogasie in die Versekeringsreg* unpublished LLM dissertation, University of South Africa (1979) 26 ff points out that an insured does not 'as a matter of law' have the right to recover from the third party but 'is subrogated to the remedies of the insured'. Van Niekerk correctly points out that subrogation is one of the *naturale* of an insurance contract and that cession to the insurer is not required; thus 'as a matter of law' the insurer has rights against the third party. This is correct; but the fact remains that the insurer exercises the rights of the insured, while the surety exercises his own rights. See also JC Sonnekus 'Beskikking deur die Versekeraar oor Versekerde Goed wat Gesteel is' 1987 *TSAR* 267 at 272-4; Stephen I Langmaid 'Some Recent Subrogation Problems in the Law of Suretyship and Insurance' (1934) 47 *Harvard LR* 976 and the discussion in Chapter XI.

There appears, however, to be no reason in principle why a contract of insurance should not be concluded, in suitable terms, to the end that the insurer guarantees to a creditor the performance by the debtor of his obligations to the creditor. Whether this is done at the instance of the creditor or of the debtor, the insurer's obligation is accessory to that of the debtor.[45] If this is at the instance of the debtor, in the sense that he pays the premium, there appears to be no conflict with Troplong's concept of suretyship in relation to insurance. Nothing, however, said by the writers on our own common law appears to deny a creditor the right of insuring his claim against his debtor by contracting for such a guarantee by an insurer.

Troplong says that on 'the introduction into suretyship of a price payable by the creditor' the contract of the debtor detaches itself 'and the insurance (the creditor) and the insurer negotiate as principals'; there is a sale and purchase of a chance. The issue must, however, depend upon the intention of the parties as expressed in their contract; it must be ascertained whether the insurer primarily promises performance by the debtor of his obligations or whether it undertakes no more than to make good the loss suffered by the insured (the creditor) in giving credit to the debtor. In the former event his liability to indemnify the creditor arises only when it has been ascertained that there has been non-performance and consequential loss, whilst in the latter event that liability exists from the beginning. The dividing line is thin and, as already said, the distinction must depend upon the expressed intention of the parties; but the consequences may, though not necessarily will, differ considerably, for example in relation to a right of recovery from the debtor.

---

[45] See *Yorkshire Insurance Co Ltd v Dippenaar and Others* 1963 (3) SA 414 (W).

CHAPTER III

The Principal Obligation

	Page
1. Principal obligation essential for surety's obligation.	38
2. Types of principal obligation	39
(a) General: principal obligation may be contractual, delictual or merely a natural obligation	39
(b) Principal obligation cannot be illegal	41
(c) Surety may be denied reliance upon principal debt's illegality by estoppel, or his knowledge of that debt's voidness or illegality.	42
(d) Principal obligation may be *ad factum praestandum* or *ad faciendum aliquid*.	43
(e) The principal obligation must not be owed by the surety	43
3. The coming into existence of the principal obligation.	46
4. Substitution of the creditor either through cession or through the operation of the rule 'huur gaat voor koop', or through the doctrine of the undisclosed principal.	47

1. Principal obligation essential for surety's obligation

As already emphasised suretyship is accessory to a principal obligation.[1] Thus, if the principal debtor's obligation is legally non-existent, for example if it is founded upon a forgery, there can be no suretyship of it;[2] nor if it is fictitious;[3] nor if it had already been discharged before the suretyship was entered upon.[4] 'Guaranteeing a non-existent debt', said Nienaber JA in *African Life Property Holdings v Score Food Holdings*,[5] 'is as pointless as multiplying by nought'. Where it is open to the debtor to attack the debt (the claim upon him) that defence (provided it is not personal to him, eg minority), is open to the surety.[6]

---

[1] In *Imperial Cold Storage and Supply Company Ltd v Julius Weil and Co* 1912 AD 747 at 750 Innes CJ said that 'suretyship could only exist as accessory to a principal debt'; and Trollip J, quoting from the first edition of this book, said in *Orkin Lingerie Co (Pty) Ltd v Melamed & Hurwitz* 1963 (1) SA 324 (W) at 326, 'the essence of suretyship is the existence of the principal obligation of the debtor to which that of the surety becomes accessory'. See also *Union Government v Van der Merwe* 1921 TPD 318 at 321, the passage quoted in Chapter II, section 1 (notes); and *Versfeld & Co v Southern Timber (Pty) Ltd* 1935 (2) PH A38 (C).
[2] *Wiehahn NO v Wouda* 1957 (4) SA 724 (W) at 726.
[3] *Trans-Drakensberg Bank Ltd v Guy* 1964 (1) SA 790 (D).
[4] Wessels para 4265.
[5] 1995 (2) SA 230 (A) at 238F.
[6] Wessels paras 3969 and 4030. This will be discussed in the chapter on Discharge of Surety (chapter XIII).

2. Types of principal obligation

(a) General: principal obligation may be contractual, delictual or merely a natural obligation

A person may bind himself as a surety to any creditor[7] and for any debtor,[8] including a debtor who has no capacity to bind himself but who is bound by the force of law, for example, if he is bound to reimburse those who have conducted his affairs.[9] But no one is bound as surety to a person to whom the principal debtor is not liable, either legally or naturally.[10]

One can stand surety for a principal debt or principal debtor not yet in existence—for example, when one stands surety for a company yet to be registered for its debts to be incurred in the future—but then the liability of the surety does not arise until the principal obligation exists.[11]

The principal debt may be created by contract[12] or may arise out of delict[13] or in any manner in which a person may become bound as a debtor to another.[14] In respect of delict the debt secured may be a liability for a delict already committed,[15] or the surety may promise that another will not commit a delict in the future;[16] the suretyship may be an undertaking that another will perform his duties, for example, in public office or as an executor or administrator of an estate.

The principal debt may be a legal obligation or a natural (but unenforceable) obligation,[17] liquid or illiquid,[18] but there may be no suretyship in respect of an illegal[19] or forbidden or impossible transaction or obligation[20] (even though it imports a natural obligation),[21] eg for a loan of money to a *filiusfamilias* contrary

---

[7] P 393, 394.
[8] *Cens For* 1.4.17.5; P 393, 394.
[9] *Ibid.*
[10] D 46.1.16, V 46.1.3, *Cens For* 1.4.17.5; P 393, 394.
[11] See *Television & Electrical Distributors (Pty) Ltd v Coetzer en Andere* 1962 (1) SA 747 (T); *United Dominions Corporation (SA) Ltd v Rokebrand* 1963 (4) SA 411 (T), *Malcolm v Cooper and Others* 1974 (4) SA 52 (C); *Trust Bank of Africa Ltd v Frysch* 1977 (3) SA 562 (A) at 584G-H as well as V 46.1.6, 8 and Gr 3.3.24. In this last-mentioned case it was held further (at 585A-D) by Corbett and Jansen JJA that it is not necessary that the suretyship contract indicate whether it precedes or follows the principal obligation. Cession of an obligation to a non-existent company is void (as opposed to an agreement so to cede once the company exists), thus one cannot stand surety for the debts 'ceded' to a non-existent company. This is presumably why *Van Eeden v Sasol Pensioenfonds* 1975 (2) SA 167 (O) was not treated as a case of suretyship of the debts of a company yet to be formed. (See further below.)
[12] D 46.1.8.1; V 46.1.7; Gr 3.3.21.
[13] D 46.1.8.5, D 46.1.56.3, D 46.1.70.5, V 46.1.7; Gr 3.3.21, *Cens For* 1.4.17.11.
[14] D 46.1.1; D 46.1.8; Gr 3.3.21; VL 4.4.3; Huber 3.26.5.
[15] D 46.1.70.5; V 46.1.7; Gr 3.3.21; VL 4.4.3; *Cens For* 1.4.17.1; Huber 3.26.5; P 395.
[16] In *African Guarantee & Indemnity Co Ltd v Thorpe* 1933 AD 330 at 338 Wessels CJ said '*in esse* there is no difference between suretyship *ex contractu* and *ex delicto*. In the latter case the suretyship contract approaches in its essence to an indemnity contract.' This latter observation must, it seems, relate to suretyship against the consequences of delict to be committed *in futuro*.
[17] D 46.1.7; D 46 1.8.2; D 46.1.16.13; D 46.1.60; Inst 3.20.1; V 46.1.6, 9; Gr 3.3.22; Sch 300; *Cens For* 1.4.17.5; Huber 3.26.13; P 376, 395; B 6; Lee *ad Gr* 246, 247; Wessels paras 1269, 1276.
[18] V 46.1.8; B 6.
[19] *Albert v Papenfus* 1964 (2) SA 713 (E) at 717, approved in *Lipschitz NO v UDC Bank Ltd* 1979 (1) SA 789 (A).
[20] D 46.1.11; D 46.1.70.5, V 46.1.9, 11; Gr 3.3.22; *Cens For* 1.4.17.6; P 366, 395; B 6.
[21] V 46.1.9, P 395.

to the SC Macedonianum,[22] or for a share of stolen property, or against the penalty for a crime. An indemnity cannot be taken against the consequences of a contemplated wrong to be committed by the indemnified.[23] Moreover, the surety cannot bind himself to undergo imprisonment or corporal punishment for another's default.[24]

There may be a valid suretyship in respect of the contract of a minor,[25] but not that of a lunatic[26] or a prodigal.[27] In the case of a minor's contract, the surety is taken to secure performance of the contract (which is not void, but voidable), despite the fact of minority, and *restitutio in integrum* allowed to the minor does not free the surety, unless restitution is founded upon the fraud of the other contracting party.[28] In the case of the prodigal and the lunatic,[29] as they are incapable of contracting, no principal debt comes into existence, and it follows that there can be no suretyship.[30] If, however, they should become bound, so also are their sureties.[31]

The position of spouses in general and of women married by community of property in particular is of some interest. In the past, there could not be a valid suretyship of the contract of a married woman subject to her husband's marital power[32] unless she was a public trader,[33] or, presumably, if the contract was for household necessaries or authorised by the husband.[34] The doctrinal basis for this was that the wife's contract in these circumstances (like that of the lunatic or prodigal) is void and so cannot support a suretyship.[35] However, this was the position prior to the Matrimonial Property Act,[36] section 14 of which provides that a wife married in community of property 'has the same powers [as her husband] with regard to the disposal of the assets of the joint estate, the contracting of

---

[22] D 46.1.11, V 46.1.5, 9; B 6.
[23] V 46.1.7, *Cens For* 1.4.17.11; P 395.
[24] V 46.1.7; Gr 3.3.21; VL 4.4.3.6; *Cens For* 1.4.17.11; Huber 3.26.6.7 and cf P 376.
[25] D 46.1.2, 25, V 46.1.9, VL 4.4.3, *Cens For* 1.4.17.5; P 376, 395; B 6, Lee *ad Gr* 246, 247.
[26] D 46.1.70.4, V 46.1.9.
[27] V 46.1 9.
[28] Gr 3.48.12; P 380; Domat 2392; Huber 3.26.12; *Estate Van der Lith v Conradie & others* (1903) 20 SC 241 at 246.
[29] D 46.1.70.4; V 46.1.9, 10.
[30] Gr 3.3.14; VL 4.4.3. P 395.
[31] V 46.1.9.
[32] V 46.1.10; VL 2.7.8; P 395; B 6; cf *Cens For* 1.4.17.5; Lee *ad Gr* 246, 247. But if one of several co-principal debtors is a woman married in community and contracting without her husband's assistance, her incapacity and the invalidity of her contract do not nullify the obligation of her co-debtors who are capable of contracting—P 395, V 46.1.10.
[33] *Moodliar v Moodley* 1958 (1) PH F44 (N).
[34] Note that where the spouses were married in community of property under the old law then even if the husband assisted the wife to make the contract *he* could not stand surety for her debts: *Nedbank Ltd v Van Zyl* 1990 (2) SA 469 (A) discussed below.
[35] HR Hahlo and Ellison Kahn *The Union of South Africa: the Development of Its Laws and Constitution* (1960) point out (at 192) that the effectiveness of such a contract remains in suspense until the husband has either ratified or repudiated it. Note that Voet (V 46.1.10) points out that the law of Utrecht was different from the law of Holland in this regard. In Utrecht the surety for a wife's unassisted contract was bound but could only be held to his promise after the dissolution of the marriage. Voet concedes that the wife is under a natural obligation but insists that not every suretyship for a natural obligation is valid.
[36] Act 88 of 1984.

debts against the joint estate and the management of the joint estate ...'. Thus the wife's contracts in respect of the joint estate will no longer be void, and they can be secured by a surety.[37]

Where the wife is not married in community of property her debts can be secured in the usual way.

(b) Principal obligation cannot be illegal

Brandt v Weber[38] is an example of an illegal principal obligation to which no suretyship could attach, namely, a sale of ammunition in contravention of the law. *Eaton Robins & Co v Nel*[39] related to a suretyship for the debts incurred by an association of more than twenty persons known to the creditor not to be registered under the then applicable legislation[40] and therefore not entitled to trade; no valid obligation arose from the supply of goods for the illegal business of the association and consequently no suretyship could come into existence. This case is distinguishable from *United Dominions Corporation (SA) Ltd v Rokebrand*[41] in that in the latter case the suretyship was for debts to be incurred after registration of the company, which as we have seen can be secured.

A liability created in contravention of section 38 of the Companies Act 61 of 1973 (which prohibits, subject to exceptions, the giving of financial assistance by a company for the purpose of or in connection with the purchase of its own shares) is invalid as a principal obligation and consequently cannot sustain a suretyship.[42]

---

[37] There are a complex range of juristic acts, however, which a spouse married in community cannot perform without the *written* consent (section 15(2)) or the consent (section 15(3)) of the other spouse. For the details see Hahlo and Kahn, *The South African Law of Husband and Wife* (5th ed, 1985) at 244-56. Transactions requiring consent and not ratified by the other spouse (which is possible in terms of section 15(4)) are apparently void unless the transaction can be brought within section 15(9)(a) which deems the transaction to have been entered into with the necessary consent where the third party concerned neither knew nor could reasonably know that the consent was lacking. Where such transaction is void there cannot, in accordance with the usual principles, be a valid suretyship in respect thereto. For discussion of the limitation of spouses married in community of property to enter into suretyships see Chapter IV, section 1.

[38] (1886) 2 SAR 98.

[39] (1909) 26 SC 365.

[40] At that time the Companies Act 46 of 1926.

[41] 1963 (4) SA 411 (T).

[42] *Albert v Papenfus* 1964 (2) SA 713 (E), approved in *Lipschitz NO v UDC Bank Ltd* 1979 (1) SA 789 (A), and followed in *Metequity Ltd NO and Another v Heel* 1997 (3) SA 432 (W) (defence available even where judgment obtained against principal debtor; discussed further in Chapter 13, section 1(f)). HR Hahlo 'Rendering Financial Assistance' (1964) 81 *SALJ* 281 expresses agreement with this, but points to the difficult position of an innocent third party as creditor. Previously Hahlo made the suggestion that there may be a remedy for unjust enrichment (HR Hahlo 'Transaction by Company in Connection with the Purchase of Its own Shares' (1952) 69 *SALJ* 367). The essentials of a surety's plea that the principal obligation offends s 38 were discussed in *Miller v Muller* 1965 (4) SA 458 (C). See also RC Beuthin 'Section 86bis(2) A New Test for 'Financial Assistance'?' (1973) 90 *SALJ* 211 and 1973 *Annual Survey* 256-8); RC Beuthin 'More about Financial Assistance' (1980) 97 *SALJ* 477 and 'Financial Assistance' 1976 *Annual Survey* 305; AN Oelofse 'Artikel 38 van die Maatskappywet' 1980 *TSAR* 47; Rudolph de Bruin 'Artikel 38(1) van die Maatskappywet: *Lipschitz v UDC Bank Ltd*' 1979 *De Rebus* 361; JS McLennan 'Financial Assistance to Acquire Shares: The Troubles Continue' (1981) 98 *SALJ* 422; Emil Brincker *Die Verbod op die Verlening van Geldelike Bystand deur 'n Maatskappy by die Verkryging van sy Aandele* unpublished LLD thesis, University of Stellenbosch (1991) 203 ff and *Hahlo's South African Company Law through the Cases* (1999) 6 ed by JT Pretorius (gen ed), PA Delport, Michele Havenga and Maria Vermaas (1999) 124 ff.

A liability in breach of section 226 of the same Act (which absolutely prohibits a company from making loans[43] to a director of its holding company and, save where all its members agree, doing the same to one of its own directors) will also not support a suretyship.[44]

The early Zimbabwean case of *Knightsbridge Investments (Pvt) Ltd v Gurland*[45] applied this principle in deciding that an instrument of debt unenforceable because it contravened the local usury legislation did not found an action against one who, in that instrument, undertook the obligations of surety.

Where an illegal provision in a contract creating the principal obligation is severable from the contract as a whole, leaving a valid contract as the basis of the principal obligation, the suretyship is not affected by the illegality. So it was held, it seems, in *Peri-Urban Areas Health Board v The South British Insurance Co Ltd*.[46] This, however, may be prejudicial and unjust to the surety, unless the question of severability is decided with reference not only to the principal contract, but also to the suretyship, for the illegal provision may afford a distinct benefit to the surety, held bound as surety for performance of the truncated principal obligation.[47]

(c) Surety may be denied reliance upon principal debt's illegality by estoppel, or his knowledge of that debt's voidness or illegality

A surety may, however, be estopped from relying upon illegality in an action brought against him by an innocent third party; for example, where the seller under hire-purchase agreements made in breach of the law discounts his rights and cedes them to the discounting house, representing the agreements to be perfectly valid and at the same time standing surety for the buyers' obligations.[48]

Also, if the surety knows that the contract of the principal debtor is void, he is taken as contracting as a principal debtor; he undertakes to secure payment to the creditor notwithstanding the grounds which protect the principal debtor.[49]

Standard Bank of SA Ltd v Neugarten and Others 1987 (3) SA 695 (W) and MJ Oosthuizen 'Sekerheidstelling in Stryd met Artikel 226 van die Maatskappywet—Enkele Aspekte' 1988 *TSAR* 133.

[43] Or providing security to any person for the director's obligations.

[44] *Neugarten and Others v Standard Bank of SA Ltd* 1989 (3) SA 797(A); *Bevray Investments (Edms) Bpk v Boland Bank Bpk en Andere* 1993 (3) SA 597 (A) (where the person to whom the loan is made is a director of the company and a director of its holding company, he is not hit by the absolute prohibition). For discussion of earlier cases see MJ Oosthuizen 'Sekerheidstelling in Stryd met Artikel 226 van die Maatskappywet—Enkele Aspekte' 1988 *TSAR* 133.

[45] 1964 (4) SA 273 (SR).

[46] 1966 (2) PH A66 (T).

[47] The decision has been the subject of discussion in a note in 1966 *Annual Survey* 144, 145.

[48] *Trust Bank van Afrika Bpk v Eksteen* 1964 (3) SA 402 (A).

[49] B 6, 10, approved in *Van Eeden v Sasol Pensioenfonds* 1975 (2) SA 167 (O) at 180A-F where a surety of a debt ceded to a non-existent company was held bound because he, as a 'director' of the company, did not deny that he knew of its non-existence. Since the surety undertook liability as co-principal debtor as well, *a fortiori,* he was bound. For a case raising similar issues and where the same result was reached see *Hutchinson v Hylton Holdings and Another* 1993 (2) SA 405 (T).

(d) Principal obligation may be ad factum praestandum or ad faciendum aliquid

Though by civil law the principal obligation was necessarily a money debt, Voet and Grotius say[50] that a promise that another will give or do something is binding.[51] In *Corrans and Another v Transvaal Government and Coull's Trustee*[52] all three members of the Bench treated it as settled law that the principal obligation might be *ad factum praestandum* or *ad faciendum aliquid*.[53] That was a case of suretyship for performance by a building contractor of his obligations under a contract for the construction of a building.[54] Suretyships of this nature are everyday occurrences in industrial circles. As a further example of a case in which the principal obligation was not a money debt, consider *Beaufort West Municipality v Krummeck's Trustees and Others*,[55] which related to a suretyship for performance by a lessee, not only of his obligation to pay the rent[56] but of all his obligations under the lease, including a provision that it was to endure for a stated term of years.

The principal obligation may be, or may include, a negative obligation, for example, by a lessee not to contravene by-laws.[57] A surety may be taken for the performance of a personal act, possible of performance only by the principal debtor[58] including one involving the exercise of personal knowledge or skill.[59] In suretyship *ad factum praestandum* special questions arise as to the rights and obligations; these will be discussed in the chapter on the Obligations of the Surety (Chapter VII).

(e) The principal obligation must not be owed by the surety

From the definition of suretyship[60] it is plain that since the surety undertakes his promise to the creditor of *another,* the surety and the principal debtor cannot be

---

[50] V 46.1.3; Gr 3.3.3. See also B 9.

[51] *De Wet en Van Wyk Die Suid-Afrikaanse Kontraktereg en Handelsreg* 5 ed (1992) vol I by JC de Wet and GF Lubbe (ed) remark (at 391) that guarantee could be distinguished from suretyship in that in the former 'iets anders as die betaling van 'n skuld deur 'n ander persoon' is guaranteed but that this should not be read as suggesting that suretyship *ad factum praestandum is* not possible.

[52] 1909 TS 605.

[53] Innes CJ at 613, Wessels J at 623, 624 and Mason J at 627.

[54] The *exceptio non causa debiti* is usually renounced in suretyships securing debts arising otherwise than from loans of money. The surety who has renounced this exceptio is not debarred from alleging and proving that there was in fact no *causa debiti*. The purpose of the renunciation is to saddle the surety with the onus of proving the absence of the *causa*. In *Dowson & Dobson Industrial Ltd v Van der Werf and Others* 1981 (4) SA 417 (C) Marais J elucidates at 431: 'The renunciation of the exception means no more than that, when the creditor asserts a claim *in terms of the suretyship*, the surety will bear the onus of establishing that *the principal debt* for which he undertook liability does not exist.... Before the defendants [the sureties] are required to discharge that onus, plaintiff [creditor] has to allege that the *causa debiti is* one in respect of which the defendants undertook liability.... That allegation remains essential to its cause of action. Only then will the renunciation of the exception *non causa debiti* have its effect.' There may be some merit in renouncing the exceptio in instances where the cause of the debt arises otherwise than from a loan of money.

[55] (1887) 5 SC 5.

[56] As in *Arenson v Bishop* 1926 CPD 73, 6 PH A48.

[57] *Segell v Kerdia Investments (Pty) Ltd* 1953 (1) SA 20 (W) at 25-7.

[58] P 396. *Segell v Kerdia Investments (Pty) Ltd* 1953 (1) SA 20 (W) at 27.

[59] *Corrans and Another v Transvaal Government and Coull's Trustee* 1909 TS 605 at 614.

[60] See Chapter II.

one and the same person.[61] At first sight it seems pointless to suppose that this could occur for if the debtor could not perform *qua* debtor, how could he perform *qua* surety? However, the situation could arise (although not under the modern system of the administration of estates) where the debtor becomes heir to the surety or vice versa. In such a situation it might be important to know what the fate of the suretyship was for if it were still valid the debtor/surety may be able to raise, say, the benefit of division as a defence. Fortunately, the old authorities make it plain that in these circumstances the surety is released[62] (but, of course, the principal debtor, or his heir, remains liable).

Recently, this same issue has arisen in a different guise. Where a spouse, married in community of property, undertakes to stand surety for the debts of his or her spouse, is that suretyship valid? Again it may seem pointless for a creditor to accept one spouse as surety for the other spouse since, being married in community, both are jointly bound for all the debts of the community.[63] However, the spouse that stands surety may own property that falls outside the community, and thus the effect of a valid suretyship will be to render that property available to the creditor.[64] Alternatively, the suretyship may have been executed while the spouses were married but in terms wide enough to cover debts incurred after their divorce.[65] If the suretyship is void *ab initio* then the question cannot arise whether the surety is liable for post-divorce debts of the other spouse; *aliter,* vice versa.

However, fundamental principle provides the straightforward answer: a surety cannot stand surety for herself.[66] Thus where a wife, married in community, purports to stand surety for her husband, she purports to stand surety in respect of a debt which she already owes. Moreover, if valid, the suretyship imposes an obligation upon the husband jointly with the wife; thus the husband is also being asked to stand surety in respect of a debt which he already owes. In these circumstances, the suretyship cannot be enforceable. That this is so has been confirmed by the Appellate Division in *Nedbank Ltd v Van Zyl*.[67] There Corbett CJ concluded that where the wife married in community had stood surety for the debts of her

---

[61] Referred to with approval in *Intercontinental Exports (Pty) Ltd v Fowles* 1999 (2) SA 1045 (A) at 1053A.

[62] D 46.1.21, D 46.3.93.2, V 46.3.20. Where, however, the principal obligation is narrower than the suretyship, eg the principal obligation is only a natural obligation, then the surety is not released: see Chapter XIII.

[63] *De Wet NO v Jurgens* 1970 (3) SA 38 (A) at 47D-E. Of course, the husband was generally responsible for the payment of the debts of the spouse and paid them out of the joint estate.

[64] These were the facts of *Reichmans (Pty) Ltd v Ramdass* 1985 (2) SA 111 (D).

[65] These were the facts of *Nedbank Ltd v Van Zyl* 1990 (2) SA 469 (A).

[66] Notwithstanding the husband's position in the past as administrator of the joint estate, the same problems could arise with the wife standing surety for the husband as with the husband standing surety for the wife. In fact all the reported cases concern the wife standing surety for the husband, thus for ease of exposition and elegance of language in what follows the wife will be treated as the surety.

[67] 1990 (2) SA 469 (A). The Matrimonial Property Act 88 of 1984 has not affected this part of the law; that Act abolished the marital power (s 11) but this difficulty arises from the institution of community property which is not abolished by the Act. Note, however, under section 15(2) of that Act the written consent of the other spouse is required before a spouse can bind himself as surety. The relevant details of the 1984 Act relevant to the capacity of spouses to enter into contracts of suretyship are discussed above, Chapter 3, Section II.

husband that 'there was ... at the time of signature of the suretyship a complete identity of surety and principal debtor: the purported effect of the transaction was to make [the husband and wife] ... co-sureties of the overdraft obligation in respect of which they were co-debtors. It was consequently a clear case of persons standing surety for their own debt and ... the suretyship was unenforceable when entered into.'[68]

However, although Corbett CJ's judgment is fully in accord with principle it is important to note that it presses the principle no further than necessary to decide the case. Thus, the learned judge made clear that the suretyship was 'unenforceable when entered into' not void *ab initio* or invalid for all time. This leaves open the question whether the surety would be liable for debts falling within the words of the suretyship, but incurred by her husband *after* they had divorced.[69]

Nedbank Ltd v Van Zyl also leaves some uncertainty over the position of partnerships: can a partner stand surety for the debts of the partnership of which he is a member? Since it is trite, exceptional cases aside, that a partnership has no legal personality[70] apart from its members,[71] it follows that if a partner stands surety for the debts of the partnership, he is standing surety for debts he already owes and the suretyship is unenforceable. However, the courts seem to have said something different. In *Standard Bank of SA Ltd v Lombard and Another*[72] Botha J said this: 'I can see no reason in principle why partners should not bind themselves to a partnership creditor in such a way that each partner is individually liable *in solidium* to the creditor for the payment of the whole of the partnership debts even during the subsistence of the partnership... .I can see no reason why the documents [in this case] should not be valid and operative as such, even if it is to be assumed that they do not qualify as suretyships *strictu sensu,* a matter on which

---

[68] At 476G-H.

[69] In *Nedbank Ltd v Van Zyl* 1990 (2) SA 469 (A) the evidence did not establish that any of the debts in respect of which the bank sought to hold the wife liable had been incurred after the divorce so the point did not need to be decided.

[70] See in this regard the excellent discussion by JJ Henning 'Partnership' in WA Joubert (ed) *The Law of South Africa* vol 19 (2006) para 277 who points out that there are two theories on the nature of a partnership. The 'entity theory' has its origin in the mercantile concept of the partnership as a body or entity separate and apart from the members composing it, and having rights and obligations distinct from those of its members. The 'aggregate theory', on the other hand, ignores the partnership and looks at the individual partners composing it. The partners are the owners of the partnership property, and the rights and liabilities of the partnership are their rights and liabilities. Any change of partners destroys the identity of the partnership. Neither the aggregate nor the entity theory can always be followed in all circumstances. While it may be true to say that the aggregate theory is normally followed in South African law, there are instances where partnerships are regarded as entities distinct from its members, for example in the case of insolvency.

[71] For example, *Strydom v Protea Eiendomsagente* 1979 (2) SA 206 (T) at 209C. Note, however, there are situations in which partnership is recognised as a separate entity: a partnership can be sequestrated without sequestrating the individual estates of the partners and the creditor of a partnership is obliged during the existence of the partnership to sue all the partners and to execute against the partnership assets before turning to the individual assets of the partnership. Thus in *Lee en 'n Ander v Maraisdrif (Edms) Bpk* 1976 (2) SA 536 (A) it was held that a member of a partnership is liable for the full amount of the partnership debt as soon as the partnership is dissolved, even though the liquidation of the partnership has not been completed. See JJ Henning 'Partnership' in WA Joubert (ed) *The Law of South Africa* vol 19 (2006) para 322 for a full discussion in this regard.

[72] 1977 (2) SA 808 (W) at 813F-H.

I need not express any firm opinion ...'. When Botha JA (as he had become) next approached the same issue in *Du Toit en 'n Ander v Barclays Nationale Bank Bpk*[73] his ideas seemed to have firmed for he said 'Na heroorweging huldig ek nog steeds ... die mening ... dat 'n kontrak waarvolgens 'n vennoot homself teenoor 'n skuldeiser van die vennootskap verbind as borg en medehoofskuldenaar *in solidium* vir die betaling van die vennootskapskuld, 'n regsgeldige en afdwingbare kontrak is'.

Now does this amount to the recognition of a further exception to the principle that a partnership is not a legal entity apart from its members? Henceforth will a separate personality of partnerships be recognised when a partner stands surety for the partnership debts? It is submitted that, notwithstanding Botha JA's dicta quoted above, this is not the case. Careful reading of these dicta reveals that the learned judge of appeal was laying down no more than that in such circumstances a *contract* will come into existence; he was not laying down that a contract of *suretyship* comes into existence. He remarks in *Lombard* that this is not suretyship *strictu sensu* and leaves its precise nature uncertain; and even in *Du Toit* he calls it not 'borgtog' but simply ' 'n regsgeldige en afdwingbare kontrak'[74].

It is submitted that his lordship was laying down no more than that it was open to a partner to agree with a creditor of the partnership that the creditor (who would normally be bound to sue the partnership first and execute against the partnership assets before turning to the individual partners) could proceed directly against him. There can be no doubt over the enforceability of such an agreement. But when a partner enters such an agreement (although it may have the form of a suretyship) he is not standing surety. Nor is juristic personality being accorded to the partnership. All that is happening is that the partner is waiving a procedural advantage that he has *qua* partner in his contract with the creditor.

3. The coming into existence of the principal obligation

The principal debt may already have come into existence before the suretyship is undertaken;[75] or the two obligations may come into being simultaneously or

---

[73] 1985 (1) SA 563 (A) at 575G. These remarks were referred to with apparent approval by Corbett CJ in *Nedbank Ltd v Van Zyl* 1990 (2) SA 469 (A) at 479G.

[74] Note that in *Mmabatho Food Corporation (Pty) Ltd v Fourie en Andere* 1985 (1) SA 318 (T) it seems to have been taken for granted by Stegmann J that a 'sleeping partner' (ie an undisclosed partner) could stand surety for the partnership. Although the judgment does not address the question crisply, the result of the case may be able to be defended on the basis that the disclosed partners have no authority to bind the 'sleeping partner' (*Eaton & Louw v Arcade Properties (Pty) Ltd* 1961 (4) SA 233 (T) at 240 (confirmed on appeal: 1962 (3) SA 255 (A)), thus the 'sleeping partner' is not directly bound to the partnership creditors and is not acting as surety for his own debt when he stands surety for the partnership. This conclusion though will have to be re-assessed should it be established that the doctrine of the undisclosed principal applies to 'sleeping partners' (left open in *Karstein v Moribe and Others* 1982 (2) SA 282 (T) at 293). The doctrine of the undisclosed principal is part of the South African law (*Cullinan v Noordkaaplandse Artappelkernmoerkwekers Koöperasie Bpk* 1972 (1) SA 761 (A)). On the applicability of this doctrine on partnerships, see Ellison Kahn (gen ed) *Contract and Mercantile Law through the Cases* II *Specific Contracts and Mercantile Law* 2 ed (1985) by David Zeffertt, JT Pretorius & Coenraad Visser 446-7.

[75] As was the case in *Glenn Brothers v Commercial General Agency Co Ltd* 1905 TS 737; and see *Managers of Oudtshoorn Public School v White* (1893) 10 SC 203 and *Capnorizas v Webber Road Mansions (Pty) Ltd and Another* 1966 (1) PH A22 (W).

in close association with each other; or a surety may undertake his liability in respect of an obligation yet to be incurred by the principal debtor.[76] In that event, however, the surety is not bound until there is a principal debtor,[77] who is himself bound, either legally or naturally. The surety may withdraw before the principal debt has come into existence unless, expressly or tacitly, he was contracted to the contrary or unless withdrawal will prejudice the creditor.[78] Such a case was *Buyskes and Others, Trustees of Du Toit v De Kock, Smuts and De Kock*,[79] in which sureties bound themselves for payment by the debtor of the price of property under a mortgage bond he was to pass, but did not, with the consequence that the sureties never became liable. *Stratton v Cleanwell Dry Cleaners (Pvt) Ltd and Another*[80] was a case of suretyship for the price of shares payable on delivery of them to the purchasers. Quénet J said[81] that the suretyship 'would only become effectual if and when the transfer of shares took place'.[82] The language of a suretyship 'in respect of the indebtedness upon any just cause of indebtedness whatsoever' was the subject of contention in *Cope v Atkinson's Motor Garages Ltd*.[83] These words were held wide enough to cover existing indebtedness and also future debts up to the figure of money stated in the suretyship. Continuing suretyships are in the category of suretyship for obligations to be incurred *in futuro*. These will be discussed in the chapter on the Obligations of the Surety (Chapter VII).

The principal obligation may incorporate by reference the obligations created by another transaction.[84] Thus a suretyship may be in respect of an obligation the amount of which is uncertain or unliquidated and is yet to be determined.[85] Before the surety can be required to pay, however, the amount must be rendered certain or liquidated.[86]

4. Substitution of the creditor through cession or through the operation of the rule 'huur gaat voor koop', or through the doctrine of the undisclosed principal

In the past there has been controversy whether, when a creditor cedes his rights of action against the principal debtor to a third party, he also cedes to the third

---

[76] V 46.1.6, 8; VdL 1.14.10; Gr 3.3.24; P 399; B 3, 9. See also *Inter-Union Finance, Ltd v Franskraalstrand (Edms) Bpk and Others* 1965 (4) SA 180 (W) at 187.

[77] D 46.1.6.2; D 46.1.38.1; Gr 3.3.24; Lee *ad Gr* 248; *Cens For* 1.4.17.6; P 399, 403. See also note 48 and text at note 12 above.

[78] P 399.

[79] (1832) 2 Menz 12.

[80] 1960 (1) SA 355 (SR).

[81] At 360.

[82] See also *United Dominions Corporation (SA) Ltd v Rokebrand* 1963 (4) SA 411 (T), a case of suretyship for debts to be incurred in the future by a company not as yet registered.

[83] 1931 AD 366.

[84] *South African Scottish Finance Corporation Ltd v Wassenaar* 1966 (2) SA 723 (A).

[85] *De Villiers v Conradie and De Vos* (1864) 5 Searle 68 at 71. An example of this is a suretyship for the liabilities to be met upon the confirmation by the court of a compromise made in respect of a company under the provisions of s 311 of the Companies Act 61 of 1973.

[86] *Milne NO v Cook and Others* 1956 (3) SA 317 (D).

party his rights against the surety securing the debt ceded.[87] In *Pizani and Another v First Consolidated Holdings (Pty) Ltd*,[88] however, the Appellate Division settled the controversy in favour of the view that cession of the debt (*in casu* rights under the leases of certain movables) also effected cession of the rights against the surety,[89] unless, of course, cedent and cessionary agree otherwise or the suretyship itself restricts cession.[90] It follows that a formal cession of the suretyship rights, either simultaneously with the cession of the debt or at some other time, is not required. If it takes place it is a 'senseless formality'.[91] This decision, which is in accordance with the weight of the authority, is to be welcomed for it establishes a clear and convenient rule. Moreover, it is in accord with the juristic nature of a cession in terms of which Miller JA said 'the cessionary veritably steps into the shoes of the cedent. Whatever claims could, but for the cession, have been enforced by the cedent may after cession be enforced only by the cessionary.'[92] The courts have 'accepted ...for more than a century that future rights can be ceded and transferred *in anticipando*'.[93] Thus there is no reason in principle why the *Pizani* principle should not apply to rights against sureties in respect of future debts.[94]

---

[87] *Friedman v Bond Clothing Manufacturers (Pty) Ltd* 1965 (1) SA 673 (T) (at 677); *J McNeil v Insolvent Estate of R Robertson* (1882) 3 NLR 190 at 193; V 18.4.12 and Sande 9.31, *inter alia*, contain authority for the view subsequently adopted in *Pizani and Another v First Consolidated Holdings (Pty) Ltd* 1979 (1) SA 69 (A). Further old authority in favour of this view will be found in JE Scholten's article 'Cession of Rights against Sureties' (1957) 74 *SALJ* 130. In *Hasson Trading Co v Hopkinson and Hopkinson* 1961 R & N 161, however, the opposite view was taken, and in *First Consolidated Holdings (Pty) Ltd v Bissett and Others* 1978 (4) SA 491 (T) Eloff J (at 495A) followed the view of Caney J in *Inter-Union Finance Ltd v Dunsterville* 1956 (4) SA 280 (D) that the rights against the surety could be ceded after cession of the debt. This view of the learned judge—which influenced the decision in the *Hasson Trading* case, and was considered in *Moss & Page Trading Co (Pty) Ltd v Spancraft Furniture Manufacturers & Shopfitters (Pty) Ltd & others* 1972 (1) SA 211 (D), as well as being followed in *Brook v Jones* 1964 (1) SA 765 (N)—appears, with respect, to have been the source of much confusion on the subject. After all, if cession of the suretyship rights after cession of the debt was to have any meaning, it implied that cession of the debt did not effect cession of the suretyship rights and hence, that a separate cession was necessary. But if this were so, it implies that in the *spatium* between cessions, the surety promises to the cedent payment of a debt which is not due to the cedent. This, it is submitted, is not suretyship, although in *Inter-Union Finance Ltd v Dunsterville* 1956 (4) SA 280 (D) the learned judge considered that it was (at 283; see *De Wet en Van Wyk Die Suid-Afrikaanse Kontraktereg en Handelsreg* 5 ed (1992) vol I by JC de Wet and GF Lubbe (ed) at 392). Here, we submit, is the fount of much of the subsequent confusion. In any event *Pizani and Another v First Consolidated Holdings (Pty) Ltd* 1979 (1) SA 69 (A) settles the point, and it is clear that a separate cession of the suretyship rights is 'a wholly unnecessary formality ...' (at 78D). See AO Karstaedt 'Cession of Rights against Sureties' (1980) 97 *SALJ* 218.
[88] 1979 (1) SA 69 (A).
[89] At 77H-78C.
[90] At 78F-H.
[91] JE Scholtens 'Cession of Rights against Sureties' (1957) 74 *SALJ* at 133.
[92] At 77 B-C.
[93] *First National Bank of SA Ltd v Lynn NO and Others* 1996 (2) SA 339 (A) at 360A-C. After all, cession of future debts is the basis of the cession of book debts (including book debts) as well as the basis of continuing suretyships.
[94] However, the opposite may have been held in *SA Breweries Ltd v Van Zyl* 2006 (1) SA 197 (SCA). In March 1999 SAB69 ceded its rights against Ray's Liquor Store to SAB98. Van Zyl was a surety to SAB69 for the debts of the liquor store 'which may at any time be or become owing'. The SCA held that only existing rights of action were ceded to SAB69 and so Van Zyl was not liable for the debts of the store contracted after the cession. The terms of the cession from SAB69 to SAB98 are not clear from the judgment, but if it transferred only the existing debts there is nothing exceptional about the judgment (although it may be doubted whether SAB98 would have agreed to such a restriction without insisting on fresh sureties). But if the court in stating that SAB69 'had no right of action

The question which was posed in *Mignoel Properties (Pty) Ltd v Kneebone*[95] was whether a principle similar to that applied in *Pizani's* case applied where the rule 'huur gaat voor koop' was involved. What had happened was that the lessor of certain immovable property had sold that property to Mignoel Properties; the lessee apparently remained in occupation but failed to pay the rent to Mignoel Properties. Thus Mignoel Properties sued the sureties for the lessee for the arrears. The sureties, however, had made their promise, not to Mignoel, but to the original lessor: did this provide them with a defence?

Although *Pizani's* case was clearly distinguishable (for there had been an express cession of the lessor's rights, and here there was no cession at all), counsel for Mignoel Properties argued that the rule 'huur gaat voor koop' implied a tacit cession of the lessor's rights (and thus the case fell within *Pizani*) while counsel for the surety contesting liability (Kneebone) contended the maxim did not depend upon tacit cession at all. 'Huur gaat voor koop' meant that the lessee had a real right; and his duty to pay the rent to the new owner was the result of the exercise of that real right to remain in occupation, not of any contractual rights between lessee and new owner. In the absence of such cession, there could be no such rights between new owner and lessee; and no opportunity for the *Pizani* principle to operate and transfer to the new owner the lessor's rights against the sureties.

However, the Appellate Division held (per Friedman AJA, Joubert, Botha, Nestadt and MT Steyn JJA concurring) that the effect of 'huur gaat voor koop' was that 'once the lessee elects to remain in the leased premises after a sale, the seller *ex lege* falls out of the picture and his place as lessor is taken by the purchaser. No new contract comes into existence; all that happens is that the purchaser is substituted for the seller as lessor without the necessity for a cession of rights or an assignment of obligations. 'On being so substituted for the seller, the purchaser acquires all the rights which the seller had in terms of the lease, except, of course, collateral rights unconnected with the lease ... [thus] the effect of the 'huur gaat voor koop' rule is that the purchaser is substituted as lessor in the place of the seller. It is a logical and natural result of such a substitution that the purchaser also acquires the rights which the seller had against the surety for the lessee's obligations under the lease.'[96] Thus the new owner could sue the sureties.

A similar *ex lege* substitution of the creditor may take place when it emerges that the creditor (or intermediary) contracted with the debtor on behalf of an undisclosed principal. On uncontroversial principles this means that on disclosure the principal steps into the shoes of the creditor succeeding to his rights and duties

---

for the future debts...and it could not cede rights that has not accrued to it" (para 9) intended to lay down a general principle it was, with respect, clearly in error. See further the discussion by JT Pretorius in 2006 *Annual Survey* 281ff.

[95] 1989 (4) SA 1042 (A).

[96] At 1050J-1051I. This conclusion following the *locus classicus* on 'huur gaat voor koop' (*Kessoopersadh en 'n Ander v Essop en 'n Ander* 1970 (1) SA 265 (A)) and approving the conclusions of Christo van Loggerenberg (in *Skuldoorname en Kontraksoorname* thesis submitted for the degree Doctor in de Rechtsgeleerdheid, University of Leiden (1981) at 293) makes it plain that neither the tacit cession approach nor the real right approach (espoused by De Wet) to 'huur gaat voor koop' is accepted by the Appellate Division. 'Huur gaat voor koop' is *sui generis*. The rule developed 'weens praktiese en billikheidsoorwegings' (*Kessoopersadh* at 283D) and its juristic basis is an *ex lege* transfer of contractual rights ('kontraksoorname wat van regsweë intree').

(the debtor having the option to sue the principal or the intermediary).[97] It is now clear from *Sasfin Bank Ltd v Soho Unit 14 CC*,[98] consistent with *Pizani* and *Mignoel Properties*, that the principal also acquires the original creditor's/intermediary's rights against sureties (unless excluded by the contract).[99] Thus in *Sasfin Bank*, the bank was the undisclosed principal of Sunlyn Investments which had contracted as lessor of certain premises with the lessee and taken sureties to secure the payment of the rent. The bank was held entitled to sue the lessee and the sureties for the arrears of rent.[100]

---

[97] *Cullinan v Noordkaaplandse Artappelkernmoerkwekers Koöperasie Bpk* 1972 (1) SA 761 (A) at 768. Of course, the doctrine of the undisclosed principal does not apply where the contract excludes it. But in the *Sasfin* case, below, the contracts expressly envisaged cession of the creditor's rights.

[98] 2006 (4) SA 513 (T).

[99] The fact that the principal did not sign the contract did not amount to a breach of section 6 of the General Law Amendment Act 50 of 1956 (which only required signature of the surety); extrinsic evidence could be used to identify the actual creditor. This is discussed in Chapter V, Section 4 (b).

[100] The discussion of the juristic basis of this substitution (or implied cession) confirms the analysis of Christo van Loggerenberg, above. *Sasfin* at paras. 26-27.

CHAPTER IV

The Surety

		Page
1.	Capacity to act as surety.	51
2.	Co-sureties and mutual sureties.	54
3.	Distinction between liability as a surety and liability as a surety and co-principal debtor.	56
	(a) Undertaking liability as surety and co-principal debtor.	56
	(b) Significance of the distinction: in general	56
	(c) Significance of the distinction: in particular.	57
	(d) Co-principal debtors and liability *in solidum*	58
4.	The requisite qualities of a surety where the debtor is obliged to find one	58
5.	The *fideiussor indemnitatis*	59
6.	Suretyship for a surety	60

1. Capacity to act as surety

In general anyone who is legally capable of contracting can bind himself as a surety.[1] And where a surety lacks the necessary mental capacity to contract the suretyship is invalid.[2] A guardian can undertake the obligation on behalf of his minor ward,[3] but it appears that an emancipated minor cannot bind himself as surety, for he may contract only in relation to his own business, not that of another.[4] In modern commerce, however, it may well be part of a minor's business to secure another's debt.[5] Moreover, Pothier[6] gives instances in which a minor might bind himself to secure the liberation of his father from prison.

---

[1] V 46.1.5; Gr 3.3.13; VL 4.4.2; Huber 3.27.1; P 387; B 10. Special rules used to apply to woman sureties; see Chapter I. Where spouses are married in community of property the provisions of Chapter III of the Matrimonial Property Act 88 of 1984, discussed below in this chapter, apply.

[2] *Eerste Nasionale Bank van SA Bpk v Saayman NO* 1997 (4) SA 302 (A) (85-year-old woman suffering from dementia, who did not understand the nature or consequences of signing the suretyship documents, lacked contractual capacity). The majority of the SCA simply followed *Pheasant v Warne* 1922 AD 481 ('could [the signer] understand and appreciate the transaction into which he purported to enter' per Innes CJ) but Olivier JA rested his judgment upon public policy—discussed below in Chapter XIII.

[3] D 46.1.8.4; V 46.1.5; Gr 3.3.13.

[4] P 389.

[5] Section 68(1) of the Mutual Building Societies Act 24 of 1965 and s 87 of the Banks Act 94 of 1990 authorize minors over 16 inter alia to pledge their deposits without the intervention of their guardians; it is remarkable, therefore, that they cannot, even if emancipated, stand surety for another.

[6] P 389.

In the past a company's power to bind itself as surety depended upon its memorandum of association setting out the company's objects.[7] If standing surety was *ultra vires* the company, then the suretyship was void. With the enactment of section 36 of the Companies Act 61 of 1973, however, this position has been drastically changed. An *ultra vires* act is not void, and neither the company nor any other person may rely in any proceedings upon the company's lack of capacity.[8] A creditor, therefore, in deciding whether to accept a company as a surety, need not, in general, concern himself with the company's capacity.

Close corporations 'have the capacity and powers of a natural person of full capacity in so far as a juristic person is capable of having such capacity or of exercising such powers'[9] and this includes the power to stand surety. But section 52 of the Close Corporations Act 69 of 1984 provides that the close corporation cannot make loans or provide security, directly or indirectly, to its members, to corporations in which any member has a more than 50% interest or to a company controlled by the close corporation's members.[10] However, these provisions do not apply where the making of the loan or the provision of security is made with the express consent in writing of all the members of the close corporation.[11] In *Hanekom v Builders Market Klerksdorp (Pty) Ltd and Others*[12] a close corporation stood surety for the debts of a private company (controlled by the close corporation's sole member) in apparent breach of section 52. That member had signed the suretyship for the close corporation but now argued that that suretyship was invalid in the absence of the express consent in writing of its sole member! The Supreme Court of Appeal rejected this argument as 'absurd'. Such 'a literal inter-

---

[7] See, for example, *Robinson v Hay* 1930 (1) PH E3 (N). See also *Harcourt v Eastman NO* 1953 (2) SA 424 (N). Cf *Marshall's Industrials Ltd v Khan and Another* 1959 (4) SA 684 (D).

[8] See SJ Naudé 'Company Contracts: The Effect of Section 36 of the New Act' (1974) 91 *SALJ* 315; MS Blackman 'The Capacity, Powers and Purposes of Companies: The Commission and the New Companies Act' (1975) 8 *CILSA* 1; ML Benade 'Exit Ultra Vires' (1972) 35 *THRHR* 281; JS McLennan 'The Ultra Vires Rule and the Turquand Rule' (1979) 96 *SALJ* 329; AN Oelofse 'Artikel 36 van die Maatskappywet versus Artikel 15A van die Akteswet' (1979) 42 *THRHR* 100, MG Fredman 'A Note on Section 36 of the Companies Act' (1982) 99 *SALJ* 283; MJ Oosthuizen 'Aanpassing van die Verteenwoordigingsreg in Maatskappyverband' 1979 *TSAR* 1; JSA Fourie 'Die Wisselwerking tussen Suid-Afrikaanse Maatskappyeregleerstukke' (1988) 51 *THRHR* 218; MS Blackman 'Directors' Duty to Exercise their Powers for an Authorised Business Purpose' (1990) 2 *SA Merc LJ* 1 and *Hahlo's South African Company Law through the Cases* 6 ed by JT Pretorius (gen ed), PA Delport, Michele Havenga and Maria Vermaas (1999) 60 ff for a general discussion of the *ultra vires* doctrine and the effect of s 36. The limitations on a company's power to provide financial assistance for the purchase of its shares or to make loans to its directors or secure their obligations (Companies Act 61 of 1973, sections 38 and 226) are discussed in Chapter III, section 2 (b).

[9] Section 2(4) of the Close Corporations Act 69 of 1984.

[10] The relevant parts of section 52 are: '(1) A corporation shall not, directly or indirectly, make a loan – *(a)* to any of its members; *(b)* to any other corporation in which one or more of its members together hold more than a 50 per cent interest; or *(c)* to any company or other juristic person (except a corporation) controlled by one or more members of the corporation, and shall not provide any security to any person in connection with any obligation of any such member, or other corporation, company or other juristic person. (2) The provisions of subsection (1) shall not apply in respect of the making of any particular loan or the provision of any particular security with the express previously obtained consent in writing of all the members of a corporation.'

[11] Section 52(2) (above).

[12] 2007 (3) SA 95 (SCA).

THE SURETY

pretation...does no more than provide a sole member of the corporation with a defence that could never have been intended by the Legislature'.[13]

In accordance with general principle a statutory corporation, such as a co-operative, must have power to enter into contracts of suretyship if such contracts are to be valid.[14] Thus, for example, section 49(1)(g) of the Co-operatives Act 91 of 1981 provides, certain special situations aside,[15] that a co-operative has power 'to guarantee obligations or to stand surety for the proper compliance therewith' provided that it 'was reasonably necessary for the carrying out of the objects of the co-operative'.

A trust cannot stand surety unless the trust deed authorises the trustees to authorise the suretyship in the particular circumstances.[16] All will depend upon the terms of the deed but the court will not be sympathetic to technical restrictions on the trust's power.[17] On the other hand, wide powers (but not express powers to stand surety) given to a trustee in the trust deed were given so as to achieve the objects of the trust, and those did not include the provision of unlimited deeds of suretyship to secure loans made to a trust beneficiary.[18]

Where spouses are married in community of property then the provisions of Chapter III of the Matrimonial Property Act 88 of 1984 are applicable.[19] Although a person married in community of property has the same powers with regard to the contracting of debts which lie against the joint estate as his or her spouse,[20] the written consent of that spouse—attested by two witnesses[21]—is required before that person can bind himself or herself as surety.[22] However, that consent is not required where the spouse enters into the suretyship 'in the ordinary course of his [or her] profession, trade or business'.[23]

In *ABSA Bpk v De Goede*[24] the Supreme Court of Appeal held that this proviso applied where a clerk and a teacher bound themselves as sureties and co-principal debtors for the overdraft of a close corporation of which they were members and which carried on a passenger transport business. The members of the close corporation were its co-managers and thus legally entitled to participate in its

---

[13] Scott JA, para 9.

[14] Implied from *Eerste Nasionale Bank van Suidelike Afrika Bpk v Noordkaap Lewendehawe Kooperasie Bpk* 1997 (1) SA 299 (A) at 307G-308A.

[15] Section 52(1) of the 1981 Act required a special resolution in certain cases but in the *Eerste Nationale Bank van Suidelike Afrika Bpk v Noordkaap Lewendehawe Kooperasie Bpk* the SCA, overruling the Northern Cape Division, found that it did not apply in the instant case.

[16] Implied by *Liebenberg NO v MGK Bedryfsmaatskappy (Pty) Ltd* 2003 (2) SA 224 (SCA) and *Potgieter en 'n Ander NNO v Shell Suid-Afrika (Edms) Bpk* 2003 (1) SA 155 (SCA).

[17] *Potgieter en 'n Ander NNO v Shell Suid-Afrika (Edms) Bpk*, above (power to stand surety for company included power to stand surety for close corporation).

[18] *Liebenberg NO v MGK Bedryfsmaatskappy (Pty) Ltd*, above.

[19] It is assumed in the following paragraphs that the spouses concerned are all married in community of property.

[20] 1984 Act, section 14 and section 15(1).

[21] Section 15(5). Where consent is not given at the time it may 'be given by ratification within a reasonable time' (section 15(4)).

[22] Section 15(2)(h).

[23] Section 15(6).

[24] 1997 (4) SA 66 (A). Followed in *Tesoriero v Bhyjo Investments Share Block (Pty) Ltd* 2000 (1) SA 167 (W) (surety for a close corporation's obligations under a lease, who owned half the corporation and was actively involved with its management, signed in the ordinary course of business).

management; as such, in signing the suretyships, the clerk and the teacher—even though they were not involved in the day to day running of the business—were acting as co-managers and thus in the course of their business as co-managers. Grosskopf JA said: ''n Lid van 'n beslote korporasie staan dus in 'n besondere verhouding tot die korporasie. Hy is regtens 'n mede-bestuurder en geregtig om deel te neem aan die dryf van die korporasie se besigheid. Daar moet egter onderskei word tussen die beslote korporasie se besigheid (bv om passasiersdienste te verskaf) en die lid se besigheid (om die beslote korporasie se besigheid te dryf en te bestuur). Wanneer hy as lid 'n regshandeling verrig wat verband hou met die gewone besigheid van die beslote korporasie, tree hy op in sy hoedanigheid as mede-bestuurder van die beslote korporasie, en dus ook in die loop van sy besigheid as sodanig.'[25] Entering into a suretyship was thus not something that the respondents ordinarily undertook in the course of their profession (or business) as a clerk or teacher, but it was something ordinarily done in their business as co-manager of a close corporation. Presumably similar principles would apply in the case of companies, so a director or chairman who binds himself for the company's debts would not require his spouse's consent. But a mere shareholder of the company with no legal right to share in the management of the company would require his spouse's consent. Suretyships entered into order to assist a friend or relative to obtain a loan would, save perhaps in special circumstances, require the surety's spouse's consent. Where spousal consent is required, but not obtained, the suretyship is invalid.[26]

2. Co-sureties and mutual sureties

Two persons, whom we may call mutual sureties, may stand surety, each for the other, in respect of the debt of that other.[27] For instance, it is not uncommon for businessmen, who are not partners, to assist each other in this way, especially in obtaining banking facilities. Co-debtors may stand surety for each other.[28]

Far more frequently, however, two or more persons may stand surety for the same principal debtor in respect of the same obligation. They are co-sureties;[29] and this is so even if they have given their undertakings in separate instruments, independently of each other, or at different times and even if unbeknown to each

---

[25] at 75E-F. Note, however, the dissent of Streicher AJA pointing out that such a construction of section 15(6) gives little protection to spouses whose estates may be placed at risk without their consent.

[26] *ABSA Bpk v Lydenburg Passasiersdienste BK* 1995 (3) SA 314 (T). This followed from the peremptory terms of section: 15(2) ('such a spouse shall not') and the fact that subsections (5) (formal requirements) and (6) (the proviso) would be irrelevant unless a breach of section 15(2)(g) led to voidness. Although *ABSA Bpk v Lydenburg Passasiersdienste BK* was overturned on appeal (*sub nom. ABSA Bpk v De Goede* 1997 (4) SA 66(A)) its correctness on this point was not challenged.

[27] V 46.1.5. Voet says of this 'especially if they are co-heirs or partners', but there appears to be no reason in principle to place any such limitation on the statement, although co-heirs and partners are, perhaps, those most likely so to secure each other's debts.

[28] Cf *Dirck's Estate v Gwadiso & Komanis' Estates* 1936 EDL 303 at 309; *Gerber v Wolson* 1955 (1) SA 158 (A).

[29] B 344; Wessels para 4115.

THE SURETY 55

other.[30] Each co-surety is liable *in solidum* for the debt of the debtor.[31] Sureties, each of whom has undertaken only a specified portion of the debt, are, however, not co-sureties; nor is one a co-surety who, along with one or more sureties for the whole debt, has secured only a portion of it.[32] The significance of distinguishing between co-sureties and ordinary sureties is that co-sureties have the benefit of division of the debt among themselves, unless this has been excluded. In terms of this benefit the surety who has paid the debt has the right to have the other or others contribute to it. We shall discuss this benefit in Chapter IX.

Co-sureties may be such for co-debtors, but two sureties, one of whom is surety for one co-debtor of the same debt and the other of whom is surety for the other co-debtor of the same debt, are not co-sureties, whether or not the co-debtors are liable jointly (each for his aliquot share of the debt) or *in solidum*.[33] The liability of co-debtors for an obligation which is not indivisible is joint, not *in solidum* unless they have undertaken liability jointly and severally or unless the law imposes that liability upon them.[34] Consequently the liability of co-sureties (or, indeed, that of a single surety) for co-debtors liable jointly relates to each co-debtor's aliquot share of the debt; each co-surety is liable *in solidum* for each such share.[35] If the suretyship is not for all the co-debtors, it follows that the surety or co-sureties is or are liable for a portion only of the debt. If, however, the co-debtors are liable *in solidum*, their sureties bear their responsibility for the whole debt.

There is no contractual privity between co-sureties merely because they are co-sureties. Each contracts with the creditor, but not necessarily with the other sureties, and the mere fact that their individual obligations are recorded in one document does not alter that situation.[36] But they may expressly contract with each other concerning the extent to which each is to contribute to the debt.[37]

Payment by one co-surety to another co-surety is not payment to the creditor, who is entitled, notwithstanding this, to have payment from the one who has paid to his co-surety.[38] The creditor cannot recover the amount so paid from the co-surety to whom it has been paid; that is a matter between the two co-sureties.

---

[30] V 46.1.22, P 424; B 344; Wessels para 4116. *Klopper v Van Straaten* (1894) 11 SC 94, *Lever v Buhrmann* 1925 TPD 254 at 262; *Moosa v Mahomed* 1939 TPD 271 at 284, 285, and *Hart v Corder* 1973 (3) SA 11 (N). *Hart's* case was approved in *Fircone Investments (Pty) Ltd v Bank of Lisbon and South Africa Ltd and Another* 1981 (3) SA 141 (W) at 142, 1982 (3) SA 700 (T) at 703 and in *De Beer v Bosman* (TPD 27 November 1990 (case 1993/90) unreported). See also JT Pretorius 'Contributions between Co-sureties' (1991) 3 *SA Merc LJ* 381 at 382. *Hart's* case is criticised for other reasons in Chapter XII.

[31] D 46.1.51 pr; Inst 3.20.4; V 46.1.22, 24; Huber 3.26.15; P 415, 426; B 343; Wessels paras 4101 4105. *Van der Vyver v De Wayer and Others* (1861) 4 Searle 27 at 29.

[32] D 46.1.43, 51 pr; V 46.1.22; P 415.

[33] D 46.1.43; D 46.1.51.2; V 46.1.22; P 419; B 344; Wessels para 1489.

[34] Nov 99.1; C 40.3; P 265; Lee Intro 294, 285; Lee ad Gr 257, 258. *De Pass v Colonial Government and Others* (1886) 4 SC 383 at 390; *Kistan and Others v Komarasamy* 1940 NPD 56; *Tucker and Another v Carruthers* 1941 AD 251 at 254.

[35] P 415, Wessels paras 4115, 4116. Cf *Henwood & Co v Westlake and Coles* (1887) 5 SC 341 at 347.

[36] D 46.1.43; D 46.1.51.1; V 46.1.22; P 445; B 344. *Kroon v Enschede and Others* 1909 TS 374 at 382, *Kalil v Standard Bank of South Africa Ltd* 1967 (4) SA 550 (A) at 556, 557. See also *Union Trust Maatskappy (Edms) Bpk v Thirion* 1965 (3) SA 648 (GW).

[37] See Chapter XII.

[38] D 46.1.25; Wessels para 4136.

Two or more signatories to an aval[39] are co-sureties whose obligations arise from the same instrument.[40]

The test by which to discover whether sureties are co-sureties was said in *Executors Estate Watson v Huneberg & Leathern*[41] to be to ascertain whether the same default on the part of the principal debtor makes them all responsible to pay the debt.

Pothier says[42] 'it is evident that a person cannot become surety for or to himself', that is to say, he cannot be the debtor and the surety for himself as such, nor be the creditor and the surety to himself for the debtor. But there appears to be no reason why he should not be a co-debtor and at the same time a surety for his associate debtors, with a consequential limitation on his right to contribution from his co-sureties.[43] Also, a person may bind himself as surety and co-principal debtor, as we have seen. It seems, too, that there is nothing against a person being a co-creditor standing surety to the other creditors of the debtor.

3. Distinction between liability as a surety and liability as surety and co-principal debtor[44]

(a) Undertaking liability as surety and co-principal debtor

A person binding himself as surety may in addition bind himself as co-principal debtor. This he may do expressly in the suretyship document, but in the absence of express undertaking to that effect, the answer to the question whether he binds himself both as surety and as co-principal debtor depends on the language of the document and on all the circumstances. Even if he signs a promissory note as maker of it, this is only one of the circumstances and is not conclusive in itself that he is a principal debtor, for evidence is admissible to show the true relationship of the parties to each other.[45]

(b) Significance of the distinction: in general

One who has bound himself as surety and co-principal debtor is, so far as the creditor is concerned, a surety who has undertaken the obligations of a co-debtor; his obligations in the latter respect are co-equal in extent with those of the principal debtor and thus of the same scope and nature;[46] he is liable with him jointly

---

[39] See Chapter V, Section 5, Avals and their liability.
[40] *Meer v General Industrial Credit Corporation (Pty) Ltd* 1947 (4) SA 330 (C).
[41] 1915 NPD 571 at 577.
[42] P 393; D 46.1.3. In *Nedbank Ltd v Van Zyl* 1990 (2) SA 469 (A) the Appellate Division confirmed that 'a contract whereby a person purports to stand surety for his own debt is not a legally enforceable one' (at 475I).
[43] Cf *Huneberg and Others v Watson's Estate* 1916 AD 116.
[44] This section was referred to with apparent approval in *Millman v Masterbond Participation Trust* 1997 (1) SA 113 (C) at 123B.
[45] See the discussion on negotiable instruments in the next chapter.
[46] Gr 3.3.29; VdK 503; VL 4.4.7; *Cens For* 1.4.17.23.

and severally.[47] The obligation of the surety and co-principal debtor becomes enforceable at the same time as that of the principal debtor.[48]

But he does not undertake a separate independent liability as a principal debtor; he is a surety.[49] Consequently, if the principal obligation is non-existent or illegal, he is not bound to the creditor.[50] In *Neon and Cold Cathode Illuminations (Pty) Ltd v Ephron*[51] the Appellate Division clarified the distinction between liability as a 'surety' and liability as a 'surety and co-principal debtor'. It was held that 'generally the only consequence ... that flows from the surety also undertaking liability as a co-principal debtor is that vis-à-vis the creditor he thereby tacitly renounces the ordinary benefits available to a surety, such as those of excussion and division, and he becomes liable jointly and severally with the principal debtor'.[52]

(c) Significance of the distinction: in particular

Thus it has been held that the surety and co-principal debtor is not entitled to the benefit of division of the debt between himself and the principal debtor, as co-debtors, even although he has not expressly renounced the benefit of division.[53] The undertaking of the obligations of surety and co-principal debtor operates as adumbrated as a renunciation of the benefit of excussion[54] and where two or more persons have undertaken those obligations, this operates as a renunciation of the benefit of division.[55] The surety and co-principal debtor is, however, entitled against the creditor to the benefit of cession of actions.[56] He has available to him the defences which are available to a surety and, in particular, is entitled to found

---

[47] *Willems v Widow Schendeler* (1835) 2 Menz 20; *Trustees of Du Toit v Executors of Smuts and De Kock* (1835) 2 Menz 24; *Van der Byl v Munnik* (1845) 2 Menz 73; *In re Deneys* (1846) 3 Menz 309; *Union Government v Van der Merwe* 1921 TPD 318 at 322; *Mahomed v Lockhat Brothers & Co Ltd* 1944 AD 230 at 238; *Business Buying & Investment Co Ltd v Linaae* 1959 (3) SA 93 (T) at 95; *Trans-Drakensberg Bank Ltd v The Master and Others* 1962 (4) SA 417 (N) at 422; *Neon and Cold Cathode Illuminations (Pty) Ltd v Ephron* 1978 (1) SA 463 (A) at 472B.

[48] *Millman v Masterbond Participation Trust* 1997 (1) SA 113 (C) at 123A in reliance upon Lotz/Henning para. 200 (as it appeared in the earlier edition).

[49] *Maasdorp v Graaff-Reinet Board of Executors* (1909) 3 Buch AC 482 at 490; *Peimer v Finbro Furnishers (Pty) Ltd* 1936 AD 177; *National Industrial Credit Corporation (Rhod) Ltd v Gumede and Another (2)* 1964 (4) SA 258 (SR) at 263; *Gurland v Caltex (Africa) Ltd* 1965 (2) SA 659 (SR) at 663; *Ideal Finance Corporation v Coetzer* 1969 (4) SA 43 (O) at 44. See also JSA Fourie 'Die Aanspreeklikheid van die Borg en die Hoofskuldenaar' (1978) 41 *THRHR* 307. The distinction will be of vital importance where the suretyship has to comply with certain formalities (Chapter V below). However, the distinction may indeed be difficult to draw in practice. See JT Pretorius 'Die Formaliteitsvereiste by Borgstelling' (1988) 10 *MB* 122 at 128.

[50] *Wiehahn NO v Wouda* 1957 (4) SA 724 (W) at 726; *Choonora v Rahim* 1960 (2) SA 504(W); *National Industrial Credit Corporation (Rhod) Ltd v Gumede and Another (2)* 1964 (4) SA 258 (SR) at 262, 263.

[51] 1978 (1) SA 463 (A).

[52] At 472B-C.

[53] D 46.1.27.4; V 46.1.22; P 417; B 344, 345; Wessels para 4117. Cf *Trustees of Du Toit v Executors of Smuts and De Kock* (1835) 2 Menz 24, *Roos v Coetzee* (1846) 2 Menz 74.

[54] V 46.1.16; Gr 3.3.29; Sch 305; VdK 503; VL 4.4.9; *Cens For* 1.4.17.23; VdL 1.14.10; B 334, 338; Wessels para 4088, Lee *ad Gr* 248, 251, 252 and Cf Huber 3.26.19.

[55] V 46.1.24; Gr 3.3.29; Sch 305, VdK 503; VL 4.49; *Cens For* 1.4.17.23; Huber 3.26.23; P 416; B 344; Wessels paras 4124, 4132. For the cases see Chapters VIII, IX. Pothier (P 408, 416) shows that there were divergent views about this in French law.

[56] *Van der Byl v Munnik* (1845) 2 Menz 73; *In re Deneys* (1846) 3 Menz 309, *Business Buying & Investment Co Ltd v Linaae* 1959 (3) SA 93 (T) at 96.

a defence against the creditor on any act or omission of the latter in relation to the principal debtor which prejudices him in the exercise of the benefit of cession of actions.[57]

So far as the principal debtor is concerned, the surety and co-principal debtor is a surety and he has against the debtor the rights of a surety, in particular the right of recourse; there is no departure from the normal relations between surety and debtor.[58]

(d) Co-principal debtors and liability in solidum

The undertaking of liability as a surety *in solidum* is not the same thing as undertaking that of a co-principal debtor. In *Van der Vyver v De Wayer and Others*[59] Watermeyer J, after examination of the controversy among the old writers on the subject (to whom can be added Voet[60] and Van der Keessel in his *Dictata*),[61] said that all co-sureties are in the nature of suretyship, liable *singuli in solidum*; the undertaking of the obligation expressly in those terms adds nothing and does not in itself make the sureties co-principal debtors; if this is intended, appropriate additional words must be used.[62]

Where one of four co-sureties for repayment of a loan was himself a recipient of the benefit of the loan, along with the principal debtor (who raised the loan for their benefit), he was held, as between himself and his co-sureties, to be a principal debtor and not entitled, to the extent he had benefited, to any contribution from his co-sureties.[63]

4. The requisite qualities of a surety where the debtor is obliged to find one

When a debtor is obliged to find a surety, there is authority for the view that the surety provided must not only be capable of binding himself, but also

(1) he must be solvent, and of sufficient means to meet the obligations he undertakes;
(2) he must have a local domicile so that he may easily be sued, if necessary: but in this respect more indulgence is shown if the surety is to be a legal and judiciary one, seeing that the debtor is acting under compulsion (*sed quaere* whether such indulgence can be claimed in these days);

---

[57] See chapter X.
[58] *Shuter v Ridgway* 1926 NPD 149; *Business Buying & Investment Co Ltd v Linaae* 1959 (3) SA 93 (T); *Taylor and Thorne NNO and Others v The Master* 1965 (1) SA 658 (N).
[59] (1861) 4 Searle 27. See also *Featherstone v Trustees of East London Angling Society and Peel* (1906) 16 CTR 112.
[60] V 46.1.24.
[61] Lee *ad Gr* 241, 242.
[62] See also Burge (B 344) and Wessels paras 4130-2.
[63] *Huneberg and Others v Watson's Estate* 1916 AD 116.

(3) he must be subject to the jurisdiction, and not be exempted from performance of the court's order and from arrest.[64]

According to Pothier,[65] the obligation to find a surety involves an obligation to replace him if he becomes insolvent or ceases to have the requisite qualities; but Voet[66] says there is no obligation to find a substitute (unless the law has compelled or the praetor ordered a surety to be found) when the surety has fallen into financial difficulties.

Pothier[67] apparently takes the view that an obligation to provide a surety is fulfilled by providing pledges if they be as good as or better than a surety, but Voet[68] distinctly says the contrary.

5. The *fideiussor indemnitatis*

A *fideiussor indemnitatis* (indemnity surety) is a special kind of surety[69] in the sense that, by the terms of his contract, with the creditor, he undertakes to do no more than indemnify him against the shortfall or loss which he may sustain through the inability of the debtor to perform his obligations. He is liable only for the deficiency after the creditor has excussed the debtor or events have happened which excuse the creditor from doing so[70] unless, of course, the terms of the contract provide otherwise.[71] The distinction between *the fideiussor indemnitatis* and the surety in the full sense is that the latter is liable (unless he has the benefit of excussion) to indemnify the creditor so soon as the principal debtor's obligation has fallen due to be performed and remains unfulfilled, while the former has the right to have the creditor ascertain his loss by excussing the principal debtor, before he calls upon the surety to pay.

---

[64] V 46.1.2, 3; P 390; V 2.8.2, 3. It may be doubted, however, whether our modern law requires strict compliance with these conditions. If a surety of insufficient means is accepted by the creditor, that is surely his own 'lookout'.

[65] P 391.

[66] V 46.1.2.

[67] P 392.

[68] V 46.1.2.

[69] Indeed, Wessels, para. 4091 suggests that the *fideiussor indemnitatis* does not even have an accessory liability but has made an independent but conditional promise. It is submitted that whether this is so depends upon the true meaning of the contract. If in fact the 'surety' has undertaken an obligation that does not depend upon the existence of the principal obligation the contract is not in truth suretyship of any kind but guarantee. See Chapter II, Section 2 (a).

[70] V 46.1.14.38. *Rogerson NO v Meyer and Berning* (1837) 2 Menz 38 at 49, 50.

[71] See *Fedbond Nominees (Pty) Ltd v Meier* 2008 (1) SA 458 (C) where Selikowitz J pointed out that the suretyship in question made the surety liable for the 'shortfall' after the other remedies had been 'exhausted'. 'Exhaustion' may entail more than mere excussion (for instance, excussion need not be proceeded with in the event of the debtor's is sequestrated). In the *Fedbond Nominees* case the creditor had settled a claim against a co-principal debtor on terms which prevented the exhaustion of any remedy against him. See the discussion of Sonnekus 'Indemniteitsborgstelling en Borgbeskerming' 2008 *TSAR* 165.

6. Suretyship for a surety

One may undertake a suretyship for a surety.[72] Sureties for a surety are *fideiussores fideiussoris,* known as rear-sureties or as '*achterborgen*'[73] and the only point that calls for special notice is in relation to the benefit of division.[74] A surety given by the debtor for reimbursement of his surety is of course the debtor's surety, and is not to be confused with a surety's surety.[75] One co-surety may indemnify the others against the consequences of the transaction.[76]

---

[72] D 46.1.8.12; V 46.1.6; Vol 1.14.10; P 398; Lee *ad Gr* 243.
[73] VdL 1.14.10.
[74] D 46.1.27.1.
[75] V 46.1.6.
[76] *Villiers v Villiers* (1843) 2 Menz 7. And *Sulski v Feldman Ltd* 1956 (1) SA 759 (A), relating to a surety given by one surety to his co-surety for the share of the former when called upon for a contribution.

CHAPTER V

The Formation of the Contract of Suretyship

		Page
1. Parties to the contract		61
2. Intention to be bound and *justa causa*		63
3. Grounds for rescission		64
4. Formalities and related questions		67
(a) The General Law Amendment Act		67
(b) The document must contain the 'terms' of the contract		69
(c) The principle of incorporation		72
(d) Rectification		73
(e) Signing the document 'in blank'		77
(f) Non-essential blank spaces		79
(g) Co-sureties and blank spaces		79
(h) Oral variations of a suretyship contract		81
5. Avals and their liability		81
6. Conditional suretyships		85
7. Stamp Duties		86

1. Parties to the contract

Suretyship is a consensual contract. It is a contract between the creditor and the surety and, subject to the requirements in regard to formalities, can be made in any manner in which a contract can be made.[1] The principal debtor need not be a

---

[1] V 46.1.1; Gr 3.3.25; VdL 1.15.10; VdK 501 ff; P 400. And see *Jurgens and Others v Volkskas Bank Ltd* 1993 (1) SA 214 (A) at 218 ('Suretyship is a bilateral jural act...It is a contract which arises from agreement between creditor and surety, and it involves acceptance of an offer...' per Hoexter JA). In *Mutual Construction Co v Victor* [2002] 3 All SA 807 (W) the defendant denied that a suretyship was concluded. The suretyship formed the last clause immediately above the space demarcated for a signature in a document headed 'Opening account form and suretyship'. The defendant contended that since the plaintiff had refused the application for credit, the suretyship, as a component of the application, never came into operation. The court found that the refusal of the application for credit was irrelevant as the suretyship was an independent contract (para 11). By signing the form, the suretyship was concluded. The surety also contended that the contract was subject to an oral suspensive condition that it would only come into operation if credit were granted. This required the rectification of the suretyship. However, this conflicted with the surety's case as pleaded and in any event the court was of the view that the suggested condition would conflict with the written terms of the contract.

party;[2] nor is it necessary that he should have given his consent.[3] If the debtor has given his consent or had knowledge that the suretyship was being undertaken, a tacit contract of mandate between debtor and surety comes into existence; the debtor is taken to have given the surety a mandate to perform his obligation if he himself fails to do so[4] and it is from the contract of mandate that the surety's right of recourse against the debtor arises.[5] If the suretyship is undertaken by the surety without the knowledge of the debtor, the surety's right of recourse against the debtor is based on *negotiorum gestio*.[6]

The creditor and the surety must each be competent to make the contract and must he *ad idem* on all the terms and conditions of the contract; all the essentials for the making of the contract must he present.[7] The ordinary rules as to offer

---

[2] D 46.1.30; P 403.

[3] *Turkstra v Massyn* 1959 (1) SA 40 (T) at 45. See also Chapter III. It is essential to the existence of a suretyship that there be a principal obligation in terms whereof someone other than the surety is the debtor. A person cannot stand as surety for his own debt (*Nedbank Ltd v Van Zyl* 1990 (2) SA 469 (A) at 475). Thus, an undertaking in a contract whereby a person purports to stand surety for his own debt is not a legally enforceable one.

[4] V 46.1.31; P 365, 429.

[5] In *Hanekom v Builders Market Klerksdorp (Pty) Ltd and Others* 2007 (3) SA 95 (SCA) the surety was a close corporation that stood surety of the debts of a private company. The appellant was the sole member of the close corporation and the only shareholder and director of the private company. The appellant also signed a suretyship in favour of the creditor in his personal capacity. After the private company was liquidated for failing to pay its debts the creditor proceeded against the close corporation as surety. The appellant now claimed that the suretyship on behalf of the close corporation was invalid because he did not obtain the prior written consent of the member of the close corporation as required by section 52 of the Close Corporations Act 69 of 1984. In other words, he maintained the suretyship was invalid because he as the sole member of the close corporation had not previously consented in writing to the suretyship that he himself executed on its behalf. Scott JA rejected this defence and held: 'I have no doubt that to give effect to the unambiguous language of section 52(2) where the close corporation has only one member in circumstances such as the present leads to an absurdity. Nothing can possibly be achieved by requiring the sole member of a close corporation before signing a suretyship on behalf of the corporation and in his personal capacity to give himself permission in writing to do so. [H]is signature on the suretyship demonstrates unequivocally his consent. ... The object of the section ... is to protect non-consenting members. In circumstances such as the present, a literal interpretation does not achieve that object; it does no more than provide a sole member of a corporation with a defence which could never have been intended by the legislature' (para 8).

[6] See the discussion in Chapter XI below. See further JE Scholtens 'Rights of Recourse of Sureties and Third Persons Who Paid Another's Debt' (1959) 76 *SALJ* 266 at 268, 269; DH van Zyl *Die Saakwaarnemingsaksie as Verrykingsaksie in die Suid-Afrikaanse Reg* thesis submitted for the degree Doctor in de Rechtsgeleerdheid, University of Leiden (1970) 150-2; *LAWSA* vol 26 (first reissue; 1997) para 207; DP Visser *Die Rol van Dwaling by die Condictio Indebiti* thesis submitted for the degree Doctor in de Rechtsgeleerdheid, University of Leiden (1985) 228 ff; Wouter de Vos *Verrykingsaanspreeklikheid in die Suid-Afrikaanse Reg* 3 ed (1987) 214-5. See also Ralph Slovenko 'Suretyship' (1965) 39 *Tulane LR* 427 at 439 ff, Morton C Campbell 'Non-consensual Suretyship' (1935) 45 *Yale LJ* 69 and Daniel Visser *Unjustified Enrichment* (2008) 565 ff.

[7] *Bouwer v Lichtenburg Co-operative Society* 1925 TPD 144 at 148. See also *Neale v Edenvale Plastic Products (Pty) Ltd* 1971 (3) SA 860 (T) and *Federated Timbers (Pretoria) (Pty) Ltd v Fourie* 1978 (1) SA 292 (T). An agreement between the debtor and a third person that the latter will pay the former's debt creates in itself no liability on the part of the third person to the creditor; no suretyship obligation arises in the absence of communication to and acceptance by the creditor (V 46.1.3). See also *De Villiers v Conradie and De Vos* (1864) 5 Searle 68 at 71 and *African Life Property Holdings (Pty) Ltd v Score Food Holdings Ltd* 1995 (2) SA 230 (A) at 239H ('mere signature by a surety to a different document, which ...is either a unilateral declaration of intent to be bound for someone else's debt or is an agreement between surety and such debtor that the surety is prepared to be so bound..., [does not] create a new suretyship' (per Nienaber JA). Naturally the surety must have contractual

and acceptance apply[8] and consequently an offer of suretyship can be withdrawn before acceptance,[9] but not after acceptance,[10] although as we have seen in discussing the principal obligation in Chapter III, if the suretyship is undertaken before the principal obligation has come into existence, there may be an opportunity for the surety to resile.

2. Intention to be bound and *justa causa*

In the making of the contract there must be a deliberate intention[11] to enter into a binding contract of suretyship.[12] There is no need—under our legal system—for a contract of suretyship to be supported by consideration.[13] All that is required is *justa causa*—a lawful reason why the parties should be bound.[14] Frequently, this will be the generosity of a person of substance in helping a friend or relative obtain credit, or helping him obtain business. Very often it is required for business transactions. But it may well be that the granting of credit to the debtor is to the advantage of the surety. For example, where debtor and surety are business associates the surety may benefit from the financial stability which his undertaking brings to the debtor's affairs.[15] The lawful reasons why sureties bind themselves are as complex and diverse as the business world itself.[16] Furthermore, a surety-

---

capacity: *Eerste Nasionale Bank van SA Bpk v Saayman NO* 1997 (4) SA 302 (A) (suretyship void where surety did not understand nature or consequences of her actions through mental illness (majority judgment)). See Chapter 3, section 1.

[8] Approved in *Volkskas Spaarbank Bpk v Van Aswegen* 1990 (3) SA 978 (A). See also *Brown & Co v Jacobson* 1915 OPD 42.

[9] *Niel & Co v Quin & O'Hea* 1903 TH 458.

[10] *Machanick v Simon* 1920 CPD 333 at 341, 342.

[11] D 46.1.8 pr; VL 4.4.5; *Cens For* 1.4.17.17.

[12] Not, for example, as a jest—cf *Moosa v Mahomed* 1939 TPD 271. See also *Keens Group Co (Pty) Ltd v Lötter* 1989 (1) SA 585 (C).

[13] Cf, however, MdeV's 'Notes on Suretyship' in (1926) 43 *SALJ* 150. With respect it appears that the learned author has failed to recognise the implications of the Appellate Division's judgment in *Conradie v Rossouw* 1919 AD 279.

[14] *Conradie v Rossouw* at 288; *Froman v Robertson* 1971 (1) SA 115 (A); *Musgrove & Watson (Rhod) Pvt v Rotta* 1978 (2) SA 918 (R) and *Saambou-Nasionale Bouvereniging v Friedman* 1979 (3) SA 978 (A). See also Schalk van der Merwe *et al Contract General Principles* 3 ed (2007)196 ff.

[15] *Goode, Durrant and Murray Ltd v Hewitt and Cornell NNO* 1961 (4) SA 286 (N) at 291; *Lategan and Another NNO v Boyes and Another* 1980 (4) SA 191 (T).

[16] LAWSA vol 26 (first reissue; 1997) para 192 argues that the *causa* for a contract of suretyship is provided by a valid principal obligation with someone other than the surety as debtor, and if a contract of suretyship is not grafted on such principal obligation it is void. The learned author argues that suretyship differs in this respect from most other contracts which require merely the serious and deliberate intention of the parties to bind themselves contractually as *causa*. It is submitted that the requirement that there should be a valid principal obligation is an incident of the accessory nature of suretyship. See also *Malan on Bills of Exchange, Cheques and Promissory Notes in South African Law* 5ed by FR Malan, JT Pretorius & SF du Toit (2009) paras 63-70. The view of *LAWSA*, however, does have the support of Jansen JA in *Saambou-Nasionale Bouvereniging v Friedman* 1979 (3) SA 978 (A) at 992A ('sonder 'n hoofooreenkoms vir die hulpooreenkoms daar geen redelike oorsaak kan wees nie') but as the judge recognises this view is not without weighty challenge. Since a valid principal obligation is in any event required, the only circumstances in which this question might become a real issue would be if there were a principal obligation but the suretyship was questioned on the basis that there was no reason for the surety to bind himself. Given the diversity of proper reasons why a person may bind themselves as a surety such a challenge seems remote and, save in far-fetched circumstances, implausible.

ship is not necessarily gratuitously undertaken; the principal debtor may pay the surety for undertaking his promise to the creditor.

3. Grounds for rescission

Since creditor and surety must be *ad idem* in making the contract, the absence of consent on the part of the surety will vitiate the contract. The principles in relation to this in the formation generally of contracts apply to the making of contracts of suretyship. Hence, fraud, whether by actual statement or by suppression of facts, duress, undue influence or mistake, whether induced by innocent misrepresentation or arising from some other cause, will be grounds for rescission of the contract of suretyship in those circumstances in which they would be grounds for rescission of any other contract.[17]

The circumstances in which mistake or *justus error* would provide a defence for a surety were set out with great clarity by Wunsh J in *Tesoriero v Bhyjo Investments Share Block (Pty) Ltd*:[18]

> The general principle, where a person who has signed a contract and wishes to escape liability on the ground of justified *error* as to the nature or contents of the document, is that he or she must show that he or she was misled as to the nature of the document or as to the terms which it contains by some act or omission (where there was a duty to inform) of the other contracting party. The misrepresentation need not have been fraudulent or negligent. The duty to inform would or could arise where the document departs from what was represented, said or agreed beforehand or where the other party realises or should realise that the signatory is under a misapprehension or where the existence of the provision or the contract is hidden or not apparent by reason of the way in which it is incorporated in a document or where the provision, not clearly presented, is unusual or would not normally be found in the contract presented for signature.

Thus mistake was successfully raised as a defence in *Prins v ABSA Bank Ltd*.[19] There the surety believed he was signing a suretyship of limited duration and for a

---

[17] *Musgrove & Watson (Rhod) (Pvt) v Rotta* 1978 (2) SA 918 (R) (court *a quo*) and 1978 (4) SA 656 (RAD); *Keens Group Co (Pty) Ltd v Lötter* 1989 (1) SA 585 (C). See also *Khan v Naidoo* 1989 (3) SA 724 (N) and JG Lotz 'Die Rol van 'n Wanvoorstelling by Wesentlike Dwaling' (1991) 3 *SA Merc LJ* 263; Schalk van der Merwe *et al Contract General Principles* 3 ed (2007)195 ff.

[18] 2000 (1) SA 167 (W) at 175F-H. This statement is supported by many cases including *George v Fairmead (Pty) Ltd* 1958 (2) SA 465 (A) at 472A-B; *Spindrifter (Pty) Ltd v Lester Donovan (Pty) Ltd* 1986 (1) SA 893 (A).

[19] 1998 (3) SA 904 (C). See Glover (1999) 62 *THRHR* 456 and JM Otto 'Verskuilde borgstellings in standaardkontrakte en *iustus error*' 2005 *TSAR Reg* 805. See also *Davids en Andere v ABSA Bank Bpk* 2005 (3) SA 361 (C) where the full bench of the Cape High Court (Fourie J with Knoll J and Bozalek J concurring) found that the sureties were not liable because of their justifiable mistake in believing that they were signing a limited suretyship whereas they were actually signing unlimited suretyships. The decision turned on the particular facts presented to the court: the sureties testified that they and their spouses were present when a bank official orally conveyed to them that they were signing for R50 000 only; the bank official did not take part in the negotiations between the parties and was responsible only for obtaining the signatures of the sureties on the document, and four years after the event he could not remember the specific incident but could merely testify about banking practice, et cetera. The format of the deed of suretyship also played an important role in determining whether the document induced the mistake on the part of the signatories: the first page of the document contained 1255 words but only five sentences. The first sentence contained 370 words and the last sentence 584 words. Fourie J said that even though the sureties did not read the documents, the question may be asked whether the sureties would have

limited amount but in fact the suretyship was for an unlimited amount and for an unlimited time. The bank official supervising the signing was aware of the surety's misapprehension but did not correct it. It was held that the surety had discharged the onus of showing that it was unreasonable to allow the bank to rely on the unlimited suretyship. In *Form-Scaff (Pty) Ltd v Fischer*[20] the suretyship undertaking was hidden in the small print of a contract headed 'Hire and sale of formwork and scaffolding' in a way that was 'calculated to lead the signatory to overlook the fact that it contained a clause purporting to constitute a surety[ship]'.[21] The signatory's ostensible agreement to the suretyship was held attributable to a *justus error* on his part and he was held not bound. Similarly in *Diners Club SA (Pty) Ltd v Livingstone and Another*[22] where the defendant had signed as an authorised signatory of Falkirk Industries (Pty) Ltd a 'Diners Club Corporate Account Enrolment Form' in the belief that the form was an application by the company and its directors for such a card. On the back of the form in 'incredibly small print' was a clause which imposed liability as surety and co-principal debtor on the signatory. 'The whole get -up of the enrolment form', said Labe J, ' is such as to mislead a person into thinking that only the company was being considered for enrolment...' In the circumstances there was a duty to alert the signatory of the liability he was undertaking which duty had not been discharged by Diners Club.

However, it should not be thought that mistake or *justus error* is a way in which a surety can readily resile from his undertakings. In accordance with well-established principles the onus rests on the surety to show, in addition to the fact that he was in *error*, that it is unreasonable to allow the creditor to enforce the apparent agreement. Thus where, as in *Roomer v Wedge Steel (Pty) Ltd*,[23] the suretyship was contained in a clause in a bold font and the contract was headed

---

understood the documents even if they had read them (at 371D-H, para 24). One aspect of the judgment that may be important is the finding by the court that the bank official did not explain the contents of the contract to the sureties and that public interest demanded that a complicated document of this nature had to be explained to the signatory, especially where the signing of the document could have such drastic consequences (at 371F-H, para 24). This view may indeed open a new can of worms and reminds one of the folly of the English and Australian law with regard to the requirement to obtain independent advice when signing a suretyship (Hermanus Lourens Janse van Rensburg *Aspects of Banker Liability: Disclosure and Other Duties of Bankers towards Customers and Sureties* unpublished LLD thesis University of South Africa (2001) 250ff; EP Ellinger, Eva Lomnicka & Richard Hooley *Modern Banking Law* 3ed (2002) 110ff). The requirement of independent advice opened the door to lots of litigation in other jurisdictions (*Royal Bank of Scotland plc v Etridge (No. 2)* [2001] 4 All E.R. 449; Debra Morris 'Surety Wives in the House of Lords: Time for Solicitors to 'Get Real'?' (2003) 11 *Feminist Legal Studies* 57; Tim Wright 'The Special Wives' Equity and the Struggle for Woman's Equality (2006) 31 *Alternative LJ* 66 and Janine Pascoe 'Woman who Guarantees Company Debts: Wife or Director?' (2003) 8 *Deakin Law Review* 13). The same will probably happen in South Africa even if the financial institution is simply required to explain the contents of the contract to the signatories.

[20] D & C LD, unreported judgment 21st August 1992 discussed in *Roomer v Wedge Steel (Pty) Ltd* 1998(1) SA 538(N) at 542A-F. No reliance seems to have been placed on the *Diners Club* case discussed below.

[21] The undertaking was in fine print with no headings or other characteristics to distinguish it from the many other clauses which applied to the company on behalf of which the signatory was signing.

[22] 1995 (4) SA 493 (W) discussed by Cilliers & Luiz (1996) 58 *THRHR* 168. See also *Diners Club SA (Pty) Ltd v Thorburn* 1990 (2) SA 870 (C).

[23] 1998 (1) SA 538(N). See to like effect *Tesoriero v Bhyjo Investments Share Block (Pty) Ltd* 2000 (1) SA 167 (W) at 175F-176J.

'Agreement of Sale and Deed of Suretyship', the surety's belief that he did not realise he was signing a suretyship did not provide a defence. The creditor reasonably relied on the surety's apparent consent.

In *Brink v Humphries*[24] the surety maintained that when he signed a credit application form on behalf of the debtor, he did not know that it contained a personal suretyship obligation. The majority of the court found on the particular facts presented to the court that the credit application form was indeed misleading and that 'the form was a trap for the unwary and that the appellant was justifiably misled by it'.[25] Cloete JA referred to several features of the form in support of this finding: the prominent heading of the document that proclaimed that it is a credit application; the particular outlay of the form, et cetera.[26] The majority of the court thus concluded that the 'conduct in furnishing the form, which was misleading, induced a fundamental mistake on the part of the appellant: He thought he was signing a credit application form on behalf of the company, whereas he was, in addition, undertaking a personal suretyship for the debts of the company. It follows that the suretyship obligation was void *ab initio* ...'.[27]

---

[24] 2005 (2) SA 419 (SCA). See also JM Otto 'Verskuilde borgstellings in standaardkontrakte en *iustus error*' 2005 *TSAR* 805 and *Blue Chip Consultants (Pty) Ltd v Shamrock* 2002 (3) SA 231 (W).

[25] At 426B-C, para 11. A copy of the relevant application form is reproduced on page 431 of the report.

[26] At 425D-426C, para 10. See also *Blue Chip Consultants (Pty) Ltd v Shamrock* 2002 (3) SA 231 (W). In *Langeveld v Union Finance Holdings (Pty) Ltd* 2007 (4) SA 572 (W) the surety raised the defence that she had signed the contract containing the suretyship undertaking in a hurry and without reading it. She claimed that no one told her she was signing as surety and that she would not have so signed had she been aware of the fact that she was signing as surety (at 574H-I, para 7). An examination of the relevant document revealed that it consisted of five different 'sections', which, according to the court, could also be described as 'blocks' (at 574B-C, para 5). The judge found that the 'suretyship section or block hardly skulks away furtively. It is not hidden in 'fine print'. It is not buried in a mountain of legalese or jargon' (at 574E, para 6). (Compare, for example, the decision in *Davids en Andere v ABSA Bank Bpk* 2005 (3) SA 361 (C), where the first page of the suretyship undertaking contained 1255 words but only five sentences. The first sentence contained 370 words and the last sentence 584 words.) Furthermore, the evidence revealed that the surety was 'no 'babe-in-the-wood', never mind an illiterate' (at 575H, para 12). She was in fact an accomplished businesswoman of many years' standing. Under these circumstances, the court held (at 575H-576A, para 12), that there 'is a strong *praesumptio hominis* (popular presumption or presumption common among persons) that anyone who has signed a document had the *animus* (intention) to enter into the transaction contained in it, and she [the surety] is burdened with the *onus* of convincing the Court that she in fact had not entered into the transaction by virtue of the maxim *caveat subscriptor* (a person who signs must be careful)'. The court remarked that *caveat subscriptor* rule is a sound principle of law that a man, when he signs a contract, is taken to be bound by the ordinary meaning and effect of the words which appear over his signature. The court concluded that the surety failed to 'discharge the *onus* of proving that she was unaware that she was signing an undertaking as surety' (at 575C, para 13). Although the judgment was delivered on the 1st of February 2007, it makes no reference to the important decision in *Brink v Humphries & Jewell (Pty) Ltd* 2005 (2) SA 419 (SCA).

[27] At 426E-F, para 12. Three other aspects of the majority judgment are important: In the first instance, the majority held that the furnishing of a document in its terms can, without more and in itself, constitute a misrepresentation (at 422B-C, para 3). Secondly, it cannot be said that a signatory's mistake is reasonable simply because it was induced by the other party. Before it can be said that the mistake is justifiable and reasonable the court has to conduct an objective enquiry whether a reasonable person would also have been misled under the circumstances (at 424 E-F, para 8). The objective enquiry primarily enables the court to prevent abuse of the *justus error* defence. Thirdly, a party who has induced a justifiable mistake in a signatory as to the contents of a document

A suretyship induced by fraud on the part of the creditor is clearly open to rescission.[28] What, however, of the situation if the debtor induces the surety by fraud to enter on the suretyship with a creditor innocent of the fraud? The implication in *Standard Bank v Du Plooy and Another; Standard Bank v Coetzee and Another*[29] appears to be that the surety is entitled to resile unless he has been negligent and by that negligence has prejudiced the creditor. On the other hand, Miller J, in *Trans-Drakensberg Bank Ltd v Guy*[30] said: 'I agree that a surety cannot rely, as against the creditor or his cessionary, on the fraud of the principal debtor.' This appears to be the better view, unless the creditor was party to the fraud.[31] The surety will have a claim for damages against the principal debtor.[32]

4. Formalities and related questions

(a) The General Law Amendment Act

At common law[33] neither writing nor any particular form was required for the making of the contract of suretyship. Section 6 of the General Law Amendment Act[34] now provides that:

---

cannot, in fairness, assert that the signatory would not have been misled had the signatory read the document carefully (at 426D-E, para 11).

Navsa JA delivered a dissenting minority judgment. He stressed that the difference between his judgment and the majority judgment relates to the application of the law to the facts (at 426H-I, para 14). The judge found that the form, 'seen as a whole, cannot be described as a trap or as a misrepresentation' (at 430D-E, para 35). Navsa JA said that it is unlikely that a 'brilliant businessman' like the appellant could have thought that credit in the amount of R50000 would be extended to a private company without any security. See JM Otto 'Verskuilde borgstellings in standaardkontrakte en *iustus error*' 2005 *TSAR* 805.

[28] Wessels paras 4270-83; *Orlando Hosking v Standard Bank of SA Ltd* (1892) 13 NLR 174 at 182; *Lewin & Adamstein v Burger* (1908) 18 CTR 160.

[29] (1899) 16 SC 161. The view implied by this case, however, is not in accord with what Wessels says in paras 3972 and 4270, referring to English decisions, namely that to escape liability the surety must show that the creditor was party to the fraud or at any rate was aware of it. In *Credit Corporation of SA Ltd v Du Preez* 1961 (4) SA 515 (T) at 517, Bresler J cites para 3972, presumably with approval, though *obiter*.

[30] 1964 (1) SA 790 (D) at 797.

[31] The Zimbabwean case of *Musgrove & Watson (Rhodesia) Ltd v Rotta* 1978 (4) SA 656 (RA) (court *a quo* 1978 (2) SA 918 (R)) can be misleading here. Respondent had been induced to sign a suretyship agreement by the fraud of the treasurer of the principal debtor. He thought his signature was required for a bookkeeping formality. The court found there was no contract and respondent was not bound; apparently allowing the surety to rely on the third party's fraud against the innocent creditor. However, this is not so. Fraud may induce a *contract,* in which case a contract comes into existence, but it is voidable at the instance of the defrauded party provided that the fraud was not the fraud of a third party. In *Rotta's* case, however, the fraud induced not a contract but a *signature,* there was 'neither a *concursus animorum* nor an *animus contrahendi*' (at 657H), and thus no basis on which Rotta could be held bound. Of course, where the 'surety' was negligent in signing a delictual action might lie. Alternatively, estoppel might prevent him denying he was bound. But in both these cases the creditor would need to show that he had relied to his detriment on the 'surety's' signature (at 657H, 658C-D, in the court *a quo* at 925E-926D). This was not the case in *Rotta*.

[32] See also JG Lotz 'Die Rol van 'n Wanvoorstelling by Wesentlike Dwaling' (1991) 3 SA *Merc LJ* 263.

[33] *Stride v Wepener* 1903 TH 383 at 386, 387; *Silver Garbus & Co (Pty) Ltd v Teichert* 1954 (2) SA 98 (N) at 105. See NJ Grové *Die Formaliteitsvereiste by Borgstelling* unpublished LLM dissertation, University of Pretoria (1984) 2 ff and JT Pretorius 'Die Formaliteitsvereiste by Borgstelling' (1988) 10 *MB* 122 for a full discussion in this regard.

[34] Act 50 of 1956, as amended (retrospectively to 22 June 1956) by section 34 of Act 80 of 1964.

> No contract of suretyship entered into after the commencement of this Act [22 June 1956] shall be valid, unless the terms thereof are embodied in a written document signed by or on behalf of the surety: Provided that nothing in this section contained shall affect the liability of the signer of an aval under the laws relating to negotiable instruments.[35]

The objects of the legislature in enacting section 6 were described by Miller JA in *Fourlamel (Pty) Ltd v Maddison*[36] in these words:

> However many objects the Legislature may have had in mind in enacting sec 6 of Act 50 of 1956, one of them was surely to achieve certainty as to the true terms agreed on and thus avoid or minimise the possibility of perjury or fraud and unnecessary litigation.... The Legislature may also have been influenced by other considerations, for example, that suretyship being an onerous obligation, involving as it does the payment of another's debts, would-be sureties should be protected against themselves to the extent that they should not be bound by any precipitate verbal undertakings to go surety for another but would be bound only after their undertaking had been recorded in a written document and signed by them or on their behalf.[37]

---

[35] The words 'or on behalf of' were inserted by the amending provision, no doubt as a consequence of the decision in *Levitan NO v Petrol Conservation (Pty) Ltd and Another* 1962 (3) SA 233 (W) that the legislation (prior to amendment) required the surety to have signed personally and that signature by an authorised agent was insufficient to make the contract. See also *Orkin Lingerie Co (Pty) Ltd v Melamed & Hurwitz* 1963 (1) SA 324 (W). *Levitan* has been the subject of adverse comment — see JF Uys 'May an Agent Sign for a Surety?' (1963) 80 *SALJ* 16 and 1962 *Annual Survey* 203. The person signing for or on behalf of the surety must have been authorised to do so. It is strange that the legislature has not required that the authority to do so be written, as it has done in the case of the sale of land. Section 2 of the Alienation of Land Act 68 of 1981 provides that no alienation of land shall be of any force 'unless it is contained in a deed of alienation signed by the parties thereto or by their agents acting on their written authority'.

[36] 1977 (1) SA 333 (A) at 342-3. It is sometimes difficult to distinguish between a suretyship and other forms of indemnity. See the discussion in Chapter II above. NJ Grové *Die Formaliteitsvereiste by Borgstelling* unpublished LLM dissertation, University of Pretoria (1984) 85-6 says the following in this regard: 'Waar borgstelling met aanverwante regsfigure soos byvoorbeeld die garansie- of versekeringskontrak vergelyk word, is daar onder regsgeleerdes onderling nie eenstemmigheid oor presies waarin die onderskeid geleë is nie. Dit veroorsaak dat daar probleme kan ontstaan indien 'n kontrak in die lig van a 6 van die Algemene Regswysigingswet van 1956 geïnterpreteer moet word. In die een geval word daar beslis dat die partye se ooreenkoms buite die bepalings van genoemde wet val en in 'n ander geval kan die partye, deur dieselfde terminologie te gebruik, 'n ooreenkoms sluit wat binne die bepalings van die wet val. In beide gevalle het die partye by die sluiting van die ooreenkoms die bedoeling gehad om gebonde te wees aan die ooreenkoms. Op 'n latere stadium, as gevolg van die bestaan van hierdie spesifieke statutêre bepaling, word die een party die geleentheid gegee om aanspreeklikheid, wat die partye geglo het bestaan, te ontduik, nieteenstaande die partye se oorspronklike bedoeling. Dit gee die buitestaander die indruk dat die stelreël *pacta servanda sunt* ondergeskik gestel word aan die formele vormvereistes. Dit het die gevolg dat tegniese verskille tussen die ooreenkomste gesoek word om sodoende te sorg dat die ooreenkoms wat die partye gesluit het, buite die bepalings van a 6 van die Algemene Regswysigingswet van 1956 val. Op hierdie wyse word die materiële reg ondergrawe en word partye uitgelewer aan 'n kasuïstiese benadering wat weer regsonsekerheid in die hand werk.' See also JT Pretorius 'Die Formaliteitsvereiste by Borgstelling' (1988) 10 *MB* 122.

[37] NJ Grové *Die Formaliteitsvereiste by Borgstelling* unpublished LLM dissertation, University of Pretoria (1984) 18-9 points out that although there is a fair amount of criticism which has been leveled against the enactment it should be pointed out that '[g]eïmpliseerd in die meeste van die kritiek teen statutêre vormvereistes is die argument dat daar gemeenregtelik in hierdie gevalle geen vormvereistes daargestel is en dat dit nie tot noemenswaardige probleme aanleiding gegee het nie. Dit word klaarblyklik afgelei uit die feit dat daar, met die gemene reg in swang, nie veel gerapporteerde beslissings oor die betrokke aspek was nie. Gerapporteerde beslissings is egter nie die enigste barometer waaraan regsekerheid gemeet word nie. Nie alle geskille tussen partye eindig in 'n geregshof nie. Vele sake word deur voornemende litigante laat vaar op sterkte van

THE FORMATION OF THE CONTRACT OF SURETYSHIP 69

Section 6 requires that the document embodying the contract of suretyship must be signed by or on behalf of the surety. The word 'sign' is derived from the Latin *signum*, a mark,[38] and it should be interpreted to mean the placing of a mark on a document identifying or representing the person signing.[39] Thus, 'signature' means any mark—whether it be a person's full name and surname, or his initials and surname, or only his initials, or a mere mark—placed on the contract with the intention of identifying the signatory. A signature need not be in ink,[40] nor be written in a specific manner[41] or in a specific place.[42] An agent must indicate that he is signing in a representative capacity in order to escape personal liability on the contract.[43]

(b) The document must contain the 'terms' of the contract
In *Sapirstein and Others v Anglo African Shipping Co (SA) Ltd*[44] the Appellate Division held that the 'terms' of a contract of suretyship, referred to in section 6, were

---

advies wat deur hulle regsverteenwoordigers aan hulle verskaf word. So byvoorbeeld kan 'n kliënt geadviseer word om sy saak teen 'n ander te laat vaar omdat probleme ondervind word om 'n mondelinge ooreenkoms tussen die partye te bewys. Sake wat aldus laat vaar word, word natuurlik nie gerapporteer nie.... Dit is dus nie 'n uitgemaakte saak dat die gemenereg meer regsekerheid daar sou stel as wat die geval met a 6 van Wet 50 van 1956 is nie.'

[38] *Putter v Provincial Insurance Co Ltd and Another* 1963 (3) SA 145 (W) at 148. See also *In re Trollip* (1895) 12 SC 243 at 246; *Ex parte Goldman and Kalmer NNO* 1965 (1) SA 464 (W) at 468 and NJ Grové *Die Formaliteitsvereiste by Borgstelling* unpublished LLM dissertation, University of Pretoria (1984) 163 ff.

[39] *In re Trollip* at 246: 'To sign one's name, as distinguished from writing one's name in full, is to make such a mark as will represent the name of the person signing the document. For that purpose it is no more necessary to write one's name in full than it is to write one's Christian names in full.' In *Van Niekerk v Smit and Others* 1952 (3) SA 17 (T) Murray J remarked at 25: 'To sign, as distinguished from writing one's own name in full is to make such a mark as will represent the name of the person signing.'

[40] *Van Niekerk v Smit and Others* at 25. See also NJ Grové *Die Formaliteitsvereiste by Borgstelling* unpublished LLM dissertation, University of Pretoria (1984) 165 and *Malan on Bills of Exchange, Cheques and Promissory Notes in South African Law* 5ed by FR Malan, JT Pretorius & SF du Toit (2009) para 71.

[41] *Ex parte Goldman and Kalmer NNO* 1965 (1) SA 464 (W) at 468.

[42] In *Standard Bank of South Africa Ltd v Bhamjee and Another* 1978 (4) SA 39 (W) Margo J remarked at 41: 'In the instant case it is only necessary to decide what is meant by the references in section 6 to the terms of the suretyship 'being embodied in a written document', and to such being 'signed' by or on behalf of the surety. In my view, section 6 means no more than that the document, irrespective of the number of pages, must be identifiable as one comprehensive and integral contract of suretyship, and that the signature therein must authenticate, or manifestly be intended to cover, the whole contract.' See further *Theunissen en Andere v Transvaalse Lewendehawe Koöp Bpk* 1988 (2) SA 493 (A) at 501-2 and NJ Grové *Die Formaliteitsvereiste by Borgstelling* unpublished LLM dissertation, University of Pretoria (1984) 167 ff.

[43] NJ Grové *Die Formaliteitsvereiste by Borgstelling* unpublished LLM dissertation, University of Pretoria (1984) 171. See also the discussion on rectification, below. Since the statute specifically requires the surety's signature, a signature affixed to an agreement in a capacity other than surety will not suffice. Thus *Steenkamp v Webster* 1955 (1) SA 524 (A) in which a company director was held bound by an agreement which he had signed on behalf of the company, and in which *inter alia* he bound himself as surety for the company's debts, would be differently decided today.

[44] 1978 (4) SA 1 (A) at 12B-D. See also *Lategan and Another NNO v Boyes and Another* 1980 (4) SA 191 (T) at 203F; *Northern Cape Co-operative Livestock Agency Ltd v John Roderick & Co Ltd* 1965 (2) SA 64 (O) at 69H; *Maxwell Furnishers v Hume* 1971 (3) SA 636 (T) at 637G-638A; *Fourlamel (Pty) Ltd v Maddison* 1977 (1) SA 333 (A) at 344H-345D; *Theunissen en Andere v Transvaalse Lewendehawe Koöp Bpk* 1988 (2) SA 493 (A) at 498; *Compaan v Dorbyl Structural Engineering (Pty) Ltd t/a Brownbuilt Metal Sections* 1983 (4) SA 107 (T) at 111 and NJ Grové 'Borgkontrakte, Mondelinge Wysigings en Kansellasie' 1983 *De Rebus* 201. It is these essentials mentioned in the text which must be 'embodied' in the writing in terms of section 6. See *Standard Bank of South Africa Ltd v Bhamjee and Another*

the identity of the creditor, the debtor, and the surety, and the nature and amount of the principal debt.[45] These had as a general rule to be capable of ascertainment by reference to the written document. Failure to include any of these terms in the writing meant that there was no compliance with section 6, and the contract was void. Although not mentioned in the *Sapirstein* case, the statute specifically requires, in addition, a signature 'by or on behalf of the surety'. Naturally, the courts take a common-sense approach to the interpretation of section 6, and thus a meticulous description of the principal debt and, presumably, the various parties, is not required.[46]

1978 (4) SA 39 (W) for the meaning of 'embodied'. The contract of suretyship may be 'embodied' in a document which consists out of more than one page (*Speech v Hill Kaplan Scott and Partners* 1981 (3) SA 332 (A) at 338-9).

[45] The actual amount of the principal debt need not be stated where the surety undertakes unlimited liability. In *Plascon-Evans Paints (Transvaal) Ltd v Virginia Glass Works (Pty) Ltd and Others* 1983 (1) SA 465 (O) Erasmus J pointed out at 470 that the duration of a surety's liability is a 'term' of the agreement of suretyship, and, as such, must be in writing. A material variation of such term must, similarly, be in writing. In *Wallace v 1662 G & D Property Investments CC* 2008 (1) SA 300 (W) the court confirmed that the *identity of the principal debtor* is indeed one of the material terms of a contract of suretyship and that unless the identity of the principal debtor is embodied in the written document, the contract will be invalid (para 32 at 308B-C. See also *Industrial Development Corporation of SA (Pty) Ltd v Silver* 2003 (1) SA 365 (SCA) where the court came to the same conclusion at 369A-B, para 5.). In *Wallace* the court dealt with two almost identical deeds of suretyship that did not identify the principal debtor. Both contracts simply referred to the principal debtor as 'the debtor' (para 6 at 302A-B). It was also common cause that neither of the deeds of suretyship made any reference to any other documents in which the identity of the principal debtor was recorded or could be ascertained with reasonable certainty (para 321 at 308A-B). There was thus no possibility of applying the concept of 'incorporation by reference' to supplement the deeds of suretyship in an effort to identify the principal debtor (see the next section below). Levenberg AJ concluded that both suretyships were invalid by reason of its failure to record an essential term of the suretyship as required by section 6 of the Act, viz. the identity of the principal debtor (para 33 at 308A-B). This conclusion is in line with the statement by Scott JA in *Industrial Development Corporation of SA (Pty) Ltd v Silver* that '[u]nless ... the identity of the principal debtor is embodied in the written document, the contract of suretyship will be invalid' (para 5 at 369A-B).

[46] In *Credit Guarantee Insurance Corporation of South Africa Ltd v Schreiber* 1987 (3) SA 523 (W) Flemming J remarked at 525: 'If parties find it impossible, impractical or inconvenient to reflect what the surety is undertaking except by an express statement of the name of the principal debtor and a definitive identification of the guaranteed debt, the parties will no doubt mention those features. But I should not commence the enquiry as if the statute insisted that a specific feature must be explicitly stated or exhaustively described. If the parties succeed in reflecting the 'terms' of the contract without mentioning eg the debtor's name, they have a valid contract. This is illustrated by *inter alia* the valid suretyship in the *Sapirstein* case which, despite additional itemisation, really related to 'any indebtedness which any of the other promisees might in future incur''. The suretyship in the *Fourlamel* case was also in wide terms similar to contracts which are frequently used by banks and other institutions. Where the surety undertook his obligation in respect of 'obligations [of the principal debtor] arising from various transactions' there was held to be compliance with section 6. These words were construed to mean 'obigations arising from all transactions of whatever nature': *Swiftair Freight CC v Singh* 1993 (1) SA 454 (D). Where the surety bound himself for the debts of 'Convenient Wholesalers' this was held to include the debts of 'Convenient Wholesalers CC'. Rectification (which would have been available) was not required: *Coca-Cola Sabco (SA) (Pty) Ltd v Muller* 1999 (4) SA 829 (E). Similarly, where the sureties undertook liability for the debts of 'companies' that were also customers of the creditor they were held liable for the debts of a close corporation in that position: *Vitamax (Pty) Ltd v Executive Catering Equipment CC and Others* 1993 (2) SA 556 (W).

THE FORMATION OF THE CONTRACT OF SURETYSHIP 71

It is sufficient if the essential terms can be properly identified.[47] The essential terms must, as a general rule, be included in the writing.[48] Extrinsic evidence may, however, be required to *identify* the essential in question.[49] For example, as in the *Sapirstein* case, where a surety undertakes to secure a debt to be incurred in the future by one of two potential debtors, extrinsic evidence will be required to identify the principal debtor *in casu*.[50] Similarly extrinsic evidence may be required to identify the debt, or its extent,[51] as well as the various parties to the contract.[52] Naturally, evidence by the parties in regard to their negotiations and

---

[47] See *Lategan and Another NNO v Boyes and Another* 1980 (4) SA 191 (T) at 203H. Thus it is possible to *amend* the principal obligation, without amending the suretyship (204A). Presumably the principal obligation could not be *replaced*, although amendment may lead to the surety's release (see Chapter XIII).

[48] There are, however, occasions when this rule is relaxed and although extrinsic evidence is needed to prove the essentials, the suretyship is valid.

[49] See *Sapirstein and Others v Anglo African Shipping Co (SA) Ltd* 1978 (4) SA 1 (A) at 12C; *African Lumber Co (Pvt) Ltd v Katz* 1978 (4) SA 432 (C) and *Asco Carbon Dioxide Ltd v Lahner* 2005 (3) SA 213 (N) at 218. In *Oranjerivier Wynkelders (Koöp) Bpk v Von Wielligh* [2002] 1 All SA 449 (C) the surety argued that the suretyship was invalid as the identity of the surety did not appear from the document. The court was satisfied that a signature appearing at the foot of the document was that of the surety as he had admitted to signing it in an affidavit furnished to resist summary judgment, and the signature read 'GJ Wielligh'. Extrinsic evidence could be used to establish that the signature was that of the surety (at 45). It was unnecessary that the name of the signatory appear under the signature. The creditor was only referred to as 'OWK' in the suretyship, which was part of an agreement of sale. In that agreement the blank space used to identify the creditor was not filled in, although it was followed by words indicating that the creditor was defined as 'OWK'. The court was satisfied that it could refer to the agreement of sale and that it was obvious that the reference to 'OWK' in the agreement of sale was to the creditor. By means of incorporation it was clear who the creditor and the surety were.

[50] Where a surety binds himself as against a creditor for the payment of the future debts of 'A and/or B', the reference to the two principal debtors envisages that either A only, or B only, or both A and B, could owe money to the creditor at a given time (*Du Toit en 'n Ander v Barclays Nasionale Bank Bpk* 1985 (1) SA 563 (A)). In such a case the identity of the principal debtor or debtors is established and there is no ambiguity which would justify a finding of non-compliance with the requirements of section 6. Extrinsic evidence may thus be necessary to identify the principal debtor.

[51] See *Lategan and Another NNO v Boyes and Another* 1980 (4) SA 191 (T) at 203H and *General Accident Insurance Company SA Ltd v Dancor Holdings (Pty) Ltd and Others* 1981 (4) SA 968 (A). And see *De Villiers v Nefdin Bank, A Division of Nedcor Bank Ltd* 1997 (2) SA 76 (E) (undertaking in respect of 'all amounts of whatever nature and/or performance of any obligation' clearly limited to the obligations of the debtor identified in the contract (and not any debtor of the bank); extrinsic evidence was allowed since it could identify the particular debt in any case).'

[52] Of course, the document itself must identify the class of potential debtors or creditors, and the extrinsic evidence then simply goes to identify which of that class is in fact the debtor or creditor. Thus to leave the creditor unnamed or to refer to the creditor as 'J Perkel, Silverman & Co (acting for and on behalf of various nominees)' is insufficient compliance with section 6 (*JPS Nominees (Pty) Ltd v Kruger* 1976 (1) SA 89 (W)). There would, however, be compliance if the creditor is defined as part of a group which could be identified without reference to the negotiations between the parties (*Federated Timbers (Pretoria) (Pty) Ltd v Fourie* 1978 (1) SA 292 (T)). Where the surety agrees to be bound to the creditor or his successors or assigns (unnamed), the agreement does not fall foul of section 6, and the creditor's cessionary can proceed against the surety (*Pizani and Another v First Consolidated Holdings (Pty) Ltd* 1979 (1) SA 69 (A) at 79F-H).

consensus is excluded,[53] for to admit such evidence would be contrary to section 6: It would amount to 'giving effect to a *consensus* not reduced to writing and embodied in the document'.[54]

(c) The principle of incorporation

Extrinsic evidence may also be admissible in accordance with the principle of incorporation. Where the suretyship document itself fails to contain an essential term, but refers to some other document which contains that term, then that other document may be incorporated in the suretyship—thereby remedying its deficiency—since *certum est quod certum reddi potest*.[55] Thus if a suretyship document does not contain the debtor's name, but in setting out the principal debt refers to an acknowledgment of debt which does name the debtor, that acknowledgment of debt can be proved to secure compliance with section 6. One point of difficulty arises in regard to this principle: is it necessary that the reference in the suretyship to the other document be sufficiently clear for it to be identified *ex facie* itself and the suretyship, or is it sufficient if the other document can be identified by

A distinction should also be drawn between a creditor and a person *solutionis causa adjectus*. The latter is only the person to whom, by agreement with the creditor, payment is to be made. He does not step into the shoes of the creditor as the person to whom the debt is owed. In *Compaan v Dorbyl Structural Engineering (Pty) Ltd t/a Brownbuilt Metal Sections* 1983 (4) SA 107 (T) the appellant had bound himself as surety and co-principal debtor on behalf of a company which was indebted to the respondent. This indebtedness was recorded on the reverse side of a series of cheques, which were made payable to the appellant's attorneys, but no mention was made of the respondent on either the face or the reverse side of the cheques. This, it was held, did not comply with the provisions of section 6 since the object of the section would be defeated if the creditor to whom the principal debt was owed included a person *solutionis causa adjectus*. 'Indeed,' said the court at 111, 'if that were the case, it could lead only to confusion in that uncertainty would exist as to whether the creditor is the person to whom in fact the principal debt is owed or merely the person to whom that debt is to be paid, which may not necessarily be one and the same person.' See also *Durity Alpha (Pty) Ltd v Vagg* 1991 (2) SA 840 (A); *Levi v Almog* 1990 (1) SA 541 (W), as discussed by AN Oelofse & JT Pretorius 'Of Suretyships, Avals and Accommodation Parties' (1991) 3 *SA Merc LJ* 260 at 262-3 and NJ Grové *Die Formaliteitsvereiste by Borgstelling* unpublished LLM dissertation, University of Pretoria (1984) 92 ff.

[53] *Sapirstein and Others v Anglo African Shipping Co (SA) Ltd* 1978 (4) SA 1 (A) at 12D.

[54] *African Lumber Co (Pvt) Ltd* 1978 (4) SA 432 (C) at 435C; *General Accident Insurance Company SA Ltd v Dancor Holdings (Pty) Ltd and Others* 1981 (4) SA 968 (A) at 978F-G. See also DT Zeffertt and A Paizes *Parol Evidence with Particular Reference to Contract* (1986) 101 ff.

[55] That the principle of incorporation applies to suretyship documents has been frequently recognised by the provincial divisions (see, for example, *Trust Bank of Africa Ltd v Cotton* 1976 (4) SA 325 (N) at 329G; *FJ Mitrie (Pty) Ltd v Madgwick and Another* 1979 (1) SA 232 (D) at 235D) but in the Appellate Division in *Fourlamel (Pty) Ltd v Maddison* 1977 (1) SA 333 (A) its applicability was only assumed (at 345E). In both *Sneech v Hill Kaplan Scott and Partners* 1981(3) SA 332(A) and *Theunissen en Andere v Transvaalse Lewendehawe Koöp Bpk* 1988 (2) SA 493 (A) the Appellate Division refrained from holding the principle of incorporation applicable to deeds of suretyship, basing its decision instead on the 'document' sought to be incorporated in fact being *part* of the suretyship document. The Appellate Division's hesitancy in this regard is difficult to understand. See now the Supreme Court of Appeal in *Industrial Development Corporation of SA (Pty) Ltd v Silver* 2003 (1) SA 365 (SCA) discussed below in note 57.

further oral evidence? Some of the older decisions are difficult to reconcile,[56] but it has since been held that identification of the other document by oral evidence should not frustrate the policy behind section 6.[57]

The parol evidence rule (sometimes called the 'integration rule') is also applicable.[58] Thus where the parties to a suretyship have reduced their agreement to writing and the writing *prima facie* accords with section 6, the surety cannot rely on any terms agreed orally with the creditor but not reduced to writing in order to have the written agreement invalidated for non-compliance with section 6.[59]

(d) Rectification

Extrinsic evidence—this time in regard to the central issue: the *consensus* of the parties—may be admissible when one of the parties seeks rectification of a

---

[56] In *Trust Bank van Afrika Bpk v Sullivan* 1979 (2) SA 765 (T) Viljoen J held that extrinsic evidence was inadmissible to identify the document referred to. He relied in the main on *Fourlamel (Pty) Ltd v Maddison* 1977 (1) SA 333 (A). In that case, however, Miller JA expressed the view that he did because oral evidence was not available. He did not intend, it is submitted, to close the door to its admission (see at 345H). Indeed in *Trust Bank of Africa Ltd v Cotton* 1976 (4) SA 325 (N) he was clearly of the opposite view. See also *FJ Mitrie (Pty) Ltd v Madgwick and Another* 1979 (1) SA 232 (D). In *Ellis v Trust Bank of Africa Ltd* 1981 (1) SA 733 (N) Kumleben J inclined to the view expressed in *Trust Bank van Afrika Bpk v Sullivan* 1979 (2) SA 765 (T), but this expression of opinion was *obiter*. See, however, *Industrial Development Corporation of SA (Pty) Ltd v Silver* 2003 (1) SA 365 (SCA), discussed below. See further JT Pretorius 'Gebrekkige Borgaktes: Inlywing by Wyse van Vergelyking' (1982) 45 *THRHR* 317 and NJ Grové *Die Formaliteitsvereiste by Borgstelling* unpublished LLM dissertation, University of Pretoria (1984) 140 ff and 1979 *Annual Survey* 166-7.

[57] In *Industrial Development Corporation of SA (Pty) Ltd v Silver* 2003 (1) SA 365 (SCA) the preliminary question the court had to decide was whether a deed of suretyship which did not identify the principal debtor as such was nevertheless valid by reason of the principle of incorporation by reference (at 367I-J, para 1). The court held that since incorporation by reference has been held to apply in the case of sale of land, there can be no justification for holding the principle not to be applicable in the case of contracts of suretyship (at 369F-G, para 6). Thus, where the suretyship document itself fails to contain an essential term, but refers to some other document which contains that term, then that other document may be incorporated in the suretyship agreement—thereby remedying the deficiency – since *certum est quod certum reddi potest*. The further question the court had to decide was whether the reference in the suretyship to the other document had to be sufficiently clear for it to be identified *ex facie* the suretyship itself or whether it was possible to lead extrinsic evidence to identify the other document to be incorporated (at 370C-D, para 9). The court pointed out that as 'a general rule the terms of a contract required by law to be in writing must appear from the document itself and may not be supplemented by extrinsic evidence' (ibid). Extrinsic evidence has, however, been allowed in a number of situations provided that such evidence is not of negotiations between the parties prior to the execution of the written agreement or of their consensus. The court referred to the conflicting decisions in this regard (at 371-2, para 11) and held that it is indeed possible to lead extrinsic evidence to identify the document as the document referred to in the deed of suretyship provided that it was clear *ex facie* the suretyship that the document sought to be incorporated did give rise to the indebtedness secured by the suretyship or that the secured debt arose from the terms of the agreement (document) sought to be incorporated (at 272 para 12). Such evidence may be given by the parties themselves or anyone else, provided that they do not testify as to some negotiation or consensus between the parties (at 371A-B, para 10). It is submitted that this decision is sound since the identification of the document sought to be incorporated by extrinsic evidence would not frustrate the policy behind section 6.

[58] The parol evidence rule lays down that where a juristic act is embodied in a particular document, that document is then conclusive of what was agreed or done and other evidence of what was agreed or done is generally excluded (*National Board (Pretoria) (Pty) Ltd and Another v Estate Swanepoel* 1975 (3) SA 16 (A) at 26).

[59] *Standard Bank of SA Ltd v Cohen (1)* 1993 (3) SA 846 (SE).

suretyship document.[60] With rectification the party seeking to have the contract rectified claims that it does not reflect what the parties agreed and seeks to have the matter put right.[61] Naturally the normal requirements for rectification will need to be proved, viz, that there was in fact consensus, but that the document does not reflect that agreement; and that third parties will not be prejudiced, etc. Rectification is not limited to cases in which the document, as signed, incorrectly reflects or omits the words which the parties intended to record. It is available where the words correctly reflect what the parties intended to record but do not reflect the parties' prior oral agreement or common intention.[62] Thus where the suretyship did not reflect the parties' prior oral agreement (to the effect that the suretyship would come into operation only if the principal debtor became liable to the creditor under a certain other transaction) rectification would be available.[63] So rectification is available not only when the words of the document are wrong but also when they do not contain the complete agreement between the parties. A clause to the effect that the writing sets out the 'entire agreement' between creditor and surety and the creditor 'shall not be bound by any undertakings,

---

[60] See, in general, *Meyer v Merchants' Trust Ltd* 1942 AD 244; NJ Grové *Die Formaliteitsvereiste by Borgstelling* unpublished LLM dissertation, University of Pretoria (1984) 101 ff; *De Wet en Van Wyk Die Suid-Afrikaanse Kontraktereg en Handelsreg* 5 ed (1992) vol I by JC de Wet and GF Lubbe (ed) 29 ff; W de Vos 'Mistake in Contract' 1976 *Acta Juridica* 177 at 186 ff; Schalk van der Merwe *et al Contract General Principles* 3 ed (2007) 178 ff and JF Malan *Aspekte van Rektifikasie in die Suid-Afrikaanse Kontraktereg,* unpublished LLD thesis, University of Pretoria (1987) 149 ff. The principles of rectification in regard to suretyship contracts were discussed in *Neuhoff v York Timbers Ltd* 1981 (4) SA 666 (T). In this case Ackermann J stressed that 'the defence of rectification of a written contract is based on the *exceptio doli generalis'* (at 673E). Notwithstanding *Bank of Lisbon and South Africa Ltd v De Ornelas and Another* 1988 (3) SA 580 (A) (ejecting the *exceptio doli generalis* from Roman-Dutch law—discussed in Chapter XIII), rectification nevertheless remains part of our law. See *Tesven CC and Another v South African Bank of Athens* 2000 (1) SA 268 (A) and *Intercontinental Exports (Pty) Ltd v Fowles* 1999 (2) SA 1045 (A) where Smallberger JA said (at 1051H): 'Rectification is a well established common-law right. It provides an equitable remedy designed to correct the failure of a written contract to reflect the true agreement between the parties to the contract.' The availability of rectification was confirmed in *Inventive Labour Structuring (Pty) Ltd v Corfe* 2006 (3) SA 107 (SCA), discussed below.

[61] See *Northern Cape Co-operative Livestock Agency Ltd v John Roderick & Co Ltd* 1965 (2) SA 64 (O); *Bardays Bank (DCO) v Bolton* 1952 (2) PH A65 (C); *Meyer v Merchants' Trust Ltd* 1942 AD 244; *Trust Bank of Africa Ltd v Frysch* 1976 (2) SA 337 (C). (Overruled on other grounds 1977 (3) SA 562 (A).) In *Mutual Construction Co v Victor* [2002] 3 All SA 807 (W) the defendant denied that a suretyship was concluded. The suretyship formed the last clause immediately above the space demarcated for a signature in a document headed 'Opening account form and suretyship'. The defendant contended that since the plaintiff had refused the application for credit, the suretyship, as a component of the application, never came into operation. The court found that the refusal of the application for credit was irrelevant as the suretyship was an independent contract (para 11). By signing the form, the suretyship was concluded. The surety also contended that the contract was subject to an oral suspensive condition that it would only come into operation if credit were granted. This required the rectification of the suretyship. However, this conflicted with the surety's case as pleaded and in any event the court was of the view that the suggested condition would conflict with the written terms of the contract.

[62] *Tesven CC and Another v South African Bank of Athens* 2000 (1) SA 268 (A) at 274G-H per Farlam AJA.

[63] In *Tesven CC and Another v South African Bank of Athens supra* the sureties alleged that such an agreement existed. The Supreme Court of Appeal rejected the view, accepted in the court *a quo,* that the parol evidence rule precluded rectification in those circumstances.

representations or warranties not expressly recorded' in the writing, does not exclude rectification.[64]

Where a material term of the agreed suretyship is erroneously recorded or not recorded at all in the document—for example the parties agree to exclude the benefit of excussion, but fail to record this in the writing—that *error* can be rectified.[65] But what is the position if the erroneous term in the document is one of the essential terms which must be included in order to ensure compliance with section 6? It is now clear that rectification is possible but the unrectified document must also be one which *ex facie* complies with the statute, that is to say, the essential terms, even if one or more of them are erroneous, must appear in the writing.[66] The dilemma facing the court in such cases is well put by Smalberger JA in *Intercontinental Exports (Pty) Ltd v Fowles*[67] in these words:

> [Rectification] enables effect to be given to the parties' actual agreement, The requirement of formal validity in the case of a deed of suretyship flows from the Legislature's perceived need to provide safeguards in such matters. To the extent that the need to satisfy the latter [formal validity] may preclude recourse to the former [actual agreement], tension will inevitably exist between the two. While care must be taken not to defeat the object of the Act, the formality requirements must not be allowed to become an unnecessary stumbling-block to rectification and, consequently, to giving effect to the true intention of the parties.

Thus *Intercontinental Exports*, where the suretyship document incorrectly named the principal debtor, the contract complied *ex facie* with section 6 and rectification could take place.

---

[64] *Standard Bank of SA Ltd v Cohen(2)* 1993 (3) SA 854 (SE) at 863C-D.
[65] See, for example, *Northern Cape Co-operative Livestock Agency Ltd v John Roderick & Co Ltd* 1965 (2) SA 64 (O) at 69H-71H and *First Rand Bank of Southern Africa Ltd v Pretorius and Another* 2002 (3) SA 489 (C). Rectification may thus be granted where the parties are all clearly identified but, by mistake common to both parties, the capacity in which the surety signed was incorrectly recorded (*Litecor Voltex (Natal) (Pty) Ltd v Jason* 1988 (2) SA 78 (D)). Rectification may also be granted to substitute the true creditor's name for a name mistakenly appearing in the contract, as the creditor's signature is not required for compliance with section 6 (*Lazarus v Gorfinkel* 1988 (4) SA 123 (C)).
[66] See *Van Wyk v Rottcher's Saw Mills (Pty) Ltd* 1948 (1) SA 983 (A) at 989; *Barclays Mortgage Nominees (Pty) Ltd v Brown* 1979 (2) PH A50 (N); *Litecor Voltex (Natal) (Pty) Ltd v Jason* 1988 (2) SA 78 (D) at 81 and *Lazarus v Gorfinkel* 1988 (4) SA 123 (C) at 131. For a criticism of the view that it is not possible to rectify a contract that is invalid for the non-compliance with statuary formalities, see *De Wet en Van Wyk Die Suid-Afrikaanse Kontraktereg en Handelsreg* 5 ed (1992) vol I by JC de Wet and GF Lubbe (ed) 325 ff; Schalk van der Merwe *et al Contract General Principles* 3 ed (2007)182 ff; NJ Grové *Die Formaliteitsvereiste by Borgstelling* unpublished LLM dissertation, University of Pretoria (1984) 112 ff and Louise Tager 'Rectification of Invalid Contracts' (1977) 94 *SALJ* 8. Notwithstanding this criticism it was held in *Intercontinental Exports (Pty) Ltd v Fowles* 1999 (2) SA 1045 (A) (following *Magwaza v Heenan* 1979(2) SA 1019(A) (no rectification of a contract for the sale of land (required by statute to be in writing) that was formally invalid) that a contract that is invalid for want of compliance with statutory formalities could not be rectified (at 1051C-G). The Supreme Court of Appeal confirmed this approach in *Inventive Labour Structuring (Pty) Ltd v Corfe* 2006 (3) SA 107 (SCA). The decisions in *Fraser and Another v Viljoen* 2008 (4) 106 (SCA) and *Just Names Properties 11 CC and Another v Fourie and Others* 2008 (1) 343 (SCA) both deal with the prescribed formalities that have to be complied with in terms of section 2 of the Alienation of Land Act 68 of 1981. Both these decisions contain extensive references to the (analogous) formalities that apply to contracts of suretyship.
[67] 1999(2) SA 1045 (A) at 1051H-I.

In *Inventive Labour Structuring (Pty) Ltd v Corfe*[68] the names of the surety and the principal debtor ('Dennis Corfe') in the suretyship were identical. The creditor claimed rectification of the document and averred that the mistake was due to an *error* common to both parties and was contrary to their intention because the surety intended to stand surety for a certain close corporation. So the court had to determine whether rectification was possible. Jafta JA confirmed the legal position as set out above and explained that, as a general rule, the determination of whether rectification of a suretyship should be ordered involves a two-stage enquiry: the first is to determine whether the formal requirements in section 6 have been met. The focal point at this stage is whether the document, on its face, constitutes a valid suretyship or not. If it does not, the enquiry ends. If it does, the enquiry then moves to the second stage, where the focus is on the question whether all the requirements for rectification have been met. If they have, rectification must be granted.[69]

The court then proceeded to enquire whether the document complied with the necessary formalities even though the names of the surety and the principal debtor were identical. It pointed out that as the names in question were those of a natural person, it rendered the contract capable of at least two interpretations: either the surety and the principal debtor are one or the same person or they are two parties with identical names. If the surety and the principal debtor were the same person, this would lead to non-compliance with the formal requirements.[70] However, as the court pointed out, where a contract is capable of more than one interpretation, one leading to invalidity and the other not, preference must be given to that which avoids the invalidity. So it was possible that the contract referred to two parties with identical names. In this regard Jafta JA quoted[71] with approval from the decision in *Intercontinental Exports (Pty) Ltd v Fowles*[72] where Smallberger JA remarked that '[e]ven if the two names [of the principal debtor and the surety] were identical, it would not follow as a matter of course that they referred to the same person. The parties might, for instance, be father and son who happen to have the same names, a not uncommon occurrence'. The court in *Inventive Labour* thus held that the contract formally complied with the requirements of section 6 and also ordered rectification in view of the fact that all the requirements for rectification had been met.[73]

---

[68] 2006 (3) SA 107 (SCA).
[69] para 6, at 110D-E.
[70] In our law a person cannot stand surety for his or her own debt (*Nedbank Ltd v Van Zyl* 1990 (2) SA 469 (A) at 475E-I.
[71] para 10, at 111D-E.
[72] 1999 (2) SA 1045 (SCA) at 1053 D-E.
[73] Unfortunately Jafta JA did not deem it necessary to determine whether the decisions in *Republican Press (Pty) Ltd v Martin Murray Associates CC and Others* 1996 (2) SA 246 (N) and *Nuform Formwork & Scaffolding (Pty) Ltd v Natscaff CC and Others* 2003 (2) SA 56 (D) were correctly decided because he was of the opinion that they could be distinguished (para 13, at 111H-I). In *Republican Press* the name of a particular company appeared in the document as both surety and principal debtor, whereas in *Nuform Formwork* the name of a close corporation was inserted in the above capacities. In both instances it was held that the suretyship did not comply with the formalities required by section 6. The upshot of this is that the distinguishing feature of *Inventive Labour* is that the identical names were those of a natural person, which rendered the document rectifiable: it probably would not have been rectifiable had the case concerned a juristic person. It is submitted that this

The *onus* of proving that the requirements for rectification are met is on the party who seeks it.[74] The practical issue is often whether a surety can resist summary judgment by showing that he has a *bona fide* defence to the claim. Here the court decides not on the whether there is a balance of probabilities in favour of the defence put forward but simply on whether the facts on which the defence is based have been fully disclosed and whether they reveal a *bona fide* defence good in law if they can be proved. Even where these requirements are not satisfied the court has a discretion to refuse summary judgment.[75]

(e) Signing the document 'in blank'

Sureties are often for reasons of commercial convenience required to sign suretyship documents 'in blank', that is to sign documents in which there are blank spaces, where the name of the debtor, the creditor and details of the debt ought to appear, leaving it to the creditor—or some other person—to fill in the details in due course in accordance with a mandate, express or implied, granted by the surety. Naturally if the creditor is fraudulent and exceeds the mandate given him to complete the document, the surety will not be bound. But suppose the document is after signature properly filled in as intended; does it comply with section 6?

The answer which the Appellate Division gave to this question in *Fourlamel (Pty) Ltd v Maddison*[76] was a clear no. The court held that section 6 required the surety to sign a written document which embodied the contract of suretyship; and that a document which omitted essentials of a suretyship could not result in a valid suretyship even if later completed as the surety and creditor intended. Miller JA said the following in this regard:

> In the case of an agreement which is not by law required to be in writing, it may be that a document signed by a party before the terms of the agreement had been embodied therein would be binding upon him in the absence of fraud or *error* in connection with

---

is indeed a fine distinction and that an element of chance actually determine the *prima facie* validity of the deed of suretyship. In *Republican Press* Hurt J made the point that 'if there *are* indeed two parties to the suretyship undertaking who have identical names, there will be no need for a rectification of the document ...' (at 251D–E). However, it has been pointed out that the 'formality requirements must not be allowed to become an unnecessary stumbling-block to rectification and, consequently, to giving effect to the true intention of the contracting parties' (per Smalberger JA in *Intercontinental Exports (Pty) Ltd v Fowles* supra para 11 at 1051I-J). Still, we believe that there is considerable merit in the view expressed by Minette Nortjé in the 1999 *Annual Survey* at 171: '[E]ither the judiciary should opt for strict formalism by refusing rectification of formal contracts, or it ought to follow an equitable approach based on the facts of each case'.

[74] *Adrianatos v Caradas' Estate and Another* 1946 CPD 455 at 458; *Bardopoulos and Macrides v Miltiadous* 1947 (4) SA 860 (W) at 863-4; *Lazarus v Gorfinkel* 1988 (4) SA 123 (C) at 131. In order to discharge such *onus* the claimant has to show on a preponderance of probability that the deed of suretyship, because of a *bona fide* mutual mistake, does not reflect the common intention or antecedent agreement of the parties (*Lazarus v Gorfinkel* 1988 (4) SA 123 (C) at 131D-F).

[75] See generally *Maharaj v Barclays National Bank Ltd* 1976 (1) SA 418(A) at 426A-E as applied in *Tesven CC and Another v South African Bank of Athens* 2000 (1) SA 268 (A) at 275D-276E.

[76] 1977 (1) SA 333 (A). A different view had been taken in the same case in the Witwatersrand Local Division (*sub nom Fourlamel (Pty) Ltd v Penguin Heating and Air Conditioning (Pty) Ltd and Others* 1975 (4) SA 501 (W)), but the Transvaal Provincial Division's view (1976 (1) SA 969 (T)) was the same as the Appellate Division's. See also DJ Joubert 'Blanko Spasies' (1973) 36 *THRHR* 285; BA Blum 'Agreements Signed in Blank' (1977) 94 *SALJ* 395 and NJ Grové *Die Formaliteitsvereiste by Borgstelling* unpublished LLM dissertation, University of Pretoria (1984) 119 ff.

the recording of the terms subsequent to his signature.... But, where the terms of a contract are required by statute to be embodied in a document and signed by a particular party as a manifestation of his assent to such terms, there are considerable difficulties, both notionally and practically, in the way of acceptance that insertion by another of the terms of the agreement after the party has appended his signature to a blank piece of paper, constitutes compliance with such statute.[77]

However, the breadth of this conclusion was doubted in *Jurgens and Others v Volkskas Bank Ltd*[78] by Hoexter JA (Hefer, Goldstone, Howie JJA and Kriegler AJA concurring). In *Fourlamel (Pty) Ltd v Maddison* the incomplete suretyships were delivered to the creditor for the creditor to complete. But in *Jurgens and Others v Volkskas Bank Ltd*, the suretyships, although incomplete when signed, were completed by the agents of the surety before delivery to the creditor. There was no way in which the creditor could tell that the documents had been signed while incomplete and the court was rightly reluctant to see that defence succeed. Hoexter JA said:

> ...it is quite immaterial whether the surety signs the document only after all the material terms have been written therein or whether the surety signs the documents first and thereafter, by his own hand or that of his agent, completes the document by filling in the material terms. In either case the surety's signature serves to authenticate the document...[79]

Jurgens and Others v Volkskas Bank Ltd reflects the commercial reality—where sureties frequently sign documents with blank spaces leaving it to their subordinates to ensure before delivery that the document is completed in accordance with the surety's wishes. Where the subordinates do complete the document in accordance with the surety's mandate and before delivery to the creditor, it would be unfair to allow the surety to evade responsibility by sheltering behind the formalities legislation—as was attempted in *Jurgens and Others v Volkskas Bank Ltd*.

---

[77] At 342. In *Ellis v Trust Bank of Africa Ltd* 1981 (1) SA 733 (N), a suretyship agreement which left blank the amount of the creditor's indebtedness was held void. See also *Commercial Bank of Namibia Ltd v Trans Continental Trading (Namibia) and Others* 1992 (2) SA 66 (Nm).

[78] 1993(1) SA 214 (A) at 222C-D.

[79] The court followed *Standard Bank of SA Ltd v Jaap de Villiers Beleggings (Edms) Bpk* 1978 (3) SA 955 (W) where the court preferred the moment of delivery of the signed document to that of signature (at 958A-G). In *Progress Knitting and Textiles Ltd v Nefic Investments (Pty) Ltd and Others* 1992 (4) SA 105 (N) a clause in the deeds of suretyship provided that the 'suretyship shall become operative and binding on acceptance by the creditor...'. By the time of acceptance of the deeds of suretyship by the creditor, the blank spaces, present when the surety had signed, had been filled in and the deeds had been completed. The acceptance of the contracts by the creditor was communicated to the sureties. Levinsohn J held that the contracts of suretyship were 'entered into' when the acceptance took place. At that time the documents had been completed and all the requisite formalities had been complied with since the sureties expressly or by necessary implication authorised whoever completed the blank spaces to do so on their behalf, a situation which would frequently occur in commercial life.

Where the surety raises the defence that the debtor's name did not appear on the document when he (the surety) signed it, the onus rests on the plaintiff creditor to show that the document complied with the statutory formalities (*Stewart & Lloyds of SA Ltd v Croydon Engineering Mining Supplies (Pty) Ltd and Others* 1981 (1) SA 305 (W)). See also AJ Kerr 'The Onus of Proof: Complete and Incomplete Contracts' (1973) 90 *SALJ* 217.

The difficulty with the approach of Hoexter JA is that, if it is 'immaterial' whether signature preceded completion, it provides no principled basis for distinguishing between such a case—where the suretyship is completed by the agent of the surety after signature by the surety – and the case where the suretyship is completed by the creditor after delivery of the document to him – which all are agreed does not result in a valid suretyship. What must be made clear is that, while the completion of a suretyship may be a process rather than a single event, and it may be 'immaterial' which event in that process occurs first, the process must be complete before delivery of the suretyship to the creditor.[80]

(f) Non-essential blank spaces

What is the position if a blank space relates to non-essential terms of the suretyship, eg one in which the upper limit of the surety's liability was to have been specified or dealing with a choice of *domicilium citandi et executandi?* In *Pizani and Another v First Consolidated Holdings (Pty) Ltd*[81] the Appellate Division considered this question. Although everything will depend on a proper interpretation of the contract, it seems clear that such blanks do not leave the contract inchoate and unenforceable.[82] Generally if a surety who signs a document in which a blank space in a clause renders that clause meaningless, this simply indicates that the clause did not apply to the suretyship thereby concluded.[83]

Of course, it may be shown that in particular circumstances the parties intended that completion of a particular clause was the *sine qua non* of their contract, in which case non-compliance would render the contract non-enforceable; but this would be because that was the parties' intention, not because the contract fell foul of section 6.

(g) Co-sureties and blank spaces

Often suretyship documents make provision for signature by a number of co-sureties and it may happen that only some of them sign, leaving blank spaces

---

[80] It may be tempting to suggest that in *Jurgens and Others v Volkskas Bank Ltd* the surety, having delivered an apparently valid suretyship to the creditor, should be estopped from raising the defence that the suretyship was only completed after signature. But this would be to allow estoppel to operate to prevent compliance with the law (section 6). See Rabie, *The Law of Estoppel in South Africa* (1991), 105-8. Interestingly though Hoexter AJA (*pere*) adopted a more flexible approach to this issue in his minority judgment in *Trust Bank van Afrika Bpk v Eksteen* 1964 (3) SA 402 (A) at 415H-416A which was followed in *Credit Corporation of SA Ltd v Botha* 1968 (4) SA 837 (N). Here a purchaser under a hire-purchase agreement was prevented from raising the defence that he had signed the agreement before it was complete and therefore it was invalid. Shearer J said that the statute was 'not designed to protect [purchasers] against persons innocent of the illegality...no consideration of public policy ... operates against the application of estoppel in [these] circumstances'(at 851F-852A). A similar approach to section 6 leaves *Fourlamel (Pty) Ltd v Maddison* intact but denies a defence in *Jurgens and Others v Volkskas Bank Ltd.*

[81] 1979 (1) SA 69 (A).

[82] At 80A-82A. A similar result was reached in *Standard Bank of SA Ltd v Jaap de Villiers Beleggings (Edms) Bpk* 1978 (3) SA 955 (W) at 959E.

[83] At 81G. This principle was applied in *Botha v Nedbank* 1981 (4) SA 949 (NC), in respect of a blank space in a clause providing that a certificate of balance issued by the manager of the 'blank' branch of the bank was sufficient proof of the principal debt and its amount. See also *Commercial Bank of Namibia Ltd v Trans Continental Trading (Namibia) and Others* 1992 (2) SA 66 (Nm).

awaiting signature in the document. Can a co-surety, who did sign, resist the creditor's claim on the grounds that these additional signatures are lacking? In *Nelson v Hodgetts Timbers (East London) (Pty) Ltd*[84] it was held that where one of two planned co-sureties did not sign the suretyship document, the surety who did sign was not bound. The essence of the court's decision was that since *inter alia* the document used the plural 'we' to refer to the co-sureties throughout, the parties' intention was to enter a contract of joint suretyship. Put differently, this was not a case in which there were to be two separate suretyship contracts which happened to be expressed in the same document.[85] Thus the second surety's signature was required for compliance with section 6.[86]

In *Industrial Development Corporation of SA Ltd v See Bee Holdings (Pty) Ltd and Others*,[87] however, Grosskopf J questioned whether it was necessary to have resort to section 6. 'When properly analysed', he said, 'the question is not one of form ... but one of substance, namely, whether the parties intended that an enforceable contract would be established even if one or more of the proposed sureties did not consent to the proposed contract. This question would have arisen even if no formalities had been required ...'.[88] This reasoning, it is submitted, is sounder than that of the Appellate Division in *Nelson v Hodgetts Timbers (East London) (Pty) Ltd.*[89]

---

[84] 1973 (3) SA 37 (A) on appeal from *Hodgetts Timbers (East London) (Pty) Ltd v HBC Properties (Pty) Ltd and Another* 1972 (4) SA 208 (E). *Nelson v Hodgetts Timbers (East London) (Pty) Ltd* 1973 (3) SA 37 (A) was followed in *Société Commerciale de Moteurs v Ackermann* 1981 (3) SA 422 (A) at 439G.

[85] At 45G-46F. The learned Chief Justice was also influenced by the fact that a surety might well wish to bind himself with a co-surety, and make his obligation conditional on his co-surety's signature; for then he would know that if called on to pay he would be able to turn to his co-surety to share the burden.

[86] There have been a number of cases in which the court has interpreted various suretyships in order to determine whether the parties' intention was that there should be joint or individual suretyship, and have consequently either held sureties liable in the absence of their co-sureties' signature or vice versa. See *Ryan Nigel Corporation (Cape) (Pty) Ltd v Peires and Another* 1976 (3) SA 660 (C); *Manufacturers Development Co (Pty) Ltd v Repcar Holdings (Pty) Ltd and Others* 1975 (2) SA 779 (W) (distinguishing *Nelson v Hodgetts Timbers (East London) (Pty) Ltd* 1973 (3) SA 37 (A) since *in casu* 'I/We' rather than 'We' was used in the document) and *Société Commerciale de Moteurs v Ackermann* 1981 (3) SA 422 (A).

[87] 1978 (4) SA 136 (C).

[88] At 138.

[89] 1973 (3) SA 37 (A). It is submitted that the court in this case should perhaps have asked what the effect would have been had the creditor released one of the co-sureties, ie that the release of a surety by the creditor is for the benefit of the other co-sureties, to the extent of such release. This would mean that the surety who did sign the deed of suretyship should, in principle, be liable for half the amount in the case of a deed of suretyship where provision is made for two co-sureties, such as in *Nelson*. There may, however, have been the implied understanding that the one co-surety would only be prepared to undertake the suretyship obligation if the other co-surety would also be liable. *Nelson's* case can thus be distinguished from those cases where the 'co-sureties' intended to undertake separate liabilities. See also NJ Grové *Die Formaliteitsvereiste by Borgstelling* unpublished LLM dissertation, University of Pretoria (1984) 172 and Ellison Kahn (gen ed) *Contract and Mercantile Law through the Cases* vol II *Specific Contracts and Mercantile Law* 2 ed (1985) by David Zeffertt, JT Pretorius & Coenraad Visser 782.

(h) Oral variations of a suretyship contract

Oral variations of a suretyship contract do not comply with section 6, and are ineffective.[90] Unless otherwise agreed, however, oral *cancellation* of a suretyship contract is possible.[91]

5. Avals and their liability

The proviso to section 6 of the General Laws Amendment Act excepts from the operation of the section 'the liability of the signer of an aval under the laws relating to negotiable instruments'. The contact of aval is one way in which the obligations of the drawer, acceptor and indorser of a negotiable instrument can

---

[90] *Oceanair (Natal) (Pty) Ltd v Sher* 1980 (1) SA 317 (D) at 322E-F; *Nedfin Bank Ltd v Muller and Others* 1981 (4) SA 229 (N) at 232B-E; *Plascon-Evans Paints (Transvaal) Ltd v Virginia Glass Works (Pty) Ltd and Others* 1983 (1) SA 465 (O) at 471; *Morgan and Another v Brittan Boustred Ltd* 1992 (2) SA 775 (A) at 782I; *Ferreira and Others v SAPDC (Trading) Ltd* 1983 (1) SA 235 (A); *African Life Property Holdings (Pty) Ltd v Score Food Holdings Ltd* 1995 (2) SA 230 (A) at 239C. Louise Tager 'The Effect of Non-variation Clauses in Contracts' (1976) 93 *SALJ* 423; NJ Grové 'Borgkontrakte, Mondelinge Wysigings en Kansellasie' 1983 *De Rebus* 201 and NJ Grové *Die Formaliteitsvereiste by Borgstelling* unpublished LLM dissertation, University of Pretoria (1984) 193 ff.

[91] *Visser v Theodore Sassen & Son (Pty) Ltd* 1982 (2) SA 320 (C). In *Tsaperas and Others v Boland Bank Ltd* 1996 (1) SA 719 (A) Harms JA doubted the correctness of the approach of Botha JA (in his minority judgment) in *Ferreira and Others v SAPDC (Trading) Ltd* to this issue (at 725B). However, he made it plain that 'there are no formalities for a valid cancellation [of a suretyship]' (at 724C).

Where two co-sureties have executed the same deed of suretyship it is possible to release the one by oral cancellation while the other remains bound (*Visser v Theodore Sassen & Son (Pty) Ltd* 1982 (2) SA 320 (C) at 322E-323H). Often, however, a co-surety's obligation will be conditional on the other surety remaining bound.

Clauses that provide that the suretyship may not be cancelled or terminated without the written agreement of the parties must be approached with care. In *Morgan and Another v Brittan Boustred Ltd* 1992 (2) SA 775 (A) it was said that although the word 'cancelled' was often used to indicate a cancellation by agreement between the parties, ie a consensual cancellation or one brought about by the exercise of a right to terminate, this was not always so. Where the contract of suretyship thus provided that a continuing suretyship 'may not be withdrawn, revoked or cancelled without the creditor's prior written consent', the clause 'was intended to deal with the situation where the surety attempts to revoke the suretyship; not with the case where there is a discharge consequent on a mutual agreement between the creditor and surety, or (*a fortiori*), where the creditor waives his rights under the suretyship' (et 784). On the other hand, a clause that provided that 'this deed of suretyship and my liabilities thereunder will only be terminated by the bank's written consent thereto' was taken by Harms JA in *Tsaperas and Others v Boland Bank Ltd* 1996 (1) SA 719 (A) to preclude an oral agreement to terminate. Unlike the clause in *Morgan and Another v Brittan Boustred Ltd* this clause covered the accrued liabilities under the suretyship which the surety had no right unilaterally to terminate. Thus this clause precluded the ending of the suretyship by an alleged oral agreement with the bank (at 724E-G). The decision in *Cecil Nurse (Pty) Ltd v Nkola* 2008 (2) SA 441 (SCA) consists mainly of an analysis of the evidence presented to the court. The most important legal principle one can extract from the decision is that where the signed contract of suretyship contains a provision that alterations to it would be binding only if agreed to in writing by the creditor, the *onus* would be on the surety to prove that the creditor had in fact agreed to any purported amendments or alterations (at 446E-F, para 19).

be secured.[92] The 'signer of an aval' is a surety who contracts his suretyship on a bill of exchange, cheque or promissory note itself by signing[93] an aval upon it, that is to say, if he qualifies his signature by words which indicate that he is a surety, or by placing his signature, without any qualifying words, on the back of the instrument before delivery of it to, or endorsement of it by, the payee.[94] Someone who signs an instrument after the payee has endorsed it specially to another, if

---

[92] Section 17 of the Bills of Exchange Amendment Act 56 of 2000 inserted a new section 54A to the Bills of Exchange Act 34 of 1964. Section 54A(1) now provides that the liabilities of the parties to a bill or note may be secured by an aval. A person may bind himself as surety for the due performance by the parties of their obligations on a bill by a contract of suretyship extraneous to the bill, or by a contract of suretyship by the bill itself, ie an aval. A contract of suretyship extraneous to the bill must comply with the requirements of section 6 (FR Malan, JT Pretorius & SF du Toit *Malan on Bills of Exchange, Cheques and Promissory Notes in South African Law* (2009) 5ed para 152 ('Malan Bills') ; AN Oelofse & JT Pretorius 'Of Suretyships, Avals and Accommodation Parties' (1991) 3 *SA Merc LJ* 260 at 262). See, in general, Malan *Bills* paras 152-4; FR Malan, AN Oelofse, W le R de Vos, JT Pretorius & C Nagel *Provisional Sentence on Bills of Exchange, Cheques and Promissory Notes* (1986) 203-23 (Malan *Provisional Sentence*); FR Malan, AN Oelofse & JT Pretorius *Proposals for the Reform of the Bills of Exchange Act, 1964* (1988) 309 ff (Malan *Proposals*;) and CJ Rowland in 'Some Aspects of the Contract of Aval' (1965) 28 *THRHR* 30. This part of the book is based on Malan *Provisional Sentence* and Malan *Proposals*.

[93] The aval's liability is founded not only on his signature (Malan *Bills* para 152; *Sonfred (Pty) Ltd v Papert* 1962 (2) SA 140 (W)), but on his intention to be bound. Malan *Bills* ibid submits that the liability of the signer of an aval arises not only from his signature and his intention to be bound but also from his delivery of the bill to the payee or the person in whose favour the suretyship is undertaken.

[94] *Moti & Co v Cassim's Trustee* 1924 AD 720 at 725, 733, 740, 744. Section 54A (2) of the Bills of Exchange Act of 1964 now provides that a 'person signs a bill or note as the signer of an aval where he signs the bill or note, and by words such as 'as aval', 'as surety' or 'as guarantor' expressly indicates that he is a surety.' The proviso to this section provides that the unqualified signature of a person other than the drawer, maker, drawee or payee made on the back of the bill or note payable to order before indorsement by the payee shall be sufficient for such indication. The plaintiff in *Constantaras v Anagnostopoulos* 1988 (3) SA 769 (W) sought provisional sentence against the defendant in respect of two cheques which the defendant had signed as surety and co-principal debtor (ie as aval) and which were subsequently dishonoured by non-payment. One of the defences raised by defendant was that he was not liable as an aval because of the sequence in which he and the drawer had put their respective signatures on the cheques: when he affixed his signature to the cheques, the cheques had not been signed as yet by the drawer. This defence was argued along the following lines: *(a)* an aval is a real undertaking of suretyship signified on and in respect of the obligation evidenced by a bill of exchange; *(b)* the document on which it is recorded must accordingly be a bill of exchange; *(c)* to this end the instrument must comply with the definitions of the terms 'bill' and 'cheque' in ss 1 and 2 of the Bills of Exchange Act 34 of 1964. It was therefore argued that since an unsigned cheque does not comply with the requirement in section 2(1) in that a bill or a cheque 'must be signed by' the drawer, the signature of an aval put on a 'cheque' before the drawer has signed it is a nullity. Kriegler J rightly rejected this defence and held that '[t]he subtlety necessarily involved in regarding the document as something unknown and unnamed until the moment the drawer has put the last dot of his signature on it, is unrealistic, not consonant with commercial or legal parlance and inconsistent with the very language of the Act' (at 772E). As pointed out in an interesting note on this case by Coenraad Visser 'Aval on an Unsigned Cheque' in (1988) 105 *SALJ* 651 at 653-5, the law may indeed be uncertain as regards the question whether the contract of aval becomes complete and irrevocable only on *delivery* of the relevant instrument. Kriegler J expressed the view that the defendant's obligations as signer of an aval arose *at the latest* on the delivery of the cheques (at 773F-H). If this view is correct it would mean that until delivery of the instrument has taken place, it would be possible, for example, for the aval to delete his signature and thus avoid liability on the bill. The learned author submits at 655 that the position needs to be clarified. See in this regard Malan *Proposals* 308 ff. See also Grové *Die Formaliteitsvereiste by Borgstelling* unpublished LLM dissertation, University of Pretoria (1984) 150 ff.

he so signs before the endorsee has signed it, is also an aval.[95] Similarly, someone who purports to accept a bill of exchange of which he is not the drawee is also an aval.[96]

Previously it was a controversial question whether the person who had signed an aval incurred the liabilities of an endorser to a holder in due course, by reason of section 54 of the Bills of Exchange Act 34 of 1964, which provides that such liability attaches to any person 'who signs a bill otherwise than as drawer or acceptor'.[97] The precise import and meaning of section 54 is not clear.[98] The main source of uncertainty is that it is not clear how to reconcile the liability created by section 54 with the South African common-law liability of aval.[99] The contract of aval is in essence a contract of suretyship. The liability of the signer of an aval, like that of other parties to an instrument, is founded on an existing contract on the instrument.[100] The difficulties encountered in reconciling the liability created by section 54 and the common-law liability of the signer of an aval have been observed by many writers and need not be detailed here.[101] The root of the problem is that, although section 54 is based on section 56 of the United Kingdom Bills of Exchange Act, English law does not recognise the institution of an aval, whereas the South African common law does.

These uncertainties have now been clarified by the Bills of Exchange Amendment Act 56 of 2000. Section 54A of the Bills of Exchange Act (inserted by s 17 of the Amendment Act) now seeks to codify the liability of the signer of an aval by

---

[95] *Moti & Co v Cassim's Trustee* 1924 AD 720 at 729.

[96] *Moti & Co v Cassim's Trustee* 1924 AD 720 at 728, 729; and see *Bentley Maudesley & Company Ltd v 'Carburol' (Pty) Ltd and Another* 1949 (4) SA 873 (C) at 876. One who signs an aval is a surety, and if there be two or more signatories to the same aval, they are co-sureties. This view is confirmed by the provisions of section 54A(2) of the Bills of Exchange Act. If the instrument be negotiated, the rights of the payee, or of the endorsee in the instance mentioned, pass with the instrument, *ipso facto*, by the mere fact of negotiation, to a subsequent holder, without the need of a further or separate cession. See *Peimer v Finbro Furnishers (Pty) Ltd* 1936 AD 177 at 186; *FJK Syndicate v Du Preez and Smit* 1943 WLD 116 at 120, 121 and *Meer v General Industrial Credit Corporation (Pty) Ltd* 1947 (3) SA 330 (C) at 336.

[97] Section 54 is based on section 56 of the United Kingdom Bills of Exchange Act of 1882 (45 & 46 Vict c 61). See also Malan *Bills* para 152, Denis V Cowen & Leonard Gering *Cowen on The Law of Negotiable Instruments in South Africa* 4 ed (1966) 223 and *De Wet & Yeats Die Suid-Afrikaanse Kontraktereg en Handelsreg* 4 ed (1978) by JC de Wet and AH van Wyk 768. Note the difficulties experienced in English law in recognising an aval validly made on a foreign bill because of the terms of section 56: *G & H Montage Gmbh v Irvani* [1990] 1 WLR 667 (CA). See Christopher Forsyth 'The Recognition of an Aval by English Courts' (1992) 42 *International and Comparative LQ* 858.

[98] Malan *Provisional Sentence* 207 ff. See also CJ Nagel *Aspekte van Voorlopige en Summiere Vonnis in die Suid-Afrikaanse Tjekreg* unpublished LLD thesis, University of Pretoria (1987) 366 ff.

[99] Malan *Bills* para 239; Malan *Provisional Sentence* 219; NJ van der Merwe 'Enkele Probleme wat uit ons Wisselwetgewing Voortspruit' (1959) 22 *THRHR* 275 and Rowland 'Some Aspects of the Contract of Aval' (1965) 28 *THRHR* 30 at 31 ff.

[100] Malan *Bills* para 237.

[101] See, for example, Rowland 'Some Aspects of the Contract of Aval' (1965) 28 *THRHR* 30 at 31 ff; Malan *Bills* paras 238-9; Cowen & Gering *Cowen on The Law of Negotiable Instruments in South Africa* 4 ed (1966) 223 ff. In the extreme it has been suggested, somewhat harshly, that section 54 leaves no room for the institution of the aval vis-à-vis a holder in due course (Van der Merwe 'Enkele Probleme wat uit ons Wisselwetgewing Voortspruit' (1959) 22 *THRHR* 275 at 281 and see *National Bank of South Africa Ltd v Seligson* 1921 WLD 108 at 116). This view has not gained general acceptance (Malan *Provisional Sentence* 220 ff; *Lion Mill Manufacturing Co (Pty) Ltd and Another v New York Shipping Co (Pty) Ltd* 1974 (4) SA 984 (T) at 990; *Moti & Co v Cassim's Trustee* 1924 AD 720 at 744; *National Acceptance Co (Pty) Ltd v Robertson and Another* 1938 CPD 175 at 179).

providing that the liabilities of the parties to a bill or note may be secured by an aval. Section 54A(2) provides for the format of the undertaking as aval: 'A person signs a bill or note as the signer of an aval where he signs the bill or note, and by words such as 'as aval', 'as surety' or 'as guarantor' expressly indicates that he is a surety' . The proviso to this section states that the unqualified signature of a person other than the drawer, maker, drawee or payee made on the back of the bill or note payable to order before indorsement by the payee is sufficient for the indication that the signatory signed as aval. Section 54A(4) provides that the signer of an aval is liable jointly and severally with and as surety for the party for whom he has given his aval or is deemed to have given his aval.[102]

If the signer of an aval qualifies his signature by adding the words 'and co-principal debtor', as, for instance, if the words ' as surety and co-principal debtor' appear above or beneath his signature, the signatory, like any other person who binds himself in such fashion, is nevertheless a surety;[103] likewise if he so signs beneath the signature of the maker.[104]

Apart from the procedure of becoming a surety by signing an aval, although it is not permissible to lead evidence to establish an oral agreement contradictory of the instrument,[105] it is permissible to lead evidence to establish a contemporaneous agreement disclosing the true relationship between the parties to the instrument. Accordingly, it is competent for a party to an instrument who, in fact, signed it as an accommodation party to establish that fact as against the accommodated party, and to do so by means of extrinsic evidence; the effect of this is that, as between them, he is a surety for the accommodated party.[106] But if two

---

[102] Section 54A(3) provides that the aval may specify for whom he has given his aval and that if he does not so specify he will be deemed to have given his aval for the drawer or the maker, as the case may be. In terms of the Roman-Dutch law, the signer of an aval could not invoke the common law privileges of a surety, namely the *beneficia excussionis et divisionis*. South African courts have thus far taken a different view and have held that the signer of an aval was entitled to the *benficia divisionis, excussionis* and *cedendarum actionum* (Malan *Bills* para 152; Malan *Provisional Sentence* 204ff). The upshot of this is that because the aval was entitled to raise these privileges his liability was not regarded as liquid and provisional sentence could not be taken against him (*Dickinson v South African General Electric Co (Pty) Ltd* 1973 (2) SA 620 (A) at 641; Malan *Bills* par 152). It is submitted that by providing in section 54A(3) that the aval is jointly and severally liable, the courts will in future revive Roman-Dutch law and regard the aval as having renounced the common-law benefits so that an action for provisional sentence would be available against the aval (Malan *Proposals* 319).

[103] *Maasdorp v Graaff-Reinet Board of Executors* (1909) 3 Buch AC 482 at 490; *Peimer v Finbro Furnishers (Pty) Ltd* 1936 AD 177. See also JSA Fourie 'Die Aanspreeklikheid van die Borg en die Hoofskuldenaar' (1978) 41 *THRHR* 307.

[104] *Shuter v Ridgway* 1926 NPD 149.

[105] *Cassiem v Standard Bank of South Africa Ltd* 1930 AD 366. See also DT Zeffertt and A Paizes *Parol Evidence with Particular Reference to Contract* (1986) 101 ff.

[106] *Gould v Ekermans* 1929 TPD 96; *De Wet v Joubert* 1931 CPD 123; *Estate Silbert & Co v De Jager* 1933 CPD 88; *Moosa v Mahomed* 1939 TPD 271 at 284; *Israelsohn v Newman* 1949 (3) SA 1178 (W) at 1182; *Israelsohn v Newman & Sons Ltd* 1949 (4) SA 300 (C) at 304, 306; *Van der Spuy v Levy* 1921 TPD 581. An accommodation party is one of the ordinary parties to a bill but is also someone who signs the instrument without receiving value for it and does so for the purpose of lending his name to some other person (Malan *Bills* para 69; Cowen & Gering *Cowen on The Law of Negotiable Instruments in South Africa* 4 ed (1966) 203 ff). Although there is some authority for the view that an accommodation party should be regarded as being in the same position as a surety (*Estate Silbert & Co v De Jager* 1933 CPD 88), the better view, it is submitted, is that an accommodation party is not a surety for the party accommodated or for anybody else, but that he incurs liability as drawer,

persons exchange promissory notes each for the same amount and due on the same date, in order to accommodate each other, these are not accommodation notes because each person receives value for what he gives, in the form of the note he receives from the other.[107]

Although extrinsic evidence is admissible to establish that a party is in truth a surety, such evidence is not available against a holder for value, to whom he is liable whether or not the holder knew, when he took the instrument, that he was an accommodation party.[108] But if the holder knows, or comes to know, of the suretyship, we suggest that, like any other creditor, he is bound in his dealings with the principal debtor and with other sureties not to act to the prejudice of the surety in question, on pain of discharging him from liability, in full or in part, depending on the circumstances.[109]

6. Conditional suretyships

Suretyship may be undertaken conditionally,[110] with the consequence that unless and until the condition is fulfilled no suretyship comes into existence, that is to say, the suretyship obligation is subject to a condition precedent.[111] Without suspending the coming into existence of the suretyship, the surety may stipulate a condition before the performance of which he cannot be sued for payment, for

---

acceptor or endorser, as the case may be (Malan *Bills* para 85; Cowen & Gering *Cowen on The Law of Negotiable Instruments in South Africa* 4 ed (1966) 203-7). In fact, the cardinal difference between an accommodation party and a surety is that an accommodation party binds himself to the holder of an instrument to pay the instrument, subject, of course, to the provisions of the Bills of Exchange Act, but irrespective of any default by the accommodated party vis-à-vis the holder (*De Wet & Yeats Die Suid-Afrikaanse Kontraktereg en Handelsreg* at 785-6; Malan *Bills* para 69). The liability of the surety, on the other hand, is conditional on the default by the principal debtor and arises only, it is submitted, when the principal debtor defaults with respect to his obligations towards the creditor (GF Lubbe 'Die Onderskeid tussen Borgtog en Ander Vorme van Persoonlike Sekerheidstelling' (1984) 47 *THRHR* 383 385-7). The aforesaid is true whether or not the surety has in fact waived the benefit of excussion. See also *Levi v Almog* 1990 (1) SA 541 (W) and AN Oelofse & JT Pretorius 'Of Suretyships, Avals and Accommodation Parties' (1991) 3 *SA Merc LJ* 260.
[107] *Consolidated Agencies v Agjee* 1948 (4) SA 179 (N).
[108] Section 26(2) of the Bills of Exchange Act 34 of 1964; *Oak v Lumsden* (1884) 3 SC 144 at 154; *Kowarsky & Co v Sable* 1923 WLD 156. See also Malan *Bills* paras 69 and CJ Nagel 'Enkele Gedagtes oor die Akkomodasiefiguur' (1986) 18 *De Jure* 23.
[109] There are conflicting decisions about this; *Kowarsky & Co v Sable* 1923 WLD 156 is against the proposition, but *Estate Silbert & Co v De Jager* 1933 CPD 88 at 97 supports it. It seems to have support also from *Gould v Ekermans* 1929 TPD 96. The facts of this case were somewhat unusual: the holder knew of the suretyship but failed to recover because of conduct on the part of his agents prejudicial to the surety. And in *Haffajee v Ramdhani* 1947 (1) SA 823 (A) at 830 SchreinerJA said 'if one party to a note stands to another in the relationship of surety to principal, he is ... entitled to the protection which the law affords to a surety, where the creditor has released the principal'. This does not appear to be limited to a release in the sense of an express abandonment of the creditor's claim, but to cover any set of circumstances which has the effect of releasing the principal, to the prejudice of the surety, in that he will then be denied his right to recourse against the principal even although he has become the holder of the note. Nevertheless, it must be noted that Schreiner JA expressly refrained from deciding the conflict between the two cases first mentioned above.
[110] D 46.1.6.1; V 46.1.3; Gr 3.3.23; Sch 302; P 371.
[111] As in *Buyskes and Others, Trustees of Du Toit v De Kock and Others* (1832) 2 Menz 12 where the suretyship was subject to the debtor passing a mortgage bond in favour of the creditor. In *Baumann v Thomas* 1920 AD 428 the surety made his undertaking subject to the provision to him of security by the principal debtor. Cf *Moosa v Schindler Lifts (SA) Ltd* 1955 (2) PH A56 (A).

example, that notice be given him of the debtor's default; or he may stipulate a condition the breach of which on the part of the creditor releases him.[112]

A surety may stipulate a place for payment or may undertake liability from a certain time or to a certain time,[113] in the sense either that he becomes surety for debts incurred before the expiration of that time or that his liability ends with the expiration of that time.[114] Or he may limit his liability to default committed by the principal debtor within a stated time. He may stipulate for remuneration[115] from the debtor[116] or for the debtor providing him (without the knowledge even of the creditor) with the promise of a further party or other security for performance of the debtor's obligations to him, the surety.[117]

A *pactum commissorium*[118] which purports to entitle the creditor to retain the security if the debt be not paid on due date is not permitted. This accords with the law in relation to pledge; such a pact is illegal in pledge as being unduly oppressive to debtors.[119] So also it may not be agreed that the debtor shall forfeit some property to the surety if the debt be not duly paid, though it is permissible, when the debt has become due, to take over the asset at a fair price.[120]

7. Stamp duties

The Stamp Duties Act 77 of 1968 has been repealed by the Revenue Laws Amendment Act 60 of 2008 and no stamp duty is payable on a contract of suretyship.

---

[112] *Texas Co (SA) Ltd v Webb and Tomlinson* 1927 NPD 24.
[113] D 46.1.6.1, Gr 3.3.23, Sch 302.
[114] Cf *Feldman Ltd v Sulski* 1954 (4) SA 665 (W), and on appeal *sub nom Sulski v Feldman Ltd* 1956 (1) SA 759 (A). See Chapter VI for the effect of such stipulations as to time.
[115] V 46.1.32.
[116] *Lever v Buhrmann* 1925 TPD 254 at 263.
[117] D 46.1.4 pr; V 46.1.6. See also *Eager v Clarke and Others* (1933) 2 Menz 15. See also *Buyskes and Others, Trustees of Du Toit v De Kock and Others* (1832) 2 Menz 12; *Baumann v Thomas* 1920 AD 428; *Rutowitz's Flour Mills v The Master and Others* 1934 TPD 163.
[118] V 46.1.32.
[119] *Mapenduka v Ashington* 1919 AD 343. For a full discussion, see *Wille's Law of Mortgage and Pledge in South Africa* (1987) 3 ed by TJ Scott and Susan Scott 124-6.
[120] V 46.1.32. See also Scott & Scott *op cit* 126.

CHAPTER VI

The Interpretation of the Contract

		Page
1. General principles		87
(a) The intention of the parties is determined by the language used in the suretyship.		88
(b) Unclear and ambiguous language: the use of 'surrounding circumstances' to determine the parties' intention		89
(c) Resolving ambiguity by restrictive interpretation in favour of the surety		90
(d) Resolving ambiguity through the assumption that the parties negotiated in good faith		91
(e) Tacit terms		91
2. Particular examples of restrictive interpretation		95
3. Whether particular words amount to undertaking liability as a surety		98

1. General principles

The general principles relating to the interpretation of contracts are applicable to the contract of suretyship.[1] Since this is the case, it may be thought that this chapter is redundant; reference can readily be made to an account of the construction of contracts in one of the standard texts dealing with the general principles of the law of contract. However, it is useful to show how the courts have applied those general principles to contracts of suretyship for, although cases on the construction of other contracts are frequently relied upon by the courts in suretyship cases, problems peculiar to the law of suretyship do arise and solutions peculiar to the law of suretyship are adopted.

---

[1] Some old and older authorities (V 46.1.12; B 40 ff; cf Wessels paras 3890-9) are open to the interpretation that an especially 'strict and adverse construction' should be given to a suretyship, in order not to burden the surety with another's obligation unless he had clearly agreed to undertake liability for that obligation. Upon analysis, however, it is clear that all that is being said is that the language used governs the transaction. See, for instance, Pothier (P 404): '[I]n order to judge of the extent of the obligation of the surety, great attention must be paid to the terms of the engagement.'

Thus rules of construction for suretyships stricter than those in use for other contracts were rejected by Innes CJ in *Glenn Brothers v Commercial General Agency Co Ltd* 1905 TS 737 where he said (at 741): 'I think the proper rule is that without bias—without prejudice one way or the other—we should ascertain from the words of the document [*in casu* a deed of suretyship] the intention of the parties, and if the words have a clear and definite meaning we should give effect to it.' See further Caney J in *Patel v Patel and Another* 1968 (4) SA 51 (D) at 55D-H and *Linford v Heynes Mathew Limited* 1915 CPD 531 at 533. It is thus clear that 'whatever the older authorities said about a strict interpretation of a suretyship contract, the general principles for the interpretation of documents apply to the interpretation of contracts of suretyship' (per Caney J in *Patel v Patel and Another* 1968 (4) SA 51 (D) at 55B).

(a) The intention of the parties is determined by the language used in the suretyship

Thus, inevitably, first and foremost, the intention of the parties must be ascertained from the language they have used in the contract itself, giving effect to the ordinary meaning of their words and to the grammatical sense in which they have expressed themselves, unless it appears from the context that both parties intended their language to bear a different meaning.[2] If that language is clear, we must give effect to it and in so doing presume that the parties knew the meaning of the words they used.[3]

The general approach of the courts was described in these graphic words by Kriegler J: 'The interpretation of a written document is not an exercise in the arcane. It is a logical process in which the interpreter seeks to ascertain the intention of the draftsman as embodied in the instrument. The mutual intention of the parties to a bilateral contract is, of course, an abstraction. The primary method to find out what the abstraction was is to ask: What did the parties say? That does not mean picking away at words like a guinea-fowl down a row of maize seed. One looks at the language used with common sense and perspective.'[4] As the last two sentences of this passage show, the courts are not irrevocably bound to a purblind literalism; they are indeed bound to consider the contract as a whole.[5] As Rumpff CJ put it in *Swart en 'n Ander v Cape Fabrix (Pty) Ltd*:[6] 'Dit is ... vanselfsprekend dat 'n mens na die betrokke woorde moet kyk met inagneming van die aard en opset van die kontrak, en ook na die samehang van die woorde in die kontrak as geheel.' Thus reading the contract as a whole may reveal that a particular word or phrase (which might have an ordinary or conventional meaning) is used in a

---

[2] Thus Harms JA remarked in *Bock and Others v Duburoro Investments (Pty) Ltd* 2004 (2) SA 242 (SCA), para. 29 '...one should begin with the terms of the deed of suretyship in order to determine the rights and obligations of the respective parties'. The Supreme Court of Appeal has several times confirmed this approach in recent years holding that the abstract values of good faith, reasonableness and equity were not independent substantive rules that courts can employ to intervene in contractual relationships (*Brisley v Drotsky* 2002(4) SA 1 (SCA), Harms, Streicher and Brand JJA at para. 22 – 25; *Afrox Healthcare Bpk v Strydom* 2002 (6) SA 21 (SCA) Brand JA at para. 32). See, particularly, Brand JA's valuable article 'The Role of Good Faith, Equity and Fairness in the South African Law of Contract: The Influence of the Common Law and the Constitution' (2009) 126 *SALJ* 71. Cf Carole Lewis 'The Demise of the *Exceptio Doli*: Is there Another Route to Contractual Equity?' (1990) 107 *SALJ* 26 and Dale Hutchison 'Non-Variation Clauses in Contract: Any Escape from the *Shifren* Straightjacket?' (2001) 118 *SALJ* 720.

Of course a clause which properly interpreted is contrary to public policy – a concept now infused with constitutional values – will not be enforced. This is discussed below in Chapter XIII, Section 4.

[3] Innes CJ expressed this in *Glenn Brothers v Commercial General Agency Co Ltd* 1905 TS 737 at 740. See also *St Patricks Mansions (Pty) Ltd v Grange Restaurant (Pty) Ltd and Another* 1949 (4) SA 57 (W) at 69; *Scottish Union & National Insurance Co Ltd v Native Recruiting Corporation Ltd* 1934 AD 458 at 465; *Patel v Patel and Another* 1968 (4) SA 51 (D); *Sassoon Confirming and Acceptance Co (Pty) Ltd v Barclays National Bank Ltd* 1974 (1) SA 641 (A); *Jonnes v Anglo-African Shipping Co (1936) Ltd* 1972 (2) SA 827 (A) at 834E and innumerable other cases.

[4] In *Bekker NO v Total South Africa (Pty) Ltd* 1990 (3) SA 159 (T) at 170G-H.

[5] See *List v Jungers* 1979 (3) SA 106 (A); *Swart en 'n Ander v Cape Fabrix (Pty) Ltd* 1979 (1) SA 195 (A); *Sassoon Confirming and Acceptance Co (Pty) Ltd v Barclays National Bank Ltd* 1974 (1) SA 641 (A) and many other cases.

[6] 1979 (1) SA 195 (A) at 202.

special or more restrictive sense in the contract. For instance, in *List v Jungers*[7] the use of the word 'guarantee' in a contract (which contained no suggestion that it was a contract accessory to a principal obligation) did not indicate that the appellant intended to bind himself as surety, although that was one of the ordinary meanings of that word. And in *Zietsman v Allied Building Society*[8] where a surety had secured the payment of 'enige bedrag wat ingevolge die gemelde verband betaalbaar mag word', he was held liable only for those sums that were payable in terms of the bond (ie the original loan) and not for other sums subsequently advanced by the creditor in later loans. Because of the wide terms of the bond these sums were secured by the bond; but they were not payable in terms of the bond and thus the surety was not liable for them. And in *Vitamax (Pty) Ptd v Executive Catering Equipment CC and Others*[9] where a surety bound himself for the debts of 'companies' this was held to include liability for the debts of a close corporation.

(b) Unclear and ambiguous language: the use of 'surrounding circumstances' to determine the parties' intention

However, there are occasions on which the court can escape from the ordinary meaning of the words used as read in the context of the contract as a whole. Where the language is unclear or ambiguous (and only then),[10] the court can, in interpreting the contract, take into account factors other than the language, the so-called 'surrounding circumstances'.[11] Thus in *Glenn Brothers v Commercial General Agency Co Ltd*,[12] Innes CJ said: 'In reading a document like this we are justified in looking at the circumstances under which the guarantee was given, and

---

[7] 1979 (3) SA 106 (A). Or see *Jonnes v Anglo-African Shipping Co (1936) Ltd* 1972 (2) SA 827 (A) where on an analysis of the contract the word 'indemnify' was not given the meaning 'to compensate for losses suffered or expenses incurred', but 'to keep free from harm or loss'. And see *Hutchinson v Hylton Holdings and Another* 1993(2) SA 405 (T) where 'guarantee [of] specific performance of this contract' was undertaking liability as a principal debtor not a surety.

[8] 1989 (3) SA 166 (O).

[9] 1993(2) SA 556(W). And to like effect see *Potgieter en 'n Ander NNO v Shell Suid-Afrika (Edms) Bpk* 2003 (1) SA 155 (SCA) (power to stand surety for company included power to stand surety for close corporation).

[10] *Cinema City (Pty) Ltd v Morgenstern Family Estates (Pty) Ltd and Others* 1980 (1) SA 796 (A) left open 'whether the stage of development has been reached where the "open sesame" of uncertainty may be dispensed with as a prerequisite to opening the door to evidence of surrounding circumstances' (at 805H-806A). In *Pritchard Properties (Pty) Ltd v Koulis* 1986 (2) SA 1 (A) the Appellate Division made it clear that this door was closed. See, however, Jansen JA's dissent in that case.

Although in *Glenn Brothers v Commercial General Agency Co Ltd* 1905 TS 737, the use of 'surrounding circumstances' was not expressly predicated upon ambiguity, Innes CJ himself required ambiguity in *Richter v Bloemfontein Town Council* 1922 AD 57 at 70 before extrinsic evidence of what the circumstances of the contract were was admissible. See also the passages from *Delmas Milling Co Ltd v Du Plessis* 1955 (3) SA 447 (A) cited at length below in note 12.

[11] 'Surrounding circumstances' were described by Schreiner JA in *Delmas Milling Co Ltd v Du Plessis* 1955 (3) SA 447 (A) at 454 as 'matters that were probably present to the minds of the parties when they contracted (but not actual negotiations or similar statements)'. Where the contract itself recites the circumstances in which the contract was entered into, it seems clear that they form part of the contract 'as a whole'.

[12] 1905 TS 737. See also *Cope v Atkinson's Motor Garages Ltd* 1931 AD 366 at 370; *Swart en 'n Ander v Cape Fabrix (Pty) Ltd* 1979 (1) SA 195 (A) at 200E-202C; *Van Rensburg v City Credit (Natal) (Pty) Ltd* 1980 (4) SA 500 (N) at 506G; *Ottosdal Ontwikkelingsmaatskappy (Edms) Bpk v KNT Bouers (Edms) Bpk* 1974 (1) SA 712 (T).

the position of the various parties concerned. That is necessary in order to enable us rightly to understand and to place ourselves in the position of the parties at the time.... [However,] I do not think we should gather from the circumstances what the parties meant, or what it is fair and equitable to think they meant, and then see whether we can ingeniously so read the document as to deduce that meaning from its language.'[13] Thus 'surrounding circumstances' can be used to give meaning to otherwise unclear or ambiguous words; they cannot be used to distort otherwise clear (but inconvenient or unfair) words.

Swart en 'n Ander v Cape Fabrix (Pty) Ltd[14] may serve as an example of the use of 'surrounding circumstances'. There was a dispute between the parties over whether the surety who had bound himself to pay 'for all amounts due for goods *purchased* from (the creditor)' (italics added) was also bound to pay for goods purchased *after* the date of the suretyship. The creditor conceded that the suretyship was ambiguous and the evidence showed that a continuing business relationship was envisaged between creditor and principal debtor with the creditor selling goods on credit to the debtor. In these circumstances, the judge in the court *a quo* concluded there was no reason to suppose that the suretyship was limited to past indebtedness, but every reason to suppose that the suretyship covered the debtor's account with the creditor on a continuing basis and was so understood by the parties. This was upheld by the Appeal Court.[15]

(c) *Resolving ambiguity by restrictive interpretation in favour of the surety*

Finally, if all else fails and there remains ambiguity, that ambiguity is resolved through the application of the maxim *verba contra stipulatorem interpretenda sunt*, treating the creditor as the stipulator.[16] As Wessels says,[17] '[T]he surety takes upon himself a debt which is not his own and therefore he is not likely to intend to charge himself by implication with more onerous duties than are expressed in the contract.' The creditor has only himself to blame if he has not seen to it that the document is expressed in terms sufficiently wide to embrace the liability to

---

[13] What was said here by Innes CJ in 1905 accords with what has since been said by Schreiner JA in *Delmas Milling Co Ltd v Du Plessis* 1955 (3) SA 447 (A) at 454. The learned judge of appeal said that where there was difficulty, even serious difficulty, in interpretation, this must be cleared up by linguistic treatment, if this can be done. 'If the difficulty cannot be cleared up with sufficient certainty by studying the language, recourse may be had to "surrounding circumstances" ... but this does not mean that if sufficient certainty can be gathered from the language alone it is nevertheless permissible to reach a different result by drawing inferences from the surrounding circumstances.' See further the discussion in *Swart en 'n Ander v Cape Fabrix (Pty) Ltd* 1979 (1) SA 195 (A) at 200E- 202C.

[14] 1979 (1) SA 195 (A). See also *Segell v Kerdia Investments (Pty) Ltd* 1953 (1) SA 20 (W). Phrases in the past tense in suretyship agreements, such as undertakings to stand surety for debts incurred for 'goods *supplied*', have frequently, and correctly, been interpreted as applying to future debts; for the parties' plain intention is that the debtor's credit be secured in respect of goods '*to be supplied*': *Linford v Heynes Mathew Limited* 1915 CPD 531 at 533. See also *Jonnes v Anglo African Shipping Co (1936) Ltd* 1972 (2) SA 827 (A).

[15] At 202E-G. The crux of the judgment in the court *a quo* is set out at 200B-E.

[16] For the general principles see D 2.14.39; V 18.1.27 and *Cairns (Pty) Ltd v Playdon & Co Ltd* 1948 (3) SA 99 (A); *Jonnes v Anglo-African Shipping Co (1936) Ltd* 1972 (2) SA 827 (A) at 835B -G.

[17] In para 3893.

which he seeks to hold the surety.[18] But this principal does not justify far-fetched defences by the surety. A 'deed of suretyship', said Harms JA in *Tsaperas and Others v Boland Bank Ltd*,[19] 'must be interpreted restrictively and in favour of the surety. It does not mean that the agreement must not be sensibly interpreted.' In principle interpretation in favour of the surety is a rule of last resort to be used only when there is no other way of cutting the Gordian knot and giving meaning to the parties' agreement,[20] but the modern tendency seems to be to rely upon it more broadly.[21]

(d) Resolving ambiguity through the assumption that the parties negotiated in good faith

Where the meaning of the words used is not ambiguous it is now clear beyond doubt that abstract principles of good faith and fairness – although they perform 'creative, informative and controlling functions' in the law of contract – cannot be relied upon to justify intervention by the judge to secure a fairer or more reasonable outcome.[22] However, the Supreme Court of Appeal has said: 'While a court is not entitled to superimpose on the clearly expressed intention of the parties its notion of fairness, the position is different where a contract is ambiguous. In such a case the principle that all contracts are governed by good faith is applied and the intention of the parties is determined on the basis that they negotiated with each other in good faith.'[23] This principle has not yet been applied in the context of the law of suretyship but there is no reason to think that it will not be.

(e) Tacit terms

One way in which the straitjacket of the ordinary meaning of the words can be escaped even where there is no ambiguity is where it is established that there is a tacit term to the contract[24] ie a term derived from the actual common intention

---

[18] Gr 3.15.9; V 18. 1.27; *Wood Bros v Gardner* (1886) 5 EDC 189 at 191; *Patel v Patel and Another* 1968 (4) SA 51 (D) at 56.

[19] 1996 (1) SA 719 (A) at 724C.

[20] *Cairns (Pty) Ltd v Playdon & Co Ltd* 1948 (3) SA 99 (A) at 124. Although *Cairns's* case was referred to, this point appears to have been overlooked by Farlam AJ in *Zietsman v Allied Building Society* 1989 (3) SA 166 (O) at 177D-E.

[21] See *Zietsman v Allied Building Society*, loc cit and there is no suggestion in *Tsaperas and Others v Boland Bank Ltd* that this was a rule of last resort.

[22] See *Brisley v Drotsky*, loc cit and *Afrox Healthcare Bpk v Strydom* loc cit. The quoted words come from Brand JA's article 'The Role of Good Faith, Equity and Fairness in the South African Law of Contract: The Influence of the Common Law and the Constitution' (2009) 126 *SALJ* 71 at 83.

[23] *South African Forestry Co Ltd v York Timbers Ltd* 2005 (3) SA 323 (SCA) at para. 30-32 (per Brandt JA, Streicher, Cameron JJA, Patel, Jafta AJJA concurring).

[24] In accordance with the approach of the Appellate Division in *Minister van Landbou-Tegniese Dienste v Scholtz* 1971 (3) SA 188 (A) at 197C-E and *Alfred McAlpine & Son (Pty) Ltd v Transvaal Provincial Administration* 1974 (3) SA 506 (A) and several other cases, the use of the words 'implied term' is eschewed where the term in question is based on an unexpressed intention of the parties. Such a term may be distinguished from a true 'implied term' ie a term imposed, in the absence on contrary agreement by the parties, by the law on that particular contract, eg the various benefits available to the surety. See the discussion in *South African Forestry Co Ltd v York Timbers Ltd* 2005 (3) SA 323 (SCA) of implied terms. Brandt JA giving the development of implied terms by the courts was an example of the 'creative and informative function performed by abstract values such as good faith and fairness' (para. 28).

(an actual tacit term) or supposed common intention (imputed tacit term) of the parties but not expressed in the writing, and which is capable of being inferred from the express terms and the surrounding circumstances.[25]

As might be expected, a tacit term will be found in a contract of suretyship in the same circumstances in which it would be found in any other contract.[26] Those circumstances were explained by Colman J in *Techni-Pak Sales (Pty) Ltd v Hall*[27] as follows: 'The court has no power to supplement the bargain between the parties by adding a term which they would have been wise to agree upon, although they did not. The fact that the suggested term would have been a reasonable one for them to adopt or that its incorporation would avoid an inequity or a hardship to one of the parties, is not enough. The suggested term must, in the first place, be one which was necessary as opposed to merely desirable, to give business efficacy to the contract; and, what is more, the court must be satisfied that it is a term which the parties themselves intended to operate if the occasion for such operation arose, although they did not express it... . That does not mean ... that the parties must consciously have visualised the situation in which the term would come into operation.'

It is important to note while a tacit term can obviously not contradict an express term, clauses that provide that the written document contains the 'entire agreement between the parties' and that no variation or modification of the contract shall be possible unless 'reduced to writing and signed by the parties' do not prevent the court from inferring a tacit term. As Nienaber JA said in *Wilkins*

---

[25] *Alfred McAlpine & Son* 1974 (3) SA 506 (A) per Corbett JA (at 531H-532A) and Rumpff ACJ (at 526); *Delfs v Kuehne & Nagel (Pty) Ltd* 1990 (1) SA 82 (A) and *Wilkins NO v Voges* 1994 (3) SA 130 (A) especially at 136H-137D (Nienaber JA). Note that JP Vorster (in 'The Influence of English Law on the Implication of Terms in the South African Law of Contract' (1987) 104 *SALJ* 588) argues that South African judges have (under the influence of the Privy Council decision of *Douglas v Baynes* [1908] AC 477, 1908 TS 1207 (overruling Innes CJ)) made errors in their reception of English law. In particular, by insisting upon basing such terms on the parties' intentions they have precluded full reliance upon the *Moorcock* doctrine *(The Moorcock* (1889) 14 PD 64 (CA) at 68) in terms of which obvious and reasonable terms not in conflict with the express terms are imposed ('implied' is the word used in the judgments) to give business efficacy to the contract even where that term was not intended by the parties. See further JP Vorster *Implied Terms in the Law of Contract in England and South Africa* unpublished PhD thesis, University of Cambridge (1987) 92 ff and 197 ff.

[26] *St Patricks Mansions (Pty) Ltd v Grange Restaurant (Pty) Ltd and Another* 1949 (4) SA 57 (W) at 71; and see FJ *Hawkes & Co Ltd v Nagel* 1957 (3) SA 126 (W)

[27] 1968 (3) SA 231 (W) at 236. The leading dictum from the Appeal Court is the following words from *Wilkins NO v Voges* 1994 (3) SA 130(A) at 136I- 137D:

'Being unspoken, a tacit term is invariably a matter of inference. It is an inference as to what both parties must or would have had in mind. The inference must be a necessary one: after all, if several conceivable terms are all equally plausible, none of them may be said to be axiomatic. The inference can be drawn from the express terms and from admissible evidence of surrounding circumstances. The onus to prove the material from which the inference is to be drawn rests on the seeking to rely on the tacit term. The practical test for determining what the parties would necessarily have agreed...is the celebrated bystander test. Since one may assume that the parties to a commercial contract are intent on concluding a contract which functions efficiently, a term will readily be imported into a contract if it is necessary to ensure its business efficacy; conversely, ...when such a term is not necessary to render the contract fully functional' it is unlikely to be so imported.

For a full discussion in the context of suretyship see *Standard Bank of SA Ltd v Durban Security Glazing (Pty) Ltd* 2000 (1) SA 146 (D) at 160H-162B.

NO v Voges:[28] 'A tacit term in a written contract, be it actual or imputed, can be the corollary of the express terms—reading, as it were, between the lines—or it can be the product of the express terms read in conjunction with evidence of admissible surrounding circumstances. Either way, a tacit term, once found to exist, is simply read or blended into the contract: as such it is 'contained' in the written deed. Not being an adjunct to but an integrated part of the contract, a tacit term does not fall foul of terms [such as those mentioned]'.

As example of the operations of these principles is found in *Standard Bank of SA Ltd v Durban Security Glazing (Pty) Ltd*[29] where the express term of the suretyship (required the surety's written notice of termination to the creditor to be accompanied by proof that the principal debtor had been informed by registered post) was held subject to a tacit term which dispensed with the requirement of notice to the principal debtor in circumstances in which it was plain that the principal debtor was fully aware of the termination (letter of termination written on principal debtor's headed note paper and signed by surety in his capacity as director of the principal debtor).

Tacit terms have become problematical in the law of suretyship where they are relied upon to restrict very wide undertakings of liability by the surety. Creditors, who generally hold the whip hand regarding the terms of the suretyship, sometimes insist on imposing upon sureties very wide obligations that appear to extend far beyond ensuring that the principal obligation is properly performed. Can such very wide suretyships be limited by a tacit term restricting the surety's liabilities to those flowing from the principal obligation? It appears that there is such a limitation, but it is unclear whether it is based upon a tacit term and, if not, what its basis is.

Van der Linden, although stating that if the terms of the suretyship are general and indefinite, the surety is bound for all the debtor's obligations flowing from the principal obligation, goes on to say that 'however wide and general a guarantee may be, it only extends to the obligations which flow from the contract [ie the principal debt] itself, and not to those which flow from any extraneous source'.[30]

Two cases may be contrasted: first, in *Hawkes, FJ, & Co Ltd v Nagel*[31] the suretyship contained wide language (the surety undertook to pay 'any and all indebtedness now or hereafter due [by the principal debtor] from whatsoever cause arising'), and the surety was held not entitled to plead a tacit term limiting his liability to indebtedness arising out of transactions between the plaintiff creditor and the debtor. Thus it was competent for the former to make a claim against the surety on a debt owed by the debtor but contained in a bill of exchange which had been endorsed to the creditor from an extraneous source.

---

[28] 1994 (3) SA 130 (A) at 144C-D; *Sweets from Heaven (Pty) Ltd and Another v Ster Kinekoor Films (Pty) Ltd and Another* 1999 (1) SA 796 (W) at 802G-I; and in a suretyship context *Standard Bank of SA Ltd v Durban Security Glazing (Pty) Ltd* 2000 (1) SA 146 (D) at 160H-I and 162I-163B (clause excluding waiver and requiring 'strict and punctual compliance...with each and every provision of the suretyship' does not exclude tacit terms).
[29] 2000 (1) SA 146 (D).
[30] VdL 1.14.10. See also Wessels paras 3907.
[31] 1957 (3) SA 126 (W). See also *Patel v Patel and Another* 1968 (4) SA 51 (D) at 56.

On the other hand, consider *Webb v Shell Zimbabwe (Pvt) Ltd.*[32] Again the suretyship was very wide ('the repayment when due of all sums of money which [the principal debtor] (hereinafter [sic] referred to as the customer) may now or from time to time hereafter owe or be indebted ... to [the creditor] from whatever cause arising [and] ... nothing excepted'). Were these words wide enough to hold the surety liable for a debt owed by the principal debtor to a third party which that third party ceded to the creditor? Beck JA held not. Relying on the words of Van der Linden cited above and a dictum of Caney J in *Patel v Patel and Another*[33] holding that even very wide words did not cover a debt from an extraneous source, the learned judge of appeal held that the suretyship contemplated a continuing trading relationship between the principal debtor and creditor (see, for instance, the use of the word 'customer' in the words cited above); and thus the suretyship 'was not meant to extend to indebtedness which [the creditor] acquired from an extraneous source unconnected with the trading relationship'.[34]

The difficulty here is that while the tacit term was argued in *Hawkes, FJ, & Co Ltd v Nagel* and rejected (on the ground that such term would be in conflict with the express terms of the contract imposing a wide liability),[35] in the authorities in which the surety has been relieved of liability for some extraneous obligation of the principal debtor it has not been made clear what the basis of that limitation is. From some points of view these cases do seem apt for analysis in terms of tacit terms. The 'officious bystander' that features prominently in the tacit terms cases might readily conclude that it was obvious and reasonable that a surety who was binding himself in order, say, that the principal debtor might be granted credit, was not undertaking to pay whichever of the principal debtor's debts might subsequently be ceded to the creditor by some third party; and that that would be obvious to the creditor too. Moreover, such a term lends 'business efficacy' to the contract (for otherwise sureties would not agree to be bound). However, whatever approach is adopted to the tacit terms question, the tacit term sought to be implied in these cases does *prima facie* appear to be contrary to the express words of the contract; it does not supplement but contradicts the terms imposing a wide liability.

In the past the *exceptio doli generalis* might have provided a solution to this problem but with the demise of that defence,[36] the question could become acute. Will the surety who has signed such a widely phrased suretyship have any defence when sued on some extraneous debt? It is submitted that where there are indications in the contract itself (such as the use of the word 'customer' in *Webb's* case) that the suretyship is linked to a particular business relationship or undertaking, then reading the contract as a whole (and the wide words in the context of the other words suggesting restriction) the wide words will not be given their

---

[32] 1982 (2) SA 763 (Z). See also *Robb NO v Standard Bank Ltd and Another* 1979 (2) SA 420 (R) at 425H-426B.
[33] 1968 (4) SA 51 (D) at 56F-G. See also *Robb NO v Standard Bank Ltd and Another* 1979 (2) SA 420 (R) at 42A-B.
[34] *Webb v Shell Zimbabwe (Pvt) Ltd* 1982 (2) SA 763 (Z) at 766H.
[35] At 130F.
[36] See *Bank of Lisbon and South Africa Ltd v De Ornelas and Another* 1988 (3) SA 580 (A) discussed in Chapter XIII.

ordinary meaning but will be given a more limited meaning. Where no such indications are to be found and there is no ambiguity to justify reliance upon the 'surrounding circumstances', then the surety unwise enough to sign a widely phrased suretyship will be liable for all the indebtedness of the principal debtor to the creditor whether flowing from the original principal debt or from some extraneous source.

2. Particular examples of restrictive interpretation

Notwithstanding that the same principles of construction are applicable to suretyship as are applicable to other contract, it is still strictly construed; and Burge[37] indicates three particular aspects in which the contract is restrictively construed. However, as will be observed in what follows, the force of these categories is on the wane. The words of the contract remain the soundest guide to the meaning of the suretyship.

(1) The surety's liability will not be extended to any other subject than that expressed or included in the suretyship contract.[38] Several examples of this principle have already been dealt with in the general discussion and Others may be readily added.[39] But many of these examples (based on old cases) have an air of unreality about them for they are unlikely to arise under modern conditions where deeds of suretyship tend to specify in wide terms, sometimes very wide terms, the liabilities of the surety; the problem in the modern cases is, as we have seen, to provide limits upon the exceptionally wide words frequently used.

---

[37] B 40 ff. See also Wessels paras 3907-27.

[38] B 46.

[39] Instances in the courts of the limitation of the surety's liability in the manner under discussion are: *Steytler v Saunders* (1883) 2 Menz 15 (suretyship for capital debt, not including collection commission) and *Dreyer v Smuts* (1828) 1 Menz 308 (suretyship for capital debt, not including interest); *The Divisional Council of Middelburg v Close* (1885) 3 SC 411 at 415; *Fauresmith Board of Executors v Blommestein* (1887) 4 CLJ 290; *Steyn NO v Borckenhagen and Venter* (1897) 14 CLJ 202; *Van der Riet v Pieters* 1879 OFS 1 are three cases of fidelity bonds for officials who broke faith in offices other than those the subject of the bonds and one (*Van der Riet v Pieters*) of suretyship for an advocate under the then applicable legislation. However, in *Parijs Municipality v AS le Roux and EH le Roux* 1916 EDL 215 sureties were held liable for rates moneys for which the town clerk (for whom they had made their promise) failed to account, it being part of his function as town clerk to act as rate collector; and *Trans-Drakensberg Bank Ltd v Guy* 1964 (1) SA 790 (D) (criticised in 1964 *Annual Survey* 136) (suretyship of price of goods not extended to a loan). See further *Barclays National Bank Ltd v Lockhat* 1978 (3) SA 922 (D), where a suretyship for the debtor's undertaking to pay the creditor's claim 'instituted in the Supreme Court ... under case No I 3948/75' was held not to cover a debt flowing from the provisional sentence granted against debtor rather than his undertaking to pay. Discussed and defended in 1978 *Annual Survey* 205 ff. A suretyship given as security for the costs of a *peregrinus* in an action in the magistrate's court does not extend to the costs of an appeal: *Campbell v Seavill* (1892) 6 HCG 156 and *Blackshire v Stegman, Esselen and Roos* 1906 TS 768. A suretyship for restitution of what was paid on provisional sentence, if the principal case went against the plaintiff, with an undertaking to conform to the judgment in the principal case, was held to extend to the costs of that case but not to those of a claim in reconvention for damages in *Beplat v Dold & Stone* (1909) 26 SC 160.

In *Moreriane v Trans-Oranje Finansierings- en Ontwikkelingskorporasie, Bpk* 1965 (1) SA 767 (T), liability under a suretyship for arrear instalments under a hire-purchase agreement was not extended to damages representing the loss of them. As against this, the language of the suretyship 'for the punctual payment of all sums due' in question in *Bester v Cape Finance Corporation* 1955 (1) PH A29 (C) was sufficiently wide to include damages after termination of the hire-purchase agreement.

However, the principle takes upon itself a modern appearance in the context of sureties for a lessee. The old authorities apply this principle to ensure that the surety for rent is not liable for wear and tear.[40] And there are old cases to similar effect: in *Arenson v Bishop*,[41] for instance, a suretyship for payment of rent was not extended to cover damages for holding over.

But, of course, the words of the suretyship must prevail. Thus in *Beaufort West Municipality v Krummeck's Trustees and Others*[42] the language of the suretyship was sufficiently wide to cover damages for cancellation of the lease. Similarly in *St Patricks Mansions (Pty) Ltd v Grange Restaurant (Pty) Ltd and Another*[43] the language covered damages for wrongful holding over and costs of ejectment proceedings. In *Segell v Kerdia Investments (Pty) Ltd*[44] the suretyship related to breaches of negative obligations under the lease and was interpreted to extend to costs of interdict proceedings to enforce compliance with the obligations.

An important question that has arisen on several occasions is whether the surety for a lessee who goes insolvent remains liable to the lessor after the lessee's trustee or liquidator has terminated the lease as he has power to do in terms of section 37(1) of the Insolvency Act 24 of 1936.[45] In *Strydom v Goldblatt*,[46] for instance, a surety binding himself as surety for 'the due fulfilment by the lessee of all its obligations in terms of the ... lease and the due payment of all amounts claimable thereunder' was held by Franklin J to escape liability for obligations flowing not from the lease, but from the lessee's liquidator's termination of the lease in terms of section 37(1). True, the proviso to that section gave the lessor a right to compensation for loss due to cancellation, but this was not a right which flowed from the lease.

This was an awkward result, for an important reason why lessors insist upon sureties for lessees is to protect themselves from such obvious consequences of the lessee's insolvency. Thus the courts were cautious; and *Strydom v Goldblatt* was not applied to similar cases with differently phrased deeds of suretyship.[47] Now with *Norex Industrial Properties (Pty) Ltd v Monarch South Africa Insurance Co Ltd*[48] the Appellate Division (in a convincing judgment from Botha JA) has overruled *Strydom v Goldblatt*. Here the surety had promised that the lessee 'will promptly and faithfully fulfil all the obligations and undertakings by it in terms

---

[40] B 48, V 46.1.12, P 404.
[41] 1926 CPD 73.
[42] (1887) 5 SC 5.
[43] 1949 (4) SA 57 (W).
[44] 1953 (1) SA 20 (W).
[45] Section 37(1) provides that a lease is not terminated by the sequestration of the lessee's estate (this is in any event the common law) but his 'trustee ... may determine the lease by notice in writing to the lessor: provided that the lessor may claim from the estate compensation for any loss which he may have sustained by reason of the non-performance of the lease'. By s 386 of the Companies Act 61 of 1973 like powers are invested in liquidators of companies.
[46] 1976 (2) SA 852 (W).
[47] See *Jayber (Pty) Ltd v Miller and Others* 1981 (2) SA 403 (N) and *Sydney Road Holdings (Pty) Ltd v Simon* 1981 (3) SA 104 (D). See also the discussion in *Pizani and Another v First Consolidated Holdings (Pty) Ltd* 1979 (1) SA 69 (A) at 82H-83C. Where the liquidator repudiates the lease (without reliance upon any statutory authority) then *a fortiori* the surety remains bound: *Somchem (Pty) Ltd v Federated Insurance Co Ltd and Another* 1983 (4) SA 609 (C) at 616H- 617B.
[48] 1987 (1) SA 827 (A).

of the said deed of lease'.' The Appellate Division rejected the defence that the liquidator's cancellation of the lease created liabilities not flowing from the lease itself but from the proviso to section 37(1) and since the surety was only liable for liabilities flowing from the lease, he was not liable for the proviso damages. Botha JA held that since the proviso spoke of loss sustained 'by reason of the non-performance' of the lease, the liability of the estate flowed from the lease. Moreover, when tested against the common law it was clear that the section was 'substantially speaking not different from what it would have been but for the section. Accordingly, [the cancellation of the lease pursuant to the section did not result] in the creation of a previously non-existent right on the part of the lessor ..., or of liabilities on the part of a liquidator not flowing from the lease itself. The true impact of the proviso ... is no more than to *preserve* for the lessor the right he would have had ... to hold the liquidator liable for the compensation of his loss, or his damages, flowing from the liquidator's decision not to continue with the lease ...'.[49] This conclusion is here supported. Not only is Botha JA's conclusion fully in accord with what the parties to such suretyships generally intend but it is also, it is submitted, common sense.

(2) The surety's liability will not be extended *de persona in personam*;[50] for example, a fidelity bond for a clerk in A's service will not operate after A has taken a partner. *Green v Beveridge*[51] was close to this; the defendant was surety to the plaintiff for the price of goods to be supplied to C, who, without the knowledge of either of them, took a partner. The plaintiff continued to give credit to C and thus the defendant was held bound. But if he had given credit to the new partnership, the surety would not have been bound.

Just as the introduction of a partner to whom, along with the original debtor, credit is given takes the case out of the suretyship contract, so the retirement of a partner from a firm the debts of which are secured by the surety, as it ends the partnership, so also it ends the surety's responsibility, except in respect of past debts.[52]

A surety for an executor of an estate is not bound for his acts committed when he is no longer functioning as executor but as administrator of the estate.[53]

(3) Nor will a suretyship be extended *a tempore ad tempus*;[54] for example, if by his contract the surety undertakes liability for debts incurred within a limited period of time, he may be sued for them after the expiration of that period, but only for

---

[49] At 839G-I.
[50] B 63.
[51] (1891) 8 SC 155.
[52] Cf *Standard Bank of SA Ltd v Lewis* 1922 TPD 285 at 289.
[53] *In re Best* (1892) 9 SC 488; *The Master v Ocean Accident and Guarantee Corporation Limited* 1937 CPD 302.
[54] B 69.

those debts incurred within the period and not those incurred beyond the time to which his liability has been limited.[55]

3. Whether particular words amount to undertaking liability as a surety

It must always be a matter of interpretation to ascertain whether what passed between the parties (the creditor and the person said to be a surety) amounts to a contract of suretyship or not. Where the suretyship is embodied in a formal document, there is not likely to be any doubt of the parties' intention in this regard, but if it is embodied in informal *writing*, such as a letter[56] (complying, as it must, with the requirements of section 6 of the General Law Amendment Act of 1956—see Chapter V), questions may readily arise as to the meaning and intention of the parties. Where the disputed suretyship is embodied in another contract then again difficult issues of interpretation may arise.

If the words used are 'stand surety for' there can hardly be any doubt of the intention to create a suretyship. The word 'guarantee', however, is not necessarily conclusive of suretyship. This word, Greenberg J said in *Walker's Fruit Farms Ltd v Sumner*,[57] is 'capable of a number of meanings, but the ordinary meaning is to assure a person of the receipt or possession of something'. He was considering the terms of a contract for the engagement of the services of a land salesman at a remuneration calculated on amounts to be received from buyers, with a 'guarantee' of a minimum monthly sum. On the other hand, in *Mouton v Die Mynwerkersunie*[58] Wessels JA said that the word guarantee, although capable of many meanings, is 'usually and more properly employed by a surety who promises to saddle himself with an obligation if the principal debtor defaults'.[59] In *Société Commerciale de Moteurs v Ackermann*[60] a statement in a letter to the creditor from the supposed surety's agent that 'all orders will in the first instance be guaranteed by' the surety was held to amount neither to a guarantee, nor an offer of a guarantee. It meant no more than that 'future orders would be accompanied by ... a guarantee by' the supposed surety. And in *Hutchinson v Hylton Holdings and Another*[61] an undertaking in a contract for the sale of land in which the representative of the purchaser

---

[55] *Van den Berg v Malherbe* (1829) 1 Menz 429; *Colonial Government v Du Toit and Muller* (1855) 2 Searle 225 and *Roodt v Botha* (1905) 22 SC 189 are examples of this. See also *Feldman Ltd v Sulski* 1954 (4) SA 665 (W), and on appeal *sub nom Sulski v Feldman Ltd* 1956 (1) SA 759 (A), in which one of the questions for decision was whether a time limit in the suretyship related to the period of time within which the liability was to be incurred, that is to say, the period during which the surety was to become liable, or whether it was a limit of time beyond which the surety's liability was discharged. For further discussion see Chapter 7, section 3.
[56] See, for example, *List v Jungers* 1979 (3) SA 106 (A).
[57] 1930 TPD 394 at 398
[58] 1977 (1) SA 119 (A). And in *Basil Read (Pty) Ltd v Beta Hotels (Pty) Ltd and Others* 2001 (2) SA 760 (C) the 'contract guarantee' required by the 'Joint Bulding Contracts Committee' for its standard form building contract was held to be 'in the nature of suretyship' (at 766D).
[59] At 136C, in fact quoting from *Hazis v Transvaal and Delagoa Bay Investment Co Ltd* 1939 AD 372 at 384. See also *List v Jungers* 1979 (3) SA 106 (A) at 117D.
[60] 1981 (3) 8A 422 (A). The quotations in the text come from the judgment at 434B and 435G respectively. Note that Jansen JA dissented on the grounds that the letter was reasonably capable of being understood as a guarantee (meaning suretyship) (at 430D).
[61] 1993(2) SA 405 (T).

undertook to 'guarantee specific performance of this contract in my personal capacity' was held to be an independent undertaking by the representative. He contracted as 'a co-principal debtor and not as surety'.[62]

The fact is, of course, that in determining whether a particular contract is one of suretyship or not, too much reliance should not be placed upon the use of a particular word—guarantee—but regard should rather be had to whether the 'surety' has undertaken, once the contract is properly interpreted, that another will perform, failing which he will perform, in which case a contract of suretyship is involved, or whether the 'surety' has undertaken a principal liability—in which case we may be dealing with guarantee proper—or whether the word has been used in another sense entirely.[63]

On various occasions use of particular words has, however, been held to indicate suretyship. Thus in *Brown, Greisler (Pty) Ltd v Wootton*[64] the term 'confirming agent' used in a commercial transaction was held to mean 'guarantor' (in the sense of surety) and the verb 'confirm' in the context meant 'to add strength to', 'to put beyond doubt', 'to assure'.

Merely to offer advice as to the financial standing of the debtor does not create the obligation of suretyship,[65] any more than does the accompanying of a customer to a shop to make a purchase;[66] payment of part of another's debt is not to be construed as an undertaking to pay the balance.[67]

It has been held that the use of the following words does not amount to an undertaking to act as surety:

(i) 'I assure you that he is an honest man and will pay';[68]
(ii) 'he is good enough: your debt will surely be paid, even if it were twice as much';[69]
(iii) 'that man is safe';[70]
(iv) 'your debt is sure to be paid';[71]
(v) 'he is a substantial person'.[72]

In *Fitzgerald v Argus Printing and Publishing Co Ltd*[73] appellant's telegram to respondents 'kindly forward Flynn's goods. Will hold myself responsible his paying your account within a fortnight' was held to create the liability of a surety, not

---

[62] Thus the representative remained liable notwithstanding the voidness of the sale to the purchaser (a company which did not come into existence).
[63] See Chapter II, generally.
[64] 1937 (1) PH A8 (W).
[65] VL 4.4.5; VdK 501; *Cens For* 1.4.17.17; P 401. There is, however, the possibility that in the appropriate circumstances a delictual remedy may be available on the grounds of negligent misrepresentation, provided all the elements or requirements of Aquilian liability have been met. see *Administrateur, Natal v Trust Bank van Afrika Bpk* 1979 (3) SA 824 (A) and *Indac Electronics (Pty) Ltd v Volkskas Bank Ltd* 1992 (1) 8A 783 (A).
[66] P401.
[67] P401.
[68] VdL 1.14.10; P 401.
[69] VL 4.4.5, Huber 3.26.4.
[70] Gr 3.3.25; Lee *ad Gr* 248.
[71] Gr 3.3.25; Lee *ad Gr* 248.
[72] VdK 501, P 401.
[73] (1907) 3 Buch AC 152.

that of a principal debtor, so that appellant was entitled to invoke the benefit of excussion; Flynn was not released, there was no *delegatio*. But in *Renou v Walcott*[74] the employer who agreed to hold himself liable for his servant's medical fees was held bound as a principal debtor, not as a surety.

The words 'I will *toch* have to pay as the mealies were mine' were held not to be a suretyship undertaking in *Bouwer v Lichtenburg Cooperative Society*.[75]

Where a building owner introduced his builder to a merchant as an honourable and trustworthy man, upon which the merchant supplied building material to the builder, the introduction was held not to constitute the owner a surety for his builder.[76] Where credit was given simply to J and appellant was told she would be held liable as surety, then though she also had the benefit of goods supplied to J it was held on appeal that she was not proved liable as a principal debtor.[77]

Where the defendant undertook to pay the debt of another for building material if the invoices were sent to him, he was held to have bound himself as the principal debtor, there being no statement by him that he would be responsible for the other paying the bills or that he would pay if the other did not do so.[78]

---

[74] (1909) 10 HCG 246. See, also, *Meyer v Coetzee* (1892) 4 SAR 252 where the defendant undertook jointly with the seller of a farm to give transfer by a stated date.

[75] 1925 TPD 144.

[76] *Bourke v Buxton and De Villiers* (1899) 3 SAR 39.

[77] *Msita v De Lange* 1921 EDL 17.

[78] Suretyship is an accessory obligation, but this was not such—*Versveld & Co v Southern Timber (Pty) Ltd* 1935 (2) PH A38 (C). A request to supply goods to another, with a promise to 'see that you get your money before anyone else is paid', is not a suretyship, for there is no undertaking to pay (*Atkinson v Aronowitz* 1933 SR 144).

CHAPTER VII

The Obligations of the Surety

	Page
1. Performance of the debtor's obligation, but no more than his obligation	101
2. Surety's obligation is to the debtor's creditor	104
3. When surety's obligation to pay becomes due	104
4. Surety's obligation when debtor's obligation is *ad factum praestandum*	106
5. Continuing suretyships	110
6. Surety's liability for interest	115
7. Surety's liability for the creditor's costs in suing the principal debtor	116
8. The effect of death	118
9. Insolvency of the principal debtor or surety	119

1. Performance of the debtor's obligation, but no more than his obligation

The surety is obliged to perform only the obligation of the principal debtor if the latter fails to do so. If the debtor's obligation is *ad factum praestandum,* the surety may be required, as we shall see, to indemnify the creditor in a money sum, unless he has the right to perform the debtor's obligation or it is agreed that he shall do so. If the principal obligation involves the exercise of personal knowledge or skill the surety's liability is, as we shall see, to pay damages, and this may be the case also where the principal obligation is negative, a subject which will also be discussed later. It is relevant whether the surety is bound for a single debtor or for one or more co-debtors.[1] He is liable *in solidum* if those for whom he is surety are liable.[2]

The surety's liability is solely for the very obligation for which he has undertaken the suretyship. This is illustrated by *Trans-Drakensberg Bank Ltd v Guy,*[3] in which case the principal obligation for which the defendant gave his undertaking was, unbeknown to him, fictitious; this was a hire-purchase agreement devised to secure for the 'buyer' a loan from the plaintiff bank, with which the 'seller' discounted the agreement. The suretyship was for payment of the price of goods said (falsely) to have been supplied under the agreement. Miller J held that the suretyship did not extend to repayment of the loan, which the defendant had never secured. The *Annual Survey*[4] criticises the decision on the ground that the surety had secured a particular debt and the fact that this, unknown to him, was

---

[1] D 46.1.40.
[2] As to this and as to co-sureties, see Chapter IV.
[3] 1964 (1) SA 790 (D) at 795, 796.
[4] 1964 *Annual Survey* 135. See also PM Nienaber 'Iets oor Verdiskontering, Estoppel en Borgtog' (1964) 27 *THRHR* 262 at 275.

a loan disguised as a hire-purchase agreement was immaterial. The decision was, however, it is submitted, correct; the rights and obligations flowing from two such different contracts are themselves completely different and, in principle, the obligation, the burden of which could fall on him, was different from what was undertaken by him.[5] For instance, had the hire-purchase agreement been genuine, there was the prospect of the defendant recovering payment from the proceeds of the goods, but not if the transaction was in fact a loan. Moreover, the surety had given his promise for the 'buyer' to the 'seller', as the creditor, and the latter had ceded his rights under the hire-purchase agreement to the plaintiff, but the creditor of the loan was the plaintiff, not by cession but as lender. The 'seller' could never have successfully sued the 'buyer', or the defendant as his surety, for repayment of the loan. The case against the plaintiff might also be put on the footing of a fraudulent non-disclosure, as Miller J pointed out;[6] the 'seller' and the 'buyer' together contrived the scheme and, while the latter actively concealed the truth from the defendant, the former may well be said to have been under a duty to disclose this to the defendant before taking him as a surety, neither leaving it to the 'buyer' to make the disclosure nor assuming that the surety was party to the scheme. On that basis also the surety was not liable, for lack of real consent in the transaction of suretyship.

The surety's liability cannot exceed that of the debtor, for the surety may undertake liability for as much as, or for less than[7] but not (effectively) for more than, the principal debtor's obligation.[8] This principle was the basis of the decisions in *Wessels v The Master of the High Court*[9] and *The Master v Western Australian Assurance Co Ltd*,[10] that sureties for the due and faithful administration of estates by executors were not liable for that amount of a loss to the estate as represented the interests of executors who were also legatees, for had they (the principal debtors) been sued for the loss to the estate, they would have been entitled to a deduction of the amounts of their legacies; their sureties were not liable for more than they were. There cannot be any doubt that in our law[11] a surety who purports to bind himself for more than the debtor's obligation is liable to the extent of the latter, no more and no less. But, as we have said,[12] a surety can be liable for a natural obligation for which the principal debtor is in not legally liable.

In ascertaining whether the surety has purported to bind himself for more than the debtor's obligation it is necessary to take into account, not merely the extent of the respective liabilities in money figures, but also all the conditions, including those as to time and place of payment and other circumstances embraced in their respective undertakings.[13] If the conditions attached to the surety's undertaking

---

[5] As Miller J pointed out at 796.
[6] At 798.
[7] Cf *Kaplan v ER Syfret & Co* 1914 CPD 1104 at 1107.
[8] D 46.1.9, 34; V 46.1.3.4; Gr 3.3.23; Huber 3.26.14; 1.4.17.6; P 368, 370; B 4; Lee *ad Gr* 247, 248. See also *MAN Truck & Bus (SA) (Pty) Ltd v Singh and Another (2)* 1976 (4) SA 266 (N).
[9] (1891) 9 SC 18.
[10] 1925 CPD 314.
[11] Cf Roman and Roman-Dutch law, to be shortly discussed.
[12] See Chapter III.
[13] D 46.1.70 pr, 1; D 46.1.49.2; V 46.1.4; Gr 3.3.23; P 370, 372, 376, 378; B4.

are more onerous than those attached to the undertaking of the principal debtor, then the suretyship is expressed to be for more than the principal debtor's obligation.[14] Voet[15] gives an example of this.

By the Roman law the surety who promised more than his principal debtor was entirely freed of obligation—no valid suretyship was created and the transaction was ineffective,[16] because the accessory cannot be greater than the principal transaction.

Among Roman-Dutch law writers there was a conflict as to the effect of an undertaking by a surety more onerous than that of the principal debtor. Groenewegen[17] took the view that the surety was bound in the strict terms of his promise and that the creditor could exact payment in terms of the undertaking. Grotius[18] said that the surety is liable on his undertaking up to the extent of the principal debtor's liability but no further; and Pothier[19] held the same view as did Voet.[20] Van der Keessel[21] and Van Leeuwen[22] said that in the event of the principal debtor's liability increasing beyond what it was at the date of the suretyship the surety is liable for the increase up to the extent of the suretyship transaction, on the tacit condition that the creditor may allow the debt to increase to that extent on the same security.

In consideration of the extent of a surety's obligation, obviously the terms in which his undertaking of liability as a surety is expressed are all-important and these must be viewed in the light of what appears in Chapter VI on Interpretation of the Contract.[23]

If nothing is said in the suretyship undertaking concerning conditions then those applicable to the principal obligation apply also to the suretyship.[24] Consequently, if the surety is bound in simple terms for a principal obligation which is subject to a term or condition, he cannot be sued until the term has expired or the condition has been fulfilled:[25] Not until the principal debt is due for fulfilment, whether by effluxion of time or performance of a condition (including a

---

[14] D 46.1.16.2, 2; D 46.1.34: D 46.1.70 pr; V 46.1.3; P 369, 371, 374.
[15] Voet *loc cit*.
[16] D 46.1.8.7; Gr 3.3.23; Sch 301; P 375; B 5.
[17] Groen *ad D* 46.1.8.7.
[18] Gr 3.3.23.
[19] P 375.
[20] V 46.1.4.
[21] VdK 499; *Dictata* (Lee *ad Gr* 247).
[22] VL 4.4.4; Kotze's note (g); *Cens For* 1.4.17.8.
[23] It may not be out of place to mention again, in relation to the use of wide language, the following cases: *Cope v Atkinson's Motor Garages Ltd* 1931 AD 366 'indebtedness on any just cause of indebtedness whatsoever'; *St Patricks Mansions (Pty) Ltd v Grange Restaurant (Pty) Ltd and* Another 1949 (4) SA 57 (W) at 67—'all and any amounts which may at any time hereafter become owing ... arising out of any cause whatsoever'; *Segell v Kerdia Investments (Pty) Ltd* 1953 (1) SA 20 (W)—'any or all rents due ... and for the due compliance with and observance by the lessee of any and all terms, conditions, stipulations and provisions'; *Hawkes, FJ, & Co Ltd v Nagel*, 1957 (3) SA 126 (W) —'for any and all indebtedness now or hereafter due to them by ... from whatsoever cause arising'. The decision in this last case is doubtful. See Chapter VI.
[24] P 371.
[25] D 46.1.57; V 46.1.4; P 370, 371; B 322, 333.

condition precedent), can a claim be made successfully against the surety.[26] But where the principal debtor was insolvent, this dispensed with notice to him to pay the debt.[27]

A surety cannot be bound for something different from that for which the principal debtor is bound, for example, one for money, the other for wheat,[28] but if the debtor is liable for money and the surety for grain of equal value the transaction is valid.[29]

2. Surety's obligation is to the debtor's creditor

The surety's obligation is to the debtor's creditor to whom he has undertaken liability as a surety and consequently he is not bound, as surety, to anyone to whom the debtor is not bound.[30] One who has undertaken liability, not as a surety, but as a principal debtor, in addition to or in place of another, as by *intercessio,* is not a surety, as we have seen in the chapter on the Definition of Suretyship (Chapter II).

Because a surety is not bound to anyone to whom the debtor is not bound, defences available to the debtor (other than those personal to him) are available also to the surety, whether they go to the root of the debtor's liability, so that he, and therefore the surety, were never bound to the creditor, or whether they are such as establish the extinction of the debtor's liability. The subject will be discussed in detail in the chapter on Discharge of the Surety (Chapter XIII).

The surety cannot be sued before the debt is actually due by the principal debtor; everything required to bring about that state of affairs must have happened.[31]

Evidently, even where both debtor and surety are liable to the creditor, the extent of the surety's obligation, and whether it is due to be performed, depends upon the extent of the debtor's obligation and, in addition, whether he is in default.[32] To these ends, where his obligation arises out of contract, it is necessary to interpret it and to examine the basis of his liability.[33] If there is a question whether the debtor is in default, it is not for the surety to decide this and to act on the assumption that he is.[34]

3. When surety's obligation to pay becomes due

If the principal debt is unliquidated or uncertain in amount, the surety cannot be called on to pay until the amount has been ascertained, as on a final balancing of

---

[26] *Willems v Widow Schendeler* (1835) 2 Menz 20; *Parker Wood & Company Ltd v Richards and Another* 1925 NLR 277 at 279; *Lindley v Ward* 1911 CPD 21 at 27, 28.
[27] *Board v De Villiers* (1840) 2 Menz 55.
[28] D 46.1.8.8; D 46.1.38, 42; V 46.1.3; *Cens For* 1.4.17.7; P 368.
[29] D 13.5.1.5.
[30] D 46.1.16; V 46.1.3; *Cens For* 1.4.17.5, P 393, 394.
[31] *Director of Public Works v Lewis, Blundell and Roberts* 1908 ORC 14; *Parker Wood & Company Ltd v Richards and Another* 1925 NLR 277.
[32] See in this regard AN Oelofse 'Enkele Gedagtes na Aanleiding van Twee Opmerkings in *Trans-Drakensberg Bank Ltd v The Master and Others* 1962 (4) SA 417 (N)' (1988) 10 *MB* 52.
[33] Cf *Western Bank Ltd v Wood* 1969 (4) SA 131 (D).
[34] *Inglis v Durban Navigation Collieries Ltd* (1908) 29 NLR 436 at 446, 447.

accounts or by other proof.[35] This is so even though the surety has bound himself up to a fixed sum;[36] or for a fixed sum,[37] for it is still necessary in either event to ascertain the amount of the principal debtor's indebtedness.[38] His liability then is limited to the ascertained figure or the amount secured, whichever is the lesser.[39]

It is for the creditor to establish the debt he claims to be owing to him.[40] If the suretyship is conditional, in the sense that the coming into existence of the surety's obligation is suspended pending performance of a condition, it is necessary for the creditor to establish the performance.[41] If, however, the condition is not such as to suspend the coming into existence of the suretyship obligation, but one before the performance of which he cannot be sued, for example, that he be given notice of the debtor's default, this is equally effective. In the absence of such a condition, the surety is not entitled to a notice.[42]

If the suretyship is undertaken from a stated time, it is necessary to show that the principal debt was incurred after that time.[43] If undertaken until the expiration of a stated period of time, a question may arise whether the stipulation as to time limits liability to debts incurred by the debtor within that time (for which it is competent thereafter to sue the surety),[44] or whether the limit of time prescribes the period during which the surety holds himself bound and may be sued, so that he is discharged if action is not commenced against him before the expiration of the time.[45] Another possibility, very similar to the one mentioned first in the preceding sentence, is that the surety binds himself for any default of the debtor

---

[35] V 46.1.8, 16. See also *Milne NO v Cook and Others* 1956 (3) SA 317 (D) at 319, 320.

[36] *J & T Anderson v Patrick & Plowright* (1904) 25 NLR 75 at 77, 79.

[37] *Wessels v The Master of the High Court* (1891) 9 SC 18.

[38] P 370.

[39] *Wessels v The Master of the High Court* (1891) 9 SC 18 at 26, which did not follow decisions *(Kennedy NO v Haarhoff* (1884) 2 HCG 215 and *Colonial Government v Goch and Chapman* (1885) 3 HCG 216) which supported the proposition that it was for the surety to disprove his liabilities or show it was less than the amount for which he had undertaken liability.

[40] It is not conclusive against the surety that the principal debtor has conceded the claim, or the amount of it—*Cullinan v Union Government* 1922 CPD 33 at 36; following *Sutherland v Snell* (1831) 1 Menz 69 and *Churchwardens of Uitenhage v Meyer and Barnard* (1835) 2 Menz 21 at 24 in both of which cases the court held that even judgment against the principal debtor was not binding on the surety, in the respect of fixing the amount of liability, on the grounds of its being *res inter alios acta* and not *res judicata* as between creditor and surety. See also *South African Independent United Order of Mechanics and Fidelity Benefit Lodge v General Accident Fire and Life Assurance Corporation Ltd* 1916 CPD 457 at 463. Likewise a sum determined in an arbitration between creditor and principal debtor is not binding on the surety (*Orphan Chamber v Cloete* (1833) 3 Menz 157). Nor is the admission by the trustee of an insolvent principal debtor of the claim against the estate binding on a surety (*J & T Anderson v Patrick & Plowright* (1904) 25 NLR 75).

[41] *Buyskes and Others, Trustees of Du Toit v De Kock and Others* (1832) 2 Menz 12; *Baumann v Thomas* 1920 AD 428.

[42] *Churchwardens of Uitenhage v Meyer and Barnard* (1835) 2 Menz 21; *South African Bank v Forde* (1886) 4 SC 287.

[43] *Colonial Government v Sandenberg, Executors of Matthiesson, and Jan W Klerk* (1834) 2 Menz 18.

[44] As in *Feldman Ltd v Sulski* 1954 (4) SA 665 (W); on appeal *sub nom Sulski v Feldman Ltd* 1956 (1) SA 759 (A).

[45] As in *Van den Berg v Malherbe* (1829) 1 Menz 429, *Colonial Government v Du Toit and Muller* (1855) 2 Searle 225 and *Roodt v Botha* (1905) 22 SC 189. Burge (B 69) must have been writing of the former when he said the surety could be sued after the expiration of time, while Grotius (Gr 3.3.23) must have been writing of the latter when he said the surety was no longer liable though the principal debtor remained bound.

committed within the stated time, for which he may be sued after the expiry of the time; but if there is no such default within the time, he is discharged.[46]

Although everything must depend on the actual words used in the suretyship, this latter possibility is attractive from a common sense and business efficiency point of view. Creditors, after all, are unlikely to agree to an arrangement in which their accrued rights—including rights very recently accrued—against the surety all vanish on a fixed date unless they have by then sued or at least demanded payment from the surety.[47] Thus in *Langston Clothing (Properties) CC v Danco Clothing (Pty) Ltd*[48] a handwritten addition to the suretyship stating that 'this surety [sic] is valid until 31 December 1994' was interpreted by the Supreme Court of Appeal, in the light of other clauses in the suretyship, as making the surety liable for debts incurred by the principal debtor prior to that date but not thereafter.[49] On the other hand, in *Boland Bank v Loeb and Others*[50] a clause that stated that 'this deed of suretyship and *the surety's liability* thereunder will be valid until the 31 December 1990' (emphasis added) was held to absolve the surety from all liability after the stated date. Providing that the surety's liability under the deed should end on that date had the effect of destroying even liability for debts incurred prior to that date.[51]

In Roman law, if a specific place for payment was laid down in terms of the principal obligation or in those of the suretyship, there was an implied condition or term that reasonable time would be allowed to enable payment to be made at that place.[52] There seems to be no such rule today; changed conditions and speed of communication have made it unnecessary.

4. Surety's obligation when debtor's obligation is *ad factum praestandum*

If the principal obligation is *ad factum praestandum*, the court will not, in the event of default on the part of the principal debtor, grant a decree of specific performance against a surety; the creditor's remedy is in damages. So it is stated without qualifi-

---

[46] Wessels paras 4221, 4222. A provision as to time may, however, not fall into any of the above categories mentioned, as in *Johannesburg Town Council v Union Assurance Society Ltd* 1928 AD 294, in which the undertaking was held to be a continuing one for a stated sum estimated in respect of the debtor's account for six weeks' charges against them.

[47] This applies particularly where the suretyship is a continuing one extending beyond liability for a single transaction. See below in section 5 of this Chapter for a detailed discussion of continuing suretyships.

[48] 1998 (4) SA 885 (A).

[49] The suretyship contained a clause permitting termination after one month's notice but requiring payment of all sums owing at that date and specifying that the surety remained liable for any debts incurred before that date but falling due for payment thereafter. In the light of this the handwritten addition simply stated the latest date for termination.

[50] 1995 (2) SA 142 (C).

[51] In *Langston Clothing (Properties) CC v Danco Clothing (Pty) Ltd* 1998 (4) SA 885 (A) the Supreme Court of Appeal made 'no comment' on the correctness of this decision (at 889A). In *Boland Bank v Loeb and Others* the judge (at 145I) rejected any distinction in this regard between continuing suretyships and suretyships for a single transaction (in respect of which creditor might more readily accept the release of the surety after a fixed period of time). But the reasoning in *Langston Clothing (Properties) CC v Danco Clothing (Pty) Ltd* is clearly influenced by the fact the case concerned a continuing suretyship.

[52] D 46.1.49.2.

cation by Innes CJ in *Corrans and Another v Transvaal Government and Coull's Trustee*.[53] There would appear, however, to be no reason why such a decree should not be made in a suitable case.[54] In general, it would not be made because of the difficulty, if not impossibility, of adequately controlling performance. But if, for instance, the undertaking by the surety was that the debtor would deliver a particular *res* and that *res* comes by some means into the possession or control of the surety, there seems little reason why specific performance could not be ordered.

Though he may not be ordered to perform, but is liable (if he does not) to indemnify the creditor against his loss by paying damages, the surety is entitled, if he wishes, to do what the debtor had undertaken to do (for example, carry out the completion of a building contract), at any rate if the creditor is willing for him to do so; the debtor cannot, as a rule, object to this.[55] The reason for this is that if the suretyship was undertaken with the debtor's consent (as it surely always is) there is an implied mandate on his part to the surety to discharge the obligation when he is called on to do so.[56]

The issue in *Corrans and Another v Transvaal Government and Coull's Trustee*[57] was whether the sureties, having completed the unperformed part of the work with the consent of the creditor (the building owner), were entitled to have the retention money (ie that portion of the contract price not paid to the contractor in instalments or as the work progressed, but retained by the owner until completion of the contract paid to them) at the time when the debtor (the building contractor) would in the normal course of events have been entitled to it, or whether the debtor's trustee in insolvency was entitled to it. No question arose regarding the payments to be made during the progress of the work, for the creditor, apparently, had paid these to the sureties as their work progressed, as it would have paid them to the contractor had he continued with his work. The court was unanimous in

---

[53] 1909 TS 605 at 613.

[54] In *Benson v SA Mutual Life Assurance Society* 1986 (1) SA 776 (A) the Appellate Division stressed that the grant or refusal of a decree of specific performance is entirely a matter for the discretion of the court in which the claim is made and that no rules should be prescribed to regulate that discretion. See Schalk van der Merwe *et al Contract General Principles* 3 ed (2007) 407 ff for a full discussion in this regard.

[55] *Corrans and Another v Transvaal Government and Coull's Trustee* 1909 TS 605. See also *Colonial Trust Corporation Ltd of Graaff Reinet v The School Board of Pearston and Others* 1916 CPD 275 at 284.

[56] Innes CJ, presiding in *Corrans and Another v Transvaal Government and Coull's Trustee* 1909 TS 605 (and Gardiner J also in at 284), left open the question whether a surety was entitled to perform the debtor's obligation against the wishes of the creditor (at 614). Clearly he is not so entitled, but must pay such sum of damages as the principal debtor is liable for, when that obligation 'involves the exercise of personal knowledge or skill, as in the painting of a picture' (*ibid*) or 'performing the duties of some office' (at 627). Wessels J (at 624) and Mason J (at 628) expressed the view that the surety was entitled (save where personal knowledge or skill is involved) to perform the debtor's obligation whether or not the creditor was willing; the creditor could not refuse to allow him to do so and insist on holding him liable in money for his loss. These statements were *obiter* because in fact the creditor in that case had agreed to the surety completing performance of the building contract. Each case must, of course, be governed by the terms of the contract; for instance, the contract concerned in *Leathern v Henwood & Co* (1887) 8 NLR 29 appeared to give the surety the right to complete the debtor's work; while the contract concerned in *Dewar v De Witt & Dickens NO* 1948 (4) SA 898 (GW) gave the creditor the right to employ another to complete the work and to charge the excess cost to the debtor or the surety.

[57] 1909 TS 605.

the conclusion that the sureties were entitled to the retention money. Innes CJ[58] and Mason J[59] took this view on the grounds that the sureties had a claim to be indemnified by the debtor and were entitled to have from the creditor all the remedies and securities held by it against the debtor; the creditor's right to the retention money as the balance of the price for the work done, due only after completion, was a right which the creditor had to reimburse itself for the cost of completing the work if the debtor defaulted and was therefore a right to which the sureties were entitled.[60] The sureties were entitled, however, not to the whole sum, but to only so much of it as was required to indemnify them. Wessels J,[61] on the other hand, considered that the sureties, in completing the work, were acting under an implied mandate from the debtor and that, in association with this, they had an implied mandate to receive on the debtor's behalf the money due under the contract; they stepped into his shoes, and the creditor had no right to retain any portion of what was due by it, for it was not concerned with accounts between sureties and debtor. On the one view the sureties derived their right to the retention money through the creditor, by a subrogation to its rights; on the other view, they derived their right from the debtor by an implied mandate. The former view does not explain how the sureties became entitled to the progress payments, if they were (a subject we shall shortly discuss), but the latter view does afford some explanation. May the simple explanation, in relation both to progress payments and retention money, not be that a surety cannot be bound more onerously than the debtor; if he binds himself in simple unqualified terms, the conditions attaching to the principal obligation apply to the suretyship? On all views in the *Corrans* case, the trustee of the debtor stood in no better a position than the debtor did and had no claim, at any rate until the sureties had been indemnified.

Three questions remain open. The first is whether the surety is entitled, against the will of the creditor, to carry out the debtor's obligation *ad factum praestandum*. The better view appears to be that, subject to the terms of the contract, he is so entitled, as Wessels and Mason JJ said, for that is the very obligation he undertook by becoming surety and the creditor accepted him as such.[62] The instances of contracts requiring the exercise of personal knowledge or skill are exceptions.

The second question is whether the building owner, as creditor, is obliged to make the progress payments to the surety or whether the latter, having stood surety for the performance of the building contractor's obligations, is entitled to no more in this respect than a right of recourse against him when he, the surety, has completed the work.[63] On the reasoning of Wessels J in the *Corrans* case[64] in

---

[58] At 614, 615.

[59] At 629, 630.

[60] Gardiner J took the same view in *Colonial Trust Corporation Ltd of Graaff Reinet v The School Board of Pearston and Others* 1916 CPD 275 at 284.

[61] At 625, 626.

[62] As is clear from *Benson v SA Mutual Life Assurance Society* 1986 (1) SA 776 (A) at 781H–783F. See also *LAWSA* vol 26 (first reissue; 1997) para 197.

[63] In *Leathern v Henwood & Co* (1887) 8 NLR 29 at 32 it seems to be implied in the judgment of Connor CJ, that the surety's right is to have the debtor cede to him his right against the creditor for the contract price when he, the surety, has completed the work in performance of his obligation as surety.

[64] *Corrans and Another v Transvaal Government and Coull's Trustee* 1909 TS 605.

relation to the retention money, the surety is entitled to the progress payments; he performs the obligation of the debtor under an implied mandate from him to do so and steps into his shoes on the performance of the contract; and consequently is entitled to receive whatever the debtor would have been entitled to receive had he properly performed. The same result is reached by application of the principle that the surety cannot oblige himself for more than the debtor's obligation, nor more onerously than the debtor has bound himself. The debtor's obligation to perform the work is subject to his right to receive progress payments (where the contract so provides) and if the surety's obligation to perform (where that rests on him) was not the same, his burden would be more onerous than that of the debtor.

The third question is whether the creditor is obliged to pay the surety, and thus is entitled to receive the whole of the contract price, or whether the surety's right is limited to so much as is required to indemnify him for the cost he has incurred in completing performance of the debtor's obligation. In other words, on whom, the creditor or the surety, lies the duty to account to the debtor or to his trustee in insolvency, or to persons to whom he has ceded his rights to payments under the contract? The answer must be that the surety is entitled to receive no more than is required to indemnify him and the creditor is obliged to pay him no more than that.[65]

Although the debtor cannot give cessions of the contract price prejudicial to the surety,[66] such cessions are valid and effective subject to the surety's rights, and so the excess over what is required to indemnify the surety must go to the debtor, his trustee or in the direction in which it has been ceded. The creditor is the person to honour the cessions and it seems to follow that, if there are no cessions, it is for him to pay the surplus to the debtor. The right of action under the contract vests in the debtor save insofar as he has ceded it and subject to the surety's right to reimbursement.[67]

If the principal obligation is negative, for instance, an undertaking by a lessee to abstain from contravening a by-law, 'performance' of the obligation consists in

---

[65] The view expressed above is consistent with the *ratio* of the decision in *BK Tooling (Edms) Bpk v Scope Precision Engineering (Edms) Bpk* 1979 (1) SA 391 (A). See also *Bermann en 'n Ander v Administrasie van Suidwes-Afrika* 1966 (2) PH A85 (SWA). Even if the surety acts under an implied mandate from the debtor, this is a mandate to perform the debtor's obligation and the *actio mandati contraria* entitles him to indemnification, as we shall see in the chapter on the surety's Right of Recourse (Chapter XI), but to no more.

[66] *Leathern v Henwood & Co* (1887) 8 NLR 29; *Colonial Trust Corporation Ltd of Graaff Reinet v The School Board of Pearston and Others* 1916 CPD 275.

[67] *Alexander NO v Administrator, Transvaal* 1974 (2) SA 248 (T) also deals with the question of retention money, but, with respect, without taking account of the difference in view between Innes CJ and Wessels J in the *Corrans* case (1909 TS 605). In *Alexander's* case a clause in the contract of suretyship provided that in the event of the contractor's default, the sureties would be in the same position as the contractor. The court was therefore correct in holding that the progress payments and retention moneys were properly paid to the sureties, leaving the sureties to account, if necessary, to the trustee of the insolvent estate of the contractor. However, the court did not distinguish between the views of the judges in *Corrans,* but simply remarked generally that the sureties in 'their contractual relationship with the building owner ... become the mandatories of the principal contractor ...' (at 255C). It is submitted that a contractual relationship with A cannot itself affect X's contractual relationship with B, but in the context this *dictum* means that the sureties acquire all the contractual rights against the owner which the contractor had.

abstention from a particular act.[68] If the act from which the principal debtor is to abstain has been done by him in breach of his obligation, it may or may not be possible for the surety to perform the obligation by restoring the situation; but, generally, it is unlikely that a court would order this, for the same reason that it is unlikely to order specific performance of a contract *ad factum praestandum*. Unless the debtor's breach is capable of remedy by the surety and he does remedy it, he is liable to the creditor for the damages for which the debtor is liable.

5. Continuing suretyships

A continuing suretyship is a suretyship for payment by a debtor of his debt arising from a series of transactions with his creditor on a running account extending into the future; the surety undertakes to pay the balance owing on this account on demand by the creditor.[69] In *SA General Electric Co (Pty) Ltd v Sharfman and Others NNO*[70] Boshoff JP explained:

> The ordinary suretyship is usually in respect of a particular debt or obligation. It is accessory to the transaction that creates the obligation of the principal debtor.... The duration of the surety's liability depends upon the terms of the deed of suretyship. Some suretyships are intended to cover a single credit and transaction only, while others, called continuing guarantees, are so framed as to apply to a series of credits and transactions. In the case of a single credit transaction the surety's liability extends only to one credit or transaction agreed upon, while in the case of a continuing guarantee the liability endures until the credits and the transactions contemplated by the parties, and covered by the guarantee, have been exhausted or until the guarantee itself has been revoked.[71]

The undertaking may thus be for an unlimited amount or may be limited to a stated sum.[72] In the former event, the surety is liable for the balance owing and unpaid by

---

[68] *Segell v Kerdia Investments (Pty) Ltd* 1953 (1) SA 20 (W) at 27.

[69] D 46.1.55; V 46.1.8. Wessels para 3992; *Glenn Brothers v Commercial General Agency Co Ltd* 1905 TS 737 at 739, 740; *Schoenfeldt v Myer and Co* 1928 TPD 468 at 470; *Johannesburg Town Council v Union Assurance Society* 1928 AD 294 at 299. See also JT Pretorius 'Continuing Suretyships' (1988) 10 *MB* 85 for further discussion in this regard.

[70] 1981 (1) SA 592 (W) at 595.

[71] Care must be taken to distinguish between, on the one hand, a suretyship in a stated sum for a single debt (for instance, for the price of goods to be supplied), which may at first sight appear to be a continuing suretyship but is not, as in *Glenn Brothers v Commercial General Agency Co Ltd* 1905 TS 737 and in *Lewis & Friedland Ltd v Tinn Bros & Lawrie* 1931 (2) PH A95 (T) and, on the other hand, a continuing suretyship limited to a stated sum, as in, for instance, *Schoenfeldt v Myer and Co* 1928 TPD 468 and *Cope v Atkinson's Motor Garages Ltd* 1931 AD 366. Which is the case in any particular substance depends on an interpretation of the contract of suretyship. See also GF Lubbe 'Die Onderskeid tussen Borgtog en Ander Vorme van Persoonlike Sekerheidstelling' (1984) 47 *THRHR* 383; JT Pretorius 'Die Formaliteitsvereiste by Borgstelling' (1988) 10 *MB* 122; *LAWSA* vol 26 para 192; NJ Grové *Die Formaliteitsvereiste by Borgstelling* unpublished LLM dissertation, University of Pretoria (1984) 70 ff.

[72] The so-called *exceptio non numeratae pecunia* may be of some relevance in this regard. Although it has been argued that this exceptio had become obsolete in the South African law (GA Mulligan 'Bonds, Negotiable Instruments, Provisional Sentence and their Mystiques' (1951) 68 *SALJ* 384 at 395), the existence of it was assumed in *Wollach v Barclays National Bank Ltd* 1983 (2) SA 543 (A) at 559–60. This *exceptio* is usually renounced where the cause of debt secured by the suretyship arises from a loan or an advance of money. The defence which is sought to be excluded or regulated is instances where a borrower of money raises the defence that no money has in fact been paid over to him. Raising the defence has the effect that despite an acknowledgment of indebtedness by the

the debtor to the creditor on a balancing of accounts between them; in the latter event, the surety's liability in respect of that balance is limited to the sum he has secured, but to this may be added interest for the whole period of the indebtedness if the terms of the suretyship, on a proper interpretation, so provide.[73] This is none the less so if the creditor has debited and capitalised interest.[74] The suretyship may

---

debtor, the onus is shifted to the creditor to prove that he has performed his part of the bargain. Renunciation of the defence results in a negative onus, that is, to prove that no money was in fact received, being placed on the debtor in an action on the merits. See *Cohen v Louis Blumberg (Pty) Ltd* 1949 (2) SA 849 (W) where Ramsbottom J stated at 851: 'The benefit of the exception is to enable a defendant to place on the plaintiff the onus of proving that the money was paid; by renouncing the benefit, the defendant takes the onus of proof on himself'.

[73] *The National Bank of South Africa v Graaf and Others* (1904) 21 SC 457; *Snaid v Volkskas Bank Ltd* 1997 (1) SA 239 (W). However, the interest may not exceed the capital sum (*LTA Construction Bpk v Administrateur, Transvaal* 1992 (1) SA 473 (A)). In *SA Breweries Ltd v Van Zyl* 2006 (1) SA 197 (SCA) the respondent (Van Zyl) was the director of a liquor store. He stood surety for its debts in favour of a division of SA Breweries Ltd, a company registered in 1969 ('SAB 69'). He bound himself as surety and co-principal debtor for money 'which may at any time be or become owing' (para 1, quoted at 199G). SAB 69 later sold its beer division business as a going concern to a company which, with two name changes and a conversion, became the appellant (referred to in the judgment as 'SAB 98'). As part of the agreement SAB 69 ceded to SAB 98 'all the seller's right, title and interest in and to debtors' and 'any outstanding orders for goods in transit' with effect from 4 March 1999 (quoted at 199G–H, para 2). After the cession SAB 98 continued to supply goods to the liquor store on credit. SAB 98 sued Van Zyl in his capacity as surety for the debts of the liquor store. Van Zyl argued that he was liable to SAB 98 only for such amounts as may have been owed by his liquor store to SAB 69 at the time of the cession. Put differently, he maintained that there was no cession in respect of debts incurred after 4 March 1999. According to him SAB 98 had never secured the debts of the liquor store after the date of the cession. The court held that Van Zyl was liable only for those debts incurred before the cession: 'The only right of action that SAB 69 [the cedent] had against its debtors and which it could cede to SAB 98 at the time of cession was the right to claim what was owed to it as at the date of the cession. It had no right of action for the future debts of its debtors and it could not cede rights that had not accrued to it. The liability of a surety being ancillary to that of the principal debtor, the respondent [Van Zyl] was accordingly only liable to be sued for payment of moneys owed to SAB 69 by [the liquor store] ... at the date of the cession ...' (para 9, at 202B–C). The problem with this quotation is that it is unclear whether it was intended to lay down a general principle. It is also not known exactly how the contract of cession was formulated. It may well be that the parties did not intend the cession to apply to future debts. That intention is manifested primarily by the way in which the cession is formulated but the judgment provides little detail of this. If the court was laying down no more than that there was no intention on this occasion to cede future debts, the decision is unexceptional. But if it was laying down a principle that the cession of future debts was not possible, it is submitted that the judgment is in error. However and at least this we can say with some certainty, that there is no general prohibition in our law against the cession of future debts (see *First National Bank of SA Ltd v Lynn NO and Others* 1996 (2) SA 339 (A) at 360A–C, where Olivier JA remarked that 'it has been accepted in commerce and by the Courts of our country for more than a century that future rights can be ceded and transferred *in anticipando*. The decisions of our Courts have thus been regarded for a very long period of time as being correct. Clearly these decisions have been acted upon and served as the basis for the general and well-known practice of taking security in the form of the cession of book debts (including future debts), cession of existing and future rights *in securitatem debiti* and factoring of existing and future rights. In these circumstances I am not inclined to hold that these decisions are wrong ...'. *Lynn* has been followed in other decisions (for example, *Byron v Duke Inc* 2002 (5) SA 483 (SCA) par 7). There is also no reason why a surety cannot undertake liability for future debts, especially with continuing suretyships and master agreements. If there had been such a prohibition, financial institutions would be in serious trouble were they, for example, to take cession of future book debts to secure an obligation, or to engage in securitization, factoring, or financing the construction of buildings by taking a cession of the rental due and to become due. If Mpati DP were to be found to have said that it was not possible to cede future debts he would clearly have been wrong. Perhaps the judgment in *SA Breweries* should rather be confined to its particular facts. See also the discussion in Chapter III note 94.

[74] *Volkskas Bpk v Meyer* 1966 (2) SA 379 (T).

furthermore be for an indefinite period of time or for a fixed term. In the former event, the suretyship may contain a provision entitling the surety to terminate the suretyship by not less than a stated period of notice to the creditor; if it does not, he nevertheless has the right to give reasonable notice to terminate the suretyship.[75] In *Kalil v Standard Bank of South Africa Ltd*[76] Williamson JA elaborated:

> Generally speaking a surety under such continuous guarantee has, apart from an express or clearly inferential provision to the contrary in his contract, a right to bring about a termination of such a continuous liability by notice duly given to the holder of the guarantee. Any such notice obviously could only relate to amounts advanced to or becoming due by the principal debtor after the notice: the surety's liability in relation to any amount due at the time of giving of the notice would remain unaffected.[77]

Although it is true, generally speaking, that a surety under a continuous suretyship has the right unilaterally to bring about the termination of the suretyship by giving due and reasonable notice to the creditor, this right is subject to the terms of the suretyship itself. Where, for example, the contract contains a provision that the suretyship shall 'remain in full force ... until the creditor/s shall have agreed in writing to cancel'[78] the suretyship, the surety's right unilaterally to terminate liability in respect of future liabilities would be severely restricted or even removed.[79] In *Oceanair (Natal) (Pty) Ltd v Sher*[80] Howard J remarked the following in this regard:

---

[75] P 399; Wessels paras 4290, 4291. Cf Jenkins & *Co v TN Price* (1903) 24 NLR 112 at 115; and see *Kalil v Standard Bank of South Africa Ltd* 1967 (4) SA 550 (A) at 555, 556.

[76] 1967 (4) SA 550 (A) at 555.

[77] See also *St Patricks Mansions (Pty) Ltd v Grange Restaurant (Pty) Ltd and Another* 1949 (4) SA 57 (W) at 71; *Diners Club South Africa (Pty) Ltd v Durban Engineering (Pty) Ltd* 1980 (3) SA 53 (A) 65, 81 (as discussed by JT Pretorius 'Borgkontrak of Vrywaringskontrak?' (1982) 45 *THRHR* 73); *SA General Electric Co (Pty) Ltd v Sharfman and Others NNO* 1981 (1) SA 592 (W) at 595; *Morgan and Another v Brittan Boustred Ltd* 1992 (2) SA 775 (A) at 784; *Langston Clothing (Properties) CC v Danco Clothing (Pty) Ltd* 1998 (4) SA 885 (A) at 888.

[78] For example, *Neuhoff v York Timbers Ltd* 1981 (4) SA 666 (T) at 676; *Oceanair (Natal) (Pty) Ltd v Sher* 1980 (1) SA 317 (D) at 319.

[79] In *Leyland Finance Co Ltd v Van Rensburg* 1970 (4) SA 145 (T) at 150 Boshoff J remarked that '[d]aar skyn ook geen beginselbesware daarteen te wees nie dat 'n borg hom verbind om sy aanspreeklikheid slegs met die skriftelike toestemming van die hoofskuldeiser te beëindig.' *SA General Electric Co (Pty) Ltd v Sharfman and Others NNO* 1981 (1) SA 592 (W) is an example of an instance where the creditor sought to preclude the surety from unilaterally withdrawing his suretyship. Apart from the fact that the suretyship contained a provision that no purported withdrawal would be effective unless the creditor consented thereto in writing, the surety undertook the liability that the suretyship 'shall remain in force as a continuing security ... notwithstanding [his] death ...' (596). The court held that the fact that the suretyship contract contained a clause precluding the surety from withdrawing his suretyship without the consent of the creditor did not preclude his executors from so doing in the absence of an express provision limiting this power of the executors (597–8). In such a case the contract of suretyship will not cover the debts incurred subsequent to the notice. By giving a promise for future liabilities, a surety undertakes an obligation which is transmitted to his estate on his death. This obligation is transmitted on his death unless before that event he terminates his obligation by proper notice, where the right to do so is not excluded by the terms of the suretyship (see below and also *Kalil v Standard Bank of South Africa Ltd* 1967 (4) SA 550 (A) at 557). In theory it would thus be possible for a surety to undertake liability under a contract of continuous suretyship which may limit the powers of the executors of his estate to terminate the suretyship in respect of future liabilities not yet incurred by the principal debtor. It is submitted that such an undertaking would make it difficult, if not impossible, to wind up such a surety's estate. It is submitted that such a clause should be void as being against public policy. See the discussion in Chapter XIII.

[80] 1980 (1) SA 317 (D) at 324.

I am of the opinion that, properly construed, the stipulation that the suretyship shall remain in force until the creditor agrees in writing to cancel it effectively removes the right of the individual surety to terminate his liability by notice or by concluding an oral agreement ... [purporting to cancel the suretyship contract]. The stipulation is valid and enforceable, and affords a sufficient basis for holding that the oral agreement is invalid and evidence of it is accordingly irrelevant and inadmissible.[81]

Where the termination of a continuing suretyship is within the exclusive discretion of the creditor,[82] the surety's position may be precarious especially if the obligations undertaken by the surety are of the widest possible nature in regard to the principal debtor's indebtedness or the obligations for which the surety undertakes liability as well as in regard to the duration of the suretyship.[83]

---

[81] See also *Plascon-Evans Paints (Transvaal) Ltd v Virginia Glass Works (Pty) Ltd and Others* 1983 (1) SA 465 (O) at 471; *Ferreira and Others v SAPDC (Trading) Ltd* 1983 (1) SA 235 (A); Louise Tager 'The Effect of Non-variation Clauses in Contracts' (1976) 93 *SALJ* 423 and NJ Grové 'Borgkontrakte, Mondelinge Wysigings en Kansellasie' 1983 *De Rebus* 201. See, however, *Morgan and Another v Brittan Boustred Ltd* 1992 (2) SA 775 (A) where it was said that although the word 'cancelled' was often used to indicate a cancellation by agreement between the parties, ie a consensual cancellation or one brought about by the exercise of a right to terminate, this was not always so. Where the contract of suretyship thus provided that the continuing suretyship 'may not be withdrawn, revoked or cancelled without the creditor's prior written consent', the clause 'was intended to deal with the situation where the surety attempts to revoke the suretyship; not with the case where there is a discharge consequent on a mutual agreement between the creditor and surety, or (*a fortiori*), where the creditor waives his rights under the suretyship' (at 784). See also *Tsaperas and Others v Boland Bank Ltd* 1996 (1) SA 719 (A) at 725.

[82] *Botha (now Griessel) and Another v Finanscredit (Pty) Ltd* 1989 (3) SA 773 (A) dealt with the interpretation of a continuing suretyship which provided that the contract 'shall not be cancelled save with the written consent of the creditor'. The court was not persuaded that this clause was improper and unconscionable, since the requirement that the accessory liability of the surety should have subsisted for so long as the principal debtor owed money to the creditor was not only commercially sound but also legally and morally unexceptionable (at 783). Hoexter JA remarked that in an investigation into whether a contract is unenforceable on the grounds of public policy it should be borne in mind: '*(a)* that, while public policy generally favours the utmost freedom of contract, it nevertheless properly takes into account the necessity for doing simple justice between man and man; and *(b)* that a court's power to declare contracts contrary to public policy should be exercised sparingly and only in cases in which the impropriety of the transaction and the element of public harm are manifest ...' (at 783). Although the exact ambit and applicability of the public policy defence remains uncertain the courts will no doubt exercise their discretion in this regard with circumspection. See also the discussion in Chapter XIII below.

[83] See in this regard *Neuhoff v York Timbers Ltd* 1981 (4) SA 666 (T); *Rand Bank Ltd v Rubenstein* 1981 (2) SA 207 (W); *Bank of Lisbon and South Africa Ltd v De Ornelas and Another* 1988 (3) SA 580 (A). In *Bank of Lisbon* the Appellate Division upheld the validity of a deed of suretyship in terms of which the sureties had bound themselves as sureties and co-principal debtors *in solidum* in favour of the creditor 'for the due payment of every sum of money which now or at any time hereafter be or become owing by the debtor to the ... [creditor] from whatsoever cause or causes arising, and for the due performance of every other obligation, howsoever arising, which the debtor may now or at any time hereafter be or become bound to perform in favour of ... [the creditor]' (at 608–9). The suretyship also contained a clause that the suretyship would 'establish a continuing [suretyship] covering liability on my/our part for whatever amount(s) and whatever other obligation(s) will be owing by the debtor to the ... [creditor] for the time being, notwithstanding any intermediate discharge or settlement of or fluctuations in the account ...' (at 609). The Appellate Division held that the *exceptio doli generalis* never formed part of the Roman-Dutch law and that that court 'has therefore previously rightly refused to exercise an equitable jurisdiction by allowing the exception *doli generalis* to be employed for the purpose of enabling a party to a valid contract to render its express terms unenforceable, or to amend or ameliorate its express terms, merely because that party would suffer hardship from the operation or enforcement of the contract' (at 610). See the discussions of this

The suretyship may provide that the amount of the principal debtor's indebtedness may be proved by means of a 'certificate of indebtedness'.[84] The purpose of such certificate clause is to facilitate proof of the amount of the principal debtor's indebtedness to the creditor at any given time.[85]

The surety may, however, attach a term the breach of which releases him from all liability, for example, a condition or term limiting the extent of supplies on credit by the creditor to the debtor, as in *Texas Co (SA) Ltd v Webb and Tomlinson*.[86] In the absence of such a term, express or implied,[87] the giving by the creditor to the debtor of credit in excess of the amount secured by the surety does not release the surety.[88]

When the surety is called on by the creditor to pay the balance of the amount owing by the debtor, in order to ascertain what that balance is, the first item on the debit side is taken to be discharged or reduced by the first item on the credit side; credits as they occur are appropriated to the earlier debits. The general rule that payments are appropriated first to interest and then to capital does not apply.[89] If, where the surety has limited his undertaking to a stated sum, the

---

decision by L Hawthorne and Ph Thomas (1989) 22 *De Jure* 143; SWJ van der Merwe, GF Lubbe and LF van Huyssteen (1989) 106 *SALJ* 235 and Michael A Lambiris (1988) 105 *SALJ* 644. See also *Sasfin (Pty) Ltd v Beukes* 1989 (1) SA 1 (A); *Botha (now Griessel) and Another v Finanscredit (Pty) Ltd* 1989 (3) SA 773 (A); *D Engineering Company (Pty) Ltd v Morkel and Others* (TPD 27 March 1992 (case A81 3/91) reported in 3 *Commercial Law Digest* 228); JT Pretorius 'Continuing Suretyships' (1988) 10 *MB* 85; Carole Lewis 'The Demise of the Exceptio Doli: Is there Another Route to Contractual Equity?' (1990) 107 *SALJ* 26; CF Forsyth & JT Pretorius 'Recent Developments in the Law of Suretyship' (1993) 5 *SA Merc LJ* 181; and the discussion in Chapter XIII below.

[84] *Astra Furnishers (Pty) Ltd v Arend and Another* 1973 (1) SA 446 (C); *Nedbank Ltd v Van der Berg and Another* 1987 (3) SA 449 (W); *Standard Bank of SA Ltd v Neugarten and Others* 1987 (3) SA 695 (W); *Sasfin (Pty) Ltd v Beukes* 1989 (1) SA 1 (A); *Nedbank Ltd v Abstein Distributors (Pty) Ltd and Others* 1989 (3) SA 750 (T); *Donelly v Barclays National Bank Ltd* 1990 (1) SA 375 (W); *Bankkorp Ltd v Hendler and Another* 1992 (4) SA 375 (W). See also Wayne Hutchinson 'Conclusive Nature of a Certificate of Balance Revisited' (1990) 107 *SALJ* 414 and Chapter XIII below.

[85] In *Senekal v Trust Bank of Africa Ltd* 1978 (3) SA 375 (A) Miller JA explained at 381–2: 'Whenever a bank claims payment of money said to be owing to it by a customer who enjoys overdraft facilities on a current account which fluctuates, possibly from day to day, it must needs rely on its books of account and other records of transactions in order to establish the amount due to it. To prove every one of the many entries in the books, which may have been made from time to time by a large number of different employees, might for obvious reasons sometimes be difficult.... The main purpose of the certificate clause was clearly to facilitate proof of the amount of the principal debtor's indebtedness to the bank at any given time. A similar purpose underlies provisions, frequently found in reducible mortgage bonds and in bonds to cover future advances, that a prescribed certificate shall be sufficient or *prima facie* proof of the amount due thereunder. In such cases the terms of the provision may show clearly that the certificate is to have evidential value only for the purpose of obtaining provisional sentence ...'. However, it has been subsequently held that such certificate cannot be a valid liquid document for the purposes of provisional sentence. See FR Malan, AN Oelofse, W de Vos, JT Pretorius & CJ Nagel *Provisional Sentence on Bills of Exchange, Cheques and Promissory Notes* (1986) 20–21 and *Wollach v Barclays National Bank Ltd* 1983 (2) SA 543 (A) for a full discussion in this regard.

[86] 1927 NPD 24.

[87] As to which see *Northern Cape Co-operative Livestock Agency Ltd v John Roderick & Co Ltd* 1965 (2) SA 64 (O) at 72.

[88] *SA Produce, Wine and Brandy Co v Mihnert* (1908) 18 CTR 700; *Rudd, Milton & Co v Dolley & Co* (1884) 3 EDC 351. And see Wessels para 3995.

[89] *Volkskas Bpk v Meyer* 1966 (2) SA 379 (T) at 382. See also *Malan on Bills of Exchange, Cheques and Promissory Notes in South African Law* 5ed by FR Malan, JT Pretorius & SF du Toit (2009) at 320 footnote 184 for a full discussion in this regard.

creditor gives the debtor credit beyond that sum, payments by the debtor are to be appropriated first to the secured sum.[90] This is in accordance with the general rule of appropriation to a debt for which there are sureties in preference to one for which there are none.[91]

6. Surety's liability for interest

If the surety has bound himself for no more than a stated sum, being the debt or part of the debt of the debtor, he is not liable, in addition, for interest chargeable against the debtor,[92] but the nature[93] of the debt (for example, a guardian's obligations to his ward, arising out of the guardianship), or the terms in which the surety has bound himself, may make him liable for the interest for which the debtor is liable.[94] Whether the terms in which the surety had bound himself go so far as to make him liable for interest is a question of interpretation of the suretyship contract.[95] If the surety has bound himself in wide general terms for performance of the debtor's obligations, without limitation, and these include a liability for interest, the surety is liable for interest.[96]

---

[90] *Northern Cape Co-operative Livestock Agency Ltd v John Roderick & Co Ltd* 1965 (2) SA 64 (O) at 73. See also *Fluxman v Brittian* 1941 AD 273 at 300.

[91] P 530. See also *Zietsman v Allied Building Society* 1989 (3) SA 166 (O).

[92] D 46.1.68.1; V 46.1.12, 13; *Cens For* 1.4.17.9, 10; P 404; B 53. See also *Dreyer v Smuts* (1828) 1 Menz 308.

[93] *Dreyer v Smuts* (1828) 1 Menz 308.

[94] *Dreyer v Smuts* (1828) 1 Menz 308. See also *Trustees of Du Toit v Executors of Smuts and De Kock* (1835) 2 Menz 24; *The National Bank of South Africa v Graaf and Others* (1904) 21 SC 457. In the latter case the surety was, indeed, held liable for compound interest. See also *Volkskas Bpk v Meyer* 1966 (2) SA 379 (T) and *Snaid v Volkskas Bank Ltd* 1997 (1) SA 239 (W). Wessels discusses the subject in paras 3900–5.

[95] *Pfeiffer v First National Bank of SA Ltd* 1998 (3) SA 1018 (SCA). Interest is capitalised whenever an agreement provides for compound interest. Capitalisation is an accounting exercise designed to simplify the calculation of compound interest. If the capitalisation of interest does not amount to a novation of the debt, the interest element cannot lose its character as interest, not only for the purposes of the *in duplum* rule, but for all purposes. All credits or payments must be appropriated first to payment of the interest element and then to capital (*Standard Bank of South Africa Ltd v Oneanate Investments (Pty) Ltd (in Liquidation)* 1998 (1) SA 811 (SCA)). A secured debt should also be paid before an unsecured debt. Good faith requires that the creditor and the debtor should as far as possible ease the burden of the surety (*Pfeiffer v First National Bank of SA Ltd* 1998 (3) SA 1018 (SCA) at 1032). The decision in *ABSA Bank Ltd t/a Volkskas Bank v Page and Another* 2002 (1) SA 617 (SCA) dealt mainly with the manner in which a court order in favour of a creditor had to be interpreted. The majority of the Supreme Court of Appeal dealt with allocation of payments and said the following: 'An unlimited suretyship covers the whole debt. A limited suretyship is no different. It does not cover only a portion of the debt. A limited surety who performs an obligation must be taken to pay a (fixed) contribution towards the whole debt. His payment means that the creditor receives a 'dividend' of fewer than one hundred cents in the rand on the *whole* debt. He does not receive payment in full of some part of the debt. Since a surety's liability is accessory, and a surety's debt cannot be greater than that of the principal debtor, payment by a principal debtor of an indebtedness which is co-extensive with the surety's liability will discharge both him and the surety. Before that, a principal debtor's payment discharges only his own debt' (at 623). Thus such a surety will be discharged from further liability only once the whole of the debt is paid. Nugent AJA, in the minority, also held that a surety who is bound to pay a limited amount will not be discharged from liability where the principal debtor merely pays an amount equivalent to the fixed amount for which the surety has undertaken liability. Such surety will only be discharged upon payment of the principal debt in full (at 624).

[96] Wessels paras 3900–5; *Snaid v Volkskas Bank Ltd* 1997 (1) SA 239 (W).

Apart from the possibility of the surety being liable for the debtor's debt for interest, he is in any event liable for interest from the time he himself is *in mora*.[97] The interest may not exceed the capital sum.[98]

7. Surety's liability for the creditor's costs in suing the principal debtor

Although the surety is liable for the principal debt he is not liable for the costs incurred by the creditor in suing the principal debtor, and failing to obtain payment from him. This is so even where the surety has the benefit of excussion, unless he has availed himself of the benefit or has requested the creditor to sue the debtor or has acquiesced in his doing so. The reason for this freedom from liability for the costs where the surety does not have the benefit of excussion is that it is then open to the creditor to sue either the debtor or the surety (and sometimes both), and if he elects to sue the debtor without reference to the surety, he takes on himself the risk of the costs. If the surety has the benefit of excussion, the creditor may not assume that he will avail himself of it. Consequently, in either event, the creditor should give the surety appropriate notice of his intention to sue the debtor so that the surety may, if he wishes, pay the debt. If he expressly avails himself of the benefit of excussion, he is liable for the costs consequently incurred, and the same situation exists if he requests the creditor to sue the debtor. If, instead of taking a stand in the matter, he remains passive after receipt of the appropriate notice, he is taken to have acquiesced in the creditor's suing the debtor and so is liable for the costs if the creditor fails to obtain payment from the debtor.[99]

In *Joubert v Vermooten*[100] Wessels J put the matter on the basis that 'if a surety guarantees a specific amount, then *prima facie* he is liable for only that amount', but if it is not paid on due date and the creditor consequently suffers damage, he is entitled to recover this from the surety. To ground that claim, however, when the damage is in the form of costs of excussing the debtor, the creditor must give the surety notice of his intention to sue the debtor. Logically, such a notice would, consequently, appear to be unnecessary where[101] the surety has, by the terms of his promise, bound himself for the costs which may be incurred by the creditor, but since the surety may elect to pay the debt rather than risk the costs

---

[97] V 46.1.13.
[98] *LTA Construction Bpk v Administrateur, Transvaal* 1992 (1) SA 473 (A); *Pfeiffer v First National Bank of SA Ltd* 1998 (3) SA 1018 (SCA) at 1026.
[99] P 404, 413. These principles were laid down in *Hurley v Marais* (1882) 2 SC 155, which appears to have been followed in *Meyer v Coetzee* 1893 OR 25, and indeed was followed in *Birch v Divisional Council of Jansenville* (1890) 7 SC 314; *Klopper v Van Straaten* (1894) 11 SC 94; *Ross & Co v Smith* (1905) 22 SC 535; *Alagerysamy v Kvalsig* 1912 NPD 25; *Joubert v Vermooten* 1912 TPD 537; *South African Independent United Order of Mechanics and Fidelity Benefit Lodge v General Accident Fire and Life Assurance Corporation Ltd* 1916 CPD 457; *Dyamola v Cohen* 1927 (1) PH A20 (E) and *Barnard v Laas* 1929 TPD 349. Wessels discusses the subject in paras 3906–8.
[100] 1912 TPD 537.
[101] As in *St Patricks Mansions (Pty) Ltd v Grange Restaurant (Pty) Ltd and Another* 1949 (4) SA 57 (W) and in *Segell v Kerdia Investments (Pty) Ltd* 1953 (1) SA 20 (W).

of proceedings against the debtor, the better view appears to be that he should be given notice. This might be put on the basis of the creditor mitigating his loss.[102]

A mere demand on or request to the surety for payment is not notice of intention to sue the debtor[103] and a mere refusal or failure on the part of the surety to pay the debt does not amount to a request to the creditor to sue the debtor; nor is it an acquiescence in his doing so.[104]

What is appropriate notice to the surety? Does it suffice to give him notice of intention to sue the debtor or must the notice warn him that he will be held liable for the costs of doing so if these are not recovered from the debtor? Although in *Hurley v Marais*[105] Smith J[106] said '... the mere fact that the creditor has notified to the surety that he intends to sue the principal is insufficient per se to render the surety liable for the costs', in none of the other cases did the language of the judgments go so far as that of the learned judge.[107]

The notice need not be in writing.[108] Properly given, it is a warning to the surety of the creditor's intention to excuss the principal debtor, and that refers to a full excussion, which includes execution after judgment and, if necessary, an appeal, for the costs of which the surety will be liable.[109] It is for the surety, having received notice of the intended action, to keep himself informed of the subsequent steps taken by the creditor.[110] The creditor must make in his summons the averments required to ground a claim for the costs.[111]

The principle applies equally where the debtor has paid the creditor, but subsequently becomes insolvent and his trustee sues the creditor for return of the money as an undue preference. If the creditor gives due notice to the surety of

---

[102] Nevertheless, as indicated in *St Patricks Mansions (Pty) Ltd v Grange Restaurant (Pty) Ltd and Another* 1949 (4) SA 57 (W) at 73, it is at least doubtful whether notice is required when the proceedings against the debtor are for his ejectment (if he is, for example, a lessee), for there is nothing the surety can do to protect himself. In essence, the surety is to be given the opportunity of protecting himself against the risk of costs by himself performing the debtor's obligation, where that is possible. See also *Barrett NO v Hassim Moti* 1925 (1) PH K6 (T), where the costs had been incurred in removing an executor from office.

[103] *Hurley v Marais* (1882) 2 SC 155 at 159, 163.

[104] *Hurley v Marais* (1882) 2 SC 155 *loc cit*.

[105] (1882) 2 SC 155.

[106] At 163.

[107] In *Klopper v Van Straaten* (1894) 11 SC 94 De Villiers CJ said 'after a surety has been informed that the principal debtor is about to be excussed, it is a legitimate inference from his silence or from his refusal to pay that he wishes the excussion to proceed' (at 99). But in *Joubert v Vermooten* 1912 TPD 537 after saying that the creditor must allege in his summons, *inter alia,* that 'he gave the surety notice that he intended to sue the principal debtor', Wessels J went on to say 'It is not sufficient for the plaintiff to have said to the defendant 'I propose to sue your son' (the principal debtor). He must give the defendant notice that he intends to sue the son for such and such an amount and will hold him (the defendant) liable for the costs' (at 539). No doubt that is the counsel of perfection, but Tindall J in *Barnard v Laas* 1929 TPD 349 expressed doubt at 356 whether Wessels J really meant that. It seems that, whatever passed between creditor and surety, in order to hold the latter liable for the costs it must be capable of being held that he requested the creditor to sue the debtor or acquiesced in his doing so. Cf *Alagerysamy v Kvalsig* 1912 NPD 25 at 26, 27.

[108] *Barnard v Laas* 1929 TPD 349.

[109] *Barnard v Laas* 1929 TPD 349.

[110] *Barnard v Laas* 1929 TPD 349. Cf Wessels para 3911. In para 3908 the learned author says, referring to English cases, that in the absence of special circumstances the surety's liability will be confined to party and party costs.

[111] *Hurley v Marais* (1882) 2 SC 155; *Joubert v Vermooten* 1912 TPD 537.

the action against him in order to afford him an opportunity of paying the debt, he can recover, not only the debt, but the costs of unsuccessfully contesting the trustee's claim, for there has been no valid payment of the debt by the debtor.'[112]

8. The effect of death

The obligations of a surety are transmitted to his estate if he dies before fulfilling them. This is in accordance with the general principle of contract that a party's obligations under his contract are transmitted to and bind his estate unless their nature involves a *delectus personae* or the terms of the contract show that it was not intended that they should be transmitted. That a surety's obligations are transmitted to his estate is clear in relation to any liability existing at the time of his death.[113]

What, however, is the effect of death of a surety on a suretyship given for a liability to be incurred in the future, including, in particular, a continuing suretyship when in fact the liability is incurred after the death in question? If the suretyship is framed in such language as expressly or impliedly makes it applicable to debts incurred after the death of the creditor (ie debts incurred to his executor or the administrator of his estate) or incurred after the principal debtor's death (by his executor or administrator), or incurred by the principal debtor after the death of the surety, that ends the inquiry; the terms of the suretyship govern the situation.

In the absence of agreement to that effect, however, it will not be taken that the surety is liable for debts to be incurred by the debtor to the estate of the creditor, nor that he has undertaken liability for debts to be incurred by the debtor's executor or administrator or by a partnership of which he has been a member during his lifetime and until his death.[114] We have indicated[115] in the chapter on Interpretation of the Contract that the surety's liability will not be extended *de persona in personam*. He gives his undertaking in reliance on, *inter alia,* the integrity and the business sense of the debtor and those of the creditor; *non constat* that he is prepared to adopt risks involved in dealings by the executor of either.

The situation needs further consideration in relation to debts incurred by the principal debtor to the creditor after the surety's death, particularly on the footing of a continuing suretyship where the terms of the undertaking do not specifically bind the estate of the surety in respect of debts incurred after his death, nor expressly limit his undertaking to those incurred during his lifetime. Wessels,[116] citing English cases, says that 'the mere fact that the surety dies does not of itself determine the guarantee'. A possible contrary contention based on the analogy of

---

[112] *Hattingh & Co v De Wet* (1904) 21 SC 212.
[113] D 46.1.4.1; Inst 3.20.2; V 46.1.26; Gr 3.3.26; *Cens For* 1.4.17.26; P 417. Likewise, if the creditor dies, his claim against the surety vests in his executor, or his successor if the debt is owing to him in an official position; so also the principal debtor's existing liability falls on his estate when he dies (or his successor in an official position) and the surety remains bound for the liability—V 46.1.8 37, P 384–5, Wessels para 3919.
[114] Wessels para 3916.
[115] Chapter VI.
[116] Wessels para 3993.

agency, that the agent's authority is terminated by the death of the principal, cannot be sustained because that relates to the agent's authority to incur liability for the principal. The introduction of the notion of the tacit contract of mandate is a matter between debtor and surety and is irrelevant to the relationship between creditor and surety, based as the latter is on an express contract by which the surety is bound to the creditor to pay the debtor's debts and continue to do so until the suretyship is terminated. He is liable to the creditor, independently of any mandate from the debtor, whatever may be the situation between surety and debtor. Nor does it lie in the mouth of the debtor to repudiate the liability to make reimbursement of what is paid on his behalf for debts incurred by him after the surety's death; it is not a case of an agent purporting to incur liability on behalf of a deceased principal, but of a deceased agent, through his executor, acting to the advantage of the principal by paying his debt.

Nor does it help to say that the creditor should protect himself by not giving credit to the debtor after the surety's death. That would be an argument based on expediency, but the question is whether or not the surety's estate is in law liable to the creditor if he does so give credit. Moreover, *non constat* that the creditor is aware of the surety's death at the time he gives credit.

The conclusion must, in accordance with the general principles of contract, be that the suretyship continues to operate and binds the surety's estate after his death. By giving an undertaking for future liabilities, the surety has undertaken an obligation which is transmitted to his estate on his death, namely, the obligation to hold himself responsible for debts to be incurred by the debtor. This obligation is transmitted on his death unless before that event he terminates his obligation by proper notice, where the right to do so is not excluded by the terms of the undertaking.[117] This conclusion is indeed implicit in the reasoning of Williamson JA in *Kalil v Standard Bank of South Africa Ltd*,[118] where he speaks of the executor of a deceased surety releasing his estate from future liability by notice of termination. He went on to say that: 'While it may be competent for a co-surety to enter into an agreement for a continuing guarantee ... debarring the executor of his estate should he come to die' from terminating the suretyship by notice 'one would expect such a material variation of the ordinary position of a co-surety to be expressly made by a clear provision therefor.' The court was dealing with a case of co-sureties, but the principle would be the same if there were but one surety.

9. Insolvency of the principal debtor or surety

That the principal debtor's estate has been declared insolvent or his estate thereafter rehabilitated does not release the surety.[119] That is indeed a contingency for which the creditor takes a surety. Further it is no bar to the creditor's action against the surety that assets in the debtor's insolvent estate remain to be recov-

---

[117] This passage was approved in *SA General Electric Co (Pty) Ltd v Sharfman and Others NNO* 1981 (1) SA 592 (W).
[118] 1967 (4) SA 550 (A) at 557.
[119] V 46.1.39; P 380. Section 139(3)*(d)* of the Insolvency Act 24 of 1936.

ered and distributed, even if the creditor will have a preference on them.[120] If the debt is not yet payable, the insolvency of the principal debtor does not make the surety immediately liable, as though it had become payable as against him.[121]

A creditor of the principal debtor is a creditor of the surety, even if the latter has the benefit of excussion.[122] 'Insolvency of a surety does not terminate the suretyship and the creditor for amounts presently payable can prove a claim', per Van den Heever JA in *Kalil v Standard Bank of South Africa Ltd.*[123] As we have seen, the creditor's claim is contingent on the principal debtor's default[124] and on excussion, if the surety has that benefit,[125] but not if he does not have that benefit.[126] In the former event, the contingency is that the creditor does not recover on excussing the principal debtor. Nor is the creditor's claim contingent on anything other than the debtor's default if the surety is a co-principal debtor with renunciation of the benefits of excussion and division and of entitlement to release on paying his share of the debt.[127]

Just as the creditor may sue the principal debtor and the surety in one action, if the latter does not have the benefit of excussion,[128] so he may prove his claim in full against their insolvent estates, if they are both insolvent, or against the estate of the one who is insolvent. If he proves against both estates, he is entitled to receive dividends from both on the full amount of his claim.[129] If, however, he has received a payment on account of his claim from the principal debtor or from his insolvent estate before proving against the estate of the surety, he may prove his claim for only the balance after deduction of what he has received, for the surety is discharged to the extent of the payment by the principal debtor or his estate.[130] The creditor may not, however, recover more than the total amount of what is owed to him, notwithstanding that he is entitled to prove against both estates. He must return any surplus, it seems, to the last payer;[131] the consequence of this will then be a matter between those who have paid—if the refund has been made to the principal debtor or his estate, the surety (or his estate) will have the right

---

[120] *Rogerson NO v Meyer and Berning* (1837) 2 Menz 38; *Consolidated Textile Mills Ltd v Weiniger* 1961 (3) SA 335 (O) at 338.
[121] *Director of Public Works v Lewis, Blundell and Roberts* 1908 ORC 14.
[122] *McLean v McLean's Trustee* 1923 AD 141 at 148.
[123] 1967 (4) SA 550 (A) at 557.
[124] See the discussion earlier in this chapter. As AN Oelofse 'Enkele Gedagtes na aanleiding van Twee Opmerkings in *Trans-Drakensberg Bank Ltd v The Master and Others* 1962 (4) SA 417 (N)' (1988) 10 *MB* 52 points out: ' 'n [B]org se aanspreeklikheid [is] altyd voorwaardelik ... of hy nou afstand gedoen het van die *beneficium excussionis* of nie.'
[125] *In re Sydserff* (1866) 5 Searle 193 (as to proof of a contingent or conditional claim, see ss 44 and 48 of the Insolvency Act 24 of 1936, the subject of discussion in Chapter XII in relation to a surety's claim on the insolvent estate of the principal debtor).
[126] *In re Deneys* (1846) 3 Menz 309.
[127] *Trans-Drakensberg Bank Ltd v The Master and Others* 1962 (4) SA 417 (N) at 422. See also GF Lubbe and AH van Wyk 'Borgstelling en Artikel 26(2) van die Insolvensiewet' (1983) 43 *THRHR* 450; CHJ Badenhorst 'Vervreemding van Goed sonder Teenwaarde ingevolge Artikel 26 van die Insolvensiewet 24 van 1926 en Ongeldige Borgstellingskontrakte' (1980) 43 *THRHR* 423.
[128] *Rogerson NO v Meyer and Berning* (1837) 2 Menz 38.
[129] *De Wet Bros v The Master and Another* 1934 CPD 427 at 430, 433.
[130] *In re Brink, ex parte Porter, Hodgson & Co* (1865) 1 Roscoe 305; *De Wet Bros v The Master and Another* 1934 CPD 427.
[131] Cf *De Wet Bros v The Master and Another* 1934 CPD 427 at 431.

of recourse, whilst if the refund is made to a co-surety, a question of contribution between co-sureties will arise.

What has been said about the effect of death of the surety on a suretyship for future liability, particularly a continuing suretyship, applies equally in the event of the insolvency of the surety; the suretyship continues to operate until the surety's trustee terminates it, as he is entitled to do unless that right has been excluded by the terms of the suretyship.[132]

---

[132] This is indeed implicit in the reasoning in the judgment in *Kalil v Standard Bank of South Africa Ltd* 1967 (4) SA 550 (A).

PART TWO

The Rights of the Surety

CHAPTER VIII

The Benefit of Excussion

	Page
1. Introduction	125
2. Absence of the debtor	126
3. The benefit is a defence to be raised by the surety	127
4. Surety's liability for the balance owing after excussion	128
5. Proof of excussion	129
6. Renunciation of the benefit	130
7. Further occasions on which the benefit is not available to the surety	132
8. Position of a surety without the benefit	134
9. The *beneficium juris, statuti, vel consuetudinis*	134
10. Procedural aspects	134
11. Delay in excussion	137

1. Introduction

The benefit of excussion (*beneficium ordinis seu excussionis*)[1] is the right of the surety against the creditor to have him proceed first against the principal debtor with a view to obtaining payment from him, if necessary by execution on his assets, before turning to the surety for payment of the debt or of so much of it as remains unpaid.[2] This is in accordance with the principle enunciated in discussing the nature of the contract of suretyship, that the surety secures performance of the obligation of the principal debtor, undertaking to pay if the latter does not do so. Where the principal debtor is absent it could, however, be difficult for the creditor to require him to follow the debtor when the surety is present and available.

---

[1] The word *'ordinis'* in the term *beneficium ordinis seu excussionis* relates to the order in which the creditor may pursue his remedies, first against the principal debtor and thereafter against the surety. That the creditor is to excuss the assets of the debtor before turning to the surety is expressed in the word *'excussionis'*, which sometimes appears as *'discussionis'*. Burge says this is the usage in the laws of France and Scotland; we find it occasionally in the judgments of our courts (B 333). See also generally Chapter I and the incisive discussion by Reinhard Zimmermann *The Law of Obligations* (1990) at 129–31 and Ralph Slovenko 'Suretyship' (1965) 39 *Tulane LR* 427 at 447 ff.

[2] *Worthington v Wilson* 1918 TPD 104 at 107. 'It is settled that every surety ... is entitled to insist on the benefit of excussion'—per Innes CJ in *Wolfson v Crowe* 1904 TS 682 at 683. There are, however, some exceptions to the rule. The principles were discussed in *Hurley v Marais* (1882) 2 SC 155 at 160 ff.

2. Absence of the debtor

It has never been clear[3] what is meant by 'absence' of the debtor. Voet[4] puts it as being beyond the jurisdiction, unless there was process for excussing him whilst in another jurisdiction. Hence he was 'absent' if he lived in another province or, if in Holland, in another city where he could not be summoned before the Provincial Court of Holland. But he was not 'absent', although physically absent, if he had attachable property within the jurisdiction, for this could be attached to found jurisdiction. Both Voet[5] and Grotius[6] say, however, that a reasonable time will be allowed to the surety to obtain the appearance of the debtor in court. Burge[7] is to the same effect.[8]

The exception relating to the absent debtor is part of our law. *Goldschmidt NO v Kinnear*[9] decided that if the debtor has left the jurisdiction of the country and there is no property of his within the jurisdiction against which the creditor can proceed, the benefit of excussion is not available to the surety.[10] Bearing in mind the provisions of section 26 of the Supreme Court Act 59 of 1959[11] (by which the civil process of any provincial or local division of the court runs throughout South Africa), it appears that absence from the Republic rather than from a province will be required.

In *Amod Moussa v Loterijman & Co*[12] the court concluded that the principal debtor was abroad when he could not be found within the country. Where the principal debtor was outside the jurisdiction when the transaction was effected and the debt payable outside the jurisdiction, it was held not to be open to the creditor, suing the surety within the jurisdiction, to take the point of the debtor being absent; having made his contract with one outside the jurisdiction, he could not complain that he was 'absent' and was required first to excuss him.[13]

How far in our law can a surety, claiming the benefit of excussion, claim a grant of time to enable him to obtain the appearance of the absent debtor? The only reported case appears to be *Worthington v Wilson*[14] in which a grant of time was refused: the principal debtor was on military service in Europe and the surety sought time until the conclusion of hostilities in which to produce him, the debtor himself being in any event protected by moratorium extended to persons on mili-

---

[3] Lee *ad Gr* 249.
[4] V 46.1.15, 18.
[5] V 46.1.18.
[6] Gr 3.3.27.
[7] B 335.
[8] Pothier says this aspect of the matter did not arise in France, where the procedure made excussion of the debtor as easy when he was absent as when he was present (P 409).
[9] (1885) 2 SAR 1 at 4.
[10] See also *Wolfson v Crowe* 1904 TS 682; *Verster, Van Wijk & Company v Pienaar* (1904) 21 SC 386; *Worthington v Wilson* 1918 TPD 104 in which, at 107, Gregorowski J with whom Mason J agreed, adopted the statement of Burge (B 335) that 'the principal debtor is said to be absent when the creditor has not the power of suing him, not only by reason of his being corporeally absent, but because he has left no attorney to represent him, or no property or assets of which the creditor may obtain possession or on which might be founded the jurisdiction of the court'.
[11] As substituted by s 5 of Act 85 of 1963.
[12] (1894) 1 OR 326.
[13] *Brandt v Weber* (1886) 2 SAR 98.
[14] 1918 TPD 104.

tary service. Such a grant of time to the surety, it was held, would be unreasonable, since the creditor's claim would be held up for an indefinite period. Gregorowski J said:[15] 'The idea of the Novel is that he shall have a *modicum temporis spatium* and shall only be entitled to this if he has a fair expectation of producing the debtor so that the suit can proceed and the creditor get his money expeditiously.' This was no positive decision that a surety has such a right, but there appears to be no reason why he should not be granted a *modicum temporis spatium* in an appropriate case. If the creditor has sued the surety because the debtor is absent, and the debtor returns before the case comes on, the benefit of excussion is not available to the surety, because an absent debtor is regarded as excussed.[16]

3. The benefit is a defence to be raised by the surety

Although sureties have the benefit of excussion (save where one of the exceptions, to be mentioned later, operates) the creditor is not obliged to proceed first against the principal debtor unless the surety avails himself of the benefit;[17] it is a dilatory defence which the surety may elect to set up if the creditor first sues him.[18] If the surety intends to raise the defence, he must do so *in initio litis*;[19] it is too late to raise it after *litis contestatio*.[20] It certainly cannot be raised for the first time on appeal.[21] If the surety disputes liability as a surety, denying the very existence of a suretyship contract, he should nevertheless raise *in initio litis* the plea of non-excussion; if he pleads to the merits and raises alternatively the special defence, the latter will be ruled out.[22] If the defence of non-excussion succeeds, the court may postpone the proceedings pending excussion of the principal debtor or, in a proper case, grant absolution against the creditor.[23]

If the surety has succeeded in raising the benefit of excussion and the creditor has excussed the principal debtor as far as possible, but without obtaining a settlement, the surety can raise the defence again if, before the creditor proceeds against him, the debtor has acquired further assets (as, for instance, by inheritance); but if proceedings have commenced against the surety and the debtor's financial position improves while the proceedings are pending, after joinder of issue, the surety is not permitted to raise the defence a second time.[24]

---

[15] At 108.
[16] V 46.1.15.
[17] V 42.3.19; VL 4.4.9; P 410; B 333; Lee *ad Gr* 251. See also Chapter I.
[18] *Hurley v Marais* (1882) 2 SC 155 at 158; *Klopper v Van Straaten* (1894) 11 SC 94 at 98; *Worthington v Wilson* 1918 TPD 104 at 107.
[19] V 46.1.15; P 410.
[20] *Rogerson NO v Meyer and Berning* (1837) 2 Menz 38 at 48; *Hurley v Marais* (1882) 2 SC 155 at 162; *Ridley v Anderson* 1911 EDL 13.
[21] *Bethlehem v Zietsman* 1908 EDC 367.
[22] *Rogerson NO v Meyer and Berning* (1837) 2 Menz 38 at 48; *Mason & Co v Booth & Co* (1903) 20 SC 645; *Jeeva Mahomed v Mahomed Valli* 1922 TPD 124 (in which, however, the parties' conduct of the trial saved the defendant from this), *Moosa v Mahomed* 1939 TPD 271.
[23] *Oslo Land Co Ltd v Temple Nourse* 1930 TPD 35. And see *Ullman Bros and Davidson v Railton* 1903 TS 596 at 601.
[24] V 46.1.15.

4. Surety's liability for the balance owing after excussion

The surety is liable for the shortfall after excussion of all the assets movable and immovable, corporeal and incorporeal, of the principal debtor.[25]

Excussion is effected by execution on the assets of the principal debtor or by proof that he has no assets on which the creditor can execute. Though the debtor is within the jurisdiction, the creditor cannot be required to excuss assets outside the jurisdiction[26] using the word 'jurisdiction' in the sense already indicated in relation to an absent debtor.[27] Pothier[28] also says that the creditor is not obliged to excuss *res litigiosa*, nor property which the principal debtor has hypothecated or pledged to a third party. This is because excussion should not be made too difficult or be prolonged. There seems, however, to be no reason why in modern procedure execution should not be effected on the debtor's interest in hypothecated or pledged property. Pothier[29] also says that the creditor is entitled to have the surety provide funds for the purpose of excussing immovables, because this is an expensive process. There seems, however, to be no reason to suppose that this is our law.

Phillip II's Placaat of 21 February 1564 specifically entitled a surety to have the creditor execute on property pledged or hypothecated to him by the principal debtor as security for the debt in question.[30] There seems to have been no unanimity amongst the writers whether this included a general bond, nor does it appear whether this right was conferred on sureties who had renounced, or otherwise did not have, the benefit of excussion.[31] *Serrurier v Langevelds*[32] decided that the Placaat applies where the surety enjoys the benefit of excussion and not where he has renounced, or otherwise does not enjoy it. The creditor may sue the latter type of surety without first excussing property pledged or hypothecated to the creditor as security for the debt.[33]

If the surety is entitled to the excussion of securities held by the creditor, the question arises whether he is entitled to have the creditor excuss co-debtors bound *in solidum* with the debtor for whom he has stood surety. Pothier[34] says he is so entitled. He puts this on the grounds of equity and also gives the reason that there is only one obligation on the part of all the debtors. On the other hand, if the surety has secured performance by only one of the several debtors, and that one fails, there is much to be said for the view that the surety must perform his

---

[25] V 46.1.15; Gr 3.3.27; B 340.
[26] V 46.1.15, P 412.
[27] *Rogerson NO v Meyer and Berning* (1837) 2 Menz 38 at 49.
[28] P 412.
[29] P 413.
[30] V 46.1.15; Gr 3.3.32; Sch 303; VL 4.4.7; *Cens For* 1.4.17.18; VdK 507, 508. B 338; Lee *Intro* 317. A translation of the text of this is to be found in *Serrurier v Langeveld* (1828) 1 Menz 316 at 317.
[31] Van der Keessel *loc cit* says that in Middelburg it was, in the instance of a special mortgage. See, in addition to the authorities cited, the discussion on this by Van der Keessel in his *Dictata* appearing in Lee *ad Gr* 255.
[32] (1828) 1 Menz 316.
[33] See also *Maasdorp v Morkel's Executor* (1828) 1 Menz 293; *Hare qq v Croeser* (1828) 1 Menz 293; *Chase v Cloete* (1828) 2 Menz 4; *Farthing v Pieters and Co* 1912 CPD 215 at 222.
[34] P 412.

obligation and pay the creditor. He will then have the right of recourse along with the right to cession of actions against the co-debtors.

5. Proof of excussion

A *nulla bona* return by the sheriff is *prima facie* evidence of excussion.[35] Where the debtor's obligation is *ad factum praestandum* and, despite judgment for specific performance, he has failed to perform and has been punished for contempt of the court's order, there has been sufficient excussion.[36] Where the principal debtor was a voluntary association, the trustees of which had mortgaged its property, execution on that property and movables in the hands of the trustees was held to be sufficient excussion without proceeding against the individual members.[37]

The purpose of the benefit of excussion is not to make matters difficult for the creditor, but to oblige him in the first instance to seek payment from the principal debtor,[38] but if the debtor cannot pay, it would be harmful to the creditor to require him to spend money and incur delay in excussing the debtor.[39] Consequently, without production of a *nulla bona* return, the creditor may establish by evidence that the debtor is in fact insolvent or that he has no attachable assets and is manifestly unable to pay or is a pauper and living on charity.[40] Where the principal debtor is deceased and the account in his estate discloses no assets available for creditors other than a preferent or secured creditor, the creditor is held relieved of excussing him.[41] It is open to the creditor who is able to show that there is no reasonable hope of a successful excussion to require of the surety who nevertheless presses for it that he give security for the costs of doing so.[42]

Sequestration of the debtor's estate operates as sufficient excussion; so too does the surrender of the debtor's estate,.[43] This applies also to a statutory assignment of the debtor's estate.[44]

The mere fact that a company or close corporation which is the principal debtor has been placed in liquidation is no ground for relieving the creditor of excussing it; there are a number of grounds on which a company or a close corporation may be wound up and it does not follow from a liquidation order that the company

---

[35] V 46.1.15; P 411. See also *Board of Executors v Ross* (1888) 6 SC 52 at 54; *Meyer v Coetzee* (1892) 4 SAR 252 at 256; *Liquidator of the Owl Syndicate v Bright* (1909) 26 SC 12 at 14.

[36] *Meyer v Coetzee* (1892) 4 SAR 252.

[37] *Featherstone v Peel* (1909) 26 SC 417.

[38] *Worthington v Wilson* 1918 TPD 104 at 105, 108, 109.

[39] B 339. Cf *Acutt v Bennett* (1906) 27 NLR 716 at 724.

[40] V 46.1.17; Sch 303; *Cens For* 1.4.17.19; B 339; Lee *ad Gr* 248. See also *Hare qq v Croeser* (1828) 1 Menz 293; *Bank of Africa v Hampson and Others* (1884) 3 HCG 1; *Acutt v Bennett* (1906) 27 NLR 716.

[41] *Hare qq v Croeser* (1828) 1 Menz 293.

[42] *Liquidator of the Owl Syndicate v Bright* (1909) 26 SC 12.

[43] V 46.1.17, 18; V 46.2.6; Huber 3.26.17; B 339. See also *Rogerson NO v Meyer and Berning* (1837) 2 Menz 38; *Wolfson v Crowe* 1904 TS 682 at 683; *Du Plessis v Greef and Walter* (1905) 22 SC 580; *Lindley v Ward 1911* CPD 21 at 26; *Gaba v Ordra Trust and Investment (Pty) Ltd and Another* 1954 (2) SA 129 (T); *Volkskas Beperk v Mohamed* 1955 (1) SA 453 (T) at 455; *Shell SA (Pty) Ltd v Guarantee Exchange International* 1986 (4) SA 7 (C).

[44] *Makda v Kalsheker* 1954 (4) SA 185 (SR).

or the close corporation is unable to pay its debts,[45] but it is open to the creditor to prove that the company or the close corporation is in fact unable to pay its debts.[46] Likewise it does not follow from the fact that a company has been put under judicial management that the creditor cannot recover payment from it.[47]

6. Renunciation of the benefit

A surety may expressly renounce the benefit of excussion,[48] but a general renunciation is not effective,[49] whether it be one of the benefit of division (for example) and all other benefits available to a surety or one in general terms of all benefits available to a surety, for it is not to be taken that a person will give away rights unless he understands what he is doing and its consequences. Van der Keessel[50] held the view that a general renunciation was effective, and so also Burge.[51] But Kotzé in his footnote to Van Leeuwen[52] says the weight of authority favours the view of Van Leeuwen that renunciation 'must be made clearly and specifically by name', and *Goldschmidt NO v Kinnear*[53] decided (Kotzé CJ presiding in a full

---

[45] *Volkskas Beperk v Mohamed* 1955 (1) SA 453 (T) at 456; *Lange Accessories (Pvt) Ltd v Fisher and Another* 1974 (1) SA 61 (R). See also *TV and Radio Guarantee Co (Pty) Ltd v Du Preez* 1986 (3) SA 866 (W) and the critical discussion of this decision in 1986 *Annual Survey* 340–1. In *Asco Carbon Dioxide Ltd v Lahner* 2005 (3) SA 213 (N) a creditor of a company (the principal debtor) applied to court for a declaratory order against the surety to restrain the surety from issuing or executing any warrant of execution in respect of a debt allegedly owed by the creditor to the surety. This is how it came about: The appellant (creditor) had previously applied for the liquidation of the principal debtor. The respondent (surety) was the director of the principal debtor. The appellant was granted leave to withdraw the application and was ordered to pay the costs of the application. The appellant then refused to pay the taxed costs and maintained that the respondent was personally indebted to the appellant in terms of the suretyship undertaking and that the appellant's indebtedness for the taxed costs was extinguished by set-off against the much larger amount owed by the respondent to the appellant (at 216D-F). We are not dealing with a creditor who is suing the surety on a debt owed, but rather with a creditor who is 'jumping the gun' by seeking to interdict the surety from executing on an order against the creditor to pay the taxed costs in the other matter, because the surety allegedly owes the creditor money and the taxed costs have been set off against that debtor. The full bench confirmed the order of the court *a quo* that the application should be dismissed. As the benefit of excussion had not been renounced the respondent (surety) was thus entitled to insist that the creditor must first excuss the principal debtor before the creditor could claim any amount from the surety. Set-off could thus not operate between the creditor and the surety, because it is a fundamental requirement for the operation of set-off that the reciprocal debts must both be payable (at 222G-H). The matter would have been quite different if the creditor had brought the action on the basis that the principal debtor was unable to pay the debt and that the surety thus did not have the benefit of excussion.

[46] *Bank of Africa v Hampson and Others* (1884) 3 HCG 1. See, however, *TV and Radio Guarantee Co (Pty) Ltd v Du Preez* 1986 (3) SA 866 (W).

[47] *Hedy (Pty) Ltd v Wellcut Garment Manufacturing Co (Pty) Ltd and Another* 1953 (2) SA 236 (C) at 240.

[48] V 42.3.19; V 46.1.16; Gr 3.3.29; Sch 303, 304; VL 4.4.8; *Cens For* 1.4.17.20, 21; VdK 502; Huber 3.26.17; P 408; Lee *ad Gr* 248, 255. See also Chapter I.

[49] V 46.1.16; VL 4.4.12, Gr 3.3.29, Huber 3.26.18; P 408.

[50] VdK 502; Lee *ad Gr* 250, 251. See also Chapter I.

[51] B 334.

[52] VL 4.4.12.

[53] (1885) 2 SAR 1 at 3, 4.

court) that a general renunciation was ineffectual. Indeed, Van Leeuwen in his *Censura Forensis*[54] requires that renunciations be explained to sureties.

Renunciation may, however, be necessarily implied (or, as some writers say, it may be tacit) as it is when the surety has bound himself as co-principal debtor.[55] Our law clearly implies renunciation in the circumstance stated unless this is excluded by the language of the document.[56] Renunciation need not be contemporaneous with the undertaking of the suretyship obligation.[57]

Renunciation is also implied when the suretyship is undertaken in a recognizance or penal bond[58] by which the surety acknowledges himself to be indebted to the creditor in a stated sum of money on the condition that, if the principal debtor pays or performs his obligation, the undertaking of the surety is to be null and void.[59] It seems that the reason for this is that the surety has taken on himself a primary obligation to pay. Where the obligation is undertaken to pay on a fixed date, as in *Hubbart v Rogers*[60] (in which the defendant secured payment of postdated cheques and undertook to pay them on demand if they were not paid by their maker on presentation), this is inconsistent with the existence of a right of excussion.[61]

The special rules regarding renunciation, which used to apply to some contracts governed by the law of Natal, no longer apply since Law 40 of 1884 (N) has been repealed.[62]

---

[54] *Loc cit.*

[55] V 46.1.16 and 24; Gr 3.3.29; Sch 305; VL 4.4.9; *Cens For* 1.4.17.23; VdK 503; VdL 1.4.10; Wessels paras 4087 and 4088; B 334, 338; Lee *ad Gr* 248, 251, 252; cf Huber 3.26.19. In France, says Pothier (P 408), there was a division of opinion about this.

[56] *Van der Vyver v De Wayer and Others* (1861) 4 Searle 27; *J & T Anderson v Patrick & Plowright* (1904) 25 NLR 75; *Fitzgerald v Argus Printing and Publishing Co Ltd* (1907) 3 Buch AC 152 at 160; *Maasdorp v Graaff-Reinet Board of Executors* (1909) 3 Buch AC 482; *Colonial Treasurer v Swart* 1910 TPD 552 at 556; *Union Government v Van der Merwe* 1921 TPD 318; *Kaplan v ER Syfret & Co* 1914 CPD 1104; *Meer v General Industrial Credit Corporation (Pty) Ltd* 1947 (4) SA 330 (C) at 335; *Gerber v Wolson* 1955 (1) SA 158 (A) at 167; *Taylor and Thorne NNO and Others v The Master* 1965 (1) SA 658 (N) at 659; *Ideal Finance Corporation v Coetzer* 1969 (4) SA 43 (O) at 44 (approved as far as this aspect is concerned by the Appellate Division in *Ideal Finance Corporation v Coetzer* 1970 (3) SA 1 (A) at 7 and 11); *JR & M Moffett (Pty) Ltd v Kolbe Eiendoms Beleggings (Edms) Bpk and Another* 1974 (2) SA 426 (O) at 432; *Mouton v Die Mynwerkersunie* 1977 (1) SA 119 (A); *Neon and Cold Cathode Illuminations (Pty) Ltd v Ephron* 1978 (1) SA 463 (A) at 472; *Standard Bank of SA Ltd v SA Fire Equipment (Pty) Ltd and Another* 1984 (2) SA 693 (C) (approved in *Muller and Others v Botswana Development Corporation Ltd* [2002] 3 All SA 663 (SCA)); *Kilroe-Daley v Barclays National Bank Ltd* 1984 (4) SA 609 (A) at 623. See also JSA Fourie 'Die Aanspreeklikheid van die Borg en die Hoofskuldenaar' (1978) 41 *THRHR* 307; GF Lubbe 'Die Onderskeid tussen Borgtog en Ander Vorme van Persoonlike Sekerheidstelling' (1984) 47 *THRHR* 383 at 386 ff and *LAWSA* vol 2 para 199 and para 203.

[57] See *H Maisels & Co (Pty) Ltd v Zirzow* 1971 (3) SA 523 (SWA).

[58] V 46.1.18; P 408.

[59] *Rogerson NO v Meyer and Berning* (1837) 2 Menz 38 at 50; *Board of Executors v Ross* (1888) 6 SC 48 at 54; *Birch v Divisional Council of Jansenville* (1890) 7 SC 314 at 317.

[60] 1915 WLD 39.

[61] Cf *Schoeman v Moller* 1951 (1) SA 456 (O).

[62] By the Suretyship Amendment Act 57 of 1971 and the Pre-Union Statute Law Revision Act 36 of 1976.

7. Further occasions on which the benefit is not available to the surety

Writers on Roman-Dutch law give a number of other circumstances, some of them out of date or doubtful, in which the benefit of excussion does not exist or is lost. Voet[63] has the case of the person who has stood surety for a debt which is only a natural obligation, with the consequence that no action can be brought against the debtor, although the surety remains liable; he has not the benefit of excussion by the very nature of the situation. Van Leeuwen[64] gives the example of a woman and a minor contracting without his guardian's authority. Burge[65] supports this. Van Leeuwen[66] also mentions the surety who falsely denies he is such. Voet,[67] however, although listing this as a principle of Roman law,[68] says it scarcely holds because penalties depriving a man of his rights have been abrogated; he refers to Groenewegen.[69] Voet's view found approval in *Fitzgerald v Argus Printing and Publishing Co Ltd*[70] and in *Jeeva Mahomed v Mahomed Valli*.[71]

According to Voet's list the benefit is not available when the debtor can protect himself by 'letters of respite';[72] this includes a statutory moratorium personal to the debtor:[73] Then comes the surety who has hindered, obstructed or prevented excussion[74] of the debtor; he can hardly be heard to complain about the lack of excussion. Burge[75] supports this. Voet[76] adds the surety who has received in advance from the debtor the amount for which he has become surety or otherwise holds property of the debtor out of which he can make payment. Burge[77] adopts these. Voet[78] also lists a number of instances which, however, he characterises as doubtful and ambiguous and to a great extent incorrect; Burge[79] says they do 'not seem to have been admitted by the law of Holland'.

In Holland the signer of an aval was taken to have renounced the benefit. Van der Keessel[80] says he became liable *in solidum*, without the benefit, and might be sued in the cambial action.[81] This, however, is not our law. In *Moti & Co v Cassim's Trustee*[82] Innes CJ examined the situation, referring to the decisions of our courts from the earliest days, and reaffirmed the principle held in them that the signer of

---

[63] V 46.1.18.
[64] VL 4.4.8; *Cens For* 1.4.17.19.
[65] B 336, 337.
[66] VL 4.4.9; *Cens For* 1.4.17.19.
[67] V 46.1.18, see also Lee *ad Gr* 249.
[68] D 46.1.10.1.
[69] Groen *ad Inst* 4.2.1.
[70] (1907) 3 Buch AC 152 at 161.
[71] 1922 TPD 124 at 128.
[72] V 46.1.18.
[73] *Worthington v Wilson* 1918 TPD 104.
[74] V 46.1.18.
[75] B 337.
[76] V 46.1.18.
[77] B 337.
[78] V 46.1.19.
[79] B 341.
[80] VdK 594.
[81] See also the discussion in FR Malan, AN Oelofse, W le R de Vos, JT Pretorius & CJ Nagel *Provisional Sentence on Bills of Exchange, Cheques and Promissory Notes* (1986) 204 ff and the authorities quoted.
[82] 1924 AD 720 at 726 ff.

an aval, if he has not signed also as a co-principal debtor, is just as much entitled to the benefit as if he had signed a separate document without renunciation of the benefit. This accords with the fact that it is not competent to bring provisional sentence proceedings against him, because of the need of extrinsic evidence of the fact of excussion.[83]

By the very nature of his contract the *fideiussor indemnitatis*,[84] liable for only a deficiency,[85] has the benefit of excussion, for the amount of the deficiency must be ascertained by that procedure.[86] A renunciation by him is consequently unavailing and ineffectual.[87] The same is the position of a surety for a debt which is illiquid; the principal debtor must at least be sued to make it a liquidated amount.[88] This would relate to a claim for damages.

Voet[89] says that if the surety sues the creditor for a debt due by the creditor to him, the creditor can set off what is owed to him by the surety's principal debtor; the surety is not entitled in that event to the benefit of excussion.

The question of excussion falls away if the surety becomes the principal debtor,[90] as he may by a process of novation, or if he succeeds to the debtor as his heir.[91] This last is certainly not part of the modern law in view of the changed position of the heir due to the introduction of our modern system of executorship and the administration of estates.

One of several co-sureties who has paid the principal debtor's debt is not entitled to assert his right to contributions from his co-sureties without first excussing the

---

[83] See below, this chapter.
[84] V 46.1.14; VL 4.4.11; *Cens For* 1.4.17.23.
[85] Above, Chapter IV (at end).
[86] Cf *Bowe v Colmar Garage (Pty) Ltd* 1955 (1) PH F34 (W)
[87] Cf *Muller v Meyer* (1828) 1 Menz 302.
[88] V 46.1.16.
[89] V 46.1.17. Percival Gane's translation sub nom *The Selective Voet, being the Commentary on the Pandects (Paris Edition of 1829) by Johannes Voet, and the Supplement to that Work by Johannes van der Linden* (1955-8)) reads: 'Then again it seems that this exception should not be allowed if a creditor is willing to set-off against his surety, when he is being sued by the surety for the payment of what he owes the surety. This is because there can be a set-off even of what is naturally due. But that a surety is naturally indebted, though he has a dilatory exception is quite clear from the fact that even when protected by the peremptory exception of division he nonetheless remains naturally a debtor to the extent that, if he has paid without raising the exception, he cannot sue in a personal action for what was paid.' In *Asco Carbon Dioxide Ltd v Lahner* 2005 (3) SA 213 (N) the court referred to both this passage and the statement in the text above and remarked that the statement in the text above must be considered in its proper context and that Voet may have been misunderstood by his peers and successors (at 221G-H). The court examined other passages from Voet and came to the conclusion that Voet merely dealt with the procedure in terms of which a surety could raise the claim in reconvention; he did not intend to convey that set-off can operate when the reciprocal debts are not payable (at 222). His lordship concluded: 'It is obviously only after both claims have become payable that set-off can operate. To that extent, the bold statement ... from Voet, that it is set-off which deprives the surety of the benefit of excussion has validly been doubted' (at 222D-E). It is submitted that the court in *Lahner* may perhaps have overlooked the fact that the appellant before the court was not claiming an amount from the surety. Rather the appellant sought an interdict to restrain the creditor from issuing a warrant of execution against the appellant. Voet deals with the situation where a surety sues the creditor and the creditor maintains that the surety owes the creditor money. Surely, the surety should not then be entitled to the benefit of excussion? The correctness of Voet 46.1.17 will have to be decided on another occasion.
[90] B 337.
[91] Sch 103; B 337; Lee *ad Gr* 248.

principal debtor; it is otherwise where the co-sureties have renounced the benefit as between themselves and the creditor in relation to the debtor.[92]

A surety who remains silent when called on to say whether or not he desires the principal debtor to be excussed and, in case he does, to provide security, does not abandon his right to have the principal debtor excussed.[93]

8. Position of a surety without the benefit

A surety who does not have the benefit of excussion is in the same situation as an ordinary debtor, indeed as the principal debtor;[94] *a fortiori* this is the case when a surety has assumed liability as surety and co-principal debtor.[95] He may be sued as soon as the principal debtor is in default. It must appear, however, that payment of the debt is actually due; it is necessary that everything shall have happened which is required to happen before the principal debtor can be sued.[96]

9. The *beneficium juris, statuti, vel consuetudinis*

Van Leeuwen in his *Roman-Dutch Law*[97] and in *Censura Forensis*[98] and Decker in note *(d)* to the former say that a surety who does not have the benefit of excussion may, nevertheless, on execution being levied against him, point out property of the principal debtor; if he does so, the creditor must suspend proceedings against the *beneficium juris, statuti, vel consuetudinis*. This benefit was mentioned in passing in *Serrurier v Langeveld*[99] but there does not appear to be any recorded instance of it being claimed in our law. Voet[100] says, however, that this 'takes place rather as a matter of fact than as a matter of right'. In Amsterdam the benefit was limited to the debtor's immovable property.

10. Procedural aspects

The creditor may join the principal debtor and the surety or sureties in one action, even sureties who have the benefit of excussion, for, as we have seen[101] it is for them to raise the defence. They may be so joined even though they are bound by separate documents.[102] But it is not essential to join sureties with the principal

---

[92] *Estate Steer v Steer* 1923 CPD 354 at 357.
[93] *Whitaker, Paterson & Brooks Ltd v Slater* (1905) 19 EDC 103. Cf *Klopper v Van Straaten* (1894) 11 SC 94 at 99.
[94] *Colonial Treasurer v Swart* 1910 TPD 551 at 556; *Estate Steer v Steer* 1923 CPD 354 at 357; *Neon and Cold Cathode Illuminations (Pty) Ltd v Ephron* 1978 (1) SA 463 (A) at 472.
[95] *Union Government v Van der Merwe* 1921 TPD 318; *Mahomed v Lockhat Brothers & Co Ltd* 1944 AD 230 at 238.
[96] *Director of Public Works v Lewis, Blundell and Roberts* 1908 ORC 14; *Parker Wood & Company Ltd v Richards and Another* 1925 NLR 277.
[97] VL 4.4.1.
[98] *Cens For* 2.1.33.27.
[99] (1828) 1 Menz 316 at 318.
[100] V 42.1.32.
[101] Above, this chapter.
[102] *Rogerson NO v Meyer and Berning* (1837) 2 Menz 38 at 48.

debtor or to join co-sureties.[103] A surety is not released by the creditor's election to make a claim on the principal debtor.[104] A creditor who has commenced action against the principal debtor is not bound to proceed to final excussion, but may, even after judgment, turn to his sureties who are such without the benefit of excussion because the sureties are bound until payment of the debt.[105]

From their very earliest decisions, South African courts departed from the wisselrecht holding that the signer of an aval could rely on the common law benefit of excussion.[106] In our modern law, the giver of an aval is deemed not to have renounced the *beneficia*.[107] This change is significant, since the courts have held that provisional sentence cannot be taken against the giver of an aval. This approach was explained by the Appellate Division in *Dickinson v South African General Electric Co (Pty) Ltd*[108] where Trollip JA said:

> [T]he liability of a person signing a promissory note as a surety without renouncing the *beneficium excussionis* is illiquid, precluding the grant of provisional sentence thereon. The manifest reason is that extrinsic evidence is required to prove the excussion of the principal debtor or exemption therefrom... . Putting it another way more germane to the present case: once the surety raises the *beneficium excussionis*, the liquidity of his liability is destroyed.[109]

However, where the signer of an aval has bound himself as surety and co-principal debtor, he is regarded as having renounced the benefit of excussion and provisional

---

[103] The old Roman law that *litis contestatio* in an action voluntarily taken against the principal debtor released the sureties and that, in an action against the sureties (or one or more sureties fewer than the whole of them), it released the principal debtor (and those sureties not sued), was abolished by Justinian. See C 8.41.28.

[104] VL 4.4.10; *Cens For* 1.4.17.22; P 406. See also *Ridley v Anderson* 1911 EDL 13 at 15.

[105] V 46.1.20; *Cens For* 1.4.17.22; P 406; Lee *ad Gr* 250. See also *J & T Anderson v Patrick & Plowright* (1904) 25 NLR 75; *Ridley v Anderson* 1911 EDL 13.

[106] See FR Malan, AN Oelofse, W le R de Vos, JT Pretorius & CJ Nagel *Provisional Sentence on Bills of Exchange, Cheques and Promissory Notes* (1986) 205 ff for a full discussion in this regard. See also FR Malan, JT Pretorius & SF du Toit *Malan on Bills of Exchange, Cheques and Promissory Notes in South African Law* (2009) 5ed paras 152–3.

[107] *Norton v Statchwell* (1840) 1 Menz 77; *De Kock v Russouw and Van der Poel* (1841) 1 Menz 78; *Coetzee v Tiran* (1880) Foord 42; *Bevern v Jacobse* (1889) 7 SC 65; *Klopper v Van Straaten* (1894) 11 SC 94; *Stephan Brothers v Engelbrecht* (1894) 11 SC 248; *Verster, Van Wijk & Company v Pienaar* (1904) 21 SC 386; *Maasdorp v Graaff-Reinet Board of Executors* (1909) 3 Buch AC 482; *Bethlehem v Zietsman* 1908 EDC 367; *Du Plessis v Greef and Walter* (1905) 22 SC 580; *Ullman Bros and Davidson v Railton* 1903 TS 596; *Moti & Co v Cassim's Trustee* 1924 AD 720; *Dickinson v South African General Electric Co (Pty) Ltd* 1973 (2) SA 620 (A).

[108] 1973 (2) SA 620 (A) at 641–2. See also *Glolec Bpk v Van Rensburg en 'n Ander* 1983 (2) SA 192 (O). However, in *TV and Radio Guarantee Co (Pty) Ltd v Du Preez* 1986 (3) SA 866 (W) provisional sentence was granted against the giver of an aval where the plaintiff alleged in the summons that the principal debtor had been placed in final liquidation by reason of its inability to pay its debts and these allegations were not denied by the defendant. See the critical discussion of this decision in 1986 *Annual Survey* 340–1.

[109] See FR Malan, AN Oelofse, W le R de Vos, JT Pretorius & CJ Nagel *Provisional Sentence on Bills of Exchange, Cheques and Promissory Notes* 205 ff for a critical discussion of the present law in this regard.

sentence may be taken against him.[110] The words 'as borge en mede-hoofskuldenaars' were taken to mean 'that the defendant is surety, but because he has consented to be a co-principal debtor, his liability is co-extensive with that of the maker, the principal debtor, and in addition he has waived the benefit of excussion'.[111]

When the document by which the suretyship was undertaken is a liquid document, and it appears on its face that the surety is not entitled to the benefit of excussion, it is competent for the creditor to bring provisional sentence proceedings against the surety: the liquidity of the document is not destroyed by the fact that the defendant is a surety.[112] But if the surety has the benefit of excussion, provisional sentence proceedings are not available to the creditor because of the need to aver, and to produce extrinsic evidence of, excussion of the principal debtor.[113]

It is, to say the least, questionable whether it is possible to contrive such statements in a provisional sentence summons as to amount to an averment of fulfilment of a simple condition[114] on which the plaintiff's claim depends, and thus to bring an action against a surety with the benefit within the principle laid down in *Union Share Agency & Investment Ltd v Spain*.[115] In *Verster, Van Wijk & Company v Pienaar*[116] De Villiers CJ said in an *obiter dictum* that he was unaware of any rule against suing a surety for provisional sentence when he himself does not claim the benefit or where, on the facts disclosed, it was clear that the benefit could not legally be claimed. He would have granted provisional sentence in the case, because the summons averred that the principal debtor was not within the jurisdiction, but for the fact that there was reason to believe that he had left assets within the jurisdiction.[117] In *Featherstone v Peel*[118] Hopley J held to be admissible

---

[110] *Arnoldi v Klazenga, Albers and Dreyer* 1905 TS 533; *Van der Vyver v De Wayer and Others* (1861) 4 Searle 27; *Wiehahn NO v Wouda* 1957 (4) SA 724 (W). See *Hedy (Pty) Ltd v Wellkut Garment Manufacturing Co (Pty) Ltd and Another* 1953 (2) SA 236 (C); *Humphreys v Bredell* 1913 TPD 86; *Union Government v Van der Merwe* 1921 TPD 318 at 322. See also FR Malan, JT Pretorius & SF du Toit *Malan on Bills of Exchange, Cheques and Promissory Notes in South African Law* (2009) 5ed para 152.

[111] *Wiehahn NO v Wouda* 1957 (4) SA 724 (W) at 725.

[112] *FJK Syndicate v Du Preez and Smit* 1943 WLD 116 at 121, 122.

[113] *Moti & Co v Cassim's Trustee* 1924 AD 720 at 726; *Peimer v Finbro Furnishers (Pty) Ltd* 1936 AD 177 at 186, 187; *FJK Syndicate v Du Preez and Smit* 1943 WLD 116; *Madnitsky v Kantor* 1952 (3) SA 491 (W) at 492, 493.

[114] A simple condition or event connotes 'a condition or event of the kind, unlikely in the nature of things, to give rise to a dispute, or, where it is disputed, is inherently capable of speedy proof by means of affidavit evidence' (per Wessels JA in *Rich and Others v Lagerwey* 1974 (4) SA 748 (A) at 755). See also *Western Bank Ltd v Pretorius* 1976 (2) SA 481 (T) at 487; *Leyland South Africa (Pty) Ltd v Booysen and Clark Motors (Pty) Ltd* 1984 (3) SA 480 (W) at 483; *Woolfsons Credit (Pty) Ltd v Holdt* 1977 (3) SA 720 (N) at 722; *Boonzaier v Kiley* 1981 (2) SA 618 (W) at 621; *Moraitis v De Canha and Another* 1984 (1) SA 420 (W) at 426 and FR Malan, AN Oelofse, W le R de Vos, JT Pretorius & CJ Nagel *Provisional Sentence on Bills of Exchange, Cheques and Promissory Notes* (1986) 18 ff.

[115] 1928 AD 74 at 78.

[116] (1904) 21 SC 386 at 388.

[117] The dictum of De Villiers CJ was referred to in *Madnitsky v Kantor* 1952 (3) SA 491 (W) and in *Hedy (Pty) Ltd v Wellkut Garment Manufacturing Co (Pty) Ltd and Another* 1953 (2) SA 236 (C), but in each of these cases the form of the summons in any event disentitled the plaintiff to provisional sentence. See also *Simon v Sacks and Another* 1927 WLD 162. It may be doubted whether the dictum of De Villiers CJ relating to the facts disclosed or the decision of Hopley J relating to admissibility would be followed today. See also *Gaba v Ordra Trust and Investment (Pty) Ltd and Another* 1954 (2) SA 129 (T); *Volkskas Beperk v Mohamed* 1955 (1) SA 453 (T) at 456.

[118] (1909) 26 SC 417.

documents annexed to the provisional sentence summons disclosing that the principal debtor had been excussed. However, in *TV and Radio Guarantee Co (Pty) Ltd v Du Preez*[119] provisional sentence was granted against the giver of an aval where the plaintiff alleged in the summons that the principal debtor had been placed in final liquidation by reason of its inability to pay its debts. Van Zyl J held that, since the allegation that the company (principal debtor) had been liquidated on the ground that it was unable to pay its debts had not been placed in dispute by the defendant, provisional sentence could be granted against the defendant without the necessity of proving excussion of the principal debtor.[120]

11. Delay in excussion

If, after the surety has claimed the benefit of excussion, the creditor delays in excussing the principal debtor, with the consequence that he fails to recover what he would have recovered had he proceeded timeously, no defence is thereby afforded the surety.[121] The benefit of excussion is for the surety, and if he elects to avail himself of it, there is normally no obligation on the creditor to act with any alacrity. The surety can protect himself from the risks by paying the creditor and suing the debtor before the latter's position worsens.[122] The situation is different, however, when the surety is liable for only the shortfall,[123] as on a *fideiussio indemnitatis*. If the creditor's delay contributes to the creation of the shortfall, for example, if by delaying he fails to recover what he would with diligence have recovered, he cannot turn to the surety for so much as he lost through his own delay. Voet[124] says this is so of any surety who has the benefit of excussion, but that would be contrary to the principle that mere delay or grant of time to the debtor does not release the surety. The subject is discussed more fully in the chapter on Discharge of the Surety.[125]

---

[119] 1986 (3) SA 866 (W).

[120] It seems, however, that Van Zyl J did not address the fundamental issue of whether the document in question was indeed a liquid document vis-à-vis the signer of the aval. The liquidity of a claim should not in principle depend on whether certain allegations made by the plaintiff are placed in dispute by the defendant. The question should rather be whether the defendant's liability is founded on a liquid document even though the liability as such may depend on the fulfilment of some simple condition or event (FR Malan, AN Oelofse, W le R de Vos, JT Pretorius & CJ Nagel *Provisional Sentence on Bills of Exchange, Cheques and Promissory Notes* (1986) 18 ff and the authorities there cited). It is important that a plaintiff should be able to predict with reasonable certainty whether he is entitled to claim provisional sentence on a particular document. This decision should not be influenced or decided by the fortuitous possibility of the defendant's placing certain allegations in dispute. See the critical discussion of this decision in 1986 *Annual Survey* 340–1.

[121] P 414.

[122] *Estate Liebenberg v Standard Bank of South Africa Ltd* 1927 AD 502 at 507.

[123] V 46.1.38; P 414.

[124] V 46.1.38.

[125] The matter of the surety's liability for the costs of excussion we have discussed in Chapter VII.

CHAPTER IX

The Benefit of Division Amongst Co-sureties

	Page
1. Introduction.	138
2. Invocation of the benefit	138
3. Benefit does not avail against insolvent or absent co-sureties	139
4. Minor co-sureties.	140
5. Further sureties who do not enjoy the benefit, and other special cases, including renunciation.	141

1. Introduction

Co-sureties, the nature of whom we have discussed in Chapter IV are, each of them, liable *in solidum*.[1] By a rescript of the Emperor Hadrian, however, any one or more of several co-sureties has, if the creditor claims payment of the whole debt, or more than his aliquot share of it, from one of them, the right to demand that the debt be divided between all the co-sureties who are solvent, so that each of them ends up paying only his aliquot share.[2]

2. Invocation of the benefit

Hadrian's rescript does not have the effect of dividing the debt *ipso jure*.[3] There must be positive action to bring this about; either one or more of the co-sureties makes the claim to a division or the creditor divides it of his own accord. While the benefit of excussion provides only a dilatory defence, the exercise of the right of division on the part of a co-surety destroys the creditor's action against him for the excess of the debt over his aliquot share.[4] The creditor is left, however, with his right to recover the balance of the debt from each of the other co-sureties, who remain liable *in solidum*; but he may be met with the same defence on the part of any of them whom he may sue for the whole balance or for more than that co-surety's aliquot share of the entire debt. In the result, the debt is divided

---

[1] D 46.1.51 pr; Inst 3.20.4; V 46.1.22, 24; Huber 3.26.15; P 415, 426; Wessels paras 4101, 4105. *Van der Vyver v De Wayer and Others* (1861) 4 Searle 27 at 29. See the discussion in Chapter I.
[2] D 46.1.28; D 46.1.51 pr; Inst 3.20.4; V 46.1.21; Gr 3.3.28; Sch 303; VL 4.4.7; *Cens For* 1.4.17.18; VdL 1.11.10; Huber 3.26.20; P 415, 418, 426; B 343; Wessels para 4102. *Van der Vyver v De Wayer and Others* (1861) 4 Searle 27; *Klopper v Van Straaten* (1894) 11 SC 94.
[3] D 46.1.26; Huber 3.26.20; Wessels para 4103.
[4] V 46.1.21; *Cens For* 1.4.17.18; P 420, 425.

for payment by those co-sureties who are solvent, each being liable for his aliquot share.[5]

3. Benefit does not avail against insolvent or absent co-sureties

Hadrian's rescript giving authority for dividing the debt among the co-sureties who are solvent excludes, in the making of the calculation, not merely a surety whose estate has been declared by the court to be insolvent, but any one of them who is in fact a pauper or impecunious.[6] The situation is not dissimilar from that relating to the benefit of excussion, where as we have seen in Chapter VIII a creditor cannot be required to excuss at his own risk an impecunious principal debtor. The onus of proving that the surety is not impecunious, and consequently is to be taken into account in the division, rests upon the co-surety who claims that he is not.[7] Voet[8] says that even if he is impecunious the creditor may be required to sue him upon the provision of security for doing so.[9] Pothier[10] says that the co-surety claiming division of the debt is entitled to it, at his own risk, upon payment of his share of the debt.

The relevant moment for ascertaining the financial position of the co-surety in question seems to be *litis contestatio*;[11] Van Leeuwen in *Censura Forensis*[12] and Grotius,[13] however, prefer the commencement of the action, while Wessels[14] says judgment is the crucial event. Impecuniosity of a co-surety subsequently occurring does not affect a division already made at the instance of a co-surety;[15] the loss falls on the creditor, not on the other co-sureties, even if the creditor is a minor.[16]

If the creditor voluntarily divides his action by claiming from the co-sureties their respective shares of the debt, he is not entitled thereafter to revive the former situation; he cannot claim from any one of them more than his aliquot share of the debt, not even if one of them was insolvent (in the sense we have indicated) before he divided the debt.[17] If he has sued only one of them, either *in solidum* or for his share of the debt, Voet[18] says he has not committed himself to a division, but Schorer,[19] referring to Neostadius, says he has done so when he has sued one

---

[5] Wessels para 4106.
[6] D 46.1.26; V 46.1.21; Gr 3.3.28; VL 4.4.8; *Cens For* 1.4.17.19; Huber 3.26.21; B 343. See also *Gerber v Wolson* 1955 (1) SA 158 (A) at 165 and *LAWSA* vol 26 para 213.
[7] D 46.1.28; V 46.1.21; B 345; Wessels para 4109.
[8] D 46.1.10 pr; V 46.1.21 Wessels para 4109.
[9] Cf *Acutt v Bennett* (1906) 27 NLR 716 at 724; *Liquidator of the Owl Syndicate v Bright* (1909) 26 SC 12 at 14.
[10] P 422; Wessels para 4109.
[11] V 46.1.21; *Cens For* 1.4.17.19; Gr 3.3.28; Sch 305; B 345.
[12] *Loc cit.*
[13] *Loc cit.*
[14] Para 4108.
[15] D 46.1.51; Inst. 3.20.4; V 46.1.21; Gr 3.3.28; *Cens For* 1.4.17.19; Huber 3.26.21; P 420, 426; B 345; Lee *ad Gr* 250; Wessels paras 4106, 4110.
[16] D 46.1.51.4; V 46.1.21; Lee *ad Gr* 250.
[17] C 8.41.16; V 46.1.26; *Cens For* 1.4.17.22; Sch 304; Huber 3.26.24; P 420; Wessels paras 4113, 4125–8; Lee, *ad Gr* 250.
[18] *Loc cit.*
[19] *Loc cit.*

only for his share of the debt. There seems much to be said for Schorer's view, for the creditor has performed an unequivocal act indicative of his decision to divide the debt, but Wessels[20] sees no reason why the creditor should not withdraw his action for a share and sue the sureties *in solidum*. When the creditor has divided the debt he cannot resile from this even if one of the co-sureties obtains *restitutio in integrum* on the grounds of minority.[21] A minor creditor, however, may obtain *restitutio* if he (or his guardian) has divided the debt or permitted this and it turns out that one of the co-sureties was insolvent before the division.[22]

In addition to the case of an insolvent surety, there are other instances in which, when the benefit is exercised, a co-surety is excluded from the calculation upon division of the debt. This is so of a co-surety who is out of the country or cannot be found.[23] Perhaps today, instead of saying 'out of the country', we should say 'absent' or 'beyond the jurisdiction' in the sense in which we discussed this in Chapter VIII.[24]

4. Minor co-sureties

When a minor undertakes a suretyship concomitantly with a major co-surety the following principles apply.[25] Even if the minor obtains *restitutio in integrum*,[26] the burden of his part of the debt is not to fall on his co-surety or co-sureties, for these bound themselves in the expectation that the debt would be divided, not necessarily being aware that he was a minor or that, if he was, he would obtain *restitutio*. But if the minor was added as a surety subsequently and he obtains *restitutio*, he is excluded from the division; the burden falls upon the original sureties, unless the creditor induced the minor into undertaking the suretyship by fraud, in which event the creditor must bear the loss when the minor escapes liability. Pothier[27] points out, however, that a co-surety should no more rely on the minor not obtaining *restitutio* than rely upon a co-surety's solvency; and as insolvency of a co-surety before division operates to the disadvantage of his co-sureties, so *restitutio* for a minor co-surety should do the same. The creditor should be entitled to make a reservation when division takes effect, that he will be entitled to proceed against the other sureties if the minor obtains *restitutio*. If he makes no such reservation he takes on himself the risk of the minor obtaining this. Van Leeuwen[28] in his *Roman-Dutch Law* makes the bald statement that the benefit of division does not exist for the co-surety of a minor. In his *Censura Forensis*[29] he says a person who is

---

[20] Wessels para 4129; see also Huber 3.26.24.
[21] P 424.
[22] D 46.1.52.1; V 46.1.21.
[23] V 46.1.21; VL 4.4.8; *Cens For* 1.4.17.2, 19; P 423; B 345; Wessels para 4133.
[24] Cf Wessels para 4133.
[25] D 46.1.48.1; V 46.1.23; Huber 3.26.26; B 346, 347; Wessels paras 4119, 4120.
[26] See, in general, *The South African Law of Persons* (2008) 3 ed by Jacqueline Heaton 100 ff.
[27] P 424; Wessels para 4121.
[28] VL 4.4.8.
[29] *Cens For* 1.4.17.19.

surety along with one who can bind himself only by the law of nature is bound *in solidum*. The weight of authority seems to be against Pothier.[30]

5. Further sureties who do not enjoy the benefit, and other special cases, including renunciation

Sureties, each of whom has undertaken liability for only a specified portion of the debt, not being co-sureties, are not entitled to the benefit of division.[31] Nor, it follows, is one who, along with sureties for the whole debt, has undertaken liability for only a specified portion of it, entitled to the benefit of division. Similarly such a surety's share is not taken into account in the division when one of the others obtains the benefit.

Two sureties, one of whom is surety for one co-debtor, and the other of whom is surety for another co-debtor, are not co-sureties and consequently neither has the benefit of division.[32]

If one of the co-sureties is bound only from a stated future date or is bound conditionally, a provisional division is effected.[33] He is taken into account along with the other co-sureties, but his liability for his aliquot share remains in suspense; if in the result he is released by the failure of the condition or if by the time for the commencement of his liability he is insolvent, the others bear his share of the burden.

Sureties for a surety, that is to say, *achterborgen,* take in the division the place of the surety for whom they are sureties (as also does a single surety for him), if he fails in his obligation or is himself excluded from the division.[34] They are not counted *per capita* in the calculation (for they are not co-sureties with him); but, so to speak, as a *stirpes* in his stead. They are entitled to a division of the debt between themselves and his co-sureties. If his means should be in issue, their means are added to his.[35] As between themselves, *achterborgen* may qualify as co-sureties for the surety and so divide between themselves the liability they bear.[36]

By the strict Roman law, a co-surety who voluntarily paid his share of the debt (or more or less than his share) remained liable to the creditor for the balance of the debt.[37] This was because he was liable *in solidum* and, as we have said, no division takes place unless claimed or unless the creditor volunteered it; if the creditor sued him for the balance and he claimed a division, he was liable for his share of that balance. In practice, however, this was not followed; the co-surety who had paid part of the debt became entitled, in fairness, to the creditor for what he had paid as against his share of the debt.[38] But, if he had overpaid, he was not

---

[30] See, however, *LAWSA* Vol 26 para 204 which favours Pothier's reasoning and argues that a minor surety ought to be excluded from a division.
[31] D 46.1.51 pr, 4; V 46.1.22; P 415.
[32] D 46.1.51.2; V 46.1.22; P 419; B 344. Co-sureties bind themselves as sureties in favour of a common principal debtor and in respect of the same principal debt.
[33] D 46.1.27.1, 4; V 46.1.22, 29; P 421; Wessels para 4114.
[34] D 46.1.27 pr; V 46.1.22; P 417, 418; B 345; Wessels para 4117.
[35] D 46.1.27.2; V 46.1.6; P 420; Wessels para 4112.
[36] D 46.1.27.1; V 46.1.22; P 417.
[37] D 46.1.51.1; V 46.1.25; P 426; Wessels para 4135. See also Chapter 1.
[38] Ibid.

entitled to any refund from the creditor. And so it is with us; any co-surety who pays the debt in full, or pays more than his share of it, cannot recover from the creditor the excess over his share.[39] He is left to his right to recover contributions from his co-sureties, a subject to be discussed in Chapter XII.

When a co-surety who has paid the debt claims repayment from one of his co-sureties, on a cession of actions from the creditor, the co-surety against whom the claim is made may exercise the benefit of division, unless this would not be available to him against the creditor.[40] If the co-surety who has paid the debt merely claims contributions of their aliquot share from his co-sureties, or any of them, the question of the benefit of division does not arise.[41]

There are further exceptions to the availability of the benefit of division to co-sureties. In the first place, one who, sued for the whole debt, fails to claim the benefit and has judgment given against him, loses the benefit.[42]

In the second place, a co-surety may expressly renounce the benefit;[43] this, to be effective, must be in specific, not general terms,[44] just as we have indicated in discussion of the conflict among the old writers on the renunciation of the benefit of excussion.

Renunciation may be implied, as indeed it is when co-sureties bind themselves in terms which make them also co-principal debtors.[45]

---

[39] D 46.1.49; V 46.1.17, 24; Gr 3.3.29; P 426; Wessels para 4105.

[40] V 46.1.29; P 445; Sande 6.33; B 351; Wessels para 4150.

[41] See, however, the discussion of *Gerber v Wolson* 1955 (1) SA 158 (A) in the following chapter.

[42] V 46.1.24; Gr 3.3.29; Huber 3.26.25; Lee *ad Gr* 251.

[43] V 46.1.24; Gr 3.3.29; Sch 304; VI 448; *Cens For* 1.4.17.19; VdK 502; Huber 3.26.23; P 416; B 345; Wessels para 4124; Lee *ad Gr* 250. Renunciation of the *exceptio de duobus vel pluribus reis debendi* may also result in co-sureties becoming jointly and severally liable. The effect of the *exceptio de duobus vel pluribus reis debendi* was explained by Rose Innes J in *Coloured Development Corporation Ltd v Sahabodien* 1981 (1) SA 868 (C) at 875: 'In terms of the bond defendant and his brother expressly waived and renounced the benefits *de duobus vel pluribus reis debendi* whereby co-debtors, who would otherwise be liable jointly *pro rata parte* without waiver of this benefit, but not jointly and severally liable *singuli in solidum,* may resist being sued singly for the full amount of the debt. The express abandonment of that defence is a decisive indication in terms of the contract that the agreement was that the defendant and his brother agreed to be bound *singuli in solidum* and that plaintiff would be entitled if it so elected to sue each alone for the full debt without joining the other.' A co-obligator who is bound jointly had the choice at common law to plead either the *beneficium duobus vel pluribus reis debendi* or the *exceptio divisionis* should he be sued for the whole debt. Renunciation of the *exceptio de duobus vel pluribus reis debendi* is the one way in which the liability of co-debtors can be made to be *in solidum*, but a more usual way is for them all to assume the liability jointly and severally as co-principal debtors.

[44] V 46.1.24; VL 4.4.12; *Cens For* 1.4.17.20, 21; Sande 638.

[45] V 46.1.24; Gr 3.3.29; Sch 305; VdK 503; VL 4.49; *Cens For* 1.4.17.23; Huber 3.26.23; P 416; B 344; Wessels paras 4124, 4132. See also *Van der Vyver v De Wayer and Others* (1861) 4 Searle 27; *J & T Anderson v Patrick & Plowright* (1904) 25 NLR 75; *Fitzgerald v Argus Printing and Publishing Co Ltd* (1907) 3 Buch AC 152 at 160; *Maasdorp v Graaff-Reinet Board of Executors* (1909) 3 Buch AC 482; *Colonial Treasurer v Swart* 1910 TPD 552 at 556; *Union Government v Van der Merwe* 1921 TPD 318; *Kaplan v ER Syfret & Co* 1914 CPD 1104; *Meer v General Industrial Credit Corporation (Pty) Ltd* 1947 (4) SA 330 (C) at 335; *Gerber v Wolson* 1955 (1) SA 158 (A) at 167; *Taylor and Thorne NNO and Others v The Master* 1965 (1) SA 658 (N) at 659; *Ideal Finance Corporation v Coetzer* 1969 (4) SA 43 (O) at 44 (approved as far as this aspect is concerned by the Appellate Division in *Ideal Finance Corporation v Coetzer* 1970 (3) SA 1 (A) at 7 and 11); *JR & M Moffett (Pty) Ltd v Kolbe Eiendoms Beleggings (Edms) Bpk and Another* 1974 (2) SA 426 (O) at 432; *Mouton v Die Mynwerkersunie* 1977 (1) SA 119 (A); *Neon and Cold Cathode Illuminations (Pty) Ltd v Ephron* 1978 (1) SA 463 (A) at 472; *Standard Bank of SA Ltd v SA Fire Equipment (Pty) Ltd and Another* 1984 (2) SA 693 (C) (approved in *Muller and Others v Botswana*

In Holland persons who had signed an aval did not enjoy the benefit. According to Van der Keessel;[46] they were bound as co-sureties who had tacitly renounced the benefit. This seems to accord with Van der Keessel's statement[47] that the benefit is 'supposed not to obtain' among merchants who secure the solvency of another. In our law, however, it seems from *Klopper v Van Straaten*[48] and *Du Plessis v Greef and Walter*[49] that those who sign an aval do enjoy the benefit. In *Soomar v Jeewa and Others*[50] Brokensha J appears to have regarded *Moti & Co v Cassim's Trustee*[51] as having decided this, but the fact is that the court was concerned only with the benefit of excussion and that it was influenced in its decision by the fact that the well-established practice in this country had been against permitting provisional sentence proceedings against those who had signed avals.[52] But this consideration has no place in relation to the benefit of division. There seems, in fact, never to have been any full canvassing of these issues in the courts. In *Klopper v Van Straaten*[53] the matter seems not to have been argued, but rather to have been assumed.[54] Comparison should be made with what has been said in Chapter VIII regarding the benefit of excussion.

Others who are not entitled to the benefit of division are co-sureties for the indivisible obligation or act,[55] for it is not possible to divide the action between the co-sureties. So far as monetary relief, such as damages, flows from non-performance of such an obligation or act, this, however, is divisible and the co-sureties are entitled to the division of it.[56] A consent to judgment contained in the contract of suretyship does not in itself amount to a renunciation of the benefit.[57] Nor are co-sureties for performance of a judgment allowed the benefit;[58] nor co-sureties for a guardian's duties towards his ward,[59] though Burge[60] says that if there are more guardians than one, the co-sureties for them are entitled to a division (the reason for this is not apparent); nor are co-sureties for the public revenue entitled to the benefit of division.[61]

Development Corporation Ltd [2002] 3 All SA 663 (SCA)); *Kilroe-Daley v Barclays National Bank Ltd* 1984 (4) SA 609 (A) at 623.

[46] VdK 594.
[47] VdK 504.
[48] (1894) 11 SC 94.
[49] (1905) 22 SC 580.
[50] 1958 (4) SA 24 (N).
[51] 1924 AD 720.
[52] See FR Malan, AN Oelofse, W le R de Vos, JT Pretorius & CJ Nagel *Provisional Sentence on Bills of Exchange, Cheques and Promissory Notes* 205 ff for a critical discussion of the present law in this regard. See also *Malan on Bills of Exchange, Cheques and Promissory Notes in South African Law* 5ed by FR Malan, JT Pretorius & SF du Toit (2009) para 152.
[53] (1894) 11 SC 94.
[54] See also *Gaba v Ordra Trust and Investments (Pty) Ltd and Another* 1954 (2) SA 129 (T); *Manufacturers Development Co (Pty) Ltd v Repcar Holdings (Pty) Ltd and Others* 1975 (2) SA 779 (W); *Industrial Development Corporation of SA Ltd v See Bee Holdings (Pty) Ltd and Others* 1978 (4) SA 136 (C).
[55] V 46.1.24; B 346; Wessels para 4134.
[56] V 46.1.24; B 346; Wessels para 4134.
[57] V 46.1.24.
[58] Sch 306; P 416, B 347.
[59] V 46.1.22, 23; Gr 3.3.28; Huber 3.26.25; P 416; B 346; Wessels para 4122.
[60] B 346.
[61] V 46.1.22; P 416.

In Roman law a surety who falsely denied that he was such did not have the benefit,[62] but Voet and Schorer, in the passages cited, add that, legal penalties having been abandoned in their day, this was no longer the law in Holland. It is not our law.

A surety cannot claim division of the debt between himself and the principal debtor,[63] not even if he is surety and co-principal debtor, for, in essence, he is a surety who undertakes additional obligations.[64] No more can the principal debtor claim a division with his surety, or a surety claim it with his *achterborg*.[65]

Voet[66] and Pothier[67] discuss at some length at what stage of litigation the benefit must be claimed. The former concludes that it must be pleaded in the suit, the latter that it can be raised up to judgment, indeed if there is an appeal (which suspends judgment) it may be raised for the first time even on appeal. In modern practice there can hardly be any doubt that it must be raised in the plea, even if that be by a permitted amendment to the plea.[68] Failure to raise it, as we have seen, amounts to a renunciation of the benefit.

On the death of a co-surety, his estate has, or has not, the benefit of division, depending upon whether or not he had it.[69]

---

[62] D 46.1.10.1; v 46.1.23; Gr 3.3.28; Sch 303; VL 4.4.9; *Cens For* 1.4.17.19; Huber 3.26.25; P 416; Wessels para 4123.
[63] V 46.1.22; P 417; B 344, 345; Wessels para 4117.
[64] *Trustees of Du Toit v Executors of Smuts and De Kock* (1835) 2 Menz 24; *Roos v Coetzee* (1846) 2 Menz 74. See also JSA Fourie 'Die Aanspreeklikheid van die Borg en die Hoofskuldenaar' (1978) 41 *THRHR* 307.
[65] V 46.1.22; P 418; B 345.
[66] V 46.1.5. 21.
[67] P 425.
[68] See also *LAWSA* Vol 26 para 204 note 18 which agrees with the above submission.
[69] V 46.1.26; P 417.

CHAPTER X

The Benefit of Cession of Actions

	Page
1. Introduction and history	145
2. The fate of other security held by the creditor	148
3. The effect of cession of actions	148
4. The controversy over the rights of a co-surety who has paid and has cession of actions against other co-sureties	149
5. Advantages of cession of actions	152
6. The pro rata reduction of the co-surety's rights against his fellows acquired by cession of actions	153
7. When a surety is entitled to cession	154
8. Inability of the creditor to give cession of actions	155
(a) Generally	155
(b) Release or abandonment or other loss of security held by creditor	156
9. Effect of renunciation of benefit	158

1. Introduction and history

In early Roman law, payment by a surety of the debt of the principal debtor discharged the debt at the moment of payment and consequently released the debtor and, because a surety's obligation is accessory to the principal obligation, released any other sureties there might be for the same debt.[1] In *Kroon v Enschede and Others*[2] Wessels J embarked on a full historical review of the situation regarding cession of actions and also regarding the right of a co-surety who has paid the debt to recover contributions from his colleagues. Although the surety, notwithstanding the discharge of the debt by his payment, could recover from the principal debtor what he had paid the creditor,[3] originally he had in Roman law no relief against his co-sureties hitherto liable with him for the debt of the principal debtor.[4] Many, but not all, of the Roman-Dutch writers say the law in their time was the same as the Roman law: without cession of actions there was no right to recover anything from the other co-sureties.[5] The reason for this was that there is no contractual privity or nexus between co-sureties; the contract of each is with the creditor.[6] It would be different if the co-sureties had contracted *inter se* each to bear his share of the debt or to regulate the method of division of

---

[1] D 46.1.39; Domat 1887; V 46.1.30; P 406, 519. See also Chapter I.
[2] 1909 TS 374. See also Susan Scott *The Law of Cession* 2 ed (1991) at 218 ff.
[3] The surety's right of recourse against the principal debtor is discussed in Chapter XI.
[4] D 46.1.39; C 841.11; P 445; Domat 1887; B 381; Wessels paras 4210, 4211; Reinhard Zimmermann *The Law of Obligations* (1990) at 134–6.
[5] See Chapter XII.
[6] P 445, B 381.

the liability among themselves.[7] The only other remedy for the co-surety who had paid the debt, against his co-sureties, was in Roman law provided by means of the benefit of cession of actions;[8] with this benefit he could sue his co-sureties on the creditor's claim. This became the Roman-Dutch law.[9] In our law, nevertheless, as will be seen in the chapter on the Right to Contributions by Co-sureties (Chapter XII), the co-surety who has paid the debt has the right, based in equity, to have each of the other co-sureties contribute his share of the debt, without reliance on a cession of actions. Nonetheless, as we shall see the benefit of cession of actions remains important.

Originally cession of actions was based on a fiction that the creditor sold his claims to the surety on payment of the debt, the price being that very payment.[10] This was plainly fictitious since the surety who paid the debt did not do so in order to buy the claims, but because he was obliged to pay it.[11]

If, on or before paying the whole debt (which he might do because he did not have the benefit of division or because he was unwilling to avail himself of it), the surety demanded of the creditor a cession of the latter's rights, the creditor was bound to give this, on pain of being met with the *exceptio cedendarum actionum*,[12] unless cession would be prejudicial to the creditor.[13] The surety having this benefit and being sued could thus put it forward as a dilatory defence; until the creditor gave him cession of actions he was not obliged to pay the debt.[14] Once he had been given cession of actions, the surety was entitled to sue not only the principal debtor (even if he had gone surety for him against his will)[15] but also his co-sureties and all other persons liable for the debt.[16] It was, however, too late to ask for cession of actions after the surety had paid the debt, unless at or before the time of payment the creditor had agreed to give cession, for the debt was extinguished by the surety's payment and nothing remained to be sold or ceded by the creditor to the surety.[17]

Some Roman-Dutch writers,[18] however, regarded this as inequitable and made an innovation in the law, to the following effect: payment of the debt by the surety was taken to have been made in his own name, in order to release only himself and not either the principal debtor or the co-sureties; as a consequence of that, it was competent for the creditor to give, and to the surety to take, cession of

---

[7] VL 4.4.14; *Cens For* 1.4.17.24. *Gerber v Wolson* 1955 (1) SA 158 (A) at 167, 178.
[8] D 46.1.36, 39; C 8.41.11; Domat 1887; B 381.
[9] V 46.1.28; Gr 3.3.31; Sch 303; VL 4.4.14; *Cens For* 1.4.17.24; VdL 1.14.10; P 445; Sande 6.32; Huber 3.26.27; B 348, 349.
[10] D 46.1.36; V 46.1.28, 30; *Cens For* 1.4.17.25; Sande 7.1; P 522, 523; B 350; Wessels para 4138.
[11] As Pothier *loc cit* points out. See also Chapter I.
[12] D 46.1.13, 17, 36; C 8.41.11; V 46.1.27, 28; Gr 3.3.31; Sch 303; VL 4.4.7, 14; *Cens For* 1.4.17.18, 24; VdL 1.14.9.7; 1.14.10; Sande 6.32, 34; P 427, 520; B 348, 350.
[13] Sande 6.35. See also Susan Scott *The Law of Cession* 2 ed (1991) at 219.
[14] D 46.1.13, 36; V 46.1.27, 28, 30; Sch 303; Sande 6.32; P 520.
[15] V 46.1.28.
[16] D 46.1.17, 36; V 46.1.27, 38; Gr 3.3.31; Sch 303; VL 4.4.7; *Cens For* 1.4.17.18; VdL 1.4.10; Huber 3.26.27; Sande 6.32, 34; P 427, 520; B 350, 351, 417.
[17] D 46.1.13, 36; V 46.1.30; Gr 3.3.31; VL 4.4.15; *Cens For* 1.4.17.25; VdL 1.14.9.7; Sande 7.1; P 520, 521; Huber 3.26.28; B 350; Wessels para 4139.
[18] Groen *ad Cod* 8.41.11; V 46.1.28, 30; VL 4.4.15; *Cens For* 1.4.17.25; Sande 6.32; 7.5; 7.11, 12; P 445; B 351; Lee *ad Gr* 253, 254; Wessels para 4140.

actions even long after payment of the debt.[19] Grotius,[20] however, was not a party to this innovation; he expressed himself in terms of the old law. Nor did Van der Keessel[21] go the whole way with the others, for both in his *Theses* and in his *Dictata* he says a subsequent cession is available if the payment was in fact made in the name of the surety, but not if in the name of the debtor. Decker's note to Van Leeuwen[22] explains Grotius on this basis. Sande[23] says the surety is presumed to have paid in his own name.[24] Pothier[25] indicates that in France cession generally took effect *ipso jure* on the surety's demand for it. Huber[26] was opposed to the modern view, on principle.

Our law is based on the equitable foundation laid by these writers.[27] Payment of the debt by the surety discharges the principal debtor's liability to the creditor, but this does not extinguish the debt, which is kept alive to enable the surety who has received cession of actions to enforce those actions, by suing the principal debtor and his co-sureties, if there are any, and third parties who may also be liable to be placed in the position the creditor was in; it is only right that the creditor who has been paid by the surety should come to his assistance and help him get back his money. The surety who obtains cession of actions from the creditor (as he may do even long after payment of the debt by him) can recoup himself from all sources from which the creditor himself could have obtained payment of his debt, save, however, that as between co-sureties payment of the full debt by one of them to the creditor extinguishes as between him and his co-sureties that share of the debt for which, as between them, he is liable.[28] In *Gerber v Wolson*[29] Van den Heever JA said in a dissenting judgment: 'If a surety pays in order to discharge the principal debtor's debt, the debt is extinguished; if, however, he pays in order to discharge his own accessory debt, he may demand cession of action from the creditor even if he does so after payment.' And, he went on:[30] 'As I understand our law, cession of action conveys to the cessionary all the rights of the cedent with its attendant privileges, save those highly personal rights which are now not relevant.'

For a proper understanding of the situation it must be appreciated that, although in Roman law there was but one debt which was extinguished by payment by the surety, in the new concept there are two or more debts or obligations each giving rise to a separate cause of action: the obligation of the principal debtor and that of the surety or of each of several co-sureties; and there may also be co-debtors.

---

[19] Cf *Pearce and Another v De Jager* 1924 CPD 455 at 466, in which, *obiter*, the modern view was accepted.
[20] Gr 3.3.31.
[21] VdK 506, Lee *ad Gr* 253, 254.
[22] *Loc cit.*
[23] *Loc cit.*
[24] See also *Pearce and Another v De Jager* 1924 CPD 455 at 464.
[25] P 445, 521B.
[26] Huber 3.26.28–30.
[27] *African Guarantee & Indemnity Co Ltd v Thorpe* 1933 AD 330 at 336 ff. See also *Gerber v Wolson* 1955 (1) SA 158 (A) at 167 and *LAWSA* vol 26 para 205.
[28] See also *Meer v General Industrial Credit Corporation (Pty) Ltd* 1947 (4) SA 330 (C) at 336–8. See also *Berzack Brothers Ltd v Iesberts and Others* 1973 (2) SA 196 (W).
[29] 1955 (1) SA 158 (A) at 167.
[30] At 173.

Although, as Van den Heever JA said[31] of the same case, they all frequently have the 'same economic content', they are different obligations. The payment by one co-surety of his obligation should consequently not affect the creditor's capacity to cede to him at any time his rights against the principal debtor and those against other co-sureties, or indeed any other rights he may have.

2. The fate of other security held by the creditor

In addition to rights of action against principal debtors, co-sureties and co-debtors, the creditor may hold securities of one nature or another from any of these for payment of his liability. The surety paying the debt has the right to cession of these so that he may enjoy the advantage of them.[32] Though the surety is clearly entitled to the securities held by the creditor when he gave his undertaking, this does not mean that he is not entitled to securities subsequently acquired as, for example, if a further surety is taken and he gives security; the authorities appear to be silent about this, but, having the right to cession of all the creditor's rights, it would follow that the surety is entitled to the cession of rights acquired after he has undertaken liability as surety. Insofar, however, as any security is held by the creditor not only for the debt in question, but also for some other debt, the surety is not entitled to the benefit of this unless he elects also to pay that other debt; and so, also, he is not entitled to a security given for the whole debt if (whether he has undertaken liability for the whole or a part) he has paid only part of the debt.[33] This is a facet of the rule that the surety is not entitled to cession insofar as it would prejudice the creditor.[34] If the creditor's claim is of a preferential nature, the right to the preference passes with the cession of the claim.[35]

3. The effect of cession of actions

The creditor may voluntarily cede his actions to anyone he pleases, in return for a money payment or other consideration[36] or by way of a gift, but to a surety who pays the debt of the principal debtor he is obliged to cede his actions in respect of that debt, thereby ceding to him all his rights flowing from the transaction.[37]

A surety who takes cession of actions has the advantage of them, like any other person who takes cession of a claim, 'subject to equities', that is to say, generally subject to any defences available to the debtor of the claim against the creditor,

---

[31] At 166, 167.
[32] C 8.41.2, 11, 14, 21; V 46.1.27, 28, *Cens For* 1.4.17.24; Huber 3.26.27, Sande 6.34, 35; P 281; 427, 521B; B 348, 352, 353; Wessels para 4146. See also *Berzack Brothers Ltd v Iesberts and Others* 1973 (2) SA 196 (W).
[33] C 8.41.2; V 46.1.27, 28; Sande 635; B 349; Wessels para 4147.
[34] *Farthing v Pieters and Co* 1912 CPD 215; *Farthing and Another v Pieters & Co* 1913 CPD 771 at 774.
[35] V 46.1.28; *Cens For* 1.4.17.24; P 521B.
[36] *African Guarantee & Indemnity Co Ltd v Thorpe* 1933 AD 330 at 338.
[37] *Estate Tudhope v Sand* (1907) 24 SC 614 at 618; *Mitchell Cotts & Co v Commissioner of Railways* 1905 TS 349 at 358; *Kroon v Enschede and Others* 1909 TS 374 at 378, 379; *Corrans and Another v Transvaal Government and Coull's Trustee* 1909 TS 605 at 614, 615; *Pearce and Another v De Jager* 1924 CPD 455; *Yorkshire Insurance Co Ltd v Barclays Bank (DC&O) Ltd* 1928 WLD 199 at 210; *African Guarantee & Indemnity Co Ltd v Thorpe* 1933 AD 330 at 338; *Meer v General Industrial Credit Corporation (Pty) Ltd* 1947 (4) SA 330 (C) at 336; *Turkstra v Massyn* 1959 (1) SA 40 (T) at 45; *Business Buying & Investment Co Ltd v Linaae* 1959 (3) SA 93 (T) at 96.

other than defences connected merely with the personal capacity of the creditor.[38] Consequently, defences open to the principal debtor against the creditor are available to him against the surety who sues him by virtue of cession of the creditor's claim; so also co-sureties have available to them defences they have against the creditor. By means of the benefit of excussion, a co-surety may require the surety who sues him by virtue of a cession, first to excuss the principal debtor, and co-sureties with the benefit of division can raise this with the result that the surety who, having paid the whole debt, claims from them is limited to recovery of an aliquot share from each of them.[39] If they have the benefit of cession of actions, any of them called on to pay can raise this against the surety holding cession of actions, who then is obliged to give cession in turn to the one called on to pay the debt.[40] Should the liability of the principal debtor (or a surety) to pay the debt be conditional on his first being given notice to do so, this may be raised against not only the creditor but also one who claims the creditor's right by virtue of a cession.[41]

4. The controversy over the rights of a co-surety who has paid and has cession of actions against other co-sureties

In the absence of the benefit of division, co-sureties liable *in solidum* ought, logically, to be liable *in solidum* to the surety who has cession of actions but, as will be seen, there was, and seemingly still is, controversy about this. The essential question is whether such a surety called for instance A can recover from B, one of several co-sureties liable *in solidum* without the benefit of division, the amount he, A, paid to the creditor less A's aliquot share of the debt, or whether he can recover from B only B's aliquot share.

Van Leeuwen,[42] in his *Censura Forensis,* appears to say that the right to cession of actions was conferred in order to entitle a co-surety who had paid the debt to recover the aliquot share of the debt owed by each of his co-sureties, even though they owed the debt *in solidum,* so as to place him in the same position as a co-debtor, who had the right without cession of actions to recover from each of the other co-debtors his share of the debt. Huber[43] speaks of cession of actions 'to the end that co-sureties may in turn reimburse and pay him their shares'.

Pothier[44] also aligns the co-sureties with co-debtors in the law of France. In the first of the passages cited Pothier discusses co-debtors who are liable *in solidum* and the right of one who has paid the debt to recover from another; he concedes that in the earlier law, if he had paid with subrogation of the creditor's rights, he could sue any of the others *in solidum,* but later decisions of the French courts had held that he could recover only the other's share of the debt. This Pothier held to be

---

[38] *Walker v Syfret NO* 1911 AD 141 at 162; *Sampson v Union and Rhodesia Wholesale Ltd (in liquidation)* 1929 AD 468 at 482. See also Susan Scott *The Law of Cession* 2 ed (1991) at 221 ff.
[39] V 46 1.29, P 445; Sande 6.33; B 351; Lee *ad Gr* 254, Wessels para 4150.
[40] V 46.1.29.
[41] *Neethling qq v Minnaar* (1830) 1 Menz 535.
[42] *Cens For* 1.4.17.24.
[43] Huber 3.26.27.
[44] P 281, 445, 523.

now the law, and presumably it was so in France. In the second passage Pothier says 'a surety may exercise the actions of the creditor against his co-sureties' when he has taken the precaution of obtaining a subrogation. He goes on to discuss the situation in the absence of a subrogation or cession of actions, saying *inter alia* that one co-surety is entitled as against another, when sued by the latter, to the benefit of division, even where he has renounced it or is excluded from it, for renunciation and exclusion 'are only in favour of the creditor'. (That this is so in the absence of cession of actions seems to be clear; the co-surety who has paid the debt can recover only the aliquot share of each of his co-sureties.) In the last cited passage Pothier applies to co-sureties the conclusion at which he had arrived in relation to co-debtors. Pothier's views, or the decisions on which they were based, were influenced by a fear of circuity of actions; if one co-debtor or co-surety sued another for the whole of the debt save his own aliquot share, the one sued, now the holder of cession of actions, is in the position of holding the creditor's rights and so can sue the one who had sued him, deducting only his aliquot share of the debt. Consequently there would be no finality; the contest would swing to and fro. This is a technical and unrealistic approach because it fails to take account of the equitable basis on which the liability is ultimately to be shared and was answered in the judgment of the court *a quo* in *Gerber v Wolson*,[45] which is dealt with hereunder.

On the other hand there is weighty authority[46] (Voet, Sande and Van der Keessel in his *Dictata*) for the proposition that when a creditor gives to a surety cession of actions against co-sureties who are such without the benefit of division, the surety is entitled to claim from any of them not merely for their aliquot shares, but *in solidum*; that is to say he acquires the creditor's rights to claim in that fashion. This is so notwithstanding that *inter se* their liability for the debt is, on equitable grounds, shared equally. The surety who has paid may select any one of his co-sureties and sue him for the whole debt (where he is not entitled to benefit of division against the creditor), less the aliquot share of the one who sues. The one sued then, being entitled to and having obtained cession of actions from the surety he has paid, can, in turn, sue one of the other co-sureties for what he has had to pay the first surety, less, again, his aliquot share of the debt. The consequence is that, ultimately, the co-sureties bear the responsibility in equal shares. If it turns out that any one of them is insolvent, suitable relief is given *inter se* to adjust the liability of that one equally amongst the others.[47]

That our law is as these three writers said it was, was confirmed in *Wolson v Gerber*.[48] Van den Heever JA agreed with this in a dissenting judgment in the same case on appeal, *sub nom Gerber v Wolson*,[49] which, by a majority, reversed the judgment of the court *a quo* in which reliance was placed on Voet, Sande and Van der Keessel and on Perezius's *Praelectiones*,[50] in preference to Pothier. On appeal

---

[45] 1955 (1) SA 158 (A).
[46] V 46.1.29; Sande 6.33; Lee *ad Gr* 254, and see Lee's View, 254.
[47] V 46.1.29; P 281; Domat 1888; B 351; Wessels para 4217.
[48] 1954 (3) SA 9 (T), where the court made reference to the *obiter* opinions expressed to this effect in *Buerger v Doll* 1923 SWA 5 and in *Meer v General Industrial Credit Corporation (Pty) Ltd* 1947 (4) SA 330 (C) at 337.
[49] Supra.
[50] *Ad* C 8.41.40.

Van den Heever JA also preferred the views of the first three writers. Although the decision of the court *a quo* was reversed, the gravamen of the decision on appeal was that the parties were not co-sureties, but co-debtors, and that, in the circumstances, their rights *inter se* were to be determined by an interpretation of the document by which they had undertaken liability to the creditor, that the renunciation in that document of the benefit of division had no reference to their relationship *inter se* and that the taking of cession of actions by one who had paid the creditor could not override or nullify the agreement between them (found in the document mentioned above) as to the shares in which they were to bear the liability. Consequently the one holding cession of actions from the creditor was entitled to recover from another no more than that for which the latter was liable under the agreement between them. What was said, particularly in the reasoning of Fagan JA, influenced largely by Pothier, appears to suggest, however, that when one of several co-sureties, not having the benefit of division, has paid the debt and obtained cession of actions, he is entitled to recover from each of the others no more than that one's aliquot share of the debt, irrespective of whether or not there is a contract between them regulating the distribution of the burden among them. There is much to be said for the view that if there is such a contract, effect must be given to it, but it does not necessarily follow that, in the absence of agreement between the co-sureties, the one suing with cession of actions is to be limited to recovering from the others their aliquot shares of the debt. Holding cession of actions he is in the position of the creditor unhampered by the existence of any such agreement with his co-sureties. If he were to be held so limited in his claim, this would make cession of actions valueless in the respect under discussion and negate all that Voet said on the subject. It would also deny the surety who has paid the debt the full advantage of a security given by one of the co-sureties to the creditor for payment of the whole debt. His resort to the security would be limited to the amount of the aliquot share of the one who gave it.[51]

With great respect to any contrary views expressed or to be implied in the judgment on appeal in *Gerber v Wolson*,[52] on principle we suggest that the views of Voet, Sande and Van der Keessel, writing on the law in the Netherlands, are to be preferred to those of Pothier, based on decisions of the French courts departing from the law as Pothier says it had been. Co-sureties are not to be assimilated to co-debtors in this respect.[53]

---

[51] Burge (B 350, 351, 417), whilst agreeing with Pothier in relation to co-debtors, appears to hold the view (although this is by no means clear) that a co-surety who has paid the debt and has obtained cession of actions is entitled to sue any of the other co-sureties *in solidum* and so recover from him unless the co-sureties have retained the benefit of division.

[52] 1955 (1) SA 158 (A).

[53] *Gerber v Wolson* 1955 (1) SA 158 (A) is indeed a difficult case to analyse. It is doubtful even whether on the facts it is concerned with co-sureties (*De Wet en Van Wyk Die Suid-Afrikaanse Kontraktereg en Handelsreg* 5 ed (1992) vol I by JC de Wet and GF Lubbe (ed) 401 note 68). The majority of the judges, except for Fagan JA, do not answer the legal question posed, as they find a tacit agreement between the co-sureties (which would, of course, govern their relations); apparently the existence of a common document under which they became sureties can give rise to the inference that the co-sureties agreed among themselves that the debt was to be divided equally and the payer could claim from each of his fellow co-sureties only his proportionate share. But say there is no common document?

The reason why Roman law denied relief against co-sureties to a surety who had paid the debt was that there was no contractual privity between co-sureties merely because they were co-sureties, not even if they undertook their obligations to the creditor by the same instrument.[54] The right conferred by cession of actions is derived directly from the creditor without being impinged on by any implied contractual rights on the part of the co-sureties *inter se*.[55] Consequently, when co-sureties have not the benefit of division, one of them who is the holder of the creditor's rights by cession is entitled to enforce his claims as the creditor could have done, that is to say, against any of the co-sureties *in solidum*, subject, on grounds of equity, to deduction of his aliquot share of the debt. But if there is an express contract between the co-sureties regulating the distribution of the burden *inter se*, it must be observed, notwithstanding the cession of the creditor's right. The contract between them cannot be evaded by taking a cession of the creditor's rights; the co-surety, party to such a contract, who has paid the debt cannot ignore his contract in order to improve his position against his colleagues.[56]

5. Advantages of cession of actions

Notwithstanding that without cession of actions a surety who pays the debt has a right of recourse against the principal debtor and also a right to contributions of their aliquot shares by co-sureties (as we shall see in the next two chapters), it is manifest that in certain circumstances it is preferable to obtain and employ cession of actions from the creditor. In addition to the fact that because he is in the position of the creditor, the surety can sue his co-sureties *in solidum* (if we are correct in the conclusion we have expressed), he has the following advantages.

First, he can recover any interest, expenses or damages the creditor could have recovered.[57] If the debt carries interest, the surety is entitled to recover the inter-

---

The case is discussed by JE Scholtens 'Recourse of a Surety Against His Co-sureties' (1955) 72 *SALJ* 355. He finds the reasoning of Greenberg JA flawed. 'Why should a proviso be made for co-debtors being solvent if the rights of the surety against his co-debtors are the same as if the surety had signed separate undertakings in respect of each portion? If this be the case the surety himself would have to bear the risk of a co-debtor being insolvent' (at 358). Moreover, why should the surety not have a right of recourse in full against each of these co-debtors?

Reference should also be made to the review of *Gerber v Wolson* 1955 (1) SA 158 (A) by P van Warmelo in 1955 *Butterworths South African Law Review* 147. See also Ellison Kahn (gen ed) *Contract and Mercantile Law through the Cases* II *Specific Contracts and Mercantile Law* 2 ed (1985) by David Zeffertt, JT Pretorius & Coenraad Visser 814–5 and Reinhard Zimmermann *The Law of Obligations* (1990) at 143 ff.

[54] Which is also our law: See Chapter IV.

[55] The introduction of the right to contributions of aliquot shares was much later, based on payment and equity, and was never a part of the Roman law, as we shall see in the chapter on that subject.

[56] In *Corrans and Another v Transvaal Government and Coull's Trustee* 1909 TS 605 at 614 and 615 Innes CJ emphasises (though he is dealing with the situation of the surety vis-à-vis the principal debtor) the fact that the surety with cession of actions is placed in possession of all the creditor's rights, action and securities; and in *African Guarantee & Indemnity Co Ltd v Thorpe* 1933 AD 330 at 336 ff similar emphasis is given to the fact that the surety is placed in possession of the rights the creditor formerly enjoyed.

[57] V 46.1.31; *Cens For* 1.4.17.24; P 440; B 365. See also *Corrans and Another v Transvaal Government and Coull's Trustee* 1909 TS 605 at 614, 615.

est the creditor could have recovered, at the same rate, until he is paid.[58] If the debt does not carry interest, the surety, having paid it, must make demand in order to put the other in *mora*, so that interest may commence to run.[59]

Secondly, if the creditor holds security for payment of the debt, whether by way of pledge or hypothecation, or if the claim on the principal debtor carries a preference over other claims, these benefits pass with cession of actions, with the consequence that the surety is able to enforce them as the creditor could have done.[60]

Thirdly, by cession of actions the surety may be placed in a position to recover from a stranger who is liable to the creditor for the debtor's debt, as, for instance, his partner;[61] or from a co-debtor for whom he was not surety.[62]

6. The pro rata reduction of the co-surety's rights against his fellows acquired by cession of action

Some writers[63] say that the cession to a co-surety of a creditor's rights against his co-sureties is a cession of part only of the creditor's claim, that is to say, with a deduction of so much as represents that co-surety's aliquot share of the debt.[64] So much of the claim is extinguished, on this view, when the co-surety in question, having paid the whole debt, seeks to claim *in solidum* from his co-sureties, but not if he claims from the principal debtor; then the cession is complete. This is, however, an untidy approach. The co-surety who pays the debt is entitled to cession of the whole claim in its entirety so that he may recover from the principal debtor; how can it be said that part of the claim is extinguished in the event of his suing his co-sureties, or any of them? There is but one cession of all the rights of the creditor.[65] Although the obligation, the debt, of the surety who has paid is

---

[58] *Pearce and Another v De Jager* 1924 CPD 455 at 458, 463.

[59] Section 1(1) of the Prescribed Rate of Interest Act 55 of 1975 provides that if a debt bears interest and the rate at which the interest is to be calculated is not governed by any other law or by an agreement or a trade custom or in any other manner, such interest shall be calculated at the rate prescribed determined according to subsec 1(2) which permits the Minister of Justice by notice in the *Government Gazette* from time to time to prescribe the rate of interest.

[60] C 8.41.2, 11, 14, 21; V 46.1.27, 28; *Cens For* 1.4.17.24; Huber 3.26.27; Sande 6.34, 35; P 281; 427, 521B; B 348, 352, 353; Wessels para 4146. See also *Berzack Brothers Ltd v Iesberts and Others* 1973 (2) SA 196 (W) and *Corrans and Another v Transvaal Government and Coull's Trustee* 1909 TS 605 at 615.

[61] *African Guarantee & Indemnity Co Ltd v Thorpe* 1933 AD 330.

[62] *African Guarantee & Indemnity Co Ltd v Thorpe* 1933 AD 330 at 341.

[63] V 46.1.29; Sande 6.33; P 522.

[64] Cf *African Guarantee & Indemnity Co Ltd v Thorpe* 1933 AD 330 at 342, 343.

[65] *Strachan v Fawcett* 1933 NPD 639. In *Strachan* the court disapproved of the decision in *Buerger v Doll* 1923 SWA 5. In *Buerger* the plaintiff and the defendant were co-sureties to the Master for the executor of an estate. The executor absconded, leaving a deficit in the estate of £50. After the executor had absconded the plaintiff proceeded against his assets and recovered £12. The plaintiff then paid the Master the £50 and proceeded against the defendant, as co-surety, for £25. The court held that the plaintiff was entitled to recover £25 from the defendant, since he, as surety, was not acting as the agent for the co-surety, and when he recovered the £12 he was acting for himself and not for and on behalf of the defendant. *De Wet & Yeats Die Suid-Afrikaanse Kontraktereg en Handelsreg* 4 ed (1978) by JC de Wet and AH van Wyk 352 note 69 submit that the decision is correct since 'die medeborg [het] nie kragtens 'n vorderingsreg wat hy van die skuldeiser verkry het teen die selfskuldenaar opgetree nie, maar eenvoudig kragtens sy reg as borg'. The effect of the decision in *Buerger's* case could be that the defendant bears a greater burden of the principal debt.

extinguished by his payment (and this in terms of money may represent the same amount as the debt of the principal debtor), the obligations of the principal debtor and of each of the co-sureties are not extinguished. The explanation surely is that, although the surety who has obtained cession of actions has now the creditor's rights in their entirety, he cannot be allowed to recover from his co-sureties, or any of them, his own aliquot share of the amount of the debt, or, if the co-sureties have agreed *inter se* on a basis for division of the debt among them, that share which is his liability under that agreement.

7. When surety is entitled to cession of actions

In order to entitle himself to cession of actions from the creditor the surety must actually pay the whole of the debt[66] or perform the obligations of the debtor under his contract if it is one *ad factum praestandum*[67] or arrive at a compromise with the creditor.[68] In short, there must be a *solutio* of the whole debt. Payment of part only of the debt (whether the whole is due or only the part paid is due), even payment of more than the surety's aliquot share of the debt, will not entitle him to cession of actions, because the creditor requires his rights in order to recover the balance of the debt. But where each of several co-sureties pays his aliquot share of the debt, each is entitled, without the debtor's consent, to cession of the portion of the claim paid by him and is entitled to sue the debtor for that portion.[69] This does not, however, appear to be a full cession of actions and indeed, generally, to be unnecessary because each co-surety has a right of recourse against the principal debtor without cession of actions.[70] That the surety is also a co-principal debtor does not deprive him of the right to cession of actions.[71]

The creditor is not obliged to tender cession when he sues the surety; his obligation is to give it when called on to do so.[72] Likewise, a surety who has paid the debt and who is suing his co-surety for a contribution is not required to tender cession of actions against the principal debtor.[73]

A cession should be expressed in explicit terms, not left to be implied, nor left in doubt; but no particular form of words is required.[74] The holder of a negotiable instrument who receives payment from a signatory to an aval on it fulfils his

---

[66] C 8.41.2; V 46.1.27, 28; Sande 635, 36; VL 4.4 15; P 520; B 346; Wessels para 4151. See also *Moosa v Mahomed* 1939 TPD 271 at 279, 285.

[67] *Corrans and Another v Transvaal Government and Coull's Trustee* 1909 TS 605 at 614, 631.

[68] *Mackenzie v Basckin* 1925 CPD 257.

[69] *Miller's Trust Foreshore Properties (Pty) Ltd v Kasimov* 1960 (4) SA 953 (C) at 958. The cession of a portion of a debt is, as a general rule, invalid. The general principle is that the position of a debtor may not be prejudiced by a cession (Susan Scott *The Law of Cession* 2 ed (1991) at 192 ff and the authorities cited). Suretyship is an exception and the cession of a portion of a claim is permissible in the case where a surety pays the debtor's creditor and thereafter obtains cession of a portion of the creditor's right.

[70] See Chapter XI.

[71] *Kotze v Meyer* (1830) 1 Menz 466; *Business Buying & Investment Co Ltd v Linaae* 1959 (3) SA 93 (T) at 96; see also *Irwin v Davies* 1937 CPD 442.

[72] *Horn v Loedolff et uxor* (1830) 1 Menz 403; *Lippert & Co v Van Rensburg* (1877) 7 Buch 42; *Lindley v Ward* 1911 CPD 21 at 27.

[73] *Estate Steer v Steer* 1923 CPD 354 at 357.

[74] VL 4.4.14; *Cens For* 1.4.17.24; P 521B; Wessels para 4559.

obligations as to cession of actions by endorsing and delivering the document to the signatory of the aval who has paid him.[75] In *Union Trust Maatskappy (Edms) Bpk v Thirion*[76] the court seems to have found some implied cession of actions, but the decision will not bear scrutiny.[77]

Special rules apply in KwaZulu-Natal where Law 9 of 1885 provides that one liable with any other person (co-debtors and co-sureties), so far as he has satisfied the obligation beyond his share, and also one who is 'liable otherwise than primary' (a surety) who has satisfied the obligation in whole or in part, in each instance shall not be prevented from recovering a contribution or indemnification, as the case may be, because he has not obtained cession of action, but shall have the same rights as if he had obtained cession. Cession operates automatically on payment.[78]

8. Inability of creditor to give cession of actions

(a) *Generally*

If the creditor has put it out of his power to give cession of actions against the principal debtor for the reason that, expressly or by his conduct, he has released the latter from his liability, either *in toto* or by accepting part payment in settlement by way of a compromise of the debt or, by his neglect, allowing judgment to go in the debtor's favour, he is not entitled to payment from the surety,[79] whose *exceptio cedendarum actionum* must succeed; indeed, the debt having been extinguished, no liability rests any longer on the surety, whose liability is accessory to that of the debtor: see the chapter on Discharge of the Surety (Chapter XIII).

If there are two or more co-debtors liable *in solidum,* release of one by the creditor releases the other or others to the extent of his aliquot share of the debt because they can no longer recover that share from him if they pay the debt; consequently, it seems, a surety is also released *pro tanto*, for his claim on the others will be reduced as their liability is reduced.[80]

The release by the creditor of one or two or more co-sureties, whether deliberately or by failure diligently to enforce his rights against him or by supinely allowing him to obtain a judgment in his favour or by entering on a compromise with him or howsoever, with the consequence that he, the creditor, is unable to give cession of actions against that co-surety, has the effect of entitling another co-surety called on to pay the debt to a rebate in the amount of his liability to the

---

[75] *Meer v General Industrial Credit Corporation (Pty) Ltd* 1947 (4) SA 330 (C) at 336. See also *Peimer v Finbro Furnishers (Pty) Ltd* 1936 AD 177 at 185; *FJK Syndicate v Du Preez and Smit* 1943 WLD 116 at 120, 121. See also *Malan on Bills of Exchange, Cheques and Promissory Notes in South African Law* 5ed by FR Malan, JT Pretorius & SF du Toit (2009) para 152 and AN Oelofse & JT Pretorius 'Of Suretyships, Avals and Accommodation Parties' (1991) 3 *SA Merc LJ* 260.

[76] 1965 (3) SA 648 (GW).

[77] See the criticism of it in 1965 *Annual Survey* 160.

[78] The preamble of Law 9 of 1885 indicates the purpose to have been to remove doubts as to how far indemnification and contribution could be enforced without a cession of action. Presumably such an implied cession extends to pass any ancillary or additional rights such as securities, pledges and hypothecations. As the position has since developed the doubts expressed in the preamble proved to be without real foundation, but that was not to be known with any certainty in 1885. Cf *Harman's Estate v Bartholomew* 1955 (2) SA 302 (N) at 309.

[79] Sande 6.43, 44; P 406, 521, 581; B 154; Wessels paras 4338, 4339.

[80] P 581, B 163, 417; Wessels para 4339.

extent that the creditor has made it impossible for him to recover. Such co-surety is entitled to a rebate to the extent that he has lost the right to a contribution from the co-surety who has been released.[81] This is so even if they are co-sureties under separate instruments.[82] Pothier[83] says that this principle has no application in relation to a surety who became bound after the others had done so, so that the others could not have been reckoning on recovering from him at the time they assumed liability. Other writers, however, do not seem to go to this length. Nor should they, because he is a co-surety[84] and in any event under cession of actions any one of them could recover from this surety and by releasing him the creditor denies his right of recovery on the part of any of the others who pay him. That is the essence of the matter.[85] Should the creditor's inability to give effective cession of actions arise from the fact that the co-surety in question is insolvent, this affords no relief to the other co-surety or co-sureties.[86]

(b) Release or abandonment or other loss of security held by creditor

The situation in relation to the creditor's inability to give fully effective cession of actions because of the release or abandonment by him of securities for payment of the debt, or their loss by reason of his acts or those of another persons, is by no means clearly defined, but the following principles appear to emerge from the authorities cited.[87] In the first place, to entitle the surety to relief there must be a duty on the part of the creditor towards him, the surety (irrespective of any duty the creditor may owe to the debtor), to protect or preserve the security. That duty may arise from contract, express or implied, or at law, independently of contract.

---

[81] V 46.1.29; Sande 6.43, 44; P 521, 581; B 155, 156, 163, 164; Wessels paras 4336, 4337. See also *Dwyer v Goldseller* 1906 TS 126 at 129; *De Charmoy and St Pol v Dhookoo* 1924 NPD 254 at 257; *Israelsohn v Newman* 1949 (3) SA 1178 (W) at 1182. See, however, *Nelson v Hodgetts Timbers (East London) (Pty) Ltd* 1973 (3) SA 37 (A) where one Van der Merwe and Nelson had bound themselves ('We, the undersigned') as sureties and co-principal debtors for all amounts due by the principal debtor to the Hodgetts Timber Company up to a maximum of R5 000. Nelson had signed the document but Van der Merwe had not signed in the place provided for his signature, above that of Nelson. It was held that the parties intended to enter into a joint contract of suretyship and that in the absence of Van der Merwe's signature the contract was invalid since it did not comply with the provisions of section 6 of the General Law Amendment Act 50 of 1956. (See Chapter V for a discussion of section 6 of the General Law Amendment Act 50 of 1956.) It is submitted that the court should have approached the problem on the same basis as what the effect would be had the creditor released one of the co-sureties, ie that the release of a surety by the creditor is for the benefit of the other co-sureties, to the extent of such release. This would mean that the surety who did sign the deed of suretyship should, in principle, be liable for half the amount in the case of a deed of where provision is made for two co-sureties, such as in *Nelson*. There may, however, have been the implied understanding that the one co-surety would only be prepared to undertake the suretyship obligation if the other co-surety would also be liable. *Nelson's* case can thus be distinguished from those cases where the 'co-sureties' intended to undertake separate liabilities (*Manufacturers Development Co (Pty) Ltd v Repcar Holdings (Pty) Ltd and Others* 1975 (2) SA 779 (W); *Industrial Development Corporation of SA Ltd v See Bee Holdings (Pty) Ltd and Others* 1978 (4) SA 136 (C)).
[82] *Moosa v Mahomed* 1929 TPD 271 at 280, 285; and see *Meer v General Industrial Credit Corporation (Pty) Ltd* 1947 (4) SA 330 (C) at 338, 339.
[83] P 521, 581; and see Wessels para 4335.
[84] See Chapter IV.
[85] This appears to be implicit in the judgment in *Moosa v Mahomed* 1939 TPD 271.
[86] V 46.1.29. See also *Vermaak v Cloete* (1836) 2 Menz 35. See, however, *LAWSA* Vol 26 para 204.
[87] Sande 6.44, 45; P 521, Wessels paras 4338 *et seq*, 4352 *et seq*.

If this exists and is breached by the creditor, whether by act of commission or of omission, with the consequence that he is unable to cede the benefit of the security to the surety from whom he claims payment, the surety is discharged from liability, whether or not the value of the security is the equal of the surety's liability or of the liability of the debtor. The *exceptio cedendarum actionum* succeeds.[88]

In the absence of an express undertaking on the part of the creditor to protect or preserve the security, the question whether a contractual duty is to be implied will be determined from all the circumstances. It will be more readily implied if he is in physical possession or in direct control of the secunty than when he is not.[89]

Free of any contractual duty, express or implied, in the matter, the creditor is not under a duty at law to be vigilant or active.[90] He is not liable for lack of vigilance or passive inactivity, unless he connives at or is in collusion with another who removes or injures the security. The surety cannot complain at the creditor's inability to give him effective cession of actions in relation to the security which he let slip through lack of vigilance.[91] It is open to the surety to exercise vigilance in order to protect his interests. He should call on the creditor to protect the security which is in danger of being lost, and if the creditor fails to do so the surety will have valid cause for complaint.[92]

The situation where the creditor fails to perfect his security is the same as where he does not see to the registration of a bond or take cession of book debts which by contract are to be security for the principal debt. It is hardly possible for him to escape the responsibility for perfecting his security, and if his failure to do so makes it impossible for him to give effective cession of actions, the surety is discharged.[93]

If the security was given by a co-surety, the same principles apply. The surety called on to pay is released to the extent of the contribution he would have been entitled to recover from the one who gave the security.[94]

---

[88] *Van Oosterzee v McRaie qq Carfrae & Co* (1828) 1 Menz 305; *Nathanson and Another v Dennill* 1904 TH 289; *Baillie v Transvaal Assets Ltd* 1923 (2) PH A21 (W); *Miller v Trust Bank of South Africa* 1965 (2) SA 447 (T); *Business Buying & Investment Co Ltd v Linaae* 1959 (3) SA 93 (T) at 96; *Barlows Tractor Co (Pty) Ltd v Townsend* 1996 (2) SA 869 (A) at 878.
[89] *Miller v Trust Bank of South Africa* 1965 (2) SA 447 (T).
[90] P 521, Wessels paras 4338 *et seq*.
[91] *McDonald v Bell* 3 Moo PCC 315, on appeal from *Bell qq Colonial Government v McDonald and Breda* (1836) 2 Menz 28; *Colonial Government v Edenborough and Another* (1886) 4 SC 290 at 298, 299; *Miller v Trust Bank of South Africa* 1965 (2) SA 447 (T).
[92] P 521.
[93] *Rosseau v Bierman* (1828) 1 Menz 338; *Kotze v Meyer* (1830) 1 Menz 466; *Meyer v Low* (1832) 2 Menz 8; *Watermeyer qq v Theron and Meyring* (1832) 2 Menz 14; *Robertson v Onkruyt* (1842) 2 Menz 59; *Irwin v Davies* 1937 CPD 442 at 449.
[94] *Dirck's Estate v Gwadiso & Komanis' Estates* 1936 EDL 303, in which the decision in *Estate Tudhope v Sand* (1907) 24 SC 614 that the surety was entitled to no relief because the creditor could still give him cession of actions, though truncated, was not followed. It is not entirely clear from the Eastern Districts case whether the court made the measure of the surety's relief the aliquot share of the other surety or the value of the last security, but the former is, by analogy, the correct conclusion. *De Wet en Van Wyk Die Suid-Afrikaanse Kontraktereg en Handelsreg* 5 ed (1992) vol I by JC de Wet and GF Lubbe (ed) 397 note 39 also do not find *Tudhope* convincing. The authors argue that although the co-surety gave the security for his obligations as *surety*, the release of the security would indeed prejudice the right of contribution which his co-sureties may have had against him as co-surety.

If the security is lost by operation of law, for example, if it is set aside under the provisions of the insolvency law, the surety has no relief.[95]

Notwithstanding what has been said, a surety who, with knowledge of the release of the security or of its non-registration, renews his obligation or acknowledges his liability, cannot complain.[96] If he consents to the non-registration of a security, *a fortiori* he cannot complain if it is not registered.[97]

It seems that in English law a surety has relief against the creditor to the extent that he suffers prejudice if he does so as a consequence of the creditor failing to exercise his right to perfect his security when he is not contractually bound to do so.[98] In *Business Buying & Investment Co Ltd v Linaae*[99] Boshoff J, in an *obiter dictum*, appears to have taken this to be our law and, indeed, to have gone further in expressing the view that the surety is entirely discharged. It is difficult to find a basis for any relief for the surety in our law as the consequence of the creditor merely failing to do something he is not bound to do.[100]

9. Effect of renunciation of benefit

Renunciation by a surety of the benefit of cession of actions does not disentitle him from having cession. The renunciation operates only to prevent the surety from delaying payment to the creditor by a dilatory exception, but he is entitled to cession of actions on or after payment.[101]

See also *LAWSA* vol 26 para 217.
[95] *Nisbet and Dickson v Thwaites* (1829) 1 Menz 427.
[96] *Meyer v Low* (1832) 2 Menz 8; *National Bank of ORC v Salkinder* 1907 OR 69.
[97] *Executors of Watermeyer v Executor of Watermeyer* (1870) 2 Buch 69.
[98] Cases on this are mentioned by Feetham J in passing in *Gould v Ekermans* 1929 TPD 96 at 103.
[99] 1959 (3) SA 93 (T) at 96.
[100] See further Chapter XIII below.
[101] V 46.1.30; Sch 303; Sande 6.41; P 445. See also *Estate Steer v Steer* 1923 CPD 354 at 357. In *Townsend v Barlows Tractor Co (Pty) Ltd and Another* 1995 (1) SA 159 (W) at 169 the court applied and approved of the above statement and held that by renouncing the benefit of cession of actions the surety did not disentitle himself from obtaining cession of actions from the creditor and that the effect of the renunciation of the benefit was simply to deprive the surety of the right to delay payment to the creditor of the debts owed to the creditor by the principal debtor until the creditor cedes to the surety his rights against the principal debtor (at 172). This view was confirmed on appeal *sub nom Barlows Tractor Co (Pty) Ltd v Townsend* 1996 (2) SA 869 (A) at 877.

CHAPTER XI

The Surety's Right of Recourse

		Page
1.	Introduction.	159
2.	Extent of the right of recourse.	161
3.	Right accrues only after payment to creditor	163
4.	Conditions attaching to the surety's payment	164
5.	When payment by the surety is not required before the right of recourse accrues	165
6.	The right of recourse against co-debtors	167
7.	Sureties without the right of recourse.	167
8.	Insolvency of the debtor.	168
9.	Proof of claims by both creditor and surety against the insolvent debtor's estate.	168

1. Introduction

The surety who has paid the debt of the principal debtor to the creditor has a right of recourse against the debtor; he is entitled to reimbursement by the principal debtor of what he has paid the creditor. This was so in Roman law, notwithstanding that payment of the debt extinguished it and released the debtor;[1] it became the Roman-Dutch law[2] and is our law.

This right of recourse is enforced by the *actio mandati*, in that the surety has paid on the mandate of the debtor, or, if he undertook the suretyship without the knowledge of the debtor, he has the *actio negotiorum gestorum*.[3] Consequently the surety needs no cession of actions from the creditor.[4] Indeed, when a surety is exercising his right of recourse, not suing under cessions of actions, it is wrong to

---

[1] D 46.1.4 pr; Inst 3.20.6; Domat 1876. See also Reinhard Zimmermann *The Law of Obligations* (1990) 117 ff and Chapter I above.

[2] V 46.1.31; Gr 3.3.30, 31; VL 4.4.13; *Cens For* 1.4.17.24; VdL 1.14.10; Huber 3.26.38; P 439; B 357; Lee *ad Gr* 252.

[3] Inst 3.20.6; D 17.1.6.2; V 46.1.28, 31; *Cens For* 1.4.17.24; P 365, 429, 440, Huber 3.26.38; B 357; Lee *ad Gr* 252; Wessels para 4156. *Kroon v Enschede and Others* 1909 TS 374 at 378; *Corrans and Another v Transvaal Government and Coull's Trustee* 1909 TS 605 at 613, 625, *Moti & Co v Cassim's Trustee* 1924 AD 720 at 738; *Rossouw and Rossouw v Hodgson & Others* 1925 AD 97 at 102; *African Guarantee & Indemnity Co Ltd v Thorpe* 1933 AD 330 at 336; *Turkstra v Massyn* 1959 (1) SA 40 (T). See JE Scholtens 'Rights of Recourse of Sureties and Third Persons Who Paid Another's Debt' (1959) 76 *SALJ* 266 at 268, 269; DH van Zyl *Die Saakwaarnemingsaksie as Verrykingsaksie in die Suid-Afrikaanse Reg* thesis submitted for the degree Doctor in de Rechtsgeleerdheid, University of Leiden (1970) 150-2; *LAWSA* Vol 26 para 207. See also Ralph Slovenko 'Suretyship' (1965) 39 *Tulane LR* 427 at 439 ff and Morton C Campbell 'Non-consensual Suretyship' (1935) 45 *Yale LJ* 69.

[4] V 46.1.28, 31; VL 4.4.13; *Cens For* 1.4.17.25; Huber 3.26.38; Gr 3.3.31; VdL 1.14.10; P 429; B 357; Lee *Intro* 318.

refer to this as 'subrogation'.[5] The surety who is exercising his right of recourse is not subrogated to the rights of the creditor. He sues in his own right and, as will be seen, his relief may differ from that he would have if he sued under cession of actions, enforcing the rights of the creditor now vested in him by virtue of the cession.[6] In certain circumstances there is an advantage in suing under cession of actions as we have seen in Chapter X.

There was controversy among the Roman jurists whether the right of recourse existed if the surety had undertaken the suretyship against the will, or contrary to the instruction, of the debtor. This controversy is discussed by Wessels.[7] Justinian[8] appeared to have settled the matter by decreeing that there was no right of recourse when, to the knowledge of the surety, the debtor had forbidden interference in his affairs. It is, however, difficult to escape the conclusion that the surety who gives his undertaking in these circumstances is either doing so with the intention of making a gift to the debtor (as a father might for a strong-headed son) or is acting with some ulterior motive in his own interests. In either event it could be argued that there is no reason why he should have a right of recourse. Moreover, the debtor may have had financial motives for refusing a surety. He may have entertained plans for effecting a compromise with his credi-

---

[5] *Turkstra v Massyn* 1959 (1) SA 40 (T) at 45, 47. In its literal sense the word 'subrogation' means the substitution of one party for another as creditor. Cf the use of 'subrogated' in this context in *Taylor and Thorne NNO and Others v The Master* 1965 (1) SA 658 (N) at 661. See also *LAWSA* sv 'Insurance' (by MFB Reinecke, SWJ van der Merwe, JP van Niekerk & PH Havenga) First Reissue vol 12 (2002) para 378).

[6] Susan Scott *The Law of Cession* 2 ed (1991) at 219-20 argues that the term 'subrogation' is to be preferred because the so-called duty to cede is enforceable only indirectly, and possibly not enforceable at all where the surety has already paid and only thereafter requests the creditor to cede his action. She prefers the approach that subrogation should take effect in these circumstances especially as sureties without cession are treated exactly the same as sureties who have obtained cession. We have, however, already pointed out in Chapter X that if the creditor holds security for payment of the principal debt, whether by way of pledge or hypothecation, or if the claim on the principal debtor carries a preference over other claims, these benefits pass with cession of actions. These benefits will not pass in the absence of a cession and it is thus not correct to say that sureties without cession are treated exactly the same as sureties who have obtained cession. The surety who is exercising his right of recourse is not subrogated to the rights of the creditor. See also Scholtens *op cit* 268, 269. JP van Niekerk *Subrogasie in die Versekeringsreg* unpublished LLM dissertation, University of South Africa (1979) 26 ff points out that subrogation is a *naturale* of an insurance contract. The insurer does not have the right, in the absence of a specific agreement, to demand a cession of action. Subrogation does not denote an actual transfer of the insured's rights against third parties in favour of the insurer; it is neither a cession nor a transfer by operation of law *The Law of South Africa* sv 'Insurance' (by MFB Reinecke, SWJ van der Merwe, JP van Niekerk & PH Havenga) First Reissue vol 12 (2002) para 378). See, further, Stephen I Langmaid 'Some Recent Subrogation Problems in the Law of Suretyship and Insurance' (1934) 47 *Harvard LR* 976; Amelia H Boss 'Suretyship and Letters of Credit: Subrogation Revisited' (1993) 34 *William and Mary Law Review* 1087; Stanley McDermott 'Fundamental Principles and Effects of Subrogation in French and Louisiana Law' (1951) 25 *Tulane LR* 358 and JP van Niekerk 'Subrogation and Cession in Insurance Law: A Basic Distinction Confounded' (1998) 10 *SA Merc LJ* 58.

[7] Wessels paras 4155, 4156. See also the *obiter dictum* in *Odendaal v Van Oudtshoorn* 1968 (3) SA 433 (T); *LAWSA* Vol 26 para 207; Wouter de Vos *Verrykingsaanspreeklikheid in die Suid-Afrikaanse Reg* 3 ed (1987) 214-15.

[8] C 2.19.24. Groenewegen *ad Cod* 2.19.24 would allow recovery to the extent that the debtor had been enriched by the surety's intervention. Voet 3.5.11 follows this line, but in 46.1.28, 33 he seems to be less definite about it. Van der Keessel, on the other hand, both in his *Theses* at 505 and in his *Dictata* (Lee *ad Gr* 252) is strongly opposed to Groenewegen's view.

tor, the probabilities of effecting which would be impossible to judge after the surety has paid the debt.[9] The course to be adopted by the surety who has given his promise against the will of the debtor is to obtain cession of actions from the creditor when he pays the debt.[10]

2. Extent of the right of recourse

The surety who has the right of recourse is entitled to complete indemnification from the debtor.[11] He is entitled to reimbursement of not only the amount of the debt he has paid, but also any damage, loss and expense incurred by him as a direct result of the fact of the debtor not having met his obligation, including any interest he has had to pay the creditor. The loss and expense includes costs incurred by the creditor in suing the principal debtor if the surety became liable for those costs.[12] The surety is however not entitled to recover from the debtor costs incurred by him in consequence of his having raised an unsupportable defence to the creditor's claim against him.[13] He should give the debtor notice of the proceedings to allow him the opportunity of opposing the claim, whether on these grounds or others, or of paying the debt.[14] Ultimately, responsibility for damage, loss and expense depends upon default. If this is on the part of the debtor, he is liable for it, but if on the part of the surety, he must bear it.[15]

Further, the surety is entitled to capitalize these additional outlays he has made by adding them to the capital debt he has paid and then to charge the debtor interest on the whole.[16] It is a moot point, however, whether the surety's interest is to be calculated from the time he paid the creditor or only after demand on the debtor to repay him. Pothier[17] says the latter, but Wessels[18] takes the former view, citing *Fryde v Fryde*[19] as authority for the proposition that the surety can recover interest on what he has paid the creditor, even though there has been no prior demand on the debtor. De Villiers J[20] did express this conclusion, but, in the first place, it seems to be *obiter*, because the surety was claiming on a bond of which he had taken cession from the creditor, and was consequently entitled to the interest the creditor was entitled to claim. In the second place, with respect to the learned judge, there appears to have been some confusion in his reasoning between, on the one hand, interest paid by the surety to the creditor and recoverable by him and, on the other hand, interest which a surety can recover in his own right on the

---

[9] After all, where the debtor forbids interference in his affairs, there can be no juristic basis for the right of recourse.

[10] V 46.1.28; Wessels para 4159.

[11] V 46.1.31; Gr 3.3.31 VL 4.4.13, *Cens For* 1.4.17.24, Huber 3.26.38, P 440; B 361; Wessels paras 4158, 4185, 4188, 4191, 4192.

[12] As to which Chapter VI.

[13] V 46.1.31; P 434; B 363; Wessels para 4189.

[14] P 434.

[15] V 46.1.31; B 362.

[16] V 46.1.1.31; *Cens For* 1.4.17.24; Huber 3.26.38; P 440; Domat 1876; B 365; Wessels para 4186, 4187.

[17] P 440.

[18] Wessels paras 4186, 4188.

[19] 1944 CPD 407.

[20] At 413, 414.

capital of his outlays in paying the creditor. *Fryde v Fryde* really concerned a third type of case: the creditor's interest after cession. The learned judge said that, so far as he had been able to discover, Pothier was the only authority supporting the view that a demand was necessary. In fact, however, Burge[21] adopts Pothier's view. The learned judge referred to an earlier passage in Burge,[22] but this is authority for the proposition that the surety is entitled to recover from the debtor interest he has paid the creditor, and has no relation to interest running upon what he has paid. The same must be said of the passage he cited from Voet.[23]

De Villiers J found support in what Wessels had said in his first edition contrary to Pothier's view, and also refers to the English law. Wessels, in his second edition,[24] argues in support of the view that no demand is necessary, citing *inter alios* Domat,[25] but although this writer says the surety is entitled to recover interest upon what he has paid, he does not say from when it is to be calculated. Nor does Voet.[26] At the end of the paragraph he does refer to a demand but this seems to relate to creditor's interest after the surety has taken cession of actions. Nor does any other writer seem to assist in answering the question.

The clue to the question whether the surety who is exercising his right of recourse, as opposed to one who is suing under cession of actions, is entitled to interest calculated from the time of payment by him to the creditor, without any prior demand on the debtor, surely is that the debtor cannot be held to be in default until demand has been made on him. He is not to know that the surety has paid the debt, nor what outlays the surety incurred to the creditor additional to the capital of the debt, and so is not in a position to know that he is indebted to the surety, nor to know the amount of his indebtedness. This supports Pothier's and Burge's conclusion that a demand by the surety is necessary before interest began to run against the debtor.

Because the surety who has made outlays additional to the debt is entitled to add them to the capital debt, he may be better off if he exercises his right of recourse than if he takes cession of actions from the creditor, for with cession he is limited to the relief the creditor could claim, and this would not necessarily include such additional outlays.[27] But, of course, there may be other advantages to be had by taking cession of actions, for example, the advantage of enforcing securities given to the creditor for payment of the debt.[28]

If the debtor and the surety have agreed on the extent to which the latter is to have recourse, he will be limited to that.[29] If the surety has made a compromise of the debt with the creditor, he cannot recover from the principal debtor, as

---

[21] B 365.
[22] B 361.
[23] V 46.1.31.
[24] Wessels paras 4186-8.
[25] Domat 1876.
[26] V 46.1.31.
[27] V 46.1.31; *Cens For* 14.17.24; P 440; B 365.
[28] *Cens For* 1.4.17.24.
[29] V 46.1.33; Wessels para 4157.

capital debt, more than he paid the creditor,[30] unless he sues under cession of actions.

3. Right accrues only after payment to creditor

Before the surety can turn to the principal debtor for indemnification, he must, generally, have paid the debt to the creditor.[31] Payment *(solutio)* may have been made on a judgment or order of the court or it may have been made voluntarily.[32] Indeed, the surety may, if he wishes to be relieved of his obligations under the suretyship, pay the creditor and proceed against the debtor,[33] but if he pays the creditor before the debt is due, he cannot recover from the debtor before that time arrives.[34] It is immaterial whether payment is made in money or in kind, by *compensatio* or by novation (including delegation by the surety of his debtor to the creditor), or by the rendering of services, so long as the creditor accepts payment in the form tendered. It must be acceptable to him as payment in discharge of the debtor's liability to him.[35] Unless, however, the creditor accepts a bill or promissory note as payment in discharge of the existing debt, the giving of such a document *prima facie* has not that effect.[36] The question truly is whether there has been a novation of the debt by the giving and acceptance of the bill or note. Payment may also take the form of performance by the surety of the debtor's obligations under a contract *ad factum praestandum*.[37]

---

[30] B 359, 361; Wessels para 4194.

[31] C 4.35.10; V 46.1.31, 34; Gr 3.3.30; VL 4.4.17; *Cens For* 1.4.17.24, 25, 27; Huber 3.26.39; P 439; Wessels paras 4158, 4161, 4198. *Van der Walt's Trustees v Van Coller* 1911 TPD 1173 at 1176; *Taylor and Thorne NNO and Others v The Master* 1965 (1) SA 658 (N) at 661; *Proksch v Die Meester en Andere* 1969 (4) SA 567 (A) at 585; *Fircone Investments (Pty) Ltd v Bank of Lisbon and South Africa Ltd and Another* 1982 (3) SA 700 (T) at 703; *Absa Bank Ltd v Scharrighuisen* [2000] 1 All SA 318 (C) at 322. And see *Estate Silbert & Co v De Jager* 1933 CPD 88 at 99, relating to an accommodation maker of a promissory note. Although *Estate Silbert* is authority for the view that an accommodation party should be regarded as being in the same position as a surety, the better view, it is submitted, is that an accommodation party is not a surety for the party accommodated or for anybody else, but that he incurs liability as drawer, acceptor or endorser, as the case may be (AN Oelofse & JT Pretorius 'Of Suretyships, Avals and Accommodation Parties' (1991) 3 *SA Merc LJ* 260 at 261. Also see *Levi v Almog* 1990 (1) SA 541 (W)).

[32] P 430; B 358.

[33] V 46.1.38; P 414; B 199; Wessels para 4165. *Estate Liebenberg v Standard Bank of South Africa Ltd* 1927 AD 502 at 507.

[34] D 46.1.31; V 46.1.33; P 439; B 358; Wessels para 4165.

[35] V 46.1.34; P 430, 431; B 358, 359; Wessels para 4161. *Rossouw and Rossouw v Hodgson & Others* 1925 AD 97 at 104 (in which the creditor accepted a bill from the sureties in payment of the debtor's liability); *Mackenzie v Baschin* 1925 CPD 257 (in which the creditors accepted a promissory note from one co-surety and gave him cession of actions against the other co-surety); *Rutowitz's Flour Mills v The Master and Others* 1934 TPD 163 at 168 (in which the surety paid the creditor by ceding to him security the debtor had given him against the possibility of his being called upon to fulfil his undertaking, with the consequence that the creditor was then entitled to enforce the security against the debtor's insolvent estate).

[36] *Ewers v The Resident Magistrate of Oudtshoorn and Another* (1880) Foord 32 at 35. See also *Malan on Bills of Exchange, Cheques and Promissory Notes in South African Law* 5ed by FR Malan, JT Pretorius & SF du Toit (2009) para 14 and *Adams v SA Motor Industry Employers Association* 1981 (3) SA 1189 (A) at 1199.

[37] *Corrans and Another v Transvaal Government and Coull's Trustee* 1909 TS 605; *LAWSA* Vol 26 para 206. Reference should be made to the discussions of this case in Chapter VI.

The surety who has paid the debt and is entitled to recourse against the principal debtor must bring his own action against him;[38] he cannot, for example, execute against the debtor on a judgment obtained by the creditor against him, the surety. If, however, the creditor has obtained judgment against the debtor and cedes that judgment to the surety, there is no reason why the surety should not execute upon it.[39]

4. Conditions attaching to the surety's payment

The surety's right to indemnification by the debtor depends upon three conditions attaching to his payment. First, the payment must have been a valid one[40] which secured the discharge of the debtor from his liability.[41] Payment to the wrong person, someone other than the creditor or his authorized agent,[42] for example, payment in kind of the goods of another, without authority, will not suffice.[43]

Secondly, the surety must not have failed to set up any defence of which he was aware and which would have been available to the debtor had the creditor sued him.[44] This does not, however, apply to a defence which one cannot honourably set up.[45] Whether prescription falls into that category appears to have been uncertain, but with us the surety dare not throw away the debtor's rights in this respect.[46] Indeed, he ought always, for his own protection, to give the debtor notice of the creditor's demand so that the debtor may proffer any defence he considers he has to the claim. In any event, ignorance on the part of the surety of a defence available to the debtor. Ignorance of law does not avail the surety if he fails to set it up, but if he fails in this, due to ignorance of fact and pays the debt, this does not debar him from recovering from the debtor who has his recourse against the creditor..[47]

If, having contested the creditor's claim, the surety pays on a judgment given against him but this judgment is plainly wrong and the surety, knowing this, fails

---

[38] V 46.1.35, Wessels paras 4207, 4208.

[39] See PM Nienaber 'Cession' in *LAWSA* vol 2 Part 2 (2003) para 41 and Susan Scott *The Law of Cession* 2 ed (1991) at 132 ff.

[40] *Devenish v Johnstone* (1847) 2 Menz 82.

[41] V 46.1.33; P 432, 436; B 369; Wessels para 4181.

[42] V 46.1.33; B 370; Wessels paras 4136, 4181. *Faure v Bosman* (1864) 5 Searle 9.

[43] P 436; B 369; Wessels para 4183.

[44] Domat 1883; V 46.1.33; P 432, 433, 441; B 366, 367; Wessels paras 4165-8. See *Incorporated General Insurances Ltd v Saayman en Andere* 1982 (1) SA 739 (T), but this was an indemnity case—not suretyship.

[45] V 46.1.31; P 434, B 363,368. In *Inter Industria Bpk v Nedbank Bpk en 'n Ander* 1989 (3) SA 33 (NC) it was held that a surety is in law entitled to refuse to make payment in terms of the contract of suretyship on the ground that the principal debtor has a counterclaim for an amount greater than the amount which the principal debtor owes the creditor, even though the counterclaim is partly for unliquidated damages. See Chapter XIII in this regard. The court also considered whether a principal debtor is *entitled* to *prevent* the surety from paying the creditor where the surety declines to raise a valid defence which is available to the principal debtor. No authority was adduced on this novel point. It was held, on the facts, that the principal debtor did have this right. The principal debtor had a legal interest in preventing payment by the surety, an interest which in the circumstances was deserving of protection even against the will of the surety.

[46] Wessels paras 4172, 4173.

[47] P 433; B 367, 368; Wessels para 4174.

to appeal or, if lacking the funds to do so, fails to give the debtor the opportunity of appealing, the surety cannot recover from the debtor.[48]

Thirdly, the debtor also must not have paid the creditor in ignorance of the fact that the surety has already done so. In other words, the surety must see to it that the debtor is informed of the fact that he has paid the debt, if it is at all possible to inform him,[49] so that the debtor does not pay again. If, however, the debtor does so pay, the surety is entitled to have from the debtor cession of the latter's right to recover one payment from the creditor by a *condictio indebiti*.[50] If the surety is unable to inform the debtor that he has paid the debt, he is entitled to recover from the debtor. If, on the other hand, the debtor has first paid the debt and did not inform the surety of this fact when able to do so (unless he was unaware of the undertaking), the surety who then pays the debt has a right of recourse against the debtor. He must, however, cede to him the right to recover one of the payments from the creditor.[51] If, however, the debtor was unaware of existence of the suretyship, it cannot be said that he was at fault in paying the debt without informing the surety of this. The surety must be content then to recover the payment from the creditor.

5. When payment by the surety is not required before the right of recourse accrues

Although, generally, as we have said, the surety must have paid the debt to the creditor before he can recover from the debtor, in certain circumstances the surety has relief without his having so paid the debt.[52] First, if it has been agreed between debtor and surety that the former will obtain the surety's discharge within a certain time or will pay the debt upon the surety being called upon to pay it, the surety is entitled to sue him for payment or to require him to pay the creditor.[53]

Secondly, when the creditor has obtained judgment against the surety, the latter is entitled to have the debtor pay the creditor or obtain his (the surety's) release.[54] The allowance of proof of debt on the part of the creditor against the

---

[48] C 4.35.10; Domat 1883; V 46.1.33; Wessels para 4176.
[49] Domat 1884; V 46.1.33; P 432, 438; Sande 6.26; B 370; Wessels paras 4179, 4180.
[50] See, in general, De Vos *op cit* 171 ff and DP Visser *Die Rol van Dwaling by die Condictio Indebiti* thesis submitted for the degree Doctor in de Rechtsgeleerdheid, University of Leiden (1985) 228 ff.
[51] Domat 1881; V 46.1.33; P 437; B 370; Wessels paras 4179, 4180. This cession operates *ipso iure*. See P 438 and Wessels para 4180.
[52] *Van der Walt's Trustees v Van Coller* 1911 TPD 1173; *Copestake and Others v Alexander, In re Fisher* (1882) 2 SC 137 at 147. In *Absa Bank Ltd v Scharrighuisen* [2000] 1 All SA 318 (C) at 324 Griesel J remarked that it is a misnomer to refer to the surety's remedies in this regard as simply as a 'right of recourse'. The court suggested that it would be more accurate and less confusing if one were to refer to it as 'anticipatory relief for surety against principal debtor', rather than to an indiscriminate 'right of recourse'. Such anticipatory relief may take different forms and would be available in the circumstances referred to above.
[53] V 46.1.34; Gr 3.3.30; *Cens For* 1.4.17.27, P 441; B 372, 373; Wessels para 4204. *Rutowitz's Flour Mills v The Master and Others* 1934 TPD 163 at 168.
[54] V 46.1.34; Gr 3.3.30; P 441; B 372; Wessels para 4199. *Van der Walt's Trustees v Van Coller* 1911 TPD 1173; *Taylor and Thorne NNO and Others v The Master* 1965 (1) SA 658 (N) and cases there cited.

insolvent estate of the surety is the equivalent of a judgment.[55] It seems, indeed, that the surety is so entitled against the debtor as soon as the creditor commences proceedings against him.[56]

Thirdly, since a creditor cannot be compelled to sue for payment before he wishes to do so[57] and, being content to receive interest on the debt and relying on the soundness of the surety, may allow the debt to remain unpaid for a long time, the surety may not only, as we have said,[58] pay it in order to obtain his discharge and exercise his right of recourse against the debtor, but as an alternative he may elect to call on the debtor to pay the debt or to provide security for payment of it.[59] What is a 'long time' is undefined and depends upon the circumstances, but some suretyships must necessarily remain in existence a very long time, by reason of their nature.[60]

Fourthly, if the principal debtor is squandering or wasting his assets with the consequence that the surety has good cause for alarm as to whether there will be anything left with which to pay the debt,[61] or if the debtor is in failing financial circumstances with that same result,[62] the surety may bring proceedings to compel the debtor to pay the creditor and, pending those proceedings, he may obtain an interdict against the disposal of assets, or possibly attach them.[63] Such an interdict or attachment would preserve the assets, but would not confer on the surety any preference over other creditors.

Fifthly, if the surety has tendered payment to the creditor and the latter has refused it, the surety depositing it as security for payment is entitled to recourse against the debtor.[64]

Sixthly, if the creditor has released the surety in circumstances which are to be construed as indicating an intention on the creditor's part to treat the debt as having been paid by the surety (in return for services rendered, for example, or by giving him a receipt or acknowledgement of payment, though none was actually made) or an intention to transfer the claim to the surety (whether by way of gift or bequest), the surety may recover from the debtor as though he had in fact paid the debt.[65] If, however, the creditor's intention was merely to release the surety from the suretyship and look to the debtor alone, the surety has no claim on the debtor.[66] In these circumstances, the creditor looks to the debtor without the support of the security he formerly had.

---

[55] *Ibid.*
[56] P 441; Huber 3 .2.44; Wessels para 4199.
[57] D 46.1.62; V 46.1.38; P 414.
[58] Above, this chapter.
[59] V 46.1.39, Gr 33.30; VL 4.4.17, 18; Sch 307; *Cens For* 1.4.17.27; Huber 3.26.43, 44; P 441; B 199, 372 373, 374; Lee *ad Gr* 253, Wessels paras 4203 4205.
[60] V 46.1.39; *Cens For* 1.4.17.27; Sch 307; Huber 3.26.44, 45; P 441, 442; B 374; Lee *ad Gr* 253.
[61] V 46.1.34; Gr 3.3.30; VL 4.4.17; *Cens For* 1.4.17.27; Huber 3.26.44; Wessels paras 4200, 4201; *Absa Bank Ltd v Scharrighuisen* [2000] 1 All SA 318 (C) at 324.
[62] VL 4.4.17; P 441; Huber 3.26.44; B 372, 373; Wessels para 4202.
[63] *Leathern v Henwood & Co* (1887) 8 NLR 29 at 32; *Rossouw and Rossouw v Hodgson & Others* 1925 AD 97 at 102.
[64] V 46.1.34.
[65] V 46.1.34; P 431; B 359; Wessels paras 4163, 4164.
[66] P 431; B 359 Wessels para 4163.

6. The right of recourse against co-debtors

A surety for co-debtors liable *in solidum* is entitled to exercise his right of recourse against any one or more of them for the whole debt.[67] If he claims from only one of those debtors who pays him in full, he must cede to him his rights against the others. Included in these rights are the creditor's rights, if the surety has obtained a cession of them,[68] but if he has not obtained cession, the co-debtor who is paying is entitled to a discharge upon payment of his aliquot share of the debt unless he is in the same position with cession of the rights of the surety as he would be with cession of the creditor's rights.[69]

If the co-debtors are not liable *in solidum,* the surety's claim against each is limited to that creditor's aliquot share of the total liability.[70]

7. Sureties without the right of recourse

Notwithstanding what has been said, however, not all sureties have the right of recourse. One who has intervened with the express intention of making a gift to the debtor of his undertaking cannot recover from him when he, the surety, pays the creditor,[71] nor can a surety for a minor who contracts without his guardian's authority, for the minor is not bound.[72] Nor can one who became surety without a mandate for a person bound only naturally, not legally, for if the latter is not legally bound to pay, the surety, though bound to pay, is not entitled to recover from him.[73] Nor a surety who for practical purposes is the real debtor[74]—for example, when negotiable instruments are exchanged between two parties and negotiated so that each party may obtain financial facilities from a third person.[75] A surety who has become such for an illegal or immoral debt[76] or has made a champertous purchase of the debt cannot recover on it.[77] Finally, if the debtor has provided the surety with funds with which to pay the debt and the surety pays it, clearly the latter cannot recover from the debtor.[78]

A *fideiussor indemnitatis* who pays the creditor before the extent of his liability has been determined by excussion of the debtor is in a curious situation. Kotzé in his note to Van Leeuwen[79] indicates that whether he could have recourse against the debtor was 'not free from doubt, although for good reasons the negative is understood'. It seems, however, unlikely that he would be denied any remedy whatsoever, considering that the debtor will have profited by the payment. The

---

[67] *Cens For* 1.4.17.24; P 440; B 364; Wessels para 4195.
[68] P 440; B 365; Wessels para 4195.
[69] P 440; B 365; cf *Gerber v Wolson* 1955 (1) SA 158 (A) at 161.
[70] *Henwood & Co v Westlake and Coles* (1887) 5 SC 341 at 347.
[71] V 46.1.33; P 380; Wessels para 4158.
[72] 46.1.33.
[73] V 46.1.33; Wessels para 4175.
[74] V 46.1.33.
[75] See *Levi v Almog* 1990 (1) SA 541 (W) and AN Oelofse & JT Pretorius 'Of Suretyships, Avals and Accommodation Parties' (1991) 3 *SA Merc LJ* 260.
[76] V 46.1.33; Wessels para 4176.
[77] V 46.1.33.
[78] *Ibid.*
[79] VL 4.4.11.

best course, if he be so minded to pay, is to obtain cession of actions from the creditor.

When a surety for a surety *(achterborg)* has paid the debt for the surety, he has recourse against the latter, who in relation to the *achterborg* is the principal debtor.[80]

8. Insolvency of the debtor

If the principal debtor's estate is sequestrated, the surety exercises his right of recourse by proving his claim against the insolvent estate. He is a creditor of the debtor.[81] If the surety has made payment *(solutio)* to the creditor in full, or, it seems, made a payment on account of the creditor's claim, he then has an unconditional claim on the debtor's estate and there is no difficulty in the way of his proving his claim as a creditor.[82] A surety who has paid the creditor part only of a secured claim cannot compete with the creditor in relation to the security in proving on the principal debtor's estate; the creditor is entitled first to the benefit of the security.[83]

If the surety has not paid the creditor's claim, he has a conditional or contingent claim on the debtor's estate.[84] Its claim is conditional on his paying the creditor.[85]

A contingent or conditional creditor is not a creditor at all until the contingency or condition has been fulfilled; only then do any rights come into existence against the assets of the debtor or any right to enforce payment against him.[86]

9. Proof of claims by both creditor and surety against the insolvent debtor's estate

On the insolvency of the principal debtor, it may happen that both the creditor and the surety prove claims against the insolvent estate. The creditor's claim is unconditional and based on the principal debt itself, and the surety's claim is

---

[80] Huber 3.26.46; P 445.

[81] *Alford and Wills v Johnson* (1865) 5 Searle 147.

[82] *Rossouw and Rossouw v Hodgson & Others* 1925 AD 97 at 103; *Taylor and Thorne NNO and Others v The Master* 1965 (1) SA 658 (N); *Ex parse Currie NO* 1966 (4) SA 546 (D) at 550; *Proksch v Die Meester en Andere* 1969 (4) SA 567 (A) at 584-5.

[83] *Farthing and Another v Pieters & Co* 1913 CPD 771 at 774.

[84] *Moti & Co v Cassim's Trustee* 1924 AD 720 at 738; *Rossouw and Rossouw v Hodgson and Others* 1925 AD 97 at 103; *Friedman v Bond Clothing Manufacturers (Pty) Ltd* 1965 (1) SA 673 (T) at 677; *Absa Bank Ltd v Scharrighuisen* [2000] 1 All SA 318 (C) at 326. In *Proksch v Die Meester en Andere* 1969 (4) SA 567 (A) it was pointed out that an inaccurate translation of a passage from Voet had been relied upon in *Rossouw and Rossouw v Hodgson and Others (supra)* but that this did not detract from the correctness of the judgment in the case. However, the liability of a surety and co-principal debtor is not contingent, unless the principal debt itself is contingent: *Millman and Another NNO v Masterbond Participation Bond Trust Managers (Pty) Ltd (under curatorship) and Others* 1997 (1) SA 113 (C). It thus follows that, in determining whether at any particular point in time the liabilities of the surety and co-principal debtor exceeded his assets for the purposes of s 26, 29 and 30 of the Insolvency Act of 1936, the obligations undertaken by him as surety and co-principal debtor must be included among his liabilities.

[85] *Taylor and Thorne NNO and Others v The Master* 1965 (1) SA 658 (N) at 661; *Ex parte Currie NO* 1966 (4) SA 546 (D) at 550.

[86] *Ex parte Currie NO* 1966 (4) SA 546 (D) at 549.

based upon his right of recourse against the debtor. It is, however, submitted that one of the objects of the Insolvency Act[87] is the distribution of the residue of the insolvent estate and the achievement of perfect equality amongst those creditors who have equal rights and no preferent or secured claims.[88] The principal debtor's estate is indebted only to the amount of the principal debt—whether that is owed to the creditor or the surety (under his right of recourse) should not make a difference in principle. Only *one* debt is owed.[89] To allow both the creditor and the surety to prove a claim in respect of the same debt would amount to duplication of liability of the principal debtor's insolvent estate, and this could only be to the prejudice of the other creditors.[90] Even if the surety's claim is valued at the difference between the creditor's claim and what he will probably receive as a dividend it would have the effect of a partial duplication of the insolvent estate's liability.[91]

---

[87] Act 24 of 1936.

[88] See, in general, *Mars The Law of Insolvency in South Africa* 9 ed (2008) by Eberhard Bertelsmann *et al* 395 ff; BH Swart *Die Rol van 'n Concursus Creditorum in die Suid-Afrikaanse Insolvensiereg* unpublished LLD thesis, University of Pretoria (1990) 294 ff; Catherine Smith *The Law of Insolvency* 3 ed (1988) 3 ff and JC Sonnekus 'Sekerheidsregte—'n Nuwe Rigting?' 1983 *TSAR* 97 at 98-99.

[89] *Mars op cit* 396; Smith *op cit* 224; Ellison Kahn (gen ed) *Contract and Mercantile Law through the Cases* II *Specific Contracts and Mercantile Law* 2 ed (1985) by David Zeffertt, JT Pretorius & Coenraad Visser 802.

[90] *Proksch v Die Meester en Andere* 1969 (4) SA 567 (A) at 586. See also *De Wet & Yeats Die Suid-Afrikaanse Kontraktereg en Handelsreg* 4 ed (1978) by JC de Wet and AH van Wyk 487.

[91] See JT Pretorius (1983) 100 *SALJ* 350 at 351. The reasoning in *Proksch's* case was accepted, apparently with approval, in *Fircone Investments (Pty) Ltd v Bank of Lisbon and South Africa Ltd and Another* 1981 (3) SA 141 (W) at 706B-E. It was held, however, that a surety who had paid to the creditor the full amount he had secured was not precluded from proving a claim in the insolvent debtor's estate, merely because the creditor proved a claim for the unsecured balance of the claim or that portion of the balance secured by another surety (at 706E-H). See also *Absa Bank Ltd v Scharrighuisen* [2000] 1 All SA 318 (C). In *BOE Bank Ltd v Bassage* 2006 (5) SA 33 (SCA) the creditor (the plaintiff in the court *a quo*) of a company held two covering mortgage bonds over its immovable property. The loan to the company was secured also by a suretyship. The respondent (defendant) undertook liability as surety and co-principal debtor, and renounced the benefits of excussion and division. When the company (principal debtor) was placed in liquidation, the creditor relied only on the two mortgage bonds as security for satisfaction of its claim against the insolvent estate of the company. The creditor did so to recover the value of its security without rendering it liable for the costs of sequestration. This is allowed in terms of section 89(2) of the Insolvency Act 24 of 1936, which reads: 'If a secured creditor (other than a secured creditor upon whose petition the estate in question was sequestrated) states in his affidavit submitted in support of his claim against the estate that he relies for the satisfaction of his claim solely on the proceeds of the property which constitutes his security, he shall not be liable for any costs of sequestration other than the costs specified in subsection (1), and other than costs for which he may be liable under paragraph (a) or (b) of the proviso to section *one hundred and six*.' The surety (respondent) argued that once the creditor had proved its claim against the principal debtor (the company) and relied solely on the mortgage bonds as security, it had no further claim could be enforced against the company. So the surety was also discharged from any liability to the creditor. The Supreme Court of Appeal (per Zulman JA), rejected this argument and held that it would not make commercial sense if it were held that a creditor who elected to rely on its security in proof of its claim thereby and without more waived or abandoned any rights that the creditor has against the surety (para 10, at 38H-I). The judge remarked that there was no intention on the part of the creditor to waive the debt to the extent that it exceeded the proceeds of the realisation of the security. Zulman JA said: 'Nor, in my opinion, does s 89(2) effect such a waiver. The operation of the section was to bring about a *pactum de non petendo,* in terms of which the [creditor]... agreed not to proceed against the company for the balance of its claim. It is true that the claim for the balance became unenforceable against the company, but the consequence is not ... that the suretyship became unenforceable' (para 9, at

It must thus be concluded that a surety who has not paid the principal debtor's debt has no claim under section 48 of the Insolvency Act against the insolvent estate of the principal debtor if the creditor has also proved his claim against the same estate.[92]

---

38 C-E). The judge concluded: 'Section 89(2) of the Insolvency Act does not state that the effect of a creditor who elects to rely on its security in proof of its claim results in the claim being extinguished entirely. The election is merely an election to execute on the claim or to prove the claim in a certain way. The object of the section is to confer a benefit on a secured creditor: it enables it to recover the value of its security without rendering itself liable for the costs of sequestration. The section goes no further than that. There is nothing to justify the construction that a creditor, by electing to rely solely on its security, abandons or waives the balance of the claim and is thereby precluded from proceeding against a surety for the balance. Indeed, if such a far-reaching consequence had been intended by the Legislature, it would have said so in unequivocal terms. The section means no more than that a creditor may limit the extent to which he will participate in the assets of the insolvent estate to the value of the asset which is his security. Once having made that election he is bound by it; he may not participate in the free residue even if his security should prove to be without value. Both the *Bank of Lisbon* [*Bank of Lisbon and South Africa Ltd v The Master* 1987 (1) SA 276 (A)] and *Absa Bank* [*Absa Bank Ltd v The Master* 1998 (4) SA 15 (N)] cases decide no more than this. But this does not mean the balance of the claim no longer exists or has been waived. It remains extant. There is no good reason why it cannot be enforced against a surety who has waived the defence of excussion, as is the position in this case' (para 8, at 37H-38B).

[92] *Proksch v Die Meester en Andere* 1969 (4) SA 567 (A) at 588; *Absa Bank Ltd v Scharrighuisen* [2000] 1 All SA 318 (C) at 326. Cf *Rossouw and Rossouw v Hodgson & Others* 1925 AD 97 where it was held that a surety was entitled to prove as a conditional creditor in the insolvent estate of the principal debtor. It is, however, important to note that this principle could only apply where the creditor does not prove a claim against the same estate.

CHAPTER XII

The Right to Contribution by Co-Sureties

		Page
1.	Introduction and juristic basis of the right to contribution	171
2.	Extent of benefit	173
3.	Prerequisites for claiming a contribution	174
4.	What if a co-surety has paid only part of the debt?	176
	(a) The decided cases	176
	(b) ASA Investments (Pty) Ltd v Smit	178
	(c) Arguments and assertions concerning the problem	179
5.	Determination of the quantum of contribution	180
6.	Procedure	183
7.	Loss of security held by creditor	183

1. Introduction and juristic basis of the right to contribution

We have seen in the chapter on Cession of Actions[1] that in Roman law the surety who had paid the debt had no relief against his co-sureties, and that many Roman-Dutch writers[2] held that to be the law in their time; others, however, took the contrary view.[3] In *Gerber v Wolson*[4] Van den Heever JA referred to the conflict but expressed no opinion upon it. There was, however, no reason why co-sureties should not contract *inter se* each to bear his share of the debt, or as to how they should bear it.[5] We have seen also that the lack of a remedy for one co-surety against his co-sureties was overcome by the giving and taking of cession of actions to and by the surety who paid the creditor, with the result that the co-surety who obtained cession of actions from the creditor became entitled to sue any one of his co-sureties *in solidum*, unless the latter had the benefit of division against the creditor. The surety who sues exercises the rights of the creditor, but must deduct his own aliquot share of the debt, for this is his share of the burden of the debt. Today, however, the position has clearly changed: Without cession of actions from the creditor, a co-surety who has paid the debt is, by our law, entitled to recover from each of the other co-sureties contributions of their aliquot shares

---

[1] Chapter X.
[2] V 46.1.28; Gr 3.3.31; Sch 303; VL 4.4.14; *Cens For* 1.4.17.24; Sande 6.32; Huber 3.26.27.
[3] As to who are co-sureties, Chapter IV.
[4] 1955 (1) SA 158 (A) at 169.
[5] VL 4.4.14; *Cens For* 1.4.17.24. *Gerber v Wolson* 1955 (1) SA 158 (A) at 167, 168. See also *Manufacturers Development Co (Pty) Ltd v Repcar Holdings (Pty) Ltd and Others* 1975 (2) SA 779 (W); *Industrial Development Corporation of SA Ltd v See Bee Holdings (Pty) Ltd and Others* 1978 (4) SA 136 (C).

of the debt. He pursues, not the rights of the creditor, but his own right based on the fact that he has paid the other's debt and on equity.

This change in the law was the subject of discussion in *Kroon v Enschede and Others*[6] in which the court followed those writers[7] who took the view contrary to those we have mentioned, on grounds of equity. Wessels J, with whom Curlewis J agreed, said[8] that towards the end of the eighteenth century it was the opinion of some Roman-Dutch jurists that 'where several sureties had agreed to become such in one instrument, they must be presumed to have intended that each one could be sued for his share by any one of them who had paid the whole debt. They came to be regarded as entitled, *ex jure* and without a formal cession, to recover from those who had signed the joint guarantee'. The court held our law to be that 'no cession of action is required where sureties guarantee a debt in one instrument, and that the right to contribution is a right which the surety possesses *de jure*'. The question was expressly left open whether or not this is so when the sureties have secured the debt independently of one another, but in *Hart v Corder*[9] the court held that even where the co-sureties became bound without knowing of each other's existence, the right to a contribution arose. This decision, it is submitted, is correct, since the surety's right to a contribution arises *ex jure* when he pays; it does not arise from an undertaking, express or implied, between sureties *inter se*.[10]

Pothier[11] says that in France a co-surety who has paid the debt is entitled without cession of actions to recover from his co-sureties their proportions of the debt. This is so notwithstanding that they do not contract any obligation with each other. Nor does Pothier make it a condition that they gave their undertakings simultaneously or by the same instrument; nor is it material whether they are bound jointly and severally or bound severally or, indeed, whether the surety claiming contribution knew, when he became bound, of the existence of the co-surety or co-sureties. The basis of the right to contributions is that by payment of

---

[6] 1909 TS 374. *Kroon's* case was followed in *Executors Estate Watson v Huneberg & Leathern* 1915 NPD 571 at 577, *Nosworthy and Another v Yorke* 1921 OPD 404 at 406; *Strachan v Fawcett* 1933 NPD 639 at 641; and in relation to avals, *Meer v General Industrial Credit Corporation (Pty) Ltd* 1947 (4) SA 330 (C) at 336.

[7] Groen *ad Cod* 8.41.11; V 46.1.30; *infin*; VdL 1.14.10, and see 1.14.9.7; P 445; B 381, 382.

[8] At 383.

[9] 1973 (3) SA 11 (N). Leon J relied on the decisions in *Kroon v Enschede and Others* 1909 TS 374, *Lever v Buhrmann* 1925 TPD 254 and *Moosa v Mahomed* 1939 TPD 271 to reach this conclusion (at 14-5). See the discussion by JT Pretorius 'A Running Contribution Between Co-sureties' (1983) 100 *SALJ* 387 at 389--90 (hereafter Pretorius 'Running Contribution'). The court in *Hart's* case seems to have overlooked the provisions of s 1 of Law 9 of 1885 (Natal) which regulates contributions between co-sureties in that province. (See Chapter X for a discussion of the position in Natal.) *Hart's* case was approved in *Fircone Investments (Pty) Ltd v Bank of Lisbon and South Africa Ltd and Another* 1981 (3) SA 141 (W) at 142, 1982 (3) SA 700 (T) at 703 and in *De Beer v Bosman* (TPD 27 November 1990 (case 1993/90) unreported). See also JT Pretorius 'Contributions between Co-sureties' (1991) 3 *SA Merc LJ* 381 at 382 (hereafter Pretorius 'Contributions').

[10] Ellison Kahn (gen ed) *Contract and Mercantile Law through the Cases II Specific Contract and Mercantile Law* 2 ed (1985) by David Zeffertt, JT Pretorius & Coenraad Visser 806; *LAWSA* Vol 26 para 212; Pretorius 'Running Contribution' 390. See also *Nelson v Hodgetts Timbers (East London) (Pty) Ltd* 1973 (3) SA 37 (A) and *Visser v Theodore Sassen & Son (Pty) Ltd* 1982 (2) SA 320 (C).

[11] P 445 Burge (B 381, 382, and see at 163, 164) follows Pothier's view.

the debt he has relieved the others of their liability and they have been enriched at his expense; equity demands that they reimburse him their aliquot shares.[12]

It is submitted that the right to a contribution is not derived from any engagement between the co-sureties, but arises from payment of the debt and on equitable considerations.[13] Because the right to a contribution arises from the fact of payment and since it is based in equity, the proper conclusion should be that the right arises where the co-sureties have undertaken liability in the same document,[14] where they have undertaken liability independently of one another, and even where the surety who is called upon to make a contribution was previously unaware of the existence of the surety who paid the debt.[15]

In *Pearce and Another v De Jager*[16] and *Estate Steer v Steer*[17] the question was raised whether it made any difference that the co-sureties were also co-principal debtors. Clearly it does not, because in relation to each other they are co-sureties. The situation is, however, different if one of them is in fact a debtor, as where the transaction was wholly or partly for his benefit. In such circumstances, the surety cannot enforce a contribution save in relation to what he has paid as a surety.[18] Likewise a co-surety who indemnifies the others against the consequences of the transaction cannot require them to contribute to the debt if he pays it.

2. Extent of benefit

It is irrelevant that the co-sureties have renounced the benefit of division. That is a matter between them and the creditor and does not entitle the surety who has paid the debt to sue any one of them otherwise than for his aliquot share of the debt, unless he sues under cession of actions from the creditor.[19] Had there, in *Pearce and Another v De Jager*[20] been no cession, the contention of counsel for the defendant should have prevailed; liability would have been limited to an aliquot share. The aim is that, as a matter of equity, each of the co-sureties shall bear his

---

[12] This is how Krause J construed the position in *Lever v Buhrmann* 1925 TPD 254 at 262 although for the purposes of the decision, he expressed the view that 'in many cases it would seem equitable' that this should be so. In passing, it may be observed that the statement by Krause J at 263 that the fiction is that 'by payment even without cession of action the surety steps into the shoes of the creditor, and so in suing his co-surety he is availing himself of a right he has bought and paid for', is, with respect, inappropriate. That is the position when the surety who pays obtains cession of actions; he steps into the shoes of the creditor, but the surety claiming contribution without cession of actions is exercising his own right, on grounds of equity. He has not the right of the creditor to sue any co-surety *in solidum* (where the benefit of division does not exist), nor the advantage of any securities the creditor may have had. It follows that in certain circumstances it is preferable to obtain cession of actions from the creditor, rather than exercise the equitable right to contribution.

[13] See note 10 above.
[14] See note 6 above.
[15] *Fircone Investments (Pty) Ltd v Bank of Lisbon and South Africa Ltd and Another* 1982 (3) SA 700 (T) at 703; *Hart v Corder* 1973 (3) SA 11 (N) at 14; *De Beer v Bosman* (TPD 27 November 1990 (case 1993/90) unreported); Wessels paras 4212, 4213; *LAWSA* Vol 26 para 212; Pretorius 'Running Contribution' 390.
[16] 1924 CPD 455 at 466.
[17] 1923 CPD 354 at 357, 358.
[18] *Huneberg and Others v Watson's Estate* 1916 AD 116.
[19] V 46.1.29; VdL 1.4.9.7; Sande 6.33; P 445; B 382, 383.
[20] 1924 CPD 455.

aliquot share of the debt,[21] so much so that if one of them is insolvent his share of the debt must be borne by the others, and to that end, readjustment will be made if payments had already been offered.[22] This readjustment will be made even if the co-sureties have by agreement indemnified each other in defined shares[23] but not where each has undertaken responsibility for only a stated figure of money which is the limit of his liability, so far as readjustment will place a greater burden upon him.[24] If the solvent co-surety has an *achterborg*, the latter will represent him in the making of his contribution.[25] Insolvency, in this context, means inability to pay, irrespective of sequestration of his estate.[26]

In addition to the amount of the debt the co-surety has paid, less his own aliquot share, he is entitled to have from his co-sureties the costs of enforcing the contribution, but (like a surety exercising his right of recourse against the debtor) he is not entitled to a contribution towards the costs incurred in defending the creditor's action against him, unless expressly or impliedly authorized by his co-sureties to defend it.[27] He is, however, entitled to interest if, after demand, the co-sureties delay in reimbursing him.[28]

3. Prerequisites for claiming a contribution

The co-surety who claims a contribution from one of his colleagues must have paid the debt.[29] In the *Lever v Buhrmann* case Krause J rejected Pothier's[30] view that a co-surety who has been sued may, before he has paid the debt, claim contributions. He must have paid; it does not suffice that the creditor has made demand upon him or even that judgment has been given against him. The occasions short of payment in which a surety has recourse against the principal debtor have no application in relation to the right to contributions from co-sureties.[31]

To entitle the co-surety to contributions from his co-sureties, it is essential that he should have been legally bound to pay[32] and his payment must have been valid and effective.[33] What we have said about this in the chapter on the Surety's Right of Recourse, and the manner in which payment may be made, applies generally

---

[21] P 445; B 381, 382.
[22] Domat 1888; B 351; Wessels para 4217.
[23] *Cloete v Bergh* (1832) 2 Menz 13.
[24] *Du Toit v Vos* (1834) 2 Menz 16.
[25] P 445
[26] *Gerber v Wolson* 1955 (1) SA 158 (A) at 165.
[27] B 388.
[28] Wessels para 4190. Wessels refers to V 46.1.31 but Voet is there discussing the claim of a surety based on cession of actions from the creditor. Nevertheless, on general principles, there is no reason why the surety who has paid should not have interest on his money after demand. Section 1(1) of the Prescribed Rate of Interest Act 55 of 1975 provides that if a debt bears interest and the rate at which the interest is to be calculated is not governed by any other law or by an agreement or a trade custom or in any other manner, it must be calculated at the rate prescribed in subsec 1(2) of the Act which entitles the Minister of Justice from time to time to prescribe the rate of interest by notice in the *Government Gazette*.
[29] *Lever v Buhrmann* 1925 TPD 254 at 262, 265.
[30] P 445; see also B 382, 383.
[31] Wessels para 4214.
[32] Wessels para 4215.
[33] Ibid.

to the present subject, as does also what has been said about the conditions attaching to payment. If one co-surety has paid the debt, payment by another is ineffective and he cannot recover contributions, but must look to the creditor for a refund on a *condictio indebiti*.[34]

When the co-sureties have the benefit of excussion, but one of them pays the debt without exercising his right to have the creditor excuss the principal debtor, it seems that his co-sureties, called on by him to make their contributions, can require him first to excuss the principal debtor by exercising his right of recourse. This is a facet of the principle that he cannot require contributions unless he was obliged to pay the debt. But if the co-sureties do not have the benefit of excussion, the one who pays the debt cannot be required by the others, called upon to make their contributions, to excuss first the principal debtor.[35] Several co-sureties who have paid the debt may join in suing the others to recover contributions.[36]

Support is found in some cases for the view that before a co-surety can turn to his fellows for a contribution, the 'ultimate burden' to be borne by the sureties, viz, the amount to be paid by the sureties once any other securities held by the creditor have been realised and any dividend due to the creditor from the debtor's insolvent estate has been fixed, must be determined. In *Berzack Brothers Ltd v Lesberts and Others*[37] a surety claimed to be entitled to a contribution from its co-sureties. The surety, however, held security in the form of a cession of book debts of the principal debtor. Although the surety had paid the creditor the full amount of the principal debt, the court held that until the extent of the 'ultimate burden' which the co-sureties would have to share had been determined, the surety who had paid was not entitled to claim a contribution from his co-surety without ceding to him a proportionate share of the benefits which he held. To allow a contribution, the court held, would be inequitable, because a surety, while holding security furnished by the principal debtor, would be able to claim from a co-surety the latter's aliquot share of the debt, leaving the co-surety with an unsecured personal claim for payment of any eventual excess.[38] In *Fircone Investments*

---

[34] See, in general, Wouter de Vos *Verrykingsaanspreeklikheid in die Suid-Afrikaanse Reg* 3 ed (1987) 171 ff, DP Visser *Die Rol van Dwaling by die Condictio Indebiti*, thesis submitted for the degree Doctor in de Rechtsgeleerdheid, University of Leiden (1985) 228 ff and Daniel Visser *Unjustified Enrichment* (2008) 648ff.

[35] *Estate Steer v Steer* 1923 CPD 354.

[36] *Kroon v Enschede and Others* 1909 TS 374 at 377.

[37] 1973 (2) SA 196 (W). See also *Fircone Investments (Pty) Ltd v Bank of Lisbon and South Africa Ltd and Another* 1982 (3) SA 700 (T).

[38] *De Wet & Yeats Die Suid-Afrikaanse Kontrakteregen Handelsreg* 4 ed (1978) by JC de Wet and AH van Wyk at 352 maintain that the decision in *Berzack's* case is unacceptable. They state that '[w]aar medeborge afstand gedoen het van die voorreg van uitskudding, rus daar geen verpligting op die borg, wat betaal het, om eers die selfskuldenaar uit te skud voordat hy teen die medeborg optree nie.' The effect of *Berzack* may well be that the surety is obliged to realize the security that he obtained from the creditor before he is entitled to claim a contribution from his co-sureties for their aliquot share of the debt. It is doubtful whether a partial cession of a claim could be validly effected, even under these circumstances (Susan Scott *The Law of Cession* 2 ed (1991) 192 and the authorities cited). Where co-sureties have renounced the benefits of order and excussion as between themselves and the principal debtor, and thereafter, the principal debtor having failed to pay, one of the sureties pays the whole debt, the latter can sue his co-sureties to recover a proportionate share of the amount he has paid without first excussing the principal debtor (*Estate Steer v Steer* 1923 CPD 354). Should a surety, however, obtain a cession of a security that is unavailable

(Pty) Ltd v Bank of Lisbon and South Africa Ltd and Another,[39] however, the nature of the 'ultimate burden' rule has been considerably clarified. It was there held that the purpose of the 'ultimate burden' rule was simply to protect a co-surety who is unable to obtain the benefit of something which another surety has received because that right was not given to him and he can never obtain it. The judgment in *Berzack's* case decided no more than that where one of the co-sureties has received a security which was a benefit that the others had not and could not receive, a mere tender by him to make payment to his co-sureties of any dividend he might receive from the insolvent estate of the principal debtor was insufficient to entitle him to claim contribution of their aliquot shares from them, because this would leave them with only an unsecured claim for payment of any eventual excess.[40] It follows that where the co-surety seeking to resist making a contribution can enjoy the same benefit as the other surety—eg by making a claim against the insolvent estate of the debtor—the 'ultimate burden' rule does not assist him.[41]

4. What if a co-surety has paid only part of the debt?

It has long been a difficult question whether a surety who has paid only *part* of the debt is entitled to look to his co-sureties for a contribution, or whether he must pay the *entire* debt before the right to a contribution arises. In *ASA Investments (Pty) Ltd v Smit*[42] it was held, contrary to the view adopted in previous editions of this work, that, where the co-sureties have executed separate deeds of suretyship, the entire debt must be paid before the surety can turn to his co-surety to ease his burden.

It seems appropriate to consider once more the arguments and authority in this regard.

(a) The decided cases

The decided cases reveal a diversity of approaches to this problem. In *Lever v Buhrmann*[43] the court stated that 'a surety has no right of action against his co-sureties until he has paid the whole debt, or more than his proportionate share thereof ...'. In that case, however, the court was dealing with the question whether a surety is entitled to claim a contribution from his co-surety before he has paid anything at all. The statement 'more than his proportionate share' seems to have

---

to his co-sureties, it could lead to a circuity of actions. Although it could be argued that a surety obtaining the security is not acting as the agent of his co-sureties (*Buerger v Doll* 1923 SWA 5), it could have the result that the principal debt is not borne on an equal basis between the co-sureties. In order to achieve equality of burdens between the co-sureties and to avoid a circuity of actions, there may indeed be merit in insisting that the co-surety who is claiming a contribution from a fellow co-surety should first realize the security that he obtained after paying the creditor. This would then be an exception to the rule that such a surety would be entitled to sue his co-surety without first excussing the principal debtor.

[39] 1982 (3) SA 700 (T).
[40] At 705.
[41] This seems to be the crucial reason for the success of the appellant in *Fircone Investments (Pty) Ltd v Bank of Lisbon and South Africa Ltd and Another* 1982 (3) SA 700 (T); but see at 705D-707C.
[42] 1980 (1) SA 897 (C).
[43] 1925 TPD 254 at 265.

been made *obiter.* In *Nosworthy and Another v Yorke*[44] the question was left undecided. In *Hoyer v Martin and Others*[45] the court held that under a contract of continuing suretyship a surety who has paid the whole of the principal debt outstanding at a particular time may claim a contribution from a co-surety even though the principal debtor may in future incur further debts for which the surety may be held liable and may claim further contributions for the co-surety. Once the surety wipes the slate clean, so to speak, by paying the whole of the outstanding debt at a particular time, he should be entitled to claim a contribution from the co-surety. The court referred to the 'rule' that a surety should not be allowed 'to claim a contribution unless the final claim by the [creditor] against the sureties had been ascertained ...' but said that 'in a proper case, this rule should give way to other equitable considerations ...'.[46]

In *Noakes v Whiteing,*[47] on the other hand, Davies J expressed the *obiter* opinion that until the creditor has been paid in full, one co-surety who has paid more than his aliquot share of the debt cannot recover from another co-surety a contribution in order to reduce what has been paid to the aliquot share of the one who has paid it. The court based this opinion on the following propositions. In the first instance, the main purpose of a contract of suretyship 'is to protect the creditor, and it would seem to follow that the rights of the sureties *inter se* should clearly be subordinate to the interests of the creditor'.[48] Secondly, there may be a conflict of interests which could arise between the creditor (still unpaid) and the surety when both of them are trying to extract payment from the co-surety at the same time. Thirdly, there seems to be nothing inequitable in requiring a surety to pay the creditor in full if he thinks that the creditor's failure to press the co-surety is to his eventual disadvantage.[49] *Noakes v Whiteing* was concerned with a situation in which one of the three co-sureties, who has paid more than half the debt, sued one of the others for a sum which would reduce his own outlay to one half, at a time when the creditor was suing the other two and it was not known whether or not the third would pay his share; the plaintiff co-surety assumed he would not do so, apparently because he was denying liability. The decision was that, even if there was a right to a contribution before payment of the whole debt, it could not be exercised until decision of the creditor's action, when it would be known whether the third co-surety was liable and the defendant co-surety's share of the debt could then be determined.[50]

---

[44] 1921 CPD 404 at 406.
[45] 1968 (2) PH A53 (D).
[46] At 198.
[47] 1968 (1) SA 302 (R).
[48] At 305.
[49] At 306. See Pretorius 'Running Contribution' 392 ff for a discussion of the merits of these arguments.
[50] In other cases the courts have frequently referred to the proposition that a surety must pay the creditor in full before his right of contribution against a co-surety arises (*Kroon v Enschede and Others* 1909 TS 374 at 379; *Estate Steer v Steer* 1923 CPD 354 at 357; *Strachan v Fawcett* 1933 NPD 639 at 642; *Moosa v Mahomed* 1939 TPD 271 at 285; *Hart v Corder* 1973 (3) SA 11 (N) at 13). The courts were not, however, called upon to decide the principle, and the references seem to have been made in passing.

(b) ASA Investments (Pty) Ltd v Smit

In *ASA Investments* the plaintiff (surety) applied for leave to amend its particulars of claim by inserting an alternative cause of action in which it claimed a contribution from the defendant, a co-surety. The defendant opposed the amendment on the ground that it was bad in law, in that a co-surety who is such by reason of having entered into a separate deed of suretyship cannot be sued by a fellow co-surety for his aliquot share until the would-be claimant surety has paid the full debt for which he and the co-surety had stood surety.[51] The court came to the conclusion that to allow the amendment would render the plaintiff's claim excipiable, and accordingly refused leave to make the amendment.

The court came to this conclusion after an examination of the common law[52] and on the basis of equity. The following arguments were advanced by the court as to why it would not serve the purposes of equity to allow one co-surety to claim a contribution from a fellow co-surety before he has paid the *whole* of the principal debt. In the first instance, a co-surety should not be allowed to become entangled in the unconcluded affairs between the creditor and Another co-surety from whom the creditor at his pleasure seeks in the first instance to get his redress in respect of the balance of the principal debt. Secondly, to allow a running contribution between co-sureties on the basis of equity would not serve the purposes of equity, since it could amount to an unjustifiable interference with the rights the creditor acquired by contract, especially where the sureties renounced the benefit of division. Thirdly, to allow such a claim by a co-surety could lead to a circuity of actions: the co-surety may have to litigate about these matters twice over—once with the co-surety claiming from him, and if this co-surety does not pay in full, then again with the creditor. This may result in his now being saddled with a greater portion of the principal debt, for the recovery of which he may again have to rely on litigation.[53] Fourthly, it may be very difficult for a co-surety to determine what his aliquot share of the debt will be until the whole of the principal debt has been paid.[54]

---

[51] At 898.
[52] At 900C-902A. The court referred to the views of Wassenaar, Lybreghts and Van der Linden. Wassenaar *Practyk Notariael* 10.25 recognises the principle that a surety who has paid the whole debt is entitled to claim contribution from a co-surety without cession of action. This right accrues only to a surety 'de gehele schuld betaalt hebbende, de helft niet'. Lybreghts *Aanmerkingen over het Redeneerend Vertoog over het Notaris-ampt van Arent Lybreghts door een Rechtsgeleerden* [LW Kramp] Vol 2 ch 52 at 673 states that unless a surety has paid the whole debt ('ten zy hy de schuld ten vollen betaalde') he would not be able to claim a cession of action from the creditor to enable him to claim a contribution from a co-surety. Van der Linden *Koopmans Handboek* 1.14.10 also mentions the requirement that the whole of the principal debt be paid before a surety will be entitled to claim a contribution from a co-surety. Similar statements were also made by Groenewegen *ad Cod* 8.40(41).11, Sande *De Actionum Cessione* 6.32, Neostadius *Hollandiae, Zelandiae, Frisaeque Curiae Decisiones* dec 12 and Willem Decker's note on Van Leeuwen's *Het Roomsch Hollandsch Recht* 4.4.15. The last-mentioned writers were not referred to in the *ASA Investments* case. See also the discussion by Pretorius 'Running Contribution' 393 ff.
[53] See further the full discussion by Pretorius 'Running Contribution' 396 ff.
[54] At 902A-903C.

(c) Arguments and assertions concerning the problem

It must be conceded that the matter is not altogether free from difficulty. The common law authorities seem to support the view taken in *ASA Investments* and the arguments raised are not, it is submitted, without merit.[55] However, the problem with the approach adopted in *ASA Investments* is that it requires the one surety from whom the creditor seeks payment to accept the risk that the other sureties may be declared insolvent or abscond. Indeed, it could be argued that it is inequitable, and even impracticable, to insist that one co-surety should have paid the entire debt (if he could indeed afford to do so) before he would be entitled to claim a contribution from his co-surety. It seems unfair to require him to accept this risk, while preventing him from taking any action to reduce it. A co-surety who has paid more than his aliquot share of the debt should be entitled to some relief. Moreover, the *ASA Investments* approach leaves entirely unsettled the problem of the continuing suretyship where it may be uncertain for a long or indefinite time when the surety will have made his final payment.

For all these reasons, it is respectfully submitted that *ASA Investments (Pty) Ltd v Smit* should not be followed.[56]

It is suggested that, bearing in mind that the right to contributions is based on equity, so that no one co-surety is to be burdened beyond the others, whether the one co-surety has paid less than, the same as, or more than his aliquot share of the whole debt, he is entitled to have from the other co-sureties contributions of their aliquot shares of what he has paid. It is true that if more than one of the co-sureties makes payments, then or later, to the creditor, a circuity of actions may follow, but this can be avoided by an expeditious disclosure amongst them of what they have paid and a balancing of accounts of one against another. Indeed, this cannot be entirely avoided, even where the whole debt is paid by all or some

---

[55] Pretorius 'Running Contribution' 393 ff. See, however, Pretorius 'Contributions' 384 ff where a more practical approach is advocated. See also *LAWSA* Vol 26 para 213.

[56] In *De Beer v Bosman* (TPD 27 November 1990 (case 1993/90) unreported) Le Roux AJ had to decide whether the surety (plaintiff) was entitled to claim a pro rata contribution from the defendant (the co-surety) before the creditor had been paid the full debt owing by the principal debtor (at 3--4). He held that the plaintiff was so entitled and the court sought to distinguish the facts before him from those of *ASA Investments* on the basis that the plaintiff had not undertaken unlimited liability as in the case of *ASA Investments*, and, by paying the full amount of her liability in terms of the suretyship, she was entitled to be discharged as surety (at 7). The judge found support for his approach in the judgment in *Fircone Investments (Pty) Ltd v Bank of Lisbon and South Africa Ltd and Another* 1982 (3) SA 700 (T) where Franklin J remarked that '[t]he right of a surety to claim a contribution from his co-sureties arises forthwith on payment by him of the debt even although, in terms of continuing guarantees given by the sureties, other sums may become due in future' (at 703F-G). (The surety's right to claim a contribution from a co-surety in the case of a continuing suretyship has always been somewhat controversial—see the discussion above at notes 47-9. Once the surety under a continuing suretyship wipes the slate clean by paying the whole of the outstanding debt at a particular time, he should in principle be entitled to claim a contribution from the co-surety.) Le Roux AJ thus concluded: 'Haar [the plaintiff's] posisie is derhalwe duidelik vir soverre dit die omvang van die betaling aanbetref en kan nie meer verander nie, selfs al verander die hoof-skuldenaar se posisie. Dit sal myns insiens onbillik teenoor haar wees om haar te laat wag vir enige *pro rata*-bydrae deur mede-borge' (at 7). See further the full discussion of this decision by Pretorius 'Contributions' 383 ff.

of the sureties making payments in varying proportions.[57] In essence, whether one pays or more than one pay towards the debt, the burden of this from time to time must be distributed equally.

5. Determination of the quantum of contribution

In arriving at the contributions, each co-surety must bring into account every benefit he receives so that the ultimate burden may be equal.[58] This would relate, for example, to the proceeds of a security held by one of the co-sureties, as also to a dividend received by one from the insolvent estate of the principal debtor.[59]

The next question is how the burden of the principal debt should be divided between co-sureties *inter se*. Roman-Dutch writers state that the principal debt should be divided on an equal basis between the co-sureties, and that each must contribute a pro rata share thereof.[60] To give effect to this principle in those cases where the co-sureties have all undertaken unlimited liability for the debts of a principal debtor or where they have undertaken equal responsibility in respect of a specific existing debt[61] should not create any difficulty. The principal debt is divided equally, so that the ultimate burden is shared on an equal basis between the number of solvent co-sureties.[62]

---

[57] There is always a possibility of a multiplicity of actions, for if the other surety were required to pay the balance of the debt and yet a third co-surety is insolvent, an action would be available to the co-surety who had first made a contribution, to recover a contribution towards what he had now been required to pay the creditor, so that each should be mulcted in one-half, instead of one-third of the debt. This, however, is always the case when it becomes necessary to make an adjustment in consequence of one of the co-sureties becoming insolvent after the others have paid their aliquot shares.

[58] *Executors Estate Watson v Huneberg & Leathern* 1915 NPD 571 at 578; *Berzack Brothers Ltd v Iesberts* 1973 (2) SA 196 (W) at 198B-C; *Fircone Investments (Pty) Ltd v Bank of Lisbon and South Africa Ltd and Another* 1982 (3) SA 700 (T) at 703H-704A.

[59] *Strachan v Fawcett* 1933 NPD 639. In *Strachan* the court disapproved of the decision in *Buerger v Doll* 1923 SWA 5. In *Buerger* the plaintiff and the defendant were co-sureties to the Master for the executor of an estate. The executor absconded, leaving a deficit in the estate of £50. After the executor had absconded the plaintiff proceeded against his assets and recovered £12. The plaintiff then paid the Master the £50 and proceeded against the defendant, as co-surety, for £25. The court held that the plaintiff was entitled to recover £25 from the defendant, since he, as surety, was not acting as the agent for the co-surety, and when he recovered the £12 he was acting for himself and not for and on behalf of the defendant. *De Wet & Yeats Die Suid-Afrikaanse Kontraktereg en Handelsreg* 4 ed (1978) by JC de Wet and AH van Wyk at 352 note 69 submit that the decision is correct since 'die medeborg [het] nie kragtens 'n vorderingsreg wat hy van die skuldeiser verkry het teen die selfskuldenaar opgetree nie, maar eenvoudig kragtens sy reg as borg'. The effect of the decision in *Buerger's* case could be that the defendant bears a greater burden of the principal debt. See also *Berzack Brothers v Iesberts* 1973 (2) SA 196 (W) where it was held that the surety who held security in the form of ceded book debts must wait until he has been paid a dividend from the debtor's insolvent estate before he can turn to his co-sureties. See the discussion in note 38 above.

[60] See Van der Linden *Koopmans Handboek* 1.14.10 ('om van elk hunner derzelver aandeel'); Wassenaar *Practyk Notariael* 10.23 ('die altijds gehouden zijn prorata ... die lasten te helpen dragen'); Lybrechts *Notaris Ampt* Vol 2 ch 34 at 284 ('dat hy van dezelve haar aandeel in de schuld moge bekomen'); Pothier *op cit* para 445 ('een gedeelte van elk zijner mede-borgen kan terug eisschen'); Neostadius *Hollandiae, Zelandiae, Frisaeque Curiae Decisiones* dec 12 and Willem Decker's note on Van Leeuwen's *Het Roomsch Hollandsch Recht* dec 12).

[61] *Gerber v Wolson* 1955 (1) SA 158 (A); *Executors Estate Watson v Huneberg & Leathern* 1915 NPD 571 at 578.

[62] A surety, in this context, would be insolvent when he is unable to pay his debts (*Gerber v Wolson* 1955 (1) SA 158 (A) at 615, *LAWSA* Vol 26 para 213).

Where co-sureties have undertaken liability on an unequal footing one could use either the 'maximum liability' principle or the 'independent liability' principle to calculate the contributions of the co-sureties *inter se*.

The 'maximum liability' approach requires that the pro rata share of each surety be calculated on the basis of his maximum liability, irrespective of what the principal debt happens to be. For example, suppose A, B, and C are co-sureties for the whole of a principal debt of R50 000, and their respective liabilities are limited to R20 000, R30 000 and R50 000 respectively. If C pays the principal debt of R50 000 claimed by the creditor, the liability will be shared as follows: A (2/10) R10 000, B (3/10) R15 000, C (5/10) R25 000.[63] The 'maximum liability' approach ensures an equal proportionate distribution of the principal debt between the co-sureties *inter se* with reference to their respective maximum liabilities. But it should be noted that the 'maximum liability' principle cannot be used in cases where one of the sureties undertakes liability for an unlimited amount, while his co-sureties limit their liability—the surety who undertakes unlimited liability has no maximum liability to use as a yardstick in order to calculate the respective proportions *inter se*.[64] The difficulties which the application of this method produces would render it, at best, unfair and, at worst, unworkable.[65]

With the 'independent liability' principle one asks what each of the sureties' independent liability would have been, and their respective contributions are then assessed with reference to the amount of the principal debt. On this method, the co-sureties who are liable to contribute to the common burden bear the principal debt equally up to the amount of their limited liability. Thus if A's liability is limited to R20 000 and B's liability is unlimited, they will share the burden of a principal debt of R10 000, equally. Each surety would independently have been liable for the full amount of the principal debt. Because their independent liability is the same (R10 000), their pro rata share is also the same (R5 000). But where the amount claimed by the creditor exceeds the limit of A's liability, the 'independent liability' principle would require a determination of the court what would have been the liability of each surety had he been the only surety. The amount claimed is then divided among the sureties pro rata to their independent liabilities. For example, if the liability of surety A is limited to R20 000 and

---

[63] The rule in English law in suretyship cases where contribution arises appears to be that where the liability of sureties is limited to fixed maxima of differing amounts, they share liability on the 'maximum liability' basis. The leading statement of this principle was made by Baron Anderson in *Pendlebury v Walker* (1841) 4 Y & C Ex 424 at 442, 160 ER 1072 at 1079: 'where the same default of the principal renders all the co-sureties responsible, all are to contribute; and then the law super-adds that which is not only the principle but the equitable mode of applying the principle, that they should all contribute equally, if each is a surety to an equal amount; and if not equally, then proportionably to the amount for which each is a surety'. Hence, in *Ellesmere Brewery Company v Cooper and Others* [1896] 1 QB 75 Lord Russell of Killowen CJ and Cave J followed *Pendleoury* and held that where there were four sureties, two for £50 each and two for £25 each for a principal debt of £48, the 'burthen is a common burthen of all, but unequally distributed' (at 80). The principal debt had thus to be divided on the basis that the £50 sureties would bear £16 each and the £25 sureties £8 each (that is, £16; £16; £8; £8 or 2:2:1:1).

[64] *De Beer v Bosman* (TPD 27 November 1990 (case 1993/90) unreported) at 8. See also Daniel Visser *Unjustified Enrichment* (2008) at 647 ff.

[65] *Commercial Union Assurance Co Ltd v Hayden* [1977] 1 QB 804 (CA) 816, [1977] All ER 441 at 447; *American Surety Co of New York v Wrightson* (1910) 16 Com Cas 37 at 55, (1910) 103 LT 663.

surety B's liability unlimited, calculation of their liability is for a principal debt of R60 000 will involve the following:

(i) A's independent liability as sole surety would be R20 000 and B's R60 000;
(ii) the principal debt should accordingly be apportioned with reference to their independent liability—2:6 between A and B;
(iii) A will thus be liable to pay R15 000 (one quarter) and B R45 000 (three quarters).[66]

On this principle, then, where the principal debt is for less than the lower upper limit on the respective liability of the co-sureties' liability, they will share the burden equally. It is only where the amount of the principal debt is not less than the highest maximum liability of any of the co-sureties that one deals with a rateable proportion.[67] It has been said that the 'independent liability' approach is a much fairer method of apportionment, since it divides the actual amount of the principal debt and does not impose an unduly onerous burden on one surety simply because a larger principal debt would still be within the limits of such surety's undertaking with the result that this method shares the burden of the principal debt as it is, not as it might have been.[68] Under certain circumstances it could be to the advantage of a co-surety with a greater maximum liability if the distribution of the principal debt between the co-sureties *inter se* were to be calculated on the 'independent liability' approach. As stated above, the 'maximum liability' approach could not be used in cases where one surety undertakes liability for an unlimited amount while his co-sureties limit their liabilities.

It is submitted that the 'independent liability' approach should be adopted in those instances where one or more of the co-sureties have undertaken liability for an unlimited amount while their co-sureties have limited their liability.[69]

---

[66] On the basis of the 'independent liability' principle the contribution between the two groups of sureties in *Ellesmere Brewery Company v Cooper and Others* [1896] 1 QB 75 would have been in the ratio 48:25.

[67] In *Commercial Union Assurance Co Ltd v Hayden* [1977] 1 QB 804 (CA), [1977] All ER 441 the Court of Appeal held that a 'rateable proportion' clause in a public liability insurance policy should be construed as requiring the application of the 'independent liability' principle. The court applied this principle mainly on the ground that it was the approach which was more likely to be intended by reasonable businessmen (at 815, 447). Cairns LJ expressed the opinion that the 'independent liability basis is much more realistic in its results' (at 816, 447). The 'independent liability' principle has indeed been used in English law to calculate the contributions of the co-sureties *inter se* where one of the co-sureties has undertaken liability for an unlimited amount and his co-sureties have limited their liability (*Naumann v Northcote* (7 February 1978, unreported, Court of Appeal: Transcript No 7835, as quoted by *Rowlatt on The Law of Principal and Surety* 5 ed (1999) by Gabriel Moss & David Marks 168 note 10)).

[68] Pretorius 'Contributions' 388 ff. See also Daniel Visser *Unjustified Enrichment* (2008) at 647 ff that supports the above approach.

[69] In *De Beer v Bosman* (TPD 27 November 1990 (case 1993/90) unreported) Le Roux AJ applied the 'independent liability' principle on the facts before him. See Pretorius 'Running Contributions' for a full discussion of this decision.

6. Procedure

Since extrinsic evidence is required to prove payment of the debt, provisional sentence proceedings are generally inappropriate for a claim for a contribution.[70]

In *Anglo African Shipping Co (1936) Ltd v Harris*[71] it was held that a surety called upon to pay could seek a declaratory order against his co-sureties in terms of section 19(1) of the Supreme Court Act 59 of 1959. It made no difference that the surety's rights, prior to payment to the creditor, were contingent.

7. Loss of security held by creditor

Notwithstanding that the surety who pays the debt does not demand cession of actions, what has been said in the chapter on Cession of Actions[72] in regard to the effects of a creditor releasing one of the co-sureties or making a compromise with him or failing to preserve a security, applies in principle in relation to a surety's right to contributions by his co-sureties. If the creditor prejudices him in this relation, he is entitled to relief against the creditor to the extent that his right to a contribution has been impaired by the creditor's conduct.[73]

---

[70] *Cloete v Eksteen* (1834) 1 Menz 71; *Neethling v Hamman* (1834) 1 Menz 71; *Gie v De Villiers* (1835) 1 Menz 63.
[71] 1977 (2) SA 213 (W).
[72] See Chapter X.
[73] See Chapter XIII.

PART THREE

The Release of the Surety

CHAPTER XIII

Discharge of the Surety

		Page
1.	Introduction	187
2.	Surety discharged: principal debtor's liability extinguished	188
	(a) Defences personal to the debtor do not avail the surety	188
	(b) Defences in rem available to the surety	189
	(c) Defences available for the benefit of third parties	190
	(d) Defences available under the National Credit Act 34 of 2005	192
	(e) Payment of the debt by the principal debtor	193
	(f) Release of the principal debtor by the creditor	194
	(g) Novation of the principal debt	195
	(h) Compromise of the principal debt	197
	(i) Delegation of the principal debtor	197
	(j) Set-off and the principal debt	198
	(k) Merger between principal debtor and creditor	199
	(l) Prescription of principal debt	200
	(m) Miscellaneous	204
3.	Surety discharged: nature of his contract	204
	(a) Payment of the principal debt by the surety	204
	(b) Effluxion of time	205
	(c) Prejudice through a material alteration in the principal debt	205
	(d) Prejudice through an extension of time	208
	(e) Prejudice through an agreement not to enforce	208
	(f) Breach of contract with the surety	209
4.	Exceptional defences and their history: the reach of public policy and the Constitution	210

1. Introduction

We are concerned in this chapter to ascertain when a person who has become bound as a surety is discharged or released from his obligations as surety or has some other defence when sued by the creditor. For clarity of exposition we may divide the various defences available to the surety into two major categories and several subcategories. The major categories are determined by whether the defence relates to the principal obligation or whether it relates to the surety's own obligation under the contract of suretyship.

Thus, first of all, since the surety's obligation is accessory to that of the principal debtor the surety will be able to raise, subject to certain exceptions to be discussed below and whose precise reach is controversial, all those defences available to the principal debtor. The surety is discharged where the principal debtor is entitled to *restitutio in integrum* on any of the grounds on which a party to a contract is entitled to resile from it as being void or voidable,[1] for example, lack of consent, mistake, illegality, fraud, misrepresentation, intimidation, undue influence or forgery.[2] These are the defences that relate to the principal obligation.

In the second place, there are those defences derived from the surety's own contract. The surety will, of course, have the defences that would be available to any contracting party under the general principles of the law of contract. Similarly, the question whether the creditor has released the surety is decided according to the usual principles of the law of contract.[3] The circumstances in which the surety appears to be bound, but is in fact not bound as a surety, because no contract of suretyship has been formed have been discussed elsewhere.[4] All this does not mean that this chapter is redundant: there are defences particular to the contract of suretyship and we will be primarily concerned with those.

2. Surety discharged: principal debtor's liability extinguished

Extinction of the principal obligation extinguishes that of the surety who is no longer bound when there is no principal debtor for whom he is obliged.[5] The operation of this principle can be exemplified under several headings.

(a)   Defences personal to the debtor do not avail the surety

Defences available to the principal debtor are available to the surety.[6] This principle is limited, however, to those defences which go to the root of the debt, and not to such defences as are personal to the debtor, ie those defences which are a personal privilege granted to the debtor.[7] This is often expressed in the decided cases by saying that the surety can avail himself of the debtor's *in rem* defences but not his *in personam* defences. This distinction was explained by Rose-Innes J in *Standard Bank of SA Ltd v SA Fire Equipment (Pty) Ltd and Another*[8] in these words:

---

[1] Domat 1873, 1889; Gr 3.48.8; P 380-1; B 218; Wessels paras 4969 *et seq*, 4030, 4040, 4265. *Estate Van der Lith v Conradie and Others* (1903) 20 SC 241 at 246.

[2] *Wiehahn NO v Wouda* 1957 (4) SA 724 (W) at 726.

[3] See, for instance, *Botha (now Griessel) and Another v Finanscredit (Pty) Ltd* 1989 (3) SA 773 (A), where the question whether an alleged waiver by the creditor of its rights had released the surety was considered according to general principles. See also *Tsaperas and Others v Boland Bank Ltd* 1996 (1) SA 719 (A). For the position of the surety where the creditor releases the principal debtor see below.

[4] See Chapter V on the Formation of the Contract.

[5] D 46.1.21; D 46.1.38.1; D 46.1.47 pr; P 377, 383, 406. *Colonial Government v Edenborough and Another* (1886) 4 SC 290 at 296; *Union Government v Van der Merwe* 1921 TPD 318 at 320-1; *Moti & Co v Cassim's Trustee* 1924 AD 720 at 737, 742, 743, 746. Alternatively, but less persuasively, it may be argued that since the principal debt is extinguished, the creditor cannot give the surety cession of actions; and the creditor must, of course, give cession of actions if he wishes to enforce his rights against the surety.

[6] Inst 4.14.4; D 46.1.32; D 46.1.69 pr, Domat 1873; VL 4.4.2; *Cens For* 1.4.17.18; P 380, 381; Wessels para 3969 *et seq*, 4030, 4038, 4040. *Worthington v Wilson* 1918 TPD 104 at 105-6; *Union Government v Pearl Assurance Co Ltd* 1933 (1) PH A12 (T); *Ideal Finance Corporation v Coetzer* 1970 (3) SA 1 (A); *Linden Duplex (Pty) Ltd v Harrowsmith* 1978 (1) SA 371 (W) at 373A.

[7] *Linden Duplex (Pty) Ltd v Harrowsmith* 1978 (1) SA 371 (W) at 373C. See also *Worthington v Wilson* 1918 TPD 104 at 110.

[8] 1984 (2) SA 693 (C) at 696C-E. See also *Cape Produce Co (PE) (Pty) Ltd v Dal Maso and Another NNO* 2001 (2) SA 182 (W); [2001] 1 All SA 627 (W).

'The contrast between defences *in rem* and *in personam* thus is that those *in rem* attach to the claim or cause of action or the obligation itself and arise from the invalidity, extinction or discharge of the obligation itself, whoever the debtor may be; those *in personam* arise from a personal immunity of the debtor from liability for an otherwise valid and existing civil or natural obligation. In the case of a defence *in personam* the obligation and the debt remain in existence ... but ... the debtor is personally immune from a claim. In the case of a defence *in rem* the law does not recognise the obligation or debt even as a natural obligation ...'.

Thus *in personam* defences include the insolvency or liquidation of the principal debtor,[9] statutory composition with creditors, exemption from execution, or legal moratorium.[10] In particular, even if the principal debtor is entitled to *restitutio in integrum* on the ground of the debtor's minority,[11] then the surety is not released, for a natural obligation will support a suretyship.[12]

The distinction between *in rem* defences and *in personam* defences is not ideal but it is useful as a rule of thumb.[13] But one should not follow rules of thumb rigidly. In particular, there may be cases in which although a defence is plainly not *in personam* it is possibly not *in rem*. These are the defences, to be discussed below, which are available to the insolvent's trustee for the protection of third parties.

(b) Defences in rem *available to the surety*

Any defences available to the principal debtor, other than those personal to him, are available to the surety. These include mistake, misrepresentation, duress, payment, compromise, novation, judgment or set-off to name just a few. Furthermore, non-performance by the creditor of his part of the contract, where that releases the debtor—for example, failure to deliver the goods sold, or the existence of defects in the goods sold entitling the debtor to redhibition—will also release the surety. Similarly, where supervening impossibility of performance re-

---

[9] Any doubt about this was stilled by the Appellate Division in *Norex Industrial Properties (Pty) Ltd v Monarch South Africa Insurance Co Ltd* 1987 (1) SA 827 (A). Botha JA, in reliance on *Liquidators, FH Clarke & Co Ltd v Nesbitt* 1906 TS 726, rejected the proposition that the lessee's insolvency (or liquidation) terminated the lease (and thus would provide the surety for the lessee with an *in rem* defence); the surety remained bound. See, further, the discussion of this case in Chapter VI concerning whether the termination of the lease by the liquidator in terms of section 37(1) of the Insolvency Act 24 of 1936 released the surety. See also AL Stander 'Borg-Aanspreeklikheid in geval van Likwidasie van Maatskappy' (1988) 21 *De Jure* 163 and *Boshoff v South African Mutual Life Assurance Society* 2000 (3) SA 597 (C).

[10] Domat 1873; Inst 4.14.4; V 46.1.39; V 46.2.6; VL 4.4.7; Cens Por 1.4.17.18; P 380; Wessels para 3969, 4030. The moratorium may be by statute or by order of court (*Worthington v Wilson* 1918 TPD 104 at 106, *Skelton v Shelvoke and Smith* (1904) 21 SC 664 at 666).

[11] Domat 1859, 1873, 1890, 2392; Gr 3.48.12; P 380-1; Wessels para 3969.

[12] See Chapter III.

[13] The learned author of 1984 *Annual Survey* 190, in commenting on *Standard Bank of SA Ltd v SA Fire Equipment (Pty) Ltd and Another* 1984 (2) SA 693 (C), is critical of the *in rem/in personam* distinction. The author argues that the court should 'revert directly to the intention of the parties to the [suretyship] contract, to determine whether the surety could raise the defence or not'. Of course, often the minds of the parties will simply not have met on the issue. In these circumstances, the distinction provides a useful rule of thumb. Note finally, however, the terminology is awkward for it is plain that throughout we are dealing with rights *in personam* not rights *in rem*.

leases the debtor from his obligation, the surety is discharged.[14] Or, alternatively, in regard to a future liability, the termination of the contract from which the principal debt arises will release the surety as well—for example, the termination of a lease, through the failure of the lessee to pay the rent, transmutes the lessee's obligation into one to pay damages to the lessor, and discharges the surety who has guaranteed the rent but not damages.[15] The subordination of the principal debtor's debt by the creditor is a defence *in rem* and the sureties are entitled to rely on such subordination.[16]

(c) Defences available for the benefit of third parties

There are, however, other cases where although the defence is plainly not *in personam*, it seems unjust not to allow the surety to rely on it. Take, for instance, a disposition without value in terms of section 26 of the Insolvency Act 24 of 1936. Section 26(1), it will be recalled, provides that the court may set aside 'every disposition of property [by an insolvent] not made for value' where at the time the liabilities of the insolvent exceeded his assets;[17] and section 26(2) provides that where such a disposition is set aside that fact 'shall not give rise to any claim in competition with the creditors of the insolvent estate'. The purpose of section 26 is 'plainly not ... to benefit the principal debtor; [section 26] was designed to bring about an equitable adjustment as between [the principal debtor's] creditors and the person to whom he has made the disposition'.[18] The debtor is prevented, if his assets exceed his liabilities, from impoverishing his estate by giving away his assets without receiving any value in return.[19]

Now suppose that a debtor, without giving value, issues an acknowledgement of debt to a creditor and prevails on a surety to guarantee payment of that debt.

---

[14] But if the impossibility is due to the destruction of the *res* to be delivered through the fault of the surety, not the debtor, then the debtor is released, but the surety, naturally, is liable for damages. P 383; Wessels para 4334.

[15] *Arenson v Bishop* 1926 CPD 73 at 75; Cf *St Patricks Mansions (Pty) Ltd v Grange Restaurant (Pty) Ltd and Another* 1949 (4) SA 57 (W) at 68 ff. Note the discussion in Chapter VI on suretyships for the obligations of lessees.

[16] In *Cape Produce Co (PE) (Pty) Ltd v Dal Maso and Another NNO* 2001 (2) SA 182 (W); [2001] 1 All SA 627 (W) Van Oosten J held that the effect of a subordination agreement is to suspend the due date for the payment of the principal debt until the happening of the events referred to in the agreement. Where the subordination agreement was agreed on by the creditor himself the subordination relates not to the person of the principal debtor but rather to the debt itself and therefore to the creditor's cause of action. The defence of subordination is not founded on any reason personal to the principal debtor but affects the enforceability of the debt itself in delaying the due date for payment, thereby attaching to the nature of the debt. It is thus a defence *in rem* and it follows that the sureties are entitled to raise the defence against the creditor's claim (at 192; 635).

[17] Who is required to prove that the liabilities of the estate exceeded its assets depends on whether the disposition took place more than two years or less than two years before sequestration. If it is proved, subsequent to the disposition, that the liabilities of the estate exceeded the assets by less than the value of the disposition, the disposition can only be set aside to that extent. See also GF Lubbe and AH van Wyk 'Borgstelling en Artikel 26(2) van die Insolvensiewet' (1983) 43 *THRHR* 450 and AN Oelofse 'Enkele Gedagtes na aanleiding van Twee Opmerkings in *Trans-Drakensberg Bank Ltd v The Master and Others* 1962 (4) SA 417 (N)' (1988) 10 *MB* 52.

[18] *Linden Duplex (Pty) Ltd v Harrowsmith* 1978 (1) SA 371 (W) at 374B.

[19] Based on a contention of counsel in Freedman and *Rossi (Pty) Ltd v Geustyn and Others* 1986 (4) SA 762 (W) at 764B.

Suppose further that the debtor is then sequestrated and the acknowledgment of debt is liable to be set aside as a 'disposition of property' in terms of section 26(1). In these circumstances, the creditor will naturally turn to the surety to make good his undertaking. Can the surety contend that section 26 does not contain a defence personal to the debtor; and thus it can be raised by the surety?

The courts have consistently thought so. First in *Linden Duplex (Pty) Ltd v Harrowsmith*,[20] Coleman J held that the surety for an acknowledgment of debt (that was liable to be set aside as a disposition without value) could raise section 26 as a defence, essentially on the ground that it was not a defence personal to the debtor; a setting aside went to the root of the debt. And this decision was followed by Van Niekerk J in *Freedman and Rossi (Pty) Ltd v Geustyn and Others*,[21] in which the learned judge rejected the criticism that had been made of the *Linden Duplex* case and expressed his approval of Coleman J's judgment. This was also the view of the court in *Millman NO and Stein NO v Kamfer*.[22]

The academic criticism referred to was primarily that of Whiting:[23] He pointed out that the setting aside of the disposition without value was 'not a defence available to the debtor at all, but a remedy available to his trustee for the benefit of his creditors. There was therefore clearly no basis for the invocation of the general rule that the surety is entitled to rely on any defence available to the principal debtor'.[24] This was countered by Van Niekerk J in *Freedman and Rossi (Pty) Ltd v Geustyn and Others*[25] by remarking that the section 26 defence 'was available to the debtor's estate. If the principal debt should be void or voidable, then the debt itself, to which the suretyship is accessory, may be attacked ...'.[26] The crux of the judge's argument here is that should the principal debt, for whatever reason, be void or voidable then there is (or will be once a voidable obligation is nullified) no principal obligation and thus there can be no suretyship. It is respectfully submitted that the logic of this argument cannot be faulted.[27]

Whiting also raised a second ground of criticism. It was argued that the setting aside of the disposition does not affect the validity of the underlying obligation: 'it merely cannot be enforced against the estate in competition with the claims of the creditors ...'.[28] Thus there remains an unenforceable obligation sufficient to support the suretyship. Van Niekerk J disagrees with this, contending that Whiting had overlooked the wide definition of 'disposition' in the Insolvency Act 1936. That definition is certainly wide enough to include the acknowledgment of debt that was the 'disposition' in question in both cases. Thus once the court had 'set

---

[20] 1978 (1) SA 371 (W).
[21] 1978 (1) SA 371 (W). For criticism, see MP Larkin 'Should the Surety get Away? Invalid Dispositions' (1987) 16 *Businessman's Law* 123.
[22] 1993 (1) SA 305 (C).
[23] See RC Whiting 'A Novel Defence for a Surety' (1978) 95 *SALJ* 25 and 1978 *Annual Survey* 217.
[24] 1978 *Annual Survey* 217.
[25] Above.
[26] At 765H-I.
[27] See also *Millman NO and Stein NO v Kamfer* 1993 (1) SA 305 (C) at 309.
[28] RC Whiting 'A Novel Defence for a Surety' (1978) 95 *SALJ* 25 at 26.

aside' the disposition no obligation remained and there was nothing to support the suretyship.[29]

Deregistration of the company which is the principal debtor provides a further example of the awkwardness that can result if too formalistic an approach is taken in this area. One might have thought that when the principal debtor (a company) is deregistered and ceases to exist that strikes at the root of the debts owed by that company and releases the surety. Where there is no debtor, there cannot be a debt; and if there is no principal debt there cannot be a suretyship. However, this is not the conclusion reached by the Appellate Division in *Traub and Kalk v Barclays National Bank Ltd*.[30] There Botha JA held that it 'is not the law that a surety is freed from liability to the creditor when the principal debtor ceases to exist. If the principal debtor is a natural person and he dies, his surety remains liable to his creditor; and a surety for a company remains liable to its creditor if it is liquidated and dissolved under s 419 of the Companies Act [61 of 1973]'. In the court *a quo*, the same conclusion was reached but on narrower grounds. Reliance was there placed on the fact that *litis contestatio* had been reached before the debtor was deregistered and, moreover, that the court had power to order the restoration of the company's registration. Thus the court concluded that, while the company was deregistered, the debt was unenforceable but not extinguished; and thus that the surety was not released.[31] It is submitted that the reasoning of the court *a quo* is sounder on this point, but the result is the same.

(d) Defences available under the National Credit Act 34 of 2005

This comprehensive reforming and regulating measure's purpose is 'to promote and advance the social and economic welfare of South Africans, [and also to] promote a fair, transparent, competitive, sustainable, responsible, efficient, effective and accessible credit market and industry, and [also] to protect consumers.'[32] The Act introduces a whole range of measures to prevent possible overspending by consumers and also to prevent money-lenders from lending money to borrowers who cannot afford to repay either the loan amount or the interest thereon. As will be seen the Act may sometimes, in addition, provide a defence to a surety.

Subject to various exceptions the Act applies to 'every credit agreement between parties dealing at arm's length and made within, or having an effect within, the Republic'.[33] A 'credit agreement' includes a 'credit guarantee' which is an

---

[29] At 766B. See also *Millman NO and Stein NO v Kamfer* 1993 (1) SA 305 (C) where Conradie J followed the decision in *Freedman and Rossi* and pointed out at 310: 'In insolvency the surety retains a right to whatever miserable dividend the principal debtor's estate might pay. It seems to me that the rationale of the rule that a defence *in rem* serves to discharge the surety's obligation is that the surety does not take on himself unqualified liability for the debtor's debt. The surety's undertaking is to see that the creditor gets paid, but he has a right of recourse against the debtor. The right of recourse is fundamental. It is that which makes the surety's obligation an accessory and not a principal one'.
[30] 1983 (3) SA 619 (A) at 633H-634A.
[31] *Barclays National Bank Ltd and Others v Traub; Barclays National Bank Ltd v Kalk* 1981 (4) SA 291 (W).
[32] s 3.
[33] s 4.

agreement in which 'a person undertakes or promises to satisfy upon demand any obligation of another consumer in terms of a credit facility or a credit transaction' to which the Act applies.[34] Thus in principle a surety (securing an obligation within the Act) will fall within the Act and will be able to claim the benefits of the Act. For instance, he may ask the court to suspend his obligations under his contract when he shows that the 'credit guarantee' was 'reckless' as defined in the Act.[35] Once suspended the surety is not obliged to make any payment due and incurs no interest under the contract.[36]

However, as is plain from the statute, the obligation secured must itself be within the Act for a 'credit guarantee' to qualify as a 'credit agreement'. Thus in *Firstrand Bank Ltd v Carl Beck (Pty) Ltd and Carl Beck*,[37] since the principal debtor fell outside the Act,[38] it followed that the surety did too. Thus the surety lost a benefit under the Act (the giving of notice before being sued by the creditor).

The Act of 2005 is a complex measure and it will be necessary to have close regard to it and the specialised writing about it to determine its impact in any particular case.[39]

(e) *Payment of the debt by the principal debtor*

When the debtor[40] pays the creditor[41] the principal obligation is terminated, and the surety discharged. Payment means payment in the sense of *solutio*, whether by the handing over of cash or its equivalent.[42] The payment must be a valid and effective payment but if it is not and the surety suffers prejudice — for example, by the insolvency of the principal debtor after he has made an invalid payment — it appears that, if he did not know of the invalidity of the payment, he is discharged.[43] Part-payment releases neither sureties nor securities nor any part thereof.[44]

The ordinary rules relating to appropriation of payments apply generally to the question of whether a particular payment discharges the debt secured by the surety or some other debt owed by the principal debtor to the creditor.[45] Subject

---

[34] s 8(5).

[35] See s 1 and s 80 for the definition of 'reckless' and ss 83-4 for the consequences thereof. Essentially a credit transaction will be reckless unless a proper assessment has taken place of the debtor's understanding of the transaction, his credit history and his ability to repay (amongst other things).

[36] s 84 (1).

[37] 2009 (3) SA 384 (T).

[38] As a juristic person the debtor had to fulfil the requirements of section 4 which it did not.

[39] JM Otto *The National Credit Act Explained* (2006); JW Scholtz *et al Guide to the National Credit Act* (2009).

[40] Or on behalf of the debtor. D 46.1.69; VL 4.4.16; *Cens For* 1.4.17.26; Wessels para 4030. If there are two or more co-debtors then payment by either will suffice. P 519.

[41] Payment must be to the creditor unless he has authorised another person to receive payment in his place. Cf *Faure v Bosman* (1864) 5 Searle 9.

[42] Wessels para 4224.

[43] P 406; Wessels paras 4224 *et seq.* Cf *Linden Duplex (Pty) Ltd v Harrowsmith* 1978 (1) SA 371 (W). If this rule seems harsh on the creditor, it should be recalled that the surety will have lost the opportunity of paying and recovering from the principal debtor.

[44] Wessels para 2277.

[45] Wessels paras 4031 *et seq*, 4228. Cf *Executors of Watermeyer v Executor of Watermeyer* (1870) 2 Buch 69 at 72. The general rules will be found in Wessels para 2308.

to these rules, the specific rules applicable to sureties are the following: Appropriation ought to be made to a debt of which the debtor is the principal debtor, rather than one for which he is only a surety.[46] Payment by the debtor must be applied to the secured debt rather than one for which there are no sureties, because the debtor is thereby released not only from the creditor, but also from the sureties.[47] If the creditor has allowed the debt to exceed the amount secured by the surety and the debtor is insolvent, any dividend from his estate must be appropriated rateably to the amount secured and to the excess.[48]

An actual tender validly made by the debtor and which the creditor is obliged to receive of the amount owing or the thing due to the creditor has the same effect as payment. The surety is discharged if the creditor refuses the tender to the prejudice of the surety.[49]

(f) Release of the principal debtor by the creditor

Release by the creditor of the principal debtor from his liability under the principal obligation, either entirely or partially, extinguishes the debt either partially or entirely and the surety is to that extent discharged from his obligation.[50] Should there be two or more co-debtors, the release of one discharges him alone, unless the intention is to extinguish the whole debt. The debt, however, is extinguished to the extent of the aliquot share of the debtor released.[51] Sureties for the debtor released are discharged with him, but if they are sureties for the other co-debtors they remain bound.[52]

The release of the debtor may be either a gratuitous discharge from liability, in which the creditor waives his entire claim, or the creditor may accept only a compounding of the debt, accepting part payment in full settlement. Whether the composition is carried out forthwith or whether it involves a future performance by the debtor, the surety is discharged.[53] A failure to claim what is due from the debtor or if he is dead, his estate, does not release the surety.[54]

Wessels[55] discusses the question whether the creditor, when he releases the debtor of part of his claim, can reserve his rights against the surety in respect of the released part of his claim. Wessels appears to conclude that he cannot, because he

---

[46] V 46.1.16; p 530; B 131; Wessels para 2308.

[47] V 46.3.16; P 530; s 131; Wessels para 2308. *Northern Cape Co-operative Livestock Agency Ltd v John Roderick & Co Ltd* 1965 (2) SA 64 (O) at 73F; *Zietsman v Allied Building Society* 1989 (3) SA 166 (O) at 178B-C; *Page v ABSA Bank Ltd t/a Volkskas Bank and Another* 2000 (2) SA 658 (EC) at 663B-G.

[48] B 136; *Alford and Wills v Johnson* (1865) 5 Searle 147, I Roscoe 269.

[49] V 46.3.29; Gr 3.40.2, 3, s 138, 144; Wessels paras 2332 *et seq*; *Arenson v Bishop* 1926 CPD 73 at 75; *St Patricks Mansions (Pty) Ltd v Grange Restaurant (Pty) Ltd and Another* 1949 (4) SA 57 (W) at 63. The authorities discuss this in relation to a payment into court.

[50] D 46.3.49 pr; P 377, 380, 521, 580; s 162; Wessels paras 4039, 4230. *Wides v Butcher and Sons* (1905) 26 NLR 578 at 584; *Moti & Co v Cassim's Trustee* 1924 AD 720 at 737.

[51] D 46.1.15.1; Gr 3.3.8; P 581; B 163; Wessels paras 1526-1530. *Dwyer v Goldseller* 1906 TS 126; *De Charmoy and St Pol v Dhookoo* 1924 NPD 254; *Boyce NO v Bloem and Others* 1960 (3) SA 855 (T) at 857.

[52] P 581; B 163.

[53] *Wides v Butcher and Sons* (1905) 26 NLR 578, *Moti & Co v Cassim's Trustee* 1924 AD 720, *Friedman v Bond Clothing Manufacturers (Pty) Ltd* 1965 (1) SA 673 (T) at 677, 680.

[54] *Colonial Treasurer v Swart* 1910 TPD 552 at 555.

[55] Paras 4244 *et seq*.

is not able to give the surety an effective cession of his claim against the debtor. This is correct.[56] Otherwise the surety would be prejudiced in the respect that his right of recourse for the released part would be valueless. There is no reason, however, why the surety should not, if he wishes, take the risk on himself by agreeing, at the time of the making of the composition or at the time of entering into the suretyship, to a reservation of rights against him. In these circumstances, notwithstanding the creditor's inability to give the surety cession of actions and that the surety has no right of recourse against the debtor, the surety is bound.[57] On the other hand, the creditor and the debtor may agree on such a reservation.[58] In that event, notwithstanding the creditor's release of the debtor, the surety, if called on to pay the released part of the debt, would be bound to pay, but he would have a right of recourse against the debtor. In reality, the release of the debtor is not a true release, but simply a *pactum de non petendo* between creditor and debtor leaving the surety's rights and obligations intact.[59] If the surety has renounced or waived the right of recourse, release by the creditor of the principal debtor does not release the surety, for he has not been deprived of his right of recourse. The release of the debtor is a personal consideration by the creditor. If a party to a negotiable instrument stands to another party to it in the relationship of surety to principal debtor (and is able to rely on that fact against the holder of the instrument), he is entitled, subject to any statutory provision, to the protection which the law affords a surety where the creditor has released the principal debtor.[60] The onus is on the surety to establish that the creditor has in fact so acted as to release him.[61]

(g) Novation of the principal debt

Novation (*novatio*)[62] may be effected by agreement between the parties (*novatio voluntaria*) or by operation of law (*novatio necessaria*), but we are here primarily concerned with the former. Such novation discharges the surety.[63] The reason for this is that the debtor's original obligation no longer exists and with it has gone

---

[56] B 154.
[57] *Bank of Africa v Vom Dorp* (1909) 26 SC 143 at 150-2; *Standard Bank of SA Ltd v Lewis* 1922 TPD 285 at 290; *Friedman v Bond Clothing Manufacturers (Pty) Ltd* 1965 (1) SA 673 (T) at 677; *Standard Bank v Lowry and Another* 1926 CPD 338 at 340. And see the remarks of Innes CJ in *Moti & Co v Cassim's Trustee* 1924 AD 720 at 739. See also *Trust Bank van Afrika Bpk v Ungerer* 1981 (2) SA 223 (W).
[58] As they did in *Israelsohn v Newman & Sons Ltd* 1949 (3) SA 1178 (W).
[59] *Natal Bank v Banfield & Co* (1885) 6 NLR 178 at 181; *Wides v Butcher and Sons* (1905) 26 NLR 578 at 584-5.
[60] *Haffajee v Ramdhani* 1947 (1) SA 823 (A).
[61] *Schonfrucht v King* 1934 (2) PH A35 (W).
[62] For the principles relating to novation see LR Caney *The Law of Novation* 2 ed (1976).
[63] D 46.1.68.2; P 380; B 166; Wessels paras 4244 *et seq*, 4256. *Colonial Government v Edenborough and Another* (1886) 4 SC 290 at 296, *Baillie v Transvaal Assets Ltd* 1923 (2) PH A21 (W); *Van Aswegen v Van Eetveld and Du Plessis* 1925 (2) PH A37 (C); *Irwin v Davies* 1937 CPD 442 at 449; *Schoeman v Moller* 1949 (3) SA 949 (O) at 955; *French v Sterling Finance Corporation (Pty) Ltd* 1961 (4) SA 732 (A); *Vaid v Ameen* 1962 (2) PH A33 (N). But the debt must, of course, be novated before this principle can operate. A custody agreement (in terms of which a defaulting hire-purchase buyer hands over possession of the *merx* to the creditor while he seeks to remedy his default) is patently not a novation of the principal debt: *Standard Credit Corporation Ltd v Laycock* 1988 (4) SA 679 (N).

the obligation of the surety unless, of course, he has agreed otherwise.[64] This is well-established and uncontroversial law.

However, in *Zimbabwe Football Association v Mafurusa*[65] Mfalila J held otherwise. He held that a novation agreement which 'only affected the extent, not the nature, of [the surety's] obligation to the plaintiff'[66] did not release the surety. Thus where a particular loan requiring the repayment of the full principal sum on a particular date was replaced,[67] without the surety's agreement, by an agreement between creditor and debtor to repay the principal sum by instalments, the surety was not released.

It is difficult to view this decision as anything other than clearly wrong. Given that the judge expressly holds that the original agreement had been novated and given that it was clear that debtor's obligations under that agreement were the only obligations secured by the surety, the surety must have been released. Not surprisingly, the decision has been strongly criticised.[68]

Since novation destroys the old obligation, with all its accessions and privileges, if the creditor effects a novation with one of several co-debtors, all co-debtors and sureties, it seems, are released from the old obligation.[69] The creditor cannot reserve his rights under the old obligation. If the creditor makes it a condition of the novation that the other co-debtors and the sureties (or any of these) are to continue to be bound to the old obligation, their agreement to this is necessary in order to make the novation effective.[70]

Compulsory or judicial novation (*novatio necessaria*), on the other hand, does not discharge sureties. True, in the old civil law *litis contestatio* between creditor and debtor caused novation, the principal debt fell away and the surety consequently was released. This, however, is not the law today.[71] The judgment does not replace the original principal debt, it merely strengthens and reinforces it.[72] Even if the creditor obtains judgment against the debtor, the surety is not released nor is this *res judicata* against the surety.[73]

---

[64] D 46.1.60; C 8.41.4; V 46.1.36; Gr 3.43.4; VdL 1.18.2; P 378, 563; B 171, 166, 172, 173, 214; Wessels paras 2426 *et seq* 4038, 4257, 4296.
[65] 1985 (3) SA 1050 (Z).
[66] At 1055D-E.
[67] That date being after the debt had fallen due so, in the absence of prejudice, the surety was not released through the grant of an extension of time. See below.
[68] 1985 *Annual Survey* 169-71.
[69] P 563 B 171, 172, Wessels paras 2426-32.
[70] C 8.41.4; V 46.2.7, 10; P 551, 563; B 172.
[71] See the discussion in *Rand Bank Ltd v De Jager* 1982 (3) SA 418 (C) at 451F-452H. See also *Swadif (Pty) Ltd v Dyke NO* 1978 (1) SA 928 (A) at 941B.
[72] See *Swadif (Pty) Ltd v Dyke NO* 1978 (1) SA 928 (A) at 940G-944H. Note, however, that in addition the judgment creates a separate cause of action from that of the original debt: *Joosab v Tayob* 1910 TS 486 at 488. This may be of consequence where the original debt is, perhaps, extinguished by prescription but the judgment debt is not. See the discussion of prescription below.
[73] V 46.2. 1; *Cens For* 1.4.34.7 as well as *Rand Bank Ltd v De Jager* 1982 (3) SA 418 (C) and *Swadif (Pty) Ltd v Dyke NO* 1978 (1) SA 928 (A).

However, if the creditor obtains judgment against the principal debtor on a basis other than for the debt secured by the surety, for example, for damages when the surety undertook that the debtor would pay by instalments, the novation substitutes a different type of liability and that which was secured goes out of existence (*Moreriane v Trans-Oranje Finansierings- en Ontwikkelingskorporasie, Bpk* 1965 (1) SA 767 (T) at 772).

The creditor can sue the debtor, change his mind, and thereupon sue the surety.[74] A judgment in favour of the principal debtor against the creditor is *res judicata* in favour of the surety.[75] The surety cannot be held liable while that judgment stands, unless he had undertaken in his contract to pay if action was brought against the debtor.[76] A statutory composition under section 119 of the Insolvency Act 24 of 1936 does not release sureties.[77] Nor are sureties released by the debtor's insolvency or his rehabilitation.[78] A composition effected by a company under the provisions of the Companies Act 61 of 1973 does not release the sureties for the company.[79] In *Friedman v Bond Clothing Manufacturers (Pty) Ltd*[80] it was decided that the creditors could cede their rights to the offeror, but reserve their rights as sureties. But this would appear to be plainly wrong.[81]

(h) Compromise of the principal debt

A compromise (*transactio*) of a disputed claim may release the surety entirely or in part. If the creditor agrees to accept less than he claims is owing, the debtor agreeing to pay this when he contends that he owes nothing or less than he is agreeing to pay, the creditor abandons the excess over what he agrees to accept and the debtor, and so his surety, is released from the excess over what is agreed as the compromise. But if what is agreed as the compromise is the performance of a new obligation on the part of the debtor, and the surety is not party to this new agreement, then the surety is entirely released.

(i) Delegation of the principal debtor

Delegation (*delegatio*) also discharges the surety, for a new debtor is substituted for the debtor whose debt the surety has secured.[82] The surety's obligation is not transferred to operate in respect of the new debtor, unless he agrees to this. If he does not agree, he is discharged.[83] If he does agree to secure the new debtor's debt then the agreement will have to comply with the formalities laid down in the General Law Amendment Act 50 of 1956.[84]

---

[74] V 46.120; V 46.2.1; VL 4.4.10. *Johannesburg Coal Agency v Hyman* 1915 WLD 98 at 99; *Cronin v Meerholz* 1920 TPD 403 at 405; *Haffajee v Ramdhani* 1947 (1) SA 823 (A) at 830.
[75] V 44.2.5, P 380, 381, Wessels paras 3973, 4041
[76] *Hastie v Dunstan* (1892) 9 SC 449.
[77] Section 120(3).
[78] Section 129(3)*(d)*. See also Chapter VII.
[79] See *Lalia v Bodasirg* 1955 (1) PH F49 (D).
[80] 1965 (1) SA 673 (T).
[81] 1956 *Annual Survey* 140 and JE Scholtens 'Cession of Rights Against Sureties' (1957) 74 *SALJ* 130.
[82] Cf *Eaton Robins & Co v Nel (2)* (1909) 26 SC 624 at 630.
[83] V 46.2.14; P 565; B 166, 171; Wessels paras 2454, 4257.
[84] See Chapter V, Section IV.

(j) Set-off and the principal debt

Set-off (*compensatio*) of debts owed by the creditor to the debtor will, where such set-off is permissible in terms of the ordinary rules,[85] discharge the surety.[86] In these circumstances the principal debt is extinguished, entirely or in part, as if it had been paid.[87] Each debt destroys the other to the extent of the lesser of the two.[88]

The surety may also rely on what the creditor owes him, but the principal debtor cannot rely on a set-off between creditor or surety.[89]

Although set-off operates by force of law, it is still necessary for the surety to plead it as a defence,[90] 'but its operation dates back to the moment when the two persons concerned were reciprocally liable to each other'.[91] The question was left open in *Miller v Muller*,[92] but it appears that the surety can raise set-off as a defence even where the debtor has not done so. This is because set-off operates automatically by operation of law. It is not necessary for the debtor to do anything to bring the defence into operation. Of course, the defence has to be pleaded by the surety, but this is simply to draw attention to its existence.[93]

It is trite that a claim for unliquidated damages is in law incapable of set-off. But it may be that the principal debtor has such a claim against the creditor. Can the surety deploy this fact against the creditor when sued by him? It might be thought that since, in the absence of a cession of actions, the surety could not bring the claim for damages against the creditor himself, neither could he raise the claim as a defence.

However, this overlooks rule 22(4) of the Uniform Rules of Court, which provides that where the defendant has a 'claim in reconvention, which, if successful, would extinguish all or part of the plaintiff's claim, the court may stay the plain-

---

[85] *Burton v Barlow Rand Ltd, t/a Barrows Tractor and Machinery Co, Burton v Thomas Barlow & Sons (Natal) Ltd* 1978 (4) SA 794 (T), is an awkward case in this regard. There it was held that a claim for damages by the debtor against the creditor which was not concerned with the nature, validity or extent of the principal debt could not, even if liquidated, be set off by the surety. Margo J said 'the company's claim for damages is not *rei cohaerens*. It arises out of a separate transaction [the principal debt]... . It is *personae cohaerens*, ie a claim personal to the principal debtor' (at 801A-B). But if set-off is available to the principal debtor for whatever reason then as a matter of law the principal debt is *pro tanto* extinguished and with it the surety's obligation to that extent. Carried to its logical conclusion Margo J's reasoning amounts to holding that set-off is an *in personam* rather than an *in rem* defence, but that is plainly contrary to the balance of authority set out in the following note and also to principle. The reasoning in *Burton's* case was disapproved of in both the more recent cases mentioned in the following note.

[86] V 16.2.11, Huber 3.41.16; B 161; Wessels para 4260; *Colonial Government v Edenborough and Another* (1886) 4 SC 290 at 296; *Divine Gates & Co v African Clothing Factory* 1930 CPD 238 at 242; *JR & M Moffett (Pty) Ltd v Kolbe Eiendoms Beleggings (Edms) Bpk and Another* 1974 (2) SA 426 (O); *Standard Bank of SA Ltd v SA Fire Equipment (Pty) Ltd and Another* 1984 (2) SA 693 (C) at 696G-H, 698B-C and 701A-B; *Inter Industria Bpk v Nedbank Bpk en 'n Ander* 1989 (3) SA 33 (NC) at 41E-F. Cf V 16.2.7; D 45.2.10 (dealing with joint and several debtors and creditors).

[87] B 181; Wessels para 4260.
[88] V 16.2.2, P 599.
[89] V 16.2.11; B 187.
[90] V 16.2.2, Cr 3.40.7; Huber 3.41.8.9; P 599; Lee ad Cr 349, Wessels paras 2492 *et seq*, 4261.
[91] *Postmaster General v Taute* 1905 TS 582 at 590.
[92] 1965 (4) SA 458 (C) at 464.
[93] V 16.2.2 p 599

tiff's claim until judgment is given in the claim in reconvention. The question that has arisen on several occasions is whether a surety could bring himself within the words of the rule and raise this dilatory plea when sued by the creditor in the circumstances set out above. In *JR & M Moffett (Pty) Ltd v Kolbe Eiendoms Beleggings (Edms) Bpk and Another*[94] Erasmus J held that the benefit of Rule 22(4) was confined to defendants who had filed counterclaims of their own. It was not available to a surety who seeks to rely on the debtor's counterclaim. However, in two later High Court decisions, *Standard Bank of SA Ltd v SA Fire Equipment (Pty) Ltd and Another*[95] and *Inter Industria Bpk v Nedbank Bpk en 'n Ander*,[96] the contrary view was taken. Rose-Innes J in the *Standard Bank of SA Ltd* case said that: 'To the extent that a surety and co-debtor has in his own right all the defences *in rem* of the principal debtor, a counterclaim giving rise to set-off upon judgment being granted is as much a defence "of the defendant" whether the defendant referred to is the principal debtor or the surety and co-debtor sued in the same action.'[97]

This question was thoughtfully considered but left open by the Supreme Court of Appeal in *Muller and Others v Botswana Development Corporation Ltd*.[98] But Mpati JA (with whom Howie and Lewis JJA agreed) indicated that he found 'the view taken by Rose-Innes J in the *Standard Bank* case...more attractive'.[99] It is submitted that the *Standard Bank* interpretation of rule 22(4) must now be considered the orthodox one. It has the advantage of 'avoiding a multiplicity of consecutive actions and cross-actions between the same parties'; it must be more sensible to adjudicate on all the claims of the parties *inter se* in the same proceedings.[100]

(k) Merger between principal debtor and creditor

Merger (*confusio*), ie 'the concurrence of the debtor and creditor in the same person in respect of the same obligation',[101] operates by force of law to discharge a surety in certain circumstances. The merger operates when the claim of the creditor against the principal debtor becomes vested in the debtor.[102] For example, the debtor may become entitled to receive the creditor's claim from the executor of the creditor's estate by virtue of a bequest or inheritance. The debtor is then discharged, since he cannot be both creditor and debtor in respect of the same debt. Since the debtor's obligation is thus extinguished, the surety's accessory obligation must also be extinguished and thus the surety is discharged.

---

[94] 1974 (2) SA 426 (O).
[95] 1984 (2) SA 693 (C).
[96] 1989 (3) SA 33 (NC).
[97] At 701A.
[98] 2003 (1) SA 651 (SCA) discussed more fully by JT Pretorius in 2003 *Annual Survey* 285-7.
[99] Para 11
[100] The cited words come from Rose-Innes J's judgment at 699B. In the *Botswana Development Corporation* case Mpati JA held (para 11) that, even where the counterclaim was made in a different forum (*in casu* Bostwana) so there were parallel proceedings, the court might exercise its discretion under rule 22(4).
[101] *Grootchwaing Salt Works Ltd v Van Tonder* 1920 AD 492 at 497.
[102] v 46.3.19; Huber 3.41.1; B 253, 255.

Although in strict law a debtor cannot be surety for himself, should there be 'merger'[103] between debtor and surety in respect of a natural principal obligation, the surety is not discharged.[104] This 'indulgence' is presumably to ensure that the creditor is not left without any claim at all after the 'merger'. In the more usual case, in which the surety steps into the shoes of a debtor who owes an enforceable obligation, the suretyship falls away. The surety is no longer entitled to the suretyship benefits,[105] but the securities given by him continue to be available to the creditor.[106]

Similarly, one person cannot be both creditor and surety for a particular debt. Thus if the creditor's claim becomes vested in the surety, the principal debt remains intact[107] but the creditor/surety claims as a creditor, not as a surety.

Where one co-creditor succeeds to another co-creditor, there is no effect on the principal debt; and the rule is the same for co-debtors.[108] A surety for co-debtors who are liable in solidum is not released if one of the co-debtors is involved in a 'merger' with another.[109] A co-surety, however, enjoys the benefit of the discharge of another co-surety's liability by merger, to the extent that he is relieved of liability for the other's aliquot share of the debt.[110] A 'merger' between co-sureties, however, does not affect the suretyship.[111]

(l) Prescription of principal debt

Prescription of the principal debt will (in terms of the Prescription Act 68 of 1969) extinguish that debt and thereby release the surety. This follows from the principle that the suretyship is accessory to the principal debt and that after its extinction there is nothing to support the suretyship.[112] Alternatively, section 10(2) provides

---

[103] The inverted commas indicate that 'merger' here is being used in a wide sense. It is not restricted to those cases in which one person becomes debtor and creditor in respect of the same obligation, but includes cases such as the one mentioned in the text: The debtor and the surety becoming the same person, eg by *delegatio*. Many of the texts deal with the position where, say, the debtor and the surety become one through the surety succeeding to the debtor or vice versa; but with the present-day system of administration of estates, this no longer occurs.

[104] v 46.3.20, Wessels para 2622.

[105] v 46.3.20, Huber 3.41.5. Note that this is a true merger. When a surety is released, his surety (achterborg) is also released (V 46.3.20; P 383, 406; Wessels para 2621). If a surety acquires the claim of the creditor and thus ceases to be surety, and subsequently cedes his claim to a third person, the suretyship is not ipso facto revived (*Cape Times Ltd v Goldsmid* 1913 WLD 17).

[106] V 46.3.20, Huber 3.41.5.

[107] V 46.3.21, P 383, B 255, 256, Wessels paras 2624, 4368.

[108] V 46.3.24.

[109] V 46.3.22.

[110] *Meer v General Industrial Credit Corporation (Pty) Ltd* 1947 (4) SA 330 (C) at 339.

[111] V 46.3.25; P 383, 406.

[112] *ABSA Bank Bpk v De Villiers* 2001 (1) SA 481 (A) and *Leipsig v Bankorp Ltd* 1994 (2) SA 128 (A) are examples of the prescription of the principal debt releasing the surety. Both turn on the application of section 13 (1) of the Prescription Act 1969 (which specifies the impediments that suspend the running of prescription until one year after the cessation of the impediment). They establish that, where the impediment is the filing of a claim against the insolvent estate of the principal debtor or against a company in liquidation (section 13(1)(g)), that impediment ceases on the confirmation of the first and final liquidation and distribution account. One year thereafter the principal debt prescribes; and if action has not by then been taken against the surety, he will be released.

that a subsidiary debt which arose from the principal debt will be extinguished at the same time as the principal debt.[113]

It has long been supposed that interruption of prescription against the debtor also interrupted prescription against the surety. C 8.39(40).4(5), Voet 46.1.36 and the decided cases prior to 1983[114] all favoured or seemed to favour this view. The result was that should, for instance, the creditor obtain judgment against the debtor but not the surety, the surety might find himself saddled with liability to pay for thirty years —the prescription period for judgment debts—even though he might have had no notice at all of the action against the debtor and had assumed that the debt which he secured had long since been paid or prescribed. This same question clearly arises in other contexts too. Thus the question arises whether an acknowledgement of debt by the debtor (which interrupted prescription against the debtor) also interrupted prescription against the surety and whether when prescription of the principal debt is suspended in accordance with the provisions of section 13(1)*(g)* of the Prescription Act, 1969, it is also suspended against the surety.

The late Professor JC de Wet argued for many years that it is unfair to the surety that interruption of prescription against the principal debtor also interrupted prescription against the surety;[115] and his view was accepted in *Rand Bank Ltd v De Jager*.[116] In this case Baker J, after a thorough analysis of the problem including an extensive review of the old authorities, came to the conclusion that C 8.39(40).4(5) (which holds that the interruption of prescription against one co-debtor also interrupts prescription against the other co-debtors), properly interpreted, did not apply to sureties but only to co-debtors *in solidum*; and thus that Voet 46.1.36, who relies on this passage, does not state the common law correctly when he says that 'an obligation against a surety is prolonged by a demand which was made on the principal debtor'.[117]

In the result the learned judge found that the taking of judgment against the debtor and one surety, unbeknown to the second surety, did not interrupt prescription against the second surety.

---

[113] Straightforward applications of this are found in *Volkskas Spaarbank Bpk v Van Aswegen* 1990 (3) SA 978 (A) and *Bankorp Ltd v Hendler and Hendler* 1992 (4) SA 375 (W).

[114] *Cronin v Meerholz* 1920 TPD 403; *Union Government v Van der Merwe* 1921 TPD 318 at 320; *Volkskas Bpk v The Master* 1975 (1) SA 69 (T). It may be doubted whether the common law was as clear as Voet and these cases suggest; after all, if this were so, it is difficult to see why the enactment of s 6(2) of the Prescription Act 18 of 1943, which enacts the rule under discussion, was necessary. The new Prescription Act 68 of 1969 contains no section similar to s 6(2). (See *Rand Bank Ltd v De Jager* 1982 (3) SA 418 (C) at 424C-H and the authorities mentioned in the following note.)

[115] *De Wet en Van Wyk Die Suid-Afrikaanse Kontraktereg en Handelsreg* 5 ed (1992) vol I by JC de Wet and GF Lubbe (ed) 399; JC de Wet in *Opiscula Miscellanea* (1979) by JJ Gaunlett (ed) at 129-30.

[116] 1982 (3) SA 418 (C).".

[117] Gane's translation. Voet also relied on D 45.1.91.4 but, as pointed out in *Rand Bank Ltd v De Jager* (at 451B), that perplexing text does not deal with the extension of the surety's period of prescription but with the replacement of the debtor's primary obligation with an obligation to pay damages where the debtor has put it out of his power to perform his own contract, ie it is not relevant to the prescription question.

Baker J's conclusion in *Rand Bank Ltd v De Jager* has long been controversial in the scholarly literature.[118] There were conflicting decisions in the provisional divisions[119] and the Supreme Court of Appeal was very cautious and did not let slip even an *obiter dictum* on the issue notwithstanding several opportunities to do so.[120] The view taken in earlier editions of this book was that the rule laid down in *Rand Bank Ltd v De Jager* was to be preferred. Not only was it principled—recognizing that the principal debt and the surety's obligation were separate and distinct—but it was fairer as it did not saddle the innocent surety with an extended prescription period. This rule may be inconvenient to a creditor but the remedy lies in his own hands: when he acts against the principal debtor he must take steps to interrupt prescription against the surety too.

But when the Supreme Court of Appeal (in *Jans v Nedcor Bank Ltd*[121]) had squarely to confront the question of whether a surety's obligation could prescribe independently of the principal debtor's obligation, it overruled *Rand Bank v De Jager*. The court (Scott JA, Vivier ADP, Farlam, Mthiyane and Lewis JJA concurring) held that whatever criticisms of principle might be made of C 8.39(40).4(5) and Voet's interpretation thereof, it was Voet's interpretation that formed the basis of the South African law on this point.

It is clear though from the judgment as a whole that it rested upon policy not upon a particular interpretation of Justinian's legislation. Suretyship was 'bur-

---

[118] See Konrad M Kritzinger 'Prescription of Suretyship for a Judgment Debt' (1983) 100 *SALJ* 35; 'Curious'(1983) 100 *SALJ* 327; JGA Kruger, '*Rand Bank Ltd v De Jager* 1982 (3) SA 418 (C)' (1983) 100 *SALJ* 754 and CF Forsyth 'Suretyship and Prescription: a New Direction' (1984) 101 *SALJ* 237. See also FW Mostert 'Verjaring by 'n Borgskuld' 1981 *TSAR* 163. For discussion of the most recent cases see CF Forsyth 'Prescription, Suretyship and the Unwelcome Revival of Correality' (1999) 11 *SA Merc LJ* 384.

[119] Cases which follow *Rand Bank Ltd v De Jager* are: *Bank of the Orange Free State v Cloete* 1985 (2) SA 859 (EC) at 864F (interruption of prescription against the principal debtor by tacit admission does not interrupt prescription against the surety); *ABSA Bank v De Villiers* 1998 (3) SA 920 (O) (confirmed on appeal on other grounds: 2001 (1) SA 481 (A) (sequestration of the principal debtor's estate (which suspended the running of prescription against the debtor in terms of section 13(1)(g) of the Prescription Act 1969) did not suspend the running of prescription against the surety); *Commissioner for Customs and Excise v Standard General Insurance Company Ltd.* [1998] 4 All SA 46 (W); (1998) CLR 469(W) (Forsyth (1999)11 *SA Merc LJ* 384) (also raised whether liquidation of the principal debtor suspended the running of prescription against the surety) (judge after analysing the old authorities (cf Forsyth (1999) at 387-9 criticising reliance upon correality) agreed with the conclusion of Baker J). Cases which do not follow *Rand Bank v De Jager* are: *Jordan & Co Ltd v Hamant Bulsara* 1992 (4) SA 457 (EC) (the creditor sued the debtor (but not the surety) but when judgment unsatisfied sued the surety but more than three years after the debt fell due; *Rand Bank* followed). (The appeal was decided without considering the *Rand Bank v De Jager* 1996 (1) SA 805 (A)); *Nedcor Bank Ltd v Sutherland* 1998 (4) SA 32 (N)(a claim by a creditor against the insolvent estate of a principal debtor, which suspends the running of prescription against the debtor in terms of section 13(1)(g) of the Prescription Act, 1969, also suspends prescription against the surety) (judgment of Mthiyane J as he then was)).

[120] In *Kilroe-Daley v Barclays National Bank Ltd* 1984 (4) SA 609 (A) at 628D an unanimous Appellate Division said that 'nothing in this judgment must be read to mean that this Court agrees or disagrees with what is said in *Rand Bank Ltd v De Jager* ...'. In *ABSA Bank Bpk v De Villiers* 2001 (1) SA 481 (A) at 488F the unanimous court found it unnecessary to decide the question and left it open.. In *Bulsara v Jordan & Co Ltd* 1996 (1) SA 805 (A) at 811E the courts said 'the correctness [of *Rand Bank v De Jager*] does not arise for decision'. And in *Louw v WP (Kooperatief) Bpk* 1998 (2) SA 418 (A) at 427H the correctness of the decision was assumed for the purposes of argument 'sonder om dit enigsins te beslis'.

[121] 2003 (6) SA 646 (SCA).

densome' but undertaken freely by sureties. 'Once having done so', said Scott JA, sureties 'cannot expect to be entitled simply to disabuse their minds of the fortunes of the principal debtor's liability and then require the law to protect them'.[122] In modern conditions,[123] an adequate surety was often a condition for the making of the loan that was the principal obligation.[124] This close link between the principal debt and the suretyship justified Voet's principle that the obligations prescribed together. Voet's view was not unfair to sureties. On the contrary it was 'convenient and equitable'.[125] Thus the 'an interruption or delay in the running of prescription in favour of the principal debtor interrupts or delays the running of prescription in favour of the surety'.[126]

That suretyship is a burdensome obligation is not in doubt. Views may differ on whether the balance between the interests of the surety and those of the creditor were struck in the most appropriate place in *Jans v Nedcor Bank Ltd*. But the Supreme Court of Appeal has now spoken and spoken unequivocally. The issue that 'has been the subject of debate for centuries' must now be taken as settled.[127]

When in *Eley (formerly Memmel) v Lynn & Main Inc*[128] counsel sought to draw a distinction between cases of 'interruption and delay' and cases where judgment had been taken against the principal debtor (to which the principle of *Jans v Nedcor Bank Ltd* did not apply). Predictably this distinction was found to be 'illusory' and rejected (by Mthiyane JA).

Finally, on the question of prescription it may be noted that creditors often require sureties to bind themselves in ever wider terms. In particular, they may ask the surety to bind himself for 'all and any indebtedness from whatsoever cause arising and of whatsoever nature' between the principal debtor and the creditor. Such words are wide enough to include indebtedness arising from a judgment debt; and thus render irrelevant whether the principle of *Rand Bank Ltd v De Jager* applies or not.[129] For example, in *EA Gani (Pty) Ltd v Francis*[130] the surety had undertaken liability to the creditor in the very wide terms set out above in respect of the indebtedness incurred by the debtor, the lessee of a motor car, to

---

[122] Para 30.
[123] And one may add in ancient conditions too.
[124] The surety often being a director of the company or a member of a close corporation to which the loan was made.
[125] Para 30-31.
[126] Para 32.
[127] Para 1.
[128] 2008 (2) SA 150 (SCA).
[129] See also the discussion in Chapter VI on other grounds on which a widely phrased suretyship might be restricted.
[130] 1984 (1) SA 462 (T). Kritzinger (1983) 100 *SALJ* 35 at 37-40 argues that the suretyship in contention in *Rand Bank Ltd v De Jager* was itself wide enough to include the judgment debt and that this was overlooked in that case. This is also the basis on which *Jordan & Co Ltd v Hamant Bulsara* 1992 (4) SA 457 (E) can be defended. The surety there undertook liability 'in respect of goods sold and delivered [by the creditor] to the debtor ... or for any other debt arising out of such transactions'. These words seem wide enough to include a judgment debt arising out of the sale of such goods. This was in fact so held on appeal: *Bulsara v Jordan & Co Ltd* 1996 (1) SA 805 (A). For discussion see C Louw (1996) 59 *THRHR* 718. Contrast, however, *Metequity Ltd NO and Another v Heel* 1997 (3) SA 432 (W) distinguishing *Bulsara v Jordan & Co Ltd* and restricting it to prescription cases.

the creditor, the lessor of the car. The lessee failed to fulfil his obligations under the lease and judgment was taken against him by the lessor. The lessee did not pay and the lessor turned to the surety. The surety's plea of prescription (which was otherwise sound) failed on appeal. Goldstone and Kirk-Cohen JJ held that 'a final judgment creates an independent cause of action enforceable as such in a court of law ... [and that] new cause of indebtedness created by the judgment falls within the wide undertaking of the defendant and it is this very judgment debt which is the plaintiff's cause of action. That cause of action has not prescribed ... the appeal must succeed.'[131]

(m) Miscellaneous

The principal debtor cannot deprive the surety of his right to rely on a defence available to the debtor by refusing to avail himself of it or by undertaking not to do so or by ratifying the contract by which the debt would, but for the defence, have come into existence, or varying it to make it valid and effective, or by way of any other act which would have the effect, if permitted, to deprive the surety of his right.[132]

Furthermore, it appears that the surety cannot deprive the principal debtor of a defence or otherwise by refusing to raise that defence when sued by the creditor. Indeed, in a proper case an interim interdict *pendente lite* will issue preventing the surety from paying the creditor.[133]

3. Surety discharged: nature of his contract

(a) Payment of the principal debt by the surety

Payment, while it discharges the surety, does not discharge the debt.[134] Consequently, that debt may be ceded to the surety when the creditor gives him cession of actions. Payment of the debt by one co-surety does not extinguish the debt, but it does extinguish between the co-sureties the share of the surety who has paid.[135]

---

[131] At 466H-467D.

[132] Domat 1873; P 380; Wessels paras 3969-71, 4040. *Lewin & Adamstein v Burger* (1908) 18 CTR 160 at 164.

[133] *Inter Industria Bpk v Nedbank Bpk en 'n Ander* 1989 (3) SA 33 (NC) at 44F-45J. The debtor had an unliquidated claim for damages against the creditor which, if successful, would have extinguished the principal debt. In these circumstances, the debtor (and the surety (see above under 'set-off')) would have a dilatory plea to stay the surety's action until the other action had been determined. The court was also influenced by the need to avoid a multiplicity of actions.

[134] *African Guarantee & Indemnity Co Ltd v Thorpe* 1933 AD 330 at 336.

[135] *Meer v General Industrial Credit Corporation (Pty) Ltd* 1947 (4) SA 330 (C). Note in this regard *Traub v Barclays National Bank Ltd; Kalk v Barclays National Bank* 1983 (3) SA 619 (A). Here the estate of one co-surety agreed with the creditor, a bank, to pay the amount outstanding to the bank (to be held in a special account) provided the bank instituted action (at the estate's expense and under its direction) forthwith against the other co-sureties. (The motivation of the estate in so agreeing was to limit the accumulation of interest on the debt while that of the bank was to ensure one way or another payment of the full amount in due course.) The bank's action against the other co-sureties was resisted on the ground that the co-sureties were prejudiced by the agreement between the first co-surety and the bank. The agreement meant, the co-sureties alleged, that since the payment into the special account did not discharge the debt, they faced a claim for the full amount rather than a claim for a pro rata contribution. Moreover, they had lost the opportunity to treat with the bank

Payment by the surety to the debtor's trustee in insolvency does not effect payment to the creditor,[136] nor does payment by one co-surety to another co-surety.[137]

With or without any payment from the debtor or the surety, the creditor may release the surety or one or more co-sureties from the obligation; this has the effect of discharging those sureties.[138] This does not release the principal debtor, but it does release the remaining sureties to the extent of the aliquot shares of the sureties who have been released.[139]

(b) Effluxion of time

A surety who has bound himself for a fixed period of time is discharged at the end of that time unless his undertaking, properly interpreted, was to be bound for the debts of the principal debtor incurred within that time, or an undertaking to be responsible for any default by the debtor during that time.[140]

A surety who has given his undertaking for an indefinite period of time may terminate his liability by giving the creditor 'reasonable notice' provided he has not agreed otherwise. A notice of withdrawal need not be in writing.[141] However, deeds of suretyship commonly provide that the suretyship shall not be cancelled 'save with the written consent of the creditor'; such clauses are valid and not contrary to public policy.[142]

If the surety and the principal debtor agree that the surety's liability is to terminate at a particular time, the surety's liability to the creditor is not *ipso facto* terminated at that time; but the debtor is then bound to secure the surety's release at the agreed time.[143]

(c) Prejudice through a material alteration in the principal debt

The creditor's dealings with the principal debtor and the other sureties must not have the effect of prejudicing the surety. If they do the surety is released.[144] The scope, but not the existence, of this duty not to prejudice has become a matter

---

but faced a 'vengeful and remorseless foe'.

This was quite rightly rejected by Botha JA, who said that the 'fact that the agreement with the estate provided the bank with a motive for enforcing its claims against the appellants, which it might otherwise not have done, is obviously not the kind of prejudice envisaged by the rule that sureties are released by conduct of the creditor which is prejudicial to them. Nor is it legally relevant that the present litigation is controlled by the estate; the Bank could lawfully have ceded its claims against the appellants to anyone, including the estate ...' (at 633E-F).

[136] *Faure v Bosman* (1864) 5 Searle 9.
[137] See Chapter IV.
[138] VL 4.4.16; B 155.
[139] See Chapter X.
[140] See Chapter VI and Chapter VII.
[141] *Jenkins & Co v TN Price* (1903) 24 NLR 112.
[142] See *Botha (now Griessel) and Another v Finanscredit (Pty) Ltd* 1989 (3) SA 773 (A) discussed in more detail below under public policy.
[143] See Chapter XI.
[144] Wessels para 4295. As suggested in Chapter V, a party to a negotiable instrument whom the holder knows or comes to know is a surety, whether as the signatory of an aval or as an accommodation party, must also not be prejudiced by the holder's actions.

of somewhat vexed debate.[145] The Supreme Court of Appeal has twice lain down that there is no general 'prejudice principle' whereby any prejudice will release the surety. 'As a general proposition' said Olivier JA in *ABSA Bank Ltd v Davidson*[146] 'prejudice caused to the surety can only release the surety (whether totally or partially) if the prejudice is the result of a breach [by the creditor] of some or other legal duty or obligation. The prime sources of a creditor's rights, duties and obligations are the principal agreement and the deed of suretyship.' Thus where, as in this case, the prejudice was caused by conduct – extending an overdraft and the cashing of certain cheques – authorised by the principal obligation and the suretyship, the surety was not released. And in *Bock and Others v Duburoro Investments (Pty) Ltd*[147] Harms JA disapproved of the criticism in the fifth edition of this book made of the passage just cited and said: 'this judgment subscribes to the law as set out in the dictum of Olivier JA.'[148]

Amid this disagreement between the Supreme Court of Appeal and *Caney* several points are clear. First, if the creditor and the debtor agree to the novation of the principal debt then the surety will be released (unless he has undertaken to be bound even when the principal debt is novated).[149] This follows from classic and uncontroversial principles. Secondly, where, as in *Davidson*, the prejudicial conduct is authorised by the principal obligation or the suretyship itself, the surety is not released. This too follows from classic and uncontroversial principles. Thirdly, where the prejudicial conduct is prohibited by the terms of the suretyship or the principal debt the surety is released.[150] Thus if a creditor having agreed only to make an advance to the principal debtor against the signatures of two out of three named persons, in fact makes the advance against the signature of only one of them,[151] the surety is released (unless his agreement is obtained to this alteration to, or mode of creation of, the principal obligation).[152] This too follows from classic and uncontroversial principle.

---

[145] See *Spur Steak Ranch Ltd v Mentz* 2000 (3) SA 755 (C) and in particular *Fry and Another v First National Bank of South Africa Ltd* 1996 (4) SA 924 (C) at 928F - 931I where Van der Westhuizen J concluded that the duty was not ejected from the law as an aspect of the *exceptio doli* (see below section 4) but grew out of the duty of creditors to act in good faith towards sureties.

[146] 2000 (1) SA 1117 (A) at 1124I-J.

[147] 2004 (2) SA 242 (SCA). See the far-reaching criticism of this case by JT Pretorius in 2004 *Annual Survey* 268ff showing inter alia that *Caney* had not misunderstood the passages from Wessels cited below. See also JT Pretorius 'Prejudice and the Surety' (2005) 17 *SA Merc LJ* 381.

[148] At 253B-C, para 21.

[149] Above this chapter, Section II *(g)*.

[150] See the discussion below under *(f) Breach of contract with the surety*.

[151] *Fry and Another v First National Bank of South Africa Ltd* 1996 (4) SA 924 (C).

[152] Wessels para 4299. *De Beers Mining Board v Olsen* (1882) 1 HCG 103 at 110; *Colonial Government v Edenborough and Another* (1886) 4 SC 290 at 296; *Larkins and Green v Bok NO* (1886) 2 SAR 108; *Nathanson and Another v Dennill* 1904 TH 289 at 292; *Van Aswegen v Van Eetveld and Du Plessis* 1925 (2) PH A37 (C); *Brinkman v McGill* 1931 AD 303; *Irwin v Davies* 1937 CPD 442; *Schoeman v Moller* 1951 (1) SA 456 (O) at 955; *Vaid v Ameen* 1962 (2) PH A33 (N); *Peri-Urban Areas Health Board v The South British Insurance Co Ltd* 1966 (2) PH A66 (T); *Lategan and Another NNO v Boyes and Another* 1980 (4) SA 191 (T); *Minister of Community Development v SA Mutual Fire and General Insurance Co Ltd* 1978 (1) SA 1020 (W). Prejudice is judged at the time when the variation is made: *Vaid v Ameen* 1962 (2) PH A33 (N).

The only point of disagreement that remains is whether, when the suretyship is silent on the issue, the creditor remains under a duty not to act in his dealings with the principal debtor in a way that prejudices the surety. Is there, in other words, an implied duty not to prejudice (either to be viewed as one of the *naturalia* of suretyship or flowing from the creditor's duty of good faith to the surety)?[153]

There is ample authority for the view that there is such an implied duty[154] and many examples of it in operation. And as will be seen in the next section, it is well established that sureties are released when a creditor allows the debtor more time to pay (since that delays the surety's right of recourse). The question really is what is the scope and reach of this implied duty, and the Supreme Court of Appeal has as yet made little contribution to that resolution. The implied duty is not in fact denied by the SCA[155] but its reach is left inchoate. It may be suggested that the duty is only engaged when the prejudice is specific, ie the surety can show one of his rights (eg the right of recourse) that has been adversely affected.

Now to return to some less controversial aspects of the duty not to prejudice. The alteration in the obligation does not release the surety if the change is not prejudicial to the surety. For example, if the creditor takes additional sureties to make the obligation even more secure, he does not release the original surety.[156]

On the other hand, it is not necessary for the original obligation to be novated for the surety to be released,[157] although its effect is the same as novation.[158] The release of the surety does not extend to the amount which was due to be paid before the alteration or variation was made.[159] The alteration may arise either from express agreement between the debtor and the creditor, or tacitly from a course of dealing between the two.[160] Where the suretyship provides for the passing of a mortgage bond as security but is silent in relation to its terms, the inclusion in the mortgage bond of fair and reasonable terms is not an alteration sufficient to release the surety.[161] Moreover, even where the suretyship agreement contains a term renouncing the standard benefits and in addition 'all legal exceptions which could be pleaded against the validity of ... this ... suretyship', this does not amount to a renunciation of the right of the surety to raise the question of a material alteration when sued on the agreement.[162]

---

[153] As suggested in *Fry and Another v First National Bank of SA Ltd* 1996 (4) SA 924 (C).

[154] See the discussion by JT Pretorius 'Prejudice and the Surety' (2005) 17 *SA Merc LJ* 381.

[155] And even if it were the remarks in the two cases were clearly *obiter* since in both the prejudicial conduct was in fact authorised by the suretyships in question, so no novel principle was raised or decided. See the discussion in 2004 *Annual Survey* 273 ff (Pretorius).

[156] V 46.1.39; *Cens For* 1.4.17.27. But the release of a surety or other security will partially release the other sureties. See Chapter X.

[157] Wessels para 4298; *Van Aswegen v Van Eetveld and Du Plessis* 1925 (2) PH A37 (C); *Irwin v Davies* 1937 CPD 442 at 449, *Schoeman v Moller* 1951 (1) SA 456 (O) at 955-6.

[158] *Colonial Government v Edenborough and Another* (1886) 4 SC 290 at 296-7.

[159] This was common cause in *Schoeman v Moller* 1951 (1) SA 456 (O).

[160] *Irwin v Davies* 1937 CPD 442 at 448; and see *Colonial Government v Edenborough and Another* (1886) 4 SC 290.

[161] *Brinkman v McGill* 1931 AD 303 at 315.

[162] *Minister of Community Development v SA Mutual Fire and General Insurance Co Ltd* 1978 (1) SA 1020 (W).

(d) Prejudice through an extension of time

One of the most common variations in the original obligation is the granting by the creditor to the debtor of further time to pay. This has the effect of prejudicing the surety for he is deprived of his right of recourse which would normally arise on the due date.[163]

Although the old authorities are not entirely harmonious on the question of the effect of an extension of time, the law was laid down by the Appellate Division in *Estate Liebenberg v Standard Bank of South Africa Ltd*.[164] The central rule is that where the creditor gives the debtor more time in which to pay before the debt falls due, and time is of the essence, that amounts to a material alteration and releases the surety.[165] Unlike in English law, should the grant be made after the debtor is in *mora*, the surety is not released.[166] This is because the surety can avoid any prejudice in such circumstances by paying the debt when it falls due and exercising his right of recourse against the debtor.[167] Of course, should the grant of time form part of a transaction which amounts to a novation of the original obligation, the surety will be released. However, if the surety can show that, notwithstanding that the debtor has fallen into *mora*, the grant of time has prejudiced him, he will be released.[168]

(e) Prejudice through an agreement not to enforce

Some authorities hold that the surety will also be released by an agreement between the creditor and debtor that the creditor will not enforce the original obligation (*pactum de non petendo*).[169] This is doubtful since the surety would, if not released, retain his right of recourse against the debtor. A mere delay by the creditor in enforcing the obligation will not release the surety,[170] for unless he has so agreed, the creditor does not have a duty to be vigilant.[171] It is for the surety to

---

[163] *Vaid v Ameen* 1962 (2) PH A33 (N).

[164] 1927 AD 502 at 520 ff. See also B 197 and Wessels para 4318.

[165] Lee *ad Gr* 248; Wessels para 4324; *Estate Liebenberg v Standard Bank of South Africa Ltd* 1927 AD 502 at 526; *Schoeman v Moller* 1951 (1) SA 456 (O); *Business Buying & Investment Co Ltd v Linaae* 1959 (3) SA 93 (T); *Vaid v Ameen* 1962 (2) PH A33 (N).

[166] Wessels paras 4321, 4325; *Beer v Roach* 1950 (4) SA 370 (C) at 379, 382, 383.

[167] *Estate Liebenberg v Standard Bank of South Africa Ltd* 1927 AD 502 at 507.

[168] *Executors of Watermeyer v Executor of Watermeyer* (1870) 2 Buch 69 at 75; *Trustees of Port Elizabeth Bank v Ogilvie* (1866) 1 Roscoe 339 at 342; *London and South Africa Bank v Behrens* 1869 NLR 189 at 198; *Meyer v Coetzee* 1893 OR 25 at 29, 30; *Colonial Government v Edenborough and Another* (1886) 4 SC 290 at 297; *Du Plessis v Miller and Carlie* 1906 TS 150 at 152; *Lindley v Ward* 1911 CPD 21 at 283-4; *Eshte Liebenberg v Standard Bank of South Africa Ltd* 1927 AD 502 at 507-8; *Gould v Ekermans* 1929 TPD 96; *Haffajee v Ramdhani* 1947 (1) SA 823 (A) at 829; *Beer v Roach* 1950 (4) SA 370 (C) at 381; *Miller v Muller* 1965 (4) SA 458 (C) at 461.

[169] Inst 4.14.4; *Cens For* 1.4.17.28; P 380; Wessels paras 4039, 4239.

[170] Bell qq *Colonial Government v McDonald and Breda* (1836) 2 Menz 28 at 34-5; *Vermaak v Cloete* (1836) 2 Menz 35; *Rogerson NO v Meyer and Berning* (1837) 2 Menz 38 at 50; *Executors of Hoets v De Vos* (1837) 2 Menz 53; *Van der Byl v Munnik* (1845) 2 Menz 73 at 74; *De Beers Mining Board v Olsen* (1882) 1 HCG 103 at 111; *Colonial Government v Edenborough and Another* (1886) 4 SC 290 at 297; *Ridley v Anderson* 1911 EDL 13 at 16; *Colonial Treasurer v Swart* 1910 TPD 552 at 557, *Gould v Ekermans* 1929 TPD 96 at 99 *Theodore v Deaconos* 1958 (3) SA 807 (SR). See also *Finansbank Bpk v Klopper* 1981 (1) SA 106 (T) holding that it is not necessary for the creditor to give notice to the surety that the principal debtor has failed to pay.

[171] *Johannesburg Town Council v Union Assurance Society Ltd* 1928 AD 294 at 300.

ensure that the debtor is observing his obligations.[172] The result is that a positive act amounting to fault by the creditor is required for the release of the surety.[173]

If, however, the surety is a *fideiussor indemnitatis*, he is released if the creditor delays in pressing for payment and eventually fails to obtain payment for the reason that the debtor has become unable to pay.[174] Although the authorities are not unanimous,[175] it appears that this privilege is enjoyed only by the *fideiussores indemnitatis* and not by ordinary sureties with the benefit of excussion.

When there is delay in payment, the surety is not without remedies. He may, of course, pay the creditor himself and exercise his right of recourse against the principal debtor.[176] Moreover, the surety can also call on the creditor to sue the debtor if a long time has passed without the creditor doing anything about the debt. The creditor cannot be forced to sue the debtor, but a failure to heed the surety's call will lead to the release of the surety.[177] There is a dispute in the authorities whether a surety without the benefit of excussion can call on the creditor to sue in this way.[178] Alternatively, the surety can turn directly to the debtor, and bring proceedings against him to protect his own interests and with a view to his own discharge from liability.[179]

Naturally, the onus is on the surety to establish that he has been released by the alteration or variation in the terms of the obligation or the extension of time; and it is on the creditor to show that the surety consented to the variation or extension, if he wishes to rely on that fact.[180]

(f) Breach of contract with the surety

A further such class of case is that in which the surety is released because the creditor is in breach of a duty undertaken either expressly or impliedly in the suretyship, and that duty formed a condition upon which basis the surety has undertaken his obligations. For example, if the surety undertakes liability on the basis that the creditor will further secure his debt by taking a mortgage bond over the debtor's property, and the creditor fails to do this, the surety is entirely

---

[172] *Estate Smuts v Behrens* 1872 NLR 71 at 75.
[173] Whether the rule is different in the cases of avals was discussed but not decided in *Theodore v Deaconos* 1958 (3) SA 807 (SR). Once more this question was left open in *Finansbank Bpk v Klopper* 1981 (1) SA 106 (T) at 114-5.
[174] The reason for this is that it is the creditor's own fault that he cannot recover from the debtor, and the surety has only promised him the difference between what he ought with diligence to be able to obtain from the debtor and the amount owing. V 46.1.38; P 414; *Overbeek v Cloete* (1831) 1 Menz 523 at 524; *Colonial Treasurer v Swart* 1910 TPD 552 at 556-7.
[175] See V 46.1.38. Cf P 414. Wessels para 4097. *Ackerman v Colonial Government* 1869 NLR 155 at 159-61.
[176] V 46.1.38 *in fine;* B 199; Wessels para 4322; *Estate Liebenberg v Standard Bank of South Africa Ltd* 1927 AD 502 at 507.
[177] D 46.1.62, V 46.1.38, P 414; Cf *Ackerman v Colonial Government* 1869 NLR 155 at 159.
[178] *Overbeek v Cloete* (1831) 1 Menz 523 at 524. Cf Lee *ad Gr* 253.
[179] See Chapter XI.
[180] *Schonfrucht v King* 1934 (2) PH A35 (W); *Peri-Urban Areas Health Board v The South British Insurance Co Ltd* 1966 (2) PH A66 (T), *Schoeman v Moller* 1951 (1) SA 456 (O) at 957; *Vaid v Ameen* 1962 (2) PH A33 (N).

released, whether or not he has suffered prejudice.[181] If, however, the condition is solely for the benefit of the creditor, the surety cannot complain if it is not enforced.[182] Although the Master of the Supreme Court has a duty to supervise the administration of estates under his control, this duty is one imposed by statute. It is not a duty owed a surety who undertakes that the executor of a deceased estate will perform his duties properly. Consequently, if the Master is negligent in his supervision, this does not release the surety.[183]

4. Exceptional defences and their history: the reach of public policy and the Constitution

Prior to 1988 it was assumed on good authority[184] that the *exceptio doli generalis* was available in exceptional cases to the surety to resist the claims of the creditor. It was believed that a 'long stop' defence existed to protect the surety where the creditor sought to use the suretyship for a purpose never contemplated by the parties even though that claim might be supported by a strict reading of the contract. The limits of the defence were, however, unclear. Perhaps the clearest example of the operation of the defence was where the creditor seeks to hold the surety responsible for some subsequent and extraneous principal debt, which although apparently within the terms of a widely phrased suretyship, was never any part of the parties' purpose in contracting that such a debt should be secured.[185]

---

[181] *Larkins and Green v Bok NO* (1886) 2 SAR 108 (undertaking that guaranteed auctioneers would sell for cash only; creditor permitting credit sales); *Texas Co (SA) Ltd v Webb and Tomlinson* 1927 NPD 24 (guarantee of payment of price of stated quantity of goods, supply of which not to be exceeded); but compare *Rudd, Milton & Co v Dolley & Co* (1884) 3 EDC 351; and see *Gould v Ekermans* 1929 TPD 96 (undertaking by creditors to use in paying the debt all moneys being collected by themselves for the debtor, breached by paying other creditors of the debtor); *Brinkman v McGill* 1931 AD 303 at 310 (mortgage bond to be, but not, obtained as security); *Irwin v Davies* 1937 CPD 442 at 450 ('first charge' to be, but not, obtained on book debts). And see *Minister of Community Development v SA Mutual Fire and General Insurance Co Ltd* 1978 (1) SA 1020 (W), *Administrator-General, South West Africa v Trust Bank of Africa Ltd* 1982 (1) SA 635 (SWA) (creditor failing to check that a builder had paid for materials used before making interim payments to him; builder's surety discharged) and *Standard Bank of SA Ltd v Cohen (2)* 1993 (3) SA 854 (SE) (no credit to be advanced before cession of book debts and advances not to exceed an agreed amount). In these last three cases the surety was in fact prejudiced.
[182] *Johannesburg Town Council v Union Assurance Society Ltd* 1928 AD 294.
[183] *The Master v General Accident, Fire and Life Assurance Corporation* 1935 CPD 389 at 396.
[184] *Rand Bank Ltd v Rubenstein* 1981 (2) SA 207 (W); *Oceanair (Natal) (Pty) Ltd v Sher* 1980 (1) SA 317 (D); *SAPDC (Trading) Ltd v Ferreira and Others* 1980 (3) SA 507 (T); *Neuhoff v York Timbers Ltd* 1981 (4) SA 666 (T) especially at 671D-673C. See also DH Botha 'Die *Exceptio Doli Generalis*, Rektifikasie en Estoppel' (1980) 43 *THRHR* 255, *Die Exceptio Doli Generalis in die Suid-Afrikaanse Reg* (1981) unpublished LLD thesis, University of the Orange Free State; JG Lotz 'Die Billikheid in die Suid-Afrikaanse Kontraktereg' (1979) unpublished inaugural lecture, University of South Africa and JT Pretorius 'Continuing Suretyships' (1988) 10 *Modern Business Law* 85.
[185] In *Rand Bank Ltd v Rubenstein* 1981 (2) SA 207 (W) such a case was described (at 214H) as 'tailor-made for the application of the general defence of the *exceptio doli*'.

Now, however, following the decision of the Appellate Division in *Bank of Lisbon and South Africa Ltd v De Ornelas and Another*[186] it has been held that the *exceptio doli generalis* never formed part of the Roman-Dutch law, notwithstanding several decisions of the Appellate Division holding or taking it for granted that it did form part of South African law.[187] The court said that 'the time had now arrived ... once and for all to bury the *exceptio doli generalis* as a superfluous, defunct anachronism. *Requiescat in pace*'.[188] The *De Ornelas* decision has been much criticised,[189] but it is the law. All things being equal, there a pressing need for some form of 'long stop' defence to ensure that the law does not become an engine of injustice.

One such alternative path to contractual equity has been to stress the importance of good faith in contract law. In a minority concurring judgment in *Eerste Nasionale Bank van Suidelike Afrika Bpk v Saayman NO*[190] Olivier JA based himself on the well recognised principle of good faith in contract which he considered had not been excluded by *Bank of Lisbon and South Africa Ltd v De Ornelas and Another*. Thus it was open to the courts in reliance on the principle of good faith to develop 'nuwe en billike regsreëls ... en regverdige oplossing vir probleme te vind waar die streng toepassing van bestaande regsreëls in 'n bepaalde situasie tot groot onbillikheid aanleiding sou gee'.[191] However, it has since become clear

---

[186] 1988 (3) SA 580 (A). What had happened was that the bank had extended overdraft facilities to a fishing company. The overdraft was secured by deeds of suretyship executed by the respondents (the joint managing directors of the company) in favour of the bank and mortgage bonds in favour of the bank passed over the respondents' dwellings. In due course the company discharged its entire indebtedness to the bank under the overdraft; and the respondents sought the cancellation of the deeds of suretyship and the mortgage bonds. However, the bank refused on the ground that it had an, as yet unsettled, claim for damages against the company arising from a forward purchase of foreign exchange which the company had, the bank alleged, unlawfully repudiated. In the deeds of suretyship the respondents had undertaken to stand surety for 'the due payment of every sum ... of money ... owing [by the company to the bank] from whatsoever cause or causes arising, and for the due performance of every other obligation, howsoever arising'. The bank relied on these words but the respondents contended that the foreign exchange transaction was not in the contemplation of the parties at the time they entered into the suretyship and securing such debts was not the purpose of the suretyship. Thus it would amount to *dolus* to enforce the strict words of the contract given that the company had discharged entirely its contemplated indebtedness to the bank.

(Compare the discussion in Chapter VI on how without reliance on the *exceptio doli* such very wide suretyships can be restricted.)

[187] *Weinerlein v Goch Buildings Ltd* 1925 AD 282; *Zuurbekom Ltd v Union Corporation Ltd* 1947 (1) SA 514 (A); *Paddock Motors (Pty) Ltd v Igesund* 1976 (3) SA 16 (A) at 27G-H (per Jansen JA).

[188] At 607B per Joubert JA; Rabie ACJ, Hefer and Grosskopf JJA concurring-Jansen JA dissenting.

[189] The detailed criticism of *De Ornelas* will be found in the 5th ed of *Caney* at 211 especially n 175. See also, Carole Lewis 'Demise of the *Exceptio Doli*; Is there Another Route to Contractual Equity?' (1990) 107 *SALJ* 26; SWJ van der Merwe, GF Lubbe and LF van Huyssteen 'The *Exceptio Doli Generalis*: *Requiescat in Pace – Vivat Aequitas*' (1989) 106 *SALJ* 235; JT Pretorius 'Continuing Suretyships' (1988) 10 *MB* 85; Michael A Lambiris 'The *Exceptio Doli Generalis*: An Obituary' (1988) 105 *SALJ* 644; L Hawthorne and Ph J Thomas 'The *Exceptio Doli*' (1989) 22 *De Jure* 143. See further R Zimmermann, 'Good Faith and Equity' in *Southern Cross: Civil Law and Common Law in South Africa* (1996) Reinhard Zimmermann and Daniel Visser (eds), 217-260, especially 255-260.

[190] 1997 (4) SA 302 (A). See Van der Merwe *et al* (1989) 106 *SALJ* 235 for earlier suggestions that greater reliance on the concept of *bona fides* to introduce equity into the law. And see Lewis (1990) 107 *SALJ* 26.

[191] At 320E.

from several later decisions of the Supreme Court of Appeal (*Brisley v Drotsky*[192] and *Afrox Healthcare Bpk v Strydom*[193]) that the abstract values of good faith, reasonableness and equity were not independent substantive rules that courts can employ to intervene in contractual relationships in the way envisaged by Olivier JA.[194] While these values might perform 'creative, informative and controlling functions through the established rules of contract law they cannot be acted upon by the courts directly'. Moreover, the Supreme Court of Appeal has held that 'experience has shown that acceptance of the notion that judges can refuse to enforce a contractual provision, merely because it offends their personal sense of fairness and equity, gives rise to intolerable legal and commercial uncertainty'.[195] The simple result is that good faith does not offer an escape in circumstances in which the strict application of the agreed terms in the particular circumstances 'tot groot onbillikheid aanleiding sou gee'.

All that remains as an exceptional defence in the kind of circumstance envisaged above is public policy. Indeed, in his dissent in *De Ornelas* Jansen JA envisaged that public policy might play such a role here.[196] And so it has proved, for in recent years public policy has been frequently raised as an exceptional defence by sureties. The courts continue to recognise the need for a defence of last resort to be raised - not to allow sureties to escape from obligations freely undertaken, but to prevent the law of contract being transformed into an engine of injustice. We shall turn shortly to consider how the principle of public policy has been applied in the context of suretyship.

But it is important to note first that the concept of public policy has itself been in the process of transformation through the influence of constitutional values. As Brand JA has remarked extra-curially, the Supreme Court of Appeal has 'employed the concept of public policy as the doctrinal gateway for the import of constitutional values into the law of contract'.[197] Where a contractual term is in conflict with a constitutional value that term will be found to be contrary to public policy and unenforceable.[198] As Ngcobo J said in *Barkhuizen v Napier:*[199] 'In my view, the proper approach to the constitutional challenges to contractual terms is to determine whether the term challenged is contrary to public policy as evidenced by the constitutional values, in particular, those found in the Bill of Rights. This approach leaves space for the doctrine of *pacta sunt servanda* to oper-

---

[192] 2002 (4) SA 1 (SCA), Harms, Streicher and Brand JJA paras 22–25. Note the dissent of Olivier JA.

[193] 2002 (6) SA 21 (SCA) Brand JA para 32.

[194] See further, particularly, Brand JA's valuable article 'The Role of Good Faith, Equity and Fairness in the South African Law of Contract: The Influence of the Common Law and the Constitution' (2009) 126 *SALJ* 71. See also his contribution 'Good Faith in Contract Law' in Reinhard Zimmermann, Daniel Visser and Kenneth Reid (eds) *Mixed Legal Systems in Comparative Perspective* (2004) at 94ff. Contrast the majority of the Supreme Court of Appeal in *NBS Boland Bank Ltd v One Berg River Drive CC* 1999 (4) SA 928 (A) (clause allowing mortgagee to increase interest rate valid but power to increase rate must be exercised reasonably).

[195] This quotation and that in the preceding sentence come from Brand JA's article at 81.

[196] At 617G.

[197] Brand, op cit 84.

[198] *Barkhuizen v Napier* 2006 (4) SA 1 (SCA) and see the same case in the Constitutional Court: *Barkhuizen v Napier* 2007 (5) SA 323 (CC).

[199] 2007 (5) SA 323 (CC) para 30.

ate, but at the same time allows courts to decline to enforce contractual terms that are in conflict with the constitutional values even though the parties may have consented to them.'

The result of this is that it will now be possible to rely upon constitutional values as a defence of last resort. Access to the courts, equality and dignity, individual autonomy and the like are likely to be the kind of constitutional value upon which reliance may be placed in the future.

No suretyship cases have as yet been decided in reliance upon constitutional values.[200] But the non-constitutional test for whether a particular clause will be found to be contrary to public policy will not lead, it is believed, to significant differences of outcome: constitutional values were already largely immanent within in the principles of public policy. But there may be differences in particular cases; thus the account of reliance upon public policy in a non-constitutional context in the suretyship cases that follows must be read subject to that caveat.

In *Botha (now Griessel) and Another v Finanscredit (Pty) Ltd,*[201] the test of public policy was considered in the context of suretyship, Hoexter JA (following the approach of Smalberger JA in *Sasfin (Pty) Ltd v Beukes*[202]) said the court should consider whether the clause was 'clearly inimical to the interest of the community, whether they are contrary to law or morality, or run counter to social or economic expedience', but should bear in mind '*(a)* that, while public policy generally favours the utmost freedom of contract, it nevertheless properly takes into account the necessity for doing simple justice between man and man; and *(b)* that a court's power to declare contracts contrary to public policy should be exercised sparingly and only in cases in which the impropriety of the transaction and the element of public harm are manifest.'[203] And in *Standard Bank of SA Ltd v Wilkinson*[204] a strong Provincial Division stressed in addition that the 'harm to the public must be substantially incontestable'. Moreover, regard should be had to the commercial context in which suretyships operate and that they are by their nature burdensome.[205] Although sometimes not fully appreciated,[206] it is clear that a public policy challenge does not offer 'a free pardon for recalcitrant ... debtors'.[207] Most challenges to clauses in contracts of suretyship on the ground of public policy have failed.

---

[200] For examples of the constitutional approach see *Barkhuizen v Napier, supra,* as well as *Brisley v Drotsky, supra,* and *Afrox Healthcare Bpk v Strydom, supra.*

[201] 1989 (3) SA 773 (A) in reliance on *Sasfin (Pty) Ltd v Beukes* 1989 (1) SA 1 (A) which also raised public policy but which was a case on cession not suretyship.

[202] 1989 (1) SA 1 (A).

[203] At 782I-783C.

[204] 1993 (3) SA 822 (C) at 826F-828G (per Tebbutt, Scott and Brand JJ).

[205] At 828I pointing out in reliance on earlier editions of this book (Chapter One, section 1 and 2) that the surety was 'born as a hostage' and his obligation was inherently burdensome.

[206] For instance, in *D Engineering Co (Pty) Ltd v Morkel and Others* (TPD 27 March 1992 (A813/91) reported in 3 *Commercial Law Digest* 228 (T). Here the judge used the much less onerous tests of whether the clauses attacked went 'beyond the reasonable business requirements of suretyship' or whether there was a 'commercial justification', for them or whether they made 'unnecessary inroads on a surety's rights'.

[207] Per Kriegler J in *Donelly v Barclays National Bank Ltd* 1990 (1) SA 375 (W) at 381F-G.

It is now necessary to outline some of the common provisions in suretyships which have survived challenge and which have not.

Botha (now Griessel) and Another v Finanscredit (Pty) Ltd concerned primarily a clause which provided that the suretyship 'shall not be cancelled save with the written consent of the creditor'. It was challenged on the ground that it was contrary to public policy. In the event Hoexter JA (with whom Nestadt and Milne JJA as well as Grosskopf and Nicholas AJJA agreed) decided that the clause was not contrary to public policy. It was commercially sound and morally unexceptionable that the sureties should be bound until the principal debtor no longer owed money to the creditor or alternative sureties acceptable to the creditor had been found. Moreover, the clause did not leave the surety 'helpless in the clutches of the plaintiff'; ie if the surety paid the principal debt the suretyship would fall away notwithstanding the clause. A clause of this nature was upheld in the context of landlord and tenant by the majority in *Brisley v Drotsky.*

Ex parte Minister of Justice: in Re Nedbank Ltd v Abstein Distributors (Pty) Ltd and Others and *Donelly v Barclays Bank Ltd*[208] related to a clause which laid down that 'a certificate of balance' provided by the creditor 'shall be ... conclusive proof of the amount of ... [the] indebtedness' of the principal debtor and due from the surety. The validity of a similar clause in a cession case was one of the issues in *Sasfin (Pty) Ltd v Beukes* and Smalberger JA said that such 'clauses purport to oust the Court's jurisdiction to enquire into the validity or accuracy of the certificate, to determine the weight to be attached thereto or to entertain any challenge directed at it other than on the ground of fraud. As such they run counter to public policy ...'.[209] After some conflicting views were expressed in the provincial divisions,[210] it is now clear that a conclusive proof clause in a suretyship contract is *contra bonos mores* and invalid.[211] It is anticipated that the access to justice provisions of the Constitution (section 34) would strengthen this result were the matter to be approached on a constitutional basis.

---

[208] 1995 (3) SA 1 (A).

[209] At 15A.

[210] *Nedbank Ltd v Van der Berg and Another* 1987 (3) SA 449 (W) (such a clause was simply 'designed to facilitate proof and did not oust the court's jurisdiction') and *Standard Bank of SA Ltd v Neugarten and Others* 1987 (3) SA 695 (W) (clause valid in the absence of fraud); *Donelly v Barclays National Bank Ltd* 1990 (1) SA 375 (W) (conclusive proof clause not contrary to public policy); *Re Nedbank Ltd v Abstein Distributors (Pty) Ltd* 1989 (3) SA 750 (T) (conclusive proof clause contrary to public policy). There have been many cases challenging a range of very various clauses in the Provincial Divisions. The outcomes of these cases are set out in tabular form in the previous edition of this book.

[211] *Ex parte Minister of Justice: in Re Nedbank Ltd v Abstein Distributors (Pty) Ltd and Others* and *Donelly v Barclays Bank Ltd* 1995 (3) SA 1 (A) per MT Steyn JA in a powerful judgment, rejecting all counter arguments, and relying on the persuasive article by Kerr (1993) 110 *SALJ* 668 and Hutchinson (1990) 107 *SALJ* 414.

General Index

ACCESSORY NATURE OF SURETYSHIP, 27-30, 32, 34 fn32, 35-7, 38, 59, 63 fn16, 89, 100 fn78, 110, 113 fn82, 115 fn95, 147, 155, 187, 191, 192 fn29, 199, 200
    essentials of, 27-8
    in Roman law, 6–20, 103
    in Roman-Dutch law, 27
ACCOMMODATION NOTES, *see* NEGOTIABLE INSTRUMENTS
ACHTERBORG (FIDEIUSSOR FIDEIUSSORUS), 60, 141, 144, 168, 174, 200 fn105
    contribution, right to, 174
    co-sureties, 60, 141, 144, 168
    division, benefit of, 141, 144, 174
    Hadrian's rescript, 16
    recourse, right of, 168
    release, 200 fn105
ACTIO MANDATI, 9-17, 31, 159
ACTIO MANDATI CONTRARIA 109
    fidepromissio, in, 9, 14
    mandatum credendae pecuniae, no relation to, 31
    origin of, 9 fn41
    recourse, right of, basis of, 14
        and see RECOURSE, RIGHT OF
ACTIO NEGOTIORUM GESTIO, 14, 17, 31, 62, 159
    and see RECOURSE, RIGHT OF, SURETY'S
ACTIONES
    constitutoria, 19
    de pecunia constituta, 9
    depensi, 8-9
    mandati, see *ACTIO MANDATI*
    sacramenti in personam, 5
    sacramenti in rem, 5
ARTIFICIAL PERSONS
    surety, as, 52-4
AUTHENTICA SI QUA MULIER, see WOMEN'S SURETYSHIP BENEFITS
AVALS, *see* NEGOTIABLE INSTRUMENTS

BENEFICIA
    renunciation of, *see* RENUNCIATION OF BENEFITS
BENEFICIUM CEDENDARUM ACTIONUM, 15, 84 fn102, 146, 155, 157
    and see BENEFIT OF CESSION OF ACTIONS
BENEFICIUM JURIS, STATUTI VEL CONSUETUDINIS, 134
BENEFICIUM ORDINIS VEL EXCUSSIONIS,
    see BENEFIT OF EXCUSSION

BENEFIT OF CESSION OF ACTIONS, 145
    advantages of, 152
    aval entitled to, 84 fn102
    co-debtor, rights of, 149, 152, 167
    contract *ad factum praestandum,* under, 43
    co-surety, release of a, effect, 155-6, 205
    creditor's duty to give cession, 146, 148, 154,
        tender unnecessary, 154
    dilatory defence, 146
    effects, 148,
    equitable foundation, 147
    exceptio cedendarum actionum, 146, 155, 157
    excussion, benefit of, after, 149
    extent of benefit, against co-sureties, 149
    inability to give cession, 155
    interest, 152-3
    Justinian's law, in, 16
    Natal statute, Law of, 25 fn195, 131, 155, 172 fn9
    subsequent cession, effect, 147
    principles, 145-6
    release,
        co-debtor, of, effect, 155, 194
        co-surety, of, effect, 155-6
        debtor, of, effect, 155, 194
        renunciation, of, effect, 158
    right of benefit,
        surety's, 146, 148
        compromise of debt, 155
    how exercised, 142
    payment a condition precedent, 142
    rights which pass, 153
    securities pass with cession, 15, 148-9, 152
    surety and co-principal debtor, 56, 154
    surety's right to benefit, 146, 151
    and see CESSION OF ACTIONS
BENEFIT OF DIVISION, 133, 138
    achterborgen (fideiussor fideiussoris), 116, 60
    apuleia, lex, compared with, 9, 15
    avals, 143
    cession of actions, after, 140, 148-9
    co-debtors, sureties for separate, 141
    conditional surety, 141
    contract to regulate *inter se,* 145, 151-2
    co-sureties, available to, 55, 138
    death of co-surety, effect, 144
    division, method of,

BENEFIT OF DIVISION *(continued)*
    provisional, 141
    time for effecting, 144
    voluntary, by creditor, 139
exceptions to, 141-4
exclusion from division, 141
    absent co-surety, 140
    impecunious co-surety, 139
    indivisible obligation, 143
    insolvent co-surety, 139
    judgment, sureties for payment of, 143
    onus, 139
    pauper co-surety, 139
false denial of suretyship, 144
furia, lex, 9, 10, 12-16
guardians' sureties, 143
Hadrian's rescript, 16, 18, 20, 138-9
    constitutum, extended to by Justinian, 21
    fideiussio fideiussoris, not applicable to, 16
    lex ciciffeia, lex cicereia principles applied to supplement, 16
    lex furia, compared with, 16
    mandatum credendae pecuniae, applicable to, 18
indivisible obligation, 143
method of division, 139
minor,
    creditor, 140
    co-surety, 140
not entitled
    false denial of suretyship, 144
    guardians, sureties for, 143
    indivisible obligations, sureties for, 143
    judgment, sureties for, 143
    public revenue, sureties for, 143
    separate co-debtors, sureties for, 141
    specified portion of debt, sureties for, 141
origin of, 138
payment, over, by co-surety, 141
plead, necessary to, 16, 138
positive action, necessary, 138
principal debtors, no division with, 144
principles, 138
provisional division, 141
public revenue, surety for, 141
renunciation, 142
    express, 142
    implied, 142

BENEFIT OF DIVISION, renunciation, implied *(continued)*
      judgment, consent to, not, 138
    Roman law, in, 23
    specific terms required, 142
  security for impecunious debtor, 139
  surety and co-principal debtor, 56, 141
  time,
    claiming division, 138
  surety bound from future date, 141
  voluntary division by creditor, 139
BENEFIT OF EXCUSSION, 125
  abandonment of right to, 134
  absent debtor, 125
  aval entitled, 132
  cession of actions, effect, 148
  co-debtors, excussion of, 128
  costs, 116
  co-sureties 133-5
  dilatory defence, 127
  exceptions to benefit,
    absent debtor, 126
    impecunious debtor, 129
    minor debtor, 132
    moratorium to debtor, 132
    natural obligation, 132
    surety hindering, 132
  excussion, manner of, *see* EXCUSSION
  false denial, effect of, 132
  fideiussor indemnitatis cannot renounce, 133
  illiquid debt, 133
  impecunious debtor, 129
  liquid document, 133
  mandatum credendae pecuniae, applied to, 18-19
  manner of excussing, *see* EXCUSSION
  minor debtor, 132
  moratorium, 132
  Natal Law, repeal of, 131
  natural obligation, 132
  novation, effect of, 133
  Novels, Justinian's, 17
  origin of, 17
  Placaat February, 128
  plead, necessary to, 127
  procedure, 127
  provisional sentence, 125
  renunciation,

BENEFIT OF EXCUSSION, renunciation *(continued)*
    aval, not, 132-3
    contemporaneous, need not be, 131
    express, not general, 130
    fideiussio indemnitatis cannot renounce, 133
    implied, 131, 142
    judgment, surety for performance, 131
    penal bond, 131
    surety and co-principal debtor, 56, 57, 131
    set-off, effect, 133
  surety and co-principal debtor, 56, 57, 131
  surety hindering or obstructing excussion, 132
  surety without benefit, position of, 132
  and see EXCUSSION
BILLS OF EXCHANGE, *see* NEGOTIABLE INSTRUMENTS
BUILDING CONTRACT
  form of suretyship penal bond, 131
  suretyship for performance, 106

CERTIFICATE OF INDEBTEDNESS, 114
CERTIFICATE OF BALANCE, 214
  public policy and, 214
  validity of clause, providing for conclusive proof thereby, 214
CESSION
  creditor's right to cede, 148
  form of, 154
  negotiable instruments, of, 154-5
  rights against pass, 153
  principal debt, of, 47-8
  creditor's right to cede, 148
  suretyship, effect on, 47-8
  and see BENEFIT OF CESSION OF ACTIONS *and* CESSION OF ACTIONS
CESSION OF ACTIONS
  advantages over right of recourse and right to contributions, 15, 145-6, 152, 160, 171-2
  benefit of division, when available, 138ff
  benefit of excussion, 149
  co-debtors
    liability of, 147, 151
    rights of, 149, 167
  co-surety
    benefit of division, when available, 138ff
    insolvent, 156
    liability of, 147-8
    release of, effect, 155-6, 205

CESSION OF ACTIONS *(continued)*
   creditor
      cession of claim by, effect on suretyship, 47-50
      duty to give cession, 145-6, 148, 154
      inability to give, effects, 155
      right to give to anyone, 148
   defences still available, 149
   effects of, 148
      aliquot share of prayer, on, 149
   express, 154
   inability to give cession, 155
   insolvent co-surety, effect, 156
   preference passes with, 148, 153
   securities pass with cession, 148
   'subject to equities', 148
   and see BENEFIT OF CESSION OF ACTIONS *and* CESSION
CO-DEBTORS
   cession of actions, right to, 148, 167
   co-debtors, claim against, 148
   division, benefit of, 138
   excussion of, 128
   liability, generally joint, 55
   merger, effect, 199
   release of one, effect, 155
   rights, *inter se*, 55, 152, 149
   surety for one, rights of, 167
   surety's rights, 148, 152, 198
   recourse, right of, 167
CLOSE CORPORATION
   capacity, 52
   surety, as, 52
COMPANY
   capacity, 52
   principal debtor, as, unregistered, 39
   surety, as, 52
COMPOSITION 189, 194, 195
   composition under Companies Act, 197
   composition under Insolvency Act, 197
COMPROMISE
   cession of actions, when entitles, 154
   effect on suretyship, 197
   right of recourse, effect on, 162-3
   right to contribution, effect on, 183
CONDICTIO INDEBITI, 175
CONDITIONAL SURETYSHIP, 85, 105
   condition precedent, 85

CONDITIONAL SURETYSHIP *(continued)*
   constitutum, 17ff
   co-surety, 141
   fideiussio, 13-14
   fideiussio indemnitatis, 14
   liability, 149
   performance, condition for, 85-6, 103, 105
CONSTITUTUM 12, 17-22
   and see PACTUM DE CONSTITUTO
CONSTITUTION OF THE RSA
   Constitutional values, 210
   and see PUBLIC POLICY
CONTINGENT CLAIM, 120
   and see INSOLVENCY
CONTINUING SURETYSHIP, 81 fn91, 106 fns 47, 51, 110-115, 118, 177, 179
   appropriation of payments, 114-5, 193
   contribution, right to, when arising, and, 177
   death, effect of, 118
   definition, 110
   termination, 112
CONTRACT *AD FACTUM PRAESTANDUM,* 101, 106-10
CONTRACT FOR BENEFIT OF THIRD PARTY
   suretyship is not, 32
CONTRACT OF SURETYSHIP
   acceptance, 63
   causa, 63
   conditional, *see* CONDITIONAL SURETYSHIP
   condition precedent, *see* CONDITIONAL SURETYSHIP
   consensual contract, 61
   consent
      debtor's, unnecessary, 61-2
      creditor and surety, between, required, 64
   defences open to principal debtor, 30 fn13,
   defences open to surety, 30, 38, 57, 64
   duress, induced by, 59, 64, 189
   essentials to be in writing, 67-8, 71-2
   formalities, 67-81
   formation of, 61ff
   fraud, induced by, 64, 67
   future debt, opportunity to resile, 63
   general principles of contract apply, 61ff
   'guarantee', distinguished from suretyship, 32
   incorporation, principle of, 72
   intention to create, 63
   interpretation of, 76,
      restrictive, 95

CONTRACT OF SURETYSHIP *(continued)*
    misrepresentation, induced by, 64
    mistake, induced by, 64
    offer, 60
    principal obligation, *see* PRINCIPAL OBLIGATION
    rectification of, 73-7
    rescission, grounds for, 64-7
    stamp duty, 86
    tacit, 62
    withdrawal of offer, 60
    and see SURETYSHIP
CONTRIBUTION, RIGHT TO, 171ff
    benefit of division does not arise, 141
    benefit of excussion, effect of, 175
    condictio indebiti, use of, when contribution not available, 175
    co-sureties, 53
        available to, 145, 171
        co-principal debtor, where co-surety is also, 170, 173
        contract regulating division *inter se,* 171
        indemnity *inter se,* 174
        insolvent co-surety, 174
        mutual sureties, distinguished from, 54
        payment by one, effect of, 172, 205
        payment by one to another, 205
        payment by, to debtor's trustee in insolvency, effect of, 205
        right to, from, 56, 58, 133, 142, 145-6, 155, 156, 171, 173
        separate instruments, by, 54, 156, 170
    equitable basis, 22ff, 147, 150
    impecunious co-surety, 139
    insolvent co-surety, 139, 173-4
    interest, 174
    payment
    part, effect of, 176
    excussion, right to have, 175
    part payment, effect, 176-80
    prejudice caused by creditor, effect, 183
    prescription, 200
    principles of, 171-3
    procedure to enforce, 183
    quantum, determination of, 180
    surety, also a debtor, effect, 173
        'ultimate burden' rule, 176
    and see BENEFIT OF CESSION OF ACTIONS
CO-PRINCIPAL DEBTOR, SURETY AND, *see* SURETY AND CO-PRINCIPAL

COSTS
    contribution, right to, 174
    creditor suing principal debtor
        surety's liability for cost of, 116
    debtor, cost of excussion of, 116

CO-SURETIES
    achterborgen, 141
    avals, 56
    bound conditionally, 141
    bound from future date, 141
    cession of action, benefit of
        division, benefit of, if sued under, 149
        excussion, benefit of, 149
    and see BENEFIT OF CESSION OF ACTIONS
    co-debtors, for, liability generally joint, 55
    sureties for separate, not co-sureties, 55,
    conditional, one co-surety, 141
    contractual privity between, none as a rule, 55, 145, 152
    contribution, right to, *see* CONTRIBUTION, RIGHT TO *and* BENEFIT OF
        CESSION OF ACTIONS
    co-principal debtors, also, effect, 56-8
    creditor's release of debtor, effect, 155
    creditor's loss of security, effect, 156
    death of one, effect on division, 144
    debtor, co-surety also, effect, 58
    definition, 54-5
    division, right to, 138ff
    and see BENEFIT OF DIVISION
    Hadrian's rescript, 16, 18, 20, 138-9
    impecunious co-surety, 139
    insolvent co-surety, 139, 174
    liability generally *in solidum,* unless, 55
        cession of actions, sued under, 145, 148-52, 171
        co-debtors, for, 54
        indivisible debt, for, 54
        specified portion of debt, for, 54
        merger between principal debtor and creditor, effect, 199
    minor co-surety, 140
    obligations *inter se,* 165
        contract to regulate, 171
    principal debt, division between, *inter se,* 180
    test of, 50 56

CREDITOR
    joinder of parties, 128, 134
    release of principal debtor by, 155ff, 192
    surety, against, 96, 127, 128, 145

CREDITOR *(continued)*
    surety's liability, 116
    and see CO-SURETIES
    cession of actions, *see* BENEFIT OF CESSION OF ACTIONS, CESSION OF ACTIONS *and* CESSION
    claim
        against insolvent debtor's estate, 168
        conditional or contingent, 168
    co-debtors, merger of, effect, 199
    fraud, minor co-surety induced by, 140
    inability to give cession of actions, 155
        and see BENEFIT OF CESSION OF ACTIONS
    minor surety, 51
    obligations
        cession of actions, to give, 142, 145, 151 146, 148,154
        condition to suretyship, to establish performance of, 105
        prejudice, sureties, not to, 156-8, 205
        securities, to perfect and to preserve, 156-8
            and see SECURITY
        vigilance, whether to exercise, 157
    onus to prove
        condition performed, 105
        liability, extent of, 104-5
    rights of, in South African law
        co-debtors, against, *see* CO-DEBTORS
        co-sureties, against, *see* CO-SURETIES
        principal debtor, against, 30
        surety, against, 101
    surety's obligations to, after death, 118-9

DAMAGES
    claim by surety against principal debtor, 67
    surety's liability for, 96, 101, 106-7, 110
    judgment for, discharging debt, 196

DEATH
    surety's, effect on obligations, 118
    surety's, effect on continuing suretyships, 118
    co-surety's, effect on division, 140, 144

DEBTOR, *see* PRINCIPAL DEBTOR

DEFENCES
    for benefit for third party, 189
    cession of creditor's rights, no defence, 47-8
    'huur gaat voor koop', no defence, 49
    justus error, 64-5
    mistake, *see justus error*

DEFENCES *(continued)*
    non-compliance with provisions of Companies Act or Close Corporations Act, 52-3
    personal, 188
    real, 1189
    surety, available to, 187

DEFINITIONS
    aval, 81-2
    co-sureties, 54-5
    fideiussor indemnitatis, 59
    intercession, 34
    surety, 28
    surety and co-principal debtor, 34
    suretyship
        proposed definition, 28

DISCUSSIONIS, BENEFIT OF, *see* BENEFIT OF EXCUSSION

DISCHARGE OF SURETY
    alteration of principal obligation, 205-7
    breach of duty by creditor, what constitutes, 156-8, 205-7
    composition, statutory, does not release, 197
    continuing suretyship, 110-15
    creditor's conduct, by
        altering principal obligation, *see above*
        delay by, *see below*
        duty, breach of, *see above*
        extension of time, granting, *see* 'time' *below*
        prejudicial conduct, 205
    delay of creditor in suing debtor, 205, 208
        fideiussor indemnitatis, effect on, 209
        passive inactivity, mere, 208-9
    delegation, 197
    insolvency, effect, *see* INSOLVENCY
    judgment, when, 197
    merger, by, 197-8
    novation, by, 195-7
    operation of law, by, 188
    prescription of principal debt, 200
        interruption of, 201
    res judicata, when, 196-7
    set-off, 198-9
    time
        effluxion of, 205
            continuing suretyship, 110
        extension of, 209

DISCLOSURE, DUTY OF, 97
DIVISION, *see* BENEFIT OF DIVISION

EXCEPTIO CEDENDARUM ACTIONUM, see BENEFIT OF CESSION OF ACTIONS
EXCEPTIO DE DUOBUS VEL PLURIBUS REIS DEBENDI, 142 fn42
EXCEPTIO DOLI GENERALIS, 210
    not part of Roman-Dutch law, 211
    public policy as substitute, 212
    rectification, and, 73-77
EXCEPTIO NON CAUSA DEBITI, 43 fn54
EXCEPTIO NON NUMERATAE PECUNIA, 110 fn72
EXCUSSION
    absent principal debtor, 126
    ad factum praestandum obligation,
        contempt of court, punishment for, 129
        avals, availability to, 132
    co-debtors, against, 128
    company
        judicial management, under, 130
        liquidation, in, 129
    costs of
        appeal, include, 113
        security if debtor impecunious, 129
        surety's liability for, 116
    delay by creditor
        effect, 137
    exempted assets, 128
    hypothecated assets, 128
    nulla bona return, 129
    Placaat of February, 128
    principal debtor
        absent, 126
        impecunious, 129
        insolvent, 129
    proof of, 129-30
    renunciation of benefit, 124-5, 130-1
    securities, upon, 128
    security for costs excussion impecunious debtor, 129
    sequestration of debtor's estate, 123, 128
    voluntary association, against, 123, 129
        and see BENEFIT OF EXCUSSION

FACTUM PRAESTANDUM, 9ff
FIDEIUSSIO, 10
    action against
        principal debtor
            classical period, 13
            Justinian, under, effect, 15, 16-17

FIDEIUSSIO (continued)
    surety
        co-surety whether released, 14
        principal debtor, whether released, 13
        constitutum, compared with, 20
    Hadrian's Rescript, 16
    mandate assimilated with, 19
    natural obligation, for, 12
    negotiorum gestio, 14
    origin of, 9ff
    Roman-Dutch law, basis of, is, 1, 21
FIDEIUSSOR FIDEIUSSORIS, see ACHTERBORG
FIDEIUSSOR INDEMNITATIS
    compared with surety, 59
    creditor's obligations, 137
    deficiency, liable for, 59,
    defined, 59
    delay of creditor causing loss, 137
    loss caused by creditor's delay, 132, 137
    recourse, right of, 167-8
FIDEPROMISSIO, 7ff
    contracted by *stipulatio,* 7
    obsolete by Justinian's time, 11
    overtaken by *fideiussio,* 11
FIDUCIA CUM CREDITORE, 57 fn28
FORMALITIES
    avals, writing not required, 68, 81
    blank spaces in documents, 77ff
        co-sureties, and, 79
        non-essential spaces, 79
        signing in blank, 77
    common law, required none, 67
    extrinsic evidence, when admissible, 71ff
        exceptions: identification, 69-71
            incorporation, 72
            rectification, 73
    oral variations, 81
    signature
        location on document, 69
        in pencil, 69
    meaning of, 69
    required, 67-9
    signing 'in blank', 77
    writing, required by statute, 67ff
        essentials required in writing, 67-8, 71-2

FRAUD
    disclosure, duty of, 31 fn18, 102

HISTORY OF SURETYSHIP, 1ff
HYPOTHECA, 7 fn28

INDEBTEDNESS, *see* CERTIFICATE OF INDEBTEDNESS
INDEMNIFICATION, 34
    delict, suretyship against, 39
    distinction, between suretyship and, 34-5
    fideiussor indemnitatis see FIDEIUSSOR INDEMNITATIS
    recourse, right of, 161-2
    suretyship is not contract of indemnity, 34-5
    surety's obligation to indemnity, 101, 107
INSOLVENCY
    claims, proof of, 120, 168
    conditional (contingent) claim, 119-20
        proof of, 168
        valuation, 169
    co-surety of, 139, 158, 173-4
    creditor's rights, 119-20, 119-20,
    discharge, no, 119
    liquidation, 129
        principal debtor, of, 119, 168
        proof of claim by both surety and creditor, 168
        recourse, right of, 168
        rehabilitation, effect, 119
        security
            payment, part, by surety, 168
            surety, of, 119
INSURANCE
    suretyship, compared with, 36-7
INTERCESSION
    indemnity may be, 35
    meaning of, 34-5
INTEREST, 111
    cession of actions, 152
    continuing suretyship, 110
    contribution, right to, 174
    recourse, right of, 161
INTERPRETATION
    Burge's three rules, 95-8
    extrinsic evidence, 89-90
    intention, ascertain, 88
    language creating suretyship
        examples, 98-100ff

INTERPRETATION *(continued)*
    principles, 87ff
        restrictive, 88-9, 90-91, 105
    surrounding circumstances, 89ff
    verba contra stipulatorem interpretenda sunt, 90

JURISTIC PERSONS *see* ARTIFICIAL PERSONS
JUSTINIAN'S LEGISLATION, 16

LEGES
    aebutia, 7
    apuleia, 9
    fideiussio, not applicable to, 9
    cicereia, 9
    fideiussio not referred to, 9
    cornelia, 11 fn58
    lex furia de sponsu, 9
    publilia, 8

MANDATE
    contract of, tacit, debtor and surety, 62
    and see ACTIO MANDATI
MANDATUM, see MANDATE
MANDATUM CREDENDAE PECUNIAE, 18
    constitutum, compared with, 10
    disappearance of, 19
        securities, creditor's duty to preserve, 18
MANDATUM QUALIFICATUM, see MANDATUM CREDENDAE PECUNIAE
MERGER, 199-200
MINOR
    co-surety, 139
    division, benefit of, 139
    emancipated, powers, 51
    excussion, benefit of, 132
    fraud, 140
    guardian's powers, 51
    principal debtor, 189
    surety, as, 51, 167
    suretyship for, 189
        surety's rights if minor not bound, 167
MUTUAL SURETIES, 54

NATURAL OBLIGATION
    excussion, benefit of, 132
    suretyship for, 11-12, 39, 102, 132, 189

NEGOTIABLE INSTRUMENTS, 68, 81, 154, 167, 195
    accommodation parties, 84-5, 163 fn31, 205 fn144
        definition, 84 fn106
    avals 56, 68, 81-5, 133, 135 fn108, 137, 143, 154, 172 fn6, 205 fn144, 209 fn173
    agreement not to enforce obligation, 209 fn173
    cession of instrument not required to pass rights, 83 fn96
    contribution, right to, 172 fn6
    co-sureties, 56
    definition, 82-3
    division, benefit of, 143
    endorser, compared with, 83ff
    excussion, benefit of, 84, 132-3, 135, 143
    exempted by statute from requirement of writing, 75 68, 81
    liability of, 68, 81-5
    provisional sentence, 137
    surety and co-principal debtor, effect of, 82
NEGOTIORUM GESTIO, 14, 17, 62,
    and see RECOURSE, RIGHT OF
NOVATION, 34, 35, 115 fn95, 133, 195
    delegation, 163
    defence available to security, 189
    law, by operation of, 195
    judgment, 196
    litis contestatio, 196
    principal debt, of, 195

OBLIGATION, *see* PRINCIPAL OBLIGATION
ONUS
    division, benefit of, to establish exclusion, 138
    liability of surety, to prove, 105
    release, to prove, 195

PACTUM COMMISSORIUM
    pledge, 86
PACTUM DE CONSTITUTO
    fideiussio, assimilated to, 21
        compared with, 18
    praetorian development, 19
    suretyship, form of, 19
    disappearance of, as, 21
    in Roman law, 17
    and see CONSTITUTUM PACTUM DE NON PETENDO
    surety, enjoys right of recourse, notwithstanding, 195
PAYMENT
    ad factum praestandum, 163

PAYMENT *(continued)*
    appropriation
        continuing suretyship, 110
    cession of actions, to entitle, 146-8, 154
        part payment, and, 154
    cession of securities, payer entitled to delivery, 148
    compromise, 154-5
    condition, dependent upon, 85
    contribution, right to, when arises 176
        part payment, effect, 176
    co-sureties, by one to another, 55, 205
        effect of payment by one, 145-8, 154, 204
        overpayment by one, 136 141-2, 154
    double payment, effect of, 1165, 175
    forfeiture for non-payment, 86
    forms of, 163
    negative obligation, 101, 109
    part payment, 176-8
    place for, stipulated, 85
    recourse, right of, condition of, 164-5
    part payment, effect of, 168, 176-8
    share, payment, effect on, 154
    surety, by, 145,159
        overpayment by one, 141-2, 154
        right to pay creditor and sue debtor, 163-4
    tender, 194
PERFORMANCE, *see* PAYMENT
PERSONAL DEFENCES *see* DEFENCES
PIGNUS (PLEDGE), 86
    pactum commissorium, 86
PRAEDES, 4ff
PRESCRIPTION
    interruption of, 201
    principal obligation, of, 200ff
PRINCIPAL DEBT, *see* PRINCIPAL OBLIGATION
PRINCIPAL DEBTOR
    ad factum praestandum contract
        required of surety, 101
        capacity, lacking, 39
    company, not registered, 39
    death of
        transmission of debt, 118
    defences open to, available to surety, 38, 104
    financial position, improvement of, 127
    force of law, bound by, 39
    impecunious, 139

PRINCIPAL DEBTOR *(continued)*
    insane, 40
    insolvent, *see* INSOLVENCY
    liquidation *see* INSOLVENCY
    minor, 40
    natural obligation, for, 38
    obligations
        surety, to, *see* RECOURSE, RIGHT OF SURETY'S
        surety, to provide, 58
    prodigal, 40
    squandering assets, 166
    surety
        debtor's obligation to provide one, 58
    married in community of property, 40ff

PRINCIPAL OBLIGATION
    absence of
        suretyship, effect on, 27, 38ff
    accessory, suretyship is, *see* ACCESSORY NATURE OF SURETYSHIP
    ad faciendum aliquid, 42-3
    ad factum praestandum, 43, 106-10, 129, 154, 163,
    cession of, by creditor, effect on suretyship, 47-50
    civil law, in, a money debt, 43
    conditions of, apply to suretyship, 102-4
    contemplated wrong, no indemnity against, 40
    contract arising out of, 39
    debtor lacking capacity, 39
    delict, arising from, 39
        future, 39
    discharged, already, 38
    do or give something, 43
    essential to suretyship, 28, 38,
    fictitious, 38, 101
    fideiussio, see FIDEIUSSIO
    fidepromissio, see FIDEPROMISSIO
    forbidden transaction, 39
    future debt, 38, 42, 43-4, 39, 46-7
        continuing suretyship, 106, 110ff
        surety not bound until debtor bound, 39
            opportunity to withdraw, unless agreed otherwise, 47
            give or do something, 43
    guardian's obligation to ward, 115
    illegal, 39, 41
        examples of, 41-2
        severability, 42
    illiquid debt, 39
    impossible to fulfil, 39

PRINCIPAL OBLIGATION *(continued)*
    incorporation by reference, 47, 70 fn45, 73 fn57
    indivisible debt
        division, benefit of, 143
        invalid, 41
    natural obligation, *see* NATURAL OBLIGATION
    negative obligation, 101, 109
        remedy, 105
    non-existent, 38
    personal act, 43
    personal knowledge and skill, 43, 101, 108
    simultaneous creation of suretyship, 46-7
    suretyship is accessory to, *see* ACCESSORY NATURE OF SURETYSHIP
        less than, for, 101
        not to exceed, 101
        onerous, more than, 102-3
    unliquidated, 39
    void
        knowledge of surety, 42
PROMISSORY NOTES, *see* NEGOTIABLE INSTRUMENTS
PUBLIC POLICY, 210-14
    certificate of balance, and, 214
    defence of, 213
    test of, 213

REAL SURETIES, *see ACHTERBORG*
RECOURSE, RIGHT OF, SURETY'S, 159ff
    achterborg, 168
    cession of actions, with, 145
    co-debtors, against, 167
        surety and co-principal debtor, 56
        compromise, effect of, 154, 155, 162
    contract *ad factum praestandum,* 43, 106, 129, 154, 163
    costs, 161
    fideiussor indemnitatis, rights of, 167
    indemnification, complete, entitled to, 161
    insolvent principal debtor, 168
    interest, 161
    negotiorum gestio, 17, 31, 62, 159
    payment
        condition of right, 164
        part payment, 176
        requisites of, 163-4
        tender of, 163, 166, 176, 194
        and see PAYMENT
    principal debtor insolvent, 168

RECOURSE, RIGHT OF, SURETY'S, principal debtor insolvent *(continued)*
    release of, effect, 194
  relief of surety, extent of, 161
  surety against will of debtor, 161
  surety and co-principal debtor, rights of, 56ff
  surety with or without knowledge of the principal debtor, *see 'negotiorum gestio'*
    above when entitled, 159ff
    without payment, in what circumstances, 165
    when not entitled, 167

RELEASE
  cession of actions, inability to give, 155
  co-debtor, release of one, effect, 155, 194
  co-surety, release of one, effect, 155, 194
    security, loss of, 156
  creditor prejudicing surety, 183, 194, 205ff
  death, *see* DEATH
  debtor, release of, 194
    effect on cession of actions, 155, 194
    effect on right of recourse, 192, 208
  judgment against debtor, 196
  onus to prove, 1195
  payment, effect of, *see* PAYMENT
  restitutio in integrum to minor debtor, 40
  security, loss or release of, 156
    cession of actions, effect on, 157, 183
    co-sureties, effect on, 157, 183
  and see DISCHARGE OF SURETY

RENUNCIATION OF BENEFITS
  cession of actions, benefit of, effect, 158
  division, benefit of, 57
    sureties and co-principal debtors, 57, 141-4
    and see BENEFIT OF DIVISION
  excussion, benefit of, 57, 130-1
  surety and co-principal debtor, 57, 131
  and see BENEFIT OF EXCUSSION
  fideiussor indemnitatis, by, 133
  illiquid debt, survey of, 133

RES JUDICATA, 196
  arbitration award, 196
    concession by principal debtor,105 fn40
    judgment against principal debtor, 196
      not binding on surety, 105 fn40, 196
  judgment for principal debtor, 197
    effect on surety, 197

ROMAN LAW, 1ff
  Roman-Dutch law developed from, 21ff

SECURITY
  cession of, *see* CESSION OF ACTIONS
  creditor
    preserve, 156
    stipulating for, 86
  debt, cession of, passes with, 148, 153
  division, benefit of impecunious surety, 139
  excussion of, 128
  insolvency, in, 168
  loss of, effect, 156
  pactum commissorium, 86
  part payment, effect, 168, 176ff
  perfect, creditor's failure to, 157-8
  preserve, creditor's failure to, 156
  release of, effect, 156
  setting aside, effect of, 158
SENATUS CONSULTUM VELIE/ANUM, see WOMEN'S SURETYSHIP BENEFITS
SET-OFF, 198
    surety suing creditor
        debt of principal debtor, 133
SOLUTIO, see PAYMENT
SPONSIO 4, 6, 7, 8, 9, 11
STAMP DUTY, 86
SURETY
  accommodation party, 84
  aval, 81
  cession of actions, benefit of, *see* BENEFIT OF CESSION OF ACTIONS
  co-debtor, surety for one not co-surety with surety for other co-debtor, 55
  co-debtors, for, 101
  company, 52
    ultra vires doctrine, 52
    competent to contract, must be, 53
  conditional creditor of principal debtor, is, 31, 168
  contract *ad factum praestandum,* 101, 106
  contribution, right to, *see* CONTRIBUTION, RIGHT TO
  co-sureties, *see* CO-SURETIES
  creditor of debtor, bound to only, 101
  debt unpaid, when no claim against insolvent estate, 170,
  debtor, promise to, to pay his debt
    not suretyship, 30
  debtors, separate, sureties for each other, 54
  defences open to principal debtor, available to surety, 30, 104, 187

SURETY *(continued)*
    definition of, 28
    division, benefit of, *see* BENEFIT OF DIVISION
    excussion, benefit of, *see* BENEFIT OF EXCUSSION
    future debt, for, 46-7
        bound, when, 47
    withdraw, whether can, 47
    knowledge of voidness of principal obligation, with, bound as principal debtor, 42
    married in community of property, 40-1, 44-5
    minor, for, 40, 167
    minor surety, 51
    mutual sureties, 54
    natural obligation, for, 39, 102, 189, 200
    negative principal obligation, 101, 109
        remedy, 110
    obligations, for, 101ff
        ad factum praestandum, contract, 101, 106
        arise, when, 31, 39
        cession of actions, sued under, 146
        co-debtors, for, 54-5, 101
        conditions of principal obligation, 103
        costs of creditor suing principal debtor, 116-18
        damages, to pay
            contract *ad factum praestandum,* 101, 106
            negative obligation, 101, 109
        death, transmission on his, 118ff
        debtor in default
            not for surety to decide, 104
        liability, extent of
            concession by debtor, effect, 105 fn40
            judgment against debtor, effect, 105 fn40
                for debtor, 197
            onus to prove, *see* ONUS
    obligation, very, for which he stood surety, 101ff
    onerous, not more, than debtor's, 102-4, 108-9
    payment, *see* PAYMENT
    perform debtor's obligation, to, 28-9, 101, 106
    personal knowledge and skill, 9101, 107 fn56, 108
    recourse, right of, *see* RECOURSE, RIGHT OF, SURETY'S
    release, *see* RELEASE
    rights of
        ad factum praestandum contract, 101, 106
        contribution, *see* CONTRIBUTION, RIGHT TO
        co-surety, against, 125, 145-6, 150, 153, 171, 183
            creditor, against, 125

SURETY (continued)
    prejudiced, not to be, 30-1, 155-8, 205-9
       recourse *see* RECOURSE, RIGHT OF, SURETY'S
    same debt as he guaranteed, no other, 101ff
       not more onerous, 102-3, 108-9
       security, *see* SECURITY
  specific performance, 106-7, 110
  surety, for a, *see ACHTERBORG*
  surety *in solidum* is not co-principal debtor, 58
  time, conditions as to, 102-6
  unliquidated debt, 100
  void or voidable principal obligation, 40-4
  and see SURETYSHIP, CONTRACT OF SURETYSHIP *and* PRINCIPAL OBLIGATION

SURETY AND CO-PRINCIPAL DEBTOR
  cession of actions, benefit of, 57-8
  debtor, relations with, 58
  defences available, 57
  defined, 56-7
  division, benefit of, 56, 57
    none with principal debtor, 57
  effect, 56
  excussion, benefit of, 57
  recourse, *see* RECOURSE, RIGHT OF, SURETY'S
  renunciation, implied, 57, 131
  surety *in solidum* is not, 58
  and see SURETY

SURETYSHIP
  accessory obligation, *see* ACCESSORY NATURE OF SURETYSHIP
  compromise, effect of, 197
  conditional, 85, 105
    division, benefit of, 138-44
  conditions of principal obligation apply, 101
  continuing, 110ff, 177, 179
    death of surety, effect on, 118
  Corpus Iuris, developed law, in, 21
  definition, 28-9
  equitable development in Roman-Dutch law, 22, 146-7
  essentials, 71-2
  insurance may be, 36-7
  intercession, a form of, 26, 34
  nature of, 25ff
  obligations involved, 26ff
  parties to it, 30
  principal obligation
    essential, 38
    and see PRINCIPAL OBLIGATION

WOMEN'S SURETYSHIP BENEFITS
   abolished, 24
   authentica si qua mulier, 24-5
   Roman to Roman-Duch law, 21-2
   senatus consultum veleianum, 24
   Suretyship Amendment Act, of, 25
      abolition of women's suretyship benefits, 25